T0305207

Migration and the Making of
Industrial São Paulo

PAULO FONTES

Migration and the Making of
Industrial São Paulo

Foreword by Barbara Weinstein

Translated from the Portuguese by Ned Sublette

Duke University Press / Durham and London / 2016

Library of Congress Cataloging-in-Publication Data
Names: Fontes, Paulo Roberto Ribeiro, author. | Sublette, Ned, [date] translator. |
Weinstein, Barbara, writer of foreword.
Title: Migration and the making of industrial São Paulo / Paulo Fontes ;
translated from the Portuguese by Ned Sublette ; foreword by Barbara Weinstein.
Other titles: Nordeste em São Paulo. English
Description: Durham : Duke University Press, 2016. | Includes bibliographical
references and index.
Identifiers: LCCN 2015043228
ISBN 9780822361152 (hardcover : alk. paper)
ISBN 9780822361343 (pbk. : alk. paper)
ISBN 9780822374299 (e-book)
Subjects: LCSH: Migrant labor—Brazil—São Paulo—History. | Migrant
Labor—Brazil—São Miguel Paulista—History. | Internal migrants—Brazil,
Northeast. | São Miguel Paulista (Brazil)—History.
Classification: LCC HD5856.B6 F6613 2016 | DDC 331.6/2098161—dc23
LC record available at http://lccn.loc.gov/2015043228

Cover art: Thomaz Farkas /Acervo Instituto Moreia Salles

We are delighted that the translation of this book was supported by the
Thomas E. Skidmore Prize, sponsored by the National Archive, Rio de Janeiro,
and the Brazilian Studies Association.

Obra publicada com o apoio do Ministério da Cultura do Brasil/
Fundação Biblioteca Nacional. Work published with the support of the
Cultural Ministry of Brazil/National Library Foundation.

MINISTÉRIO DA CULTURA
Fundação BIBLIOTECA NACIONAL

CONTENTS

The immigrant alighting on American shores to take up residence in Brazil or Argentina or the United States has long received a warm welcome from historians and social scientists. Typically figured as hardworking and forward-looking, those migrating from Europe across the Atlantic have been depicted as audacious, socially mobile, and prepared for modern political participation, whether in its liberal or left-wing variants. By contrast, the internal migrant arriving in the large urban area via third-class railroad cars or rickety flatbed trucks has not enjoyed an enthusiastic reception from the scholarly community.[1] Those flocking to the major Latin American cities from the countryside have been judged considerably less well prepared for the demands of "modern" urban life, and the first wave of social science research on internal migration associated them with a distorted modernity characterized by hyper-urbanization and populist demagoguery. In many ways, this massive movement of millions of rural and small-town dwellers to the larger metropolitan areas, from the 1930s to the 1970s, can be considered the most transformative social phenomenon in the recent history of Latin America, and in Brazil it produced, among other consequences, the most important labor leader and most beloved politician in the nation's history, Luiz Inácio Lula da Silva. Yet it took many decades before scholars began to shift away from their largely negative assessment of the participants in this great migration and what their actions and decisions meant for Latin American society. Even as more and more research demonstrated that claims about the internal migrants' stubborn traditionalism or political naiveté were little better than stereotypes, one could still perceive in the academy, especially among those who studied labor movements in Latin America, a certain nostalgia for the European immigrants, with their supposedly acute sense of solidarity, aptitude for labor militancy, and immunity to the blandishments of mainstream politicians.

So even now, when serious scholars would no longer think to describe internal migrants as "docile workers" or "co-opted clients," we are very fortunate to have a study of the single largest internal migration—the tidal wave of Brazilians, mainly with origins in the northeastern states, who moved to the burgeoning industrial center of São Paulo in the middle decades of the twentieth century—widely available to students of Latin American labor, politics, and urban life. Paulo Fontes has emerged as a central figure in the cohort of Brazilian labor historians whose publications are transforming our view of politics and social life in this period.[2] *Migration and the Making of Industrial São Paulo* is an extraordinary work of historical research and interpretation that replaces earlier scholars' "common sense" about northeastern migrants, not with an opposite, celebratory portrait of social struggle and political militancy, but with a nuanced depiction of the many different challenges faced and difficult choices made by the members of the community he studied and the way in which their largely *nordestino* origins influenced how they were treated and how they viewed themselves.

The place that Fontes decided to study—São Miguel Paulista, a peripheral precinct of the state capital—was an especially fortuitous choice because the district, dominated by the Nitro Química factory complex in the period in question, drew an unusually large influx of transplanted Brazilians (mainly from the Nordeste [Northeast], but also from the central state of Minas Gerais and the interior of São Paulo) to a locale that already included a small coterie of middle-class and upper-class families, as well as workers who were native *paulistanos* (i.e., residents of the capital). São Miguel could almost be regarded as a "company town," but one embedded in urban São Paulo. As such, it has the virtue of providing us insight into a specific, and perhaps singular, community while enabling us to reconsider a whole range of earlier assumptions about nordestinos based on either overly aggregated statistics or excessively isolated case studies.

The early chapters of *Migration and the Making of Industrial São Paulo* explore the shared experiences that produced a particular nordestino identity among the migrants in this community, starting with the ordeal of traveling 1,500 miles or more to their destination. Indeed, the migrant family precariously perched on a *pau-de-arara* (flatbed truck) has become one of the defining symbols of the journey from the Nordeste (although many migrants traveled at least part of the way by riverboat or train). New arrivals would typically tap into a network of already settled friends or relatives to find a place to live and later draw on a culture of reciprocal labor (*mutirão*) when building a more permanent home. Then there was the encounter with paulistano prejudice against the growing population of nordestinos, often referred to as *baianos*—in this context, a racialized term that linked all northeasterners, regardless of place of origin, to Brazil's most "African" state—or, as some paulistanos liked to facetiously remark, "From Minas up, it's all Bahia." These slights and hardships reinforced a sense of their common northeastern origins among the new residents of São Miguel, although Fontes is quick to note that in some contexts affiliation with a particular northeastern locale might take precedence over a broader collective sense of nordestino identity. Similarly, nordestino workers in the Nitro Química plant could draw on shared notions of masculinity and manly dignity in confrontations with foremen, but appeals to masculinity could also trigger conflicts between workers or among residents and feed stereotypes that exaggerated nordestinos' proclivity for violent behavior.

Although Fontes carefully identifies the fault lines within São Miguel and does justice to the heterogeneity of the local nordestino population, his discussion of labor struggles and political activism demonstrates that residents regularly and often successfully coalesced around certain class- and community-based concerns and that their identity as nordestinos served as a source of unity and empathy rather than as an impediment to labor militancy. According to the author, "The friendships and the complex of social relations formed in the places of origin and expanded in the factory and the neighborhood were frequently the basis for the elaboration of cohesion and solidarity. They were essential for the formation of a class identity." Thus, the workers at Nitro Química—overwhelmingly of northeastern origin—were among the most unified and assertive of the adherents to the famous Strike of 400,000 in 1957. As Herbert Gutman argued several decades ago about immigrants and labor militancy in the United States, ethno-cultural practices unrelated to the industrial order can be quickly invested with new meanings that may solidify class identities.[3] Or as one Nordeste-born official of the Chemical Workers Union bluntly put it, "The Bahians . . . believed in me because I also drank *cachaça*, danced *forró*, raised hell."

Sporadic episodes of labor protest did much to shape the culture and character of São Miguel, but even more formative were the ongoing struggles to secure the most basic urban services from the municipal administration. Residents recall arriving home covered in dust or mud from long walks on unpaved roads, made even more hazardous at night by the lack of street lighting. Severely inadequate bus and train service deterred many workers from seeking employment elsewhere, despite the difficult and dangerous working conditions in the Nitro Química plant, because it could mean enduring a commute of two hours or more. Therefore, community residents consistently supported candidates for political office, such as Adhemar de Barros and Jânio Quadros, who seemed most likely to deliver on promises of better services. Here one might, at first glance, conclude that this is a familiar story of politically immature clients looking to populist political bosses (especially the unsavory Adhemar, who would later support the military coup) to attend to their needs. But the vigorous social movements that took the form of neighborhood associations campaigning for lighting, paving, sanitation, running water, schools, and sports facilities indicate that residents of São Miguel also viewed this as a process that had to come from below. Indeed, the plethora of clubs and organizations that constituted the dense civic life of this community should be a revelation for anyone who doubts the associational aptitudes of rural migrants. Perhaps even more striking were the local election results during periods in which the Brazilian Communist Party (Partido Comunista Brasileiro; PCB) could legally run candidates. Repeatedly, São Miguel Paulista was among the districts of São Paulo that gave the PCB its highest vote totals. While we cannot abstract from electoral statistics what voting for communists meant to individual voters in São Miguel, such evidence certainly throws into question the idea that nordestinos ignored class-based political appeals in favor of top-down promises from mainstream politicians.

Any appreciation of *Migration and the Making of Industrial São Paulo* would be incomplete without due acknowledgment of the exhaustive and imaginative research that made the book possible. For his evidence Fontes mined the periodical press (including Nitro Química's internal newsletter), minutes of municipal council and state assembly meetings, electoral bulletins, criminal proceedings, institutional archives, personal papers, even diplomatic correspondence regarding major strikes and communist activity in São Paulo. However, two types of sources particularly stand out as imparting depth and texture to his narrative. One is the material consulted in the Departamento de Ordem Político e Social (DOPS) files housed in the Public Archive of the State of São Paulo, which have only been available to researchers since the 1990s. The *prontuários* (records) from São Miguel contain information on everything from a boardinghouse whose female owner had been accused of rent gouging and the employment trajectory of a former machine assistant to the visit by Luís Carlos Prestes, secretary-general of the PCB, to São Miguel in 1947 and the frequency of threats and violence at political rallies. Not only do these reports provide a wealth of detail that might not be available from other sources, but they also offer fascinating insight into how information was gathered, worded, and delivered to police authorities.

Even more crucial to the way Fontes is able to capture the voices and experiences of the nordestinos who populate this historical landscape is the rich collection of nearly one hundred oral histories at his disposal, forty of them from his own interviews and the rest collected by other scholars. To be sure, using oral sources for social and political history is not startlingly new, but it *is* rare for a historian to be able to draw on so many different accounts and perspectives. Fontes also offers a beautiful example of how print and oral sources can be layered to illuminate the workings of memory—in this case, the nearly universal claim that São Miguel in the immediate postwar decades was a tight-knit community where one could walk alone at night and not worry about being robbed or assaulted and "where nobody even knew what the word 'rape' meant." Yet the newspapers from those years are replete with reporting about robberies, armed attacks, and homicides. Clearly, São Miguel was never the crime-free zone that Fontes's interviewees remember. But compared with the skyrocketing rates of violent crime that have become the norm in the area since the 1980s, one can imagine that those postwar decades seemed peaceable indeed.

For historians there are few processes of more obvious consequence than the massive movement of human beings, whether forced, voluntary, or a mixture of the two. The transatlantic slave trade, widely recognized as one of history's great human tragedies, has been subjected to every form of historical scrutiny. The wave of European immigration to the Americas in the late nineteenth and early twentieth centuries has produced a vast and sophisticated historiography. But the migration of millions from the countryside (or from smaller cities) to major metropolitan areas, a process that virtually reshaped Latin America in the second half of the twentieth century and made it the most urbanized region of the world, is only beginning to get the careful consideration from historians that it deserves. For anyone seeking a better understanding of what this migration meant—for the migrants themselves and for the new worlds they helped create—*Migration and the Making of Industrial São Paulo* is the perfect place to start.

New York City

ACKNOWLEDGMENTS

This is a revised and modified version of the book *Um Nordeste em São Paulo.
Trabalhadores migrantes em São Miguel Paulista (1945–66)*, published in 2008
by the Getúlio Vargas Foundation. It was originally a doctoral dissertation
from the postgraduate program in social history at the Institute of Philoso-
phy and Human Sciences of the State University of Campinas (Universidade
Estadual de Campinas; UNICAMP). I begin by thanking Michael Hall, my former adviser. My time with Michael allowed me to understand the real meaning of "sensei," the Japanese term used by Eric Hobsbawm in *On History*: "an
intellectual master to whom one owes a debt that cannot be repaid."

This work is certainly the result of the fantastic academic environment of
the History Department at UNICAMP, in which I had the privilege of being a
student. There I built a long relationship of friendship and intellectual partnership with Alexandre Fortes, Antonio Luigi Negro, Fernando Teixeira da
Silva, and Hélio da Costa. Without them, this journey would not have begun.
I also thank the professors of UNICAMP, in particular Claudio Batalha, Marco
Aurélio Garcia, Sidney Chalhoub, and Silvia Lara who were fundamental to
my formation as a historian. This book in many ways is also the result of intellectual contributions and conversations with many colleagues and teachers. I
especially thank José Ricardo Ramalho, José Sérgio Leite Lopes, Maria Célia
Paoli, Adriano Duarte, Fabiane Popinigis, Cristiana Schettini, Francisco Barbosa de Macedo, John French, Leon Fink, Marcel Van der Linden, Rossana
Barragán, Neville Kirk, Mirta Lobato, Huw Beynon, and Samita Sen.

I was invariably well attended and well received at all of the institutions, archives, and libraries where I conducted my research. I thank the staff and the
directors of those organizations. This work was enriched by the international
academic experience that I had the opportunity to acquire over the past few
years. In 2004 and 2006–2007, respectively, I was a visiting professor at Duke
University and Princeton University in the United States. More recently, in

2013–14, I was visiting scholar at the International Institute of Social History in Amsterdam and at the Re: Work Institute of Berlin's Humboldt University. These were fascinating experiences that transformed my academic understanding, as well as my professional and personal life. I greatly appreciate the staff, teachers, students, and friends who welcomed me so kindly at these institutions.

I am also grateful to colleagues at the School of Social Sciences at the Getúlio Vargas Foundation, where I have worked since 2008. In particular, I thank my students Felipe Ribeiro, Luciana Wollmann, Claudiane Torres, Flavia Véras, and Heliene Nagavasa, who with enthusiasm, dedication, and academic competence have helped me to build the Laboratory for Studies of the Worlds of Labor and Social Movements at that institution. I also thank Marieta Moraes Ferreira of the Editora da Fundação Getúlio Vargas.

This book was the winner of the first Thomas Skidmore Prize, sponsored by the Brazilian National Archives and the Brazilian Studies Association; funds from the award made the translation of this work into English possible. I thank the jury and particularly Professor James Green, the jury chair, who is an example to us all of the good combination of academic excellence and political commitment.

Larissa Rosa Corrêa, my wife and companion, I will get straight to the point: I love you a lot! Thank you for being in my life.

MAP 1. Direction of Internal Migration, Brazil 1950s–1970s

NORTH

NORTHEAST

WEST CENTRAL

SOUTHEAST

São Paulo

SOUTH

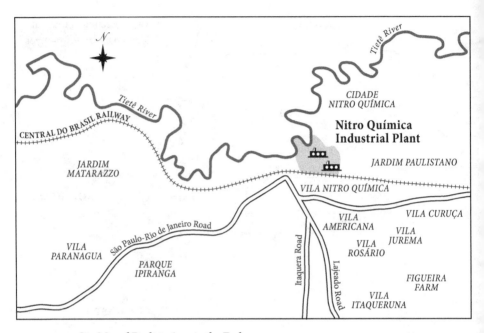

MAP 2. São Miguel Paulista Area in the Early 1950s

INTRODUCTION

You leave your home / You think you'll go to heaven
The dream comes crashing down / And you land in São Miguel.
—EDVALDO SANTANA, "Streets of São Miguel," 2000

Beginning in the 1940s, São Paulo underwent an extraordinary urban and industrial expansion unlike anything else in the world at that time. The city's rapid economic development posed innumerable challenges to its workers, in terms of both workplace issues and living conditions. Issues of infrastructure—transportation, sanitation, paving, education, health facilities, and so on—emerged as acute problems, as did real estate speculation, and the labor market was transformed by accelerating industrialization and the growth and diversification of the service sector. These phenomena intruded directly into workers' lives, along with high prices, competition, and internal divisions within the working class. Meanwhile, massive migration from rural areas (particularly from the Nordeste [Northeast], Minas Gerais, and the interior of the state of São Paulo) profoundly altered the social composition of the urban working class, resulting in fundamental political and cultural changes.

The period from 1945 to 1964 was marked by new models of political interaction, generally characterized by the term "populism," which established specific relations of conflict and reciprocity between workers and the state within a dynamic system of alliances and disputes.[1] In the context of São Paulo, this phenomenon resulted not only in *trabalhismo getulista*,[2] but also in the emergence of political forces linked to the figures of Adhemar de Barros and Jânio Quadros. In addition, the communist left was active and relatively strong at various moments during this period, although it was clandestine for much of the time.

Workers expressed and confronted their challenges during this period by means of a series of strategies. Their social networks, usually rooted in informal relationships among family, friends, countrymen, and community members, were fundamental not only to the process of migration from rural areas to the city, but also to dealing with problems of urban life and dilemmas at work. These networks were the grounding for the creation of a wave of popular associations, and, more broadly, for much of the political action taken by São Paulo's popular classes at that time.

Unions formed one axis of the workers' strength, but workers' resources were not limited to unions, nor were workers' efforts restricted to confronting industrialists. Quite the contrary: recreational, educational, charitable, ethnic, mutual, cooperative, religious, artistic, cultural, and neighborhood associations formed a complex, heterogeneous range of organizations that clearly announced the formation of a multifaceted group with diverse community values. Despite the variety of these associations, it is possible to find common spaces of speech and action among many of them, particularly at such critical times as the so-called Strike of 400,000 in 1957.[3]

This book analyzes the experience of the period 1945–66 in the São Paulo *bairro* (neighborhood) of São Miguel Paulista, where the processes of industrialization, urbanization, migration, and class formation presented a particularly intricate cross-section of relationships. São Miguel Paulista was formerly a small, isolated village on the outskirts of São Paulo, but its face was altered radically in the late 1930s, when Nitro Química (commonly called "Nitro" by its workers and by residents of São Miguel) set up a large factory there that made artificial fibers and chemical products. Nitro Química subsequently became one of Brazil's largest companies, decisively influencing the development and social life of São Miguel in the process.

The Nitro workforce was mostly composed of rural migrants, especially *nordestinos* (northeasterners), who came to live in the area around the factory and in various newly built workers' settlements. An active process of real estate subdivision made São Miguel into one of São Paulo's fastest-growing districts and one of the best examples of the city's peripheral expansion, while its strong migrant presence gave it a reputation as one of the first strongholds of northeasterners in the city.

Nitro Química's management system combined paternalism and nationalism with an extensive system of benefits. While this model contained elements present in corporate ideology and in the Brazilian state's national-developmentalist ideology of the time, it also had a system of tight control and repression, which often relied on the state's police apparatus. Despite this repression, workers in São Miguel Paulista developed a strong sense of community and class identity, mobilizing at times around local organizations—notably, the Chemical Workers Union. The poor condition of the neighborhood's urban infrastructure, which was contrary to many migrants' expectations for the capital city, created a space for the activation of various political currents that sought to relate to this new contingent of workers. While the Brazilian Communist Party (Partido Comunista Brasileiro; PCB) was quite successful in this regard, other political currents that emerged in the late 1940s and 1950s were connected to the two most prominent São Paulo political figures of the time: Adhemar de Barros and Jânio Quadros.[4]

The study of the Northeastern migrant laborers who came to São Miguel Paulista in waves over a period of nearly fifty years provides a platform from which to question and problematize previous academic arguments that have privileged the "rural origins of the Brazilian proletariat" as the explanation for its alleged apathy and lack of class-consciousness. It also provides a way to understand relationships among regional characteristics, migration, and working-class culture.

My narrative analyzes the history of workers in São Miguel beginning in 1945, when Getúlio Vargas's dictatorial Estado Novo (New State) fell, the country democratized, and Nitro Química emerged from the Second World War as one of Brazil's strongest companies. It ends in 1966, with the crisis-driven dismissal of nearly a third of Nitro Química's employees, profoundly altering the relationship between company and community and symbolizing the end of the era in which São Miguel was practically an industrial city contained within São Paulo.

While the factory constituted a fundamental space for the creation of a working-class identity, the neighborhood also played a central role in creating a strong sense of community that interacted with that identity. Through the study of São Miguel Paulista and Nitro Química, then, this book seeks to deepen the analysis of relations between the spheres of work and community.

Class, Community, and Neighborhoods

Social historians have diversified their analyses of workers' lives in recent decades. While the organized labor movement is still an important object of study, so are the multiple dimensions of class experience, and everyday working-class culture, gender, family, leisure, and sociability among workers have all become relevant to scholarly works on the history of labor.[5]

Unions, political parties, strikes, labor relations, labor procedures within firms—these basic themes make up the "nucleus of the discipline," to use Daniel James's term.[6] But it has been some time since labor historians confined their studies to these topics. For many, the challenge has been to develop an approach that incorporates them into the broader perspective of working-class experience.

My trajectory in undertaking the present study has followed this development in labor historiography. In *Trabalhadores e cidadãos* (Workers and Citizens), I sought to connect the Nitro workers' history with that of the company, tracing the development of a strong factory culture and a militant political and union tradition amid the fissures and ambiguities of the system of corporate domination.[7] Thus the workers' union and its struggles, particularly the big strike of 1957, were highlighted in that work.

From that study, it seemed clear to me that there was a need to advance the understanding of workers' social history in the hope of deepening the understanding of their relationships, both during the migration process and in their everyday urban experience. My attention was drawn in particular to the strong sense of community that developed in São Miguel Paulista. In this work, my emphasis has shifted from factory and union struggles to migration, the neighborhood, and social relations.

By connecting these overlapping perspectives, I hope to arrive at a more complex analysis of the lived working-class experience. I am trying to grasp some of the fundamental changes that occurred in Brazil during the second half of the twentieth century—industrialization, urbanization, the new postwar political context, and rural-urban migration—from the perspective of how people acted on (or were involved in) these processes in their everyday lives. In stressing the importance of everyday reality to the process of class formation, I have taken care not to depoliticize it but, instead, to demonstrate its vital importance in building social networks and a public space where workers could construct identities and fight for rights.[8]

This book investigates the social networks created by workers, first during the migration process and subsequently in the workplace and at home in São

Paulo. It also attempts to understand how these same workers affected the process of urbanization to become key political actors in the life of the city, often linking community organizations with union- and working-class-based political parties and establishing tense reciprocal relationships with political leaders. This study, then, seeks to contribute to a more multifaceted understanding of the political experience of the working class in those years. At the same time, by emphasizing the importance of internal migrations in the process of formation of the working class, I hope to stimulate a more comprehensive analysis of the history of Brazilian labor by integrating the currently disjunctive studies of international and national migration.[9]

My research into São Miguel's history reveals a defiant articulation by local workers of a specific notion of community, associated in turn with a strong class identity. Accordingly, one of the goals of this book is to improve understanding of the concept of community and its possible relation to the idea of class.

In recent years, many historians have sought to study communities not only as places but as sets of social relations. This approach has helped me understand links, networks, and relationships among workers, as well as their collective action. Many of these studies have emphasized community life and workers' ties to their cities and neighborhoods, from which they derive assistance and mutual aid, collective solidarity, and common culture. Since all of this is central to the formation and the experience of the working class, its study, then, is necessary for all those interested in analyzing "life beyond work."[10]

Critics have pointed out problems in the indiscriminate use by labor historians of the concept of "community." Many studies have presented unity and solidarity among workers not as the result of a deliberate, historically constructed human effort but as a consequence of community, a kind of "ecological factor" that explains class-consciousness.[11] More recently, however, sociologists and historians have emphasized the importance of space to the process of class formation.[12] In this approach, a space, like a social network, comes to be seen as a base, a "habitat," where collective action is created. In this conceptualization, space is not only a locus where class formation occurs; it is part of the process.

The process of class formation thus has a double dynamic. It "involves the construction of far-reaching social relations, connecting members of the class through different places"—by means of unions and political parties, for example. But it also requires "the construction of dense connections that allowed the construction of identities of solidarity and community over time and in the absence of formal organization. In this sense, the class could be 'extracted' from the 'community' and from personal relationships that lead to social solidarity."[13]

Analyzing neighborhoods and geographical spaces as communities only makes sense, therefore, when in a given context its residents hold a common understanding and share a language. Such language can, in certain circumstances, overlap with a language of class and with other notions of community, such as those based on place of residence, place of work, and a common ethnic or migrant background. That, in my opinion, is what happened in São Miguel Paulista. Neighborhoods do not just turn into communities by themselves; social networks constructed and articulated by residents create them, and space is an important component of these social networks.

Historians, geographers, urbanists, and social scientists in different national situations have been highlighting the relationships between urban space and the working class. These scholars emphasize that spatial organization not only affects workers, influencing decisively their access to material and symbolic resources while framing social networks and experiences; it is also affected by them.[14]

This emphasis on urban space is one of the concerns of recent historiographical studies of Brazilian labor.[15] In addition to the traditional aspects of the inner world of the workplace and the processes and relationships of work, these new studies ask fundamental questions for a more comprehensive understanding of class formation in Brazil. Treading a similar path, this book seeks to understand, by means of a specific study, the formation of class in its relationship with a number of complex social and political processes. The broad framework of this study will thus include the connections between migrants and their social networks; connections between workplace and neighborhood; issues of urbanization; the local and national political scene; family and gender relations; the vicissitudes of economic development and the job market; and organizational experiences both formal and informal.

Rural Origin, Workers, and Politics

The analysis of rural migrations and their interaction with the formation of the Brazilian working class also has a history. Between the mid-1950s and mid-1960s, a number of sociological studies probed the intense transformations the country underwent beginning in the 1930s, and especially after the Second World War.[16]

Buoyed by the notion of modernization, these analyses systematized in academic language the then contemporary vision of a supposed structural division in Brazil between rural "backwardness" and urban "progress."[17] Migration was thereby seen as the passage of archaic societies and cultures to the cities, which were understood to be spaces of industrial development and modernity, so that migrants would traverse "literally in a few days several epochs of socioeconomic evolution."[18]

According to this line of thought, the possibilities opened up by urbanization and industrialization represented a more advanced stage of development and, possibly, upward social and economic mobility. Migrants were seen as "fleeing the timid, unassisted, hopeless condition of the rural areas" and heading "to São Paulo, in order to progress, to *enjoy civilization*."[19]

Although, as the Brazilian sociologist Eder Sader has stated, migration was viewed optimistically as a higher stage in the lives of those thousands who moved to the cities, the image of the migrant was a negative one.[20] In Sader's vision, the first generations of migrants, mostly employed at unskilled jobs in modern factories and urban service sectors, were still permeated by traditional culture, owing to their recent rural origin. Inexperienced in the urban industrial world, they adjusted precariously to this new reality and did not identify with their condition as laborers, in a kind of "adaptive apathy."[21]

In this view, domestic migrant workers were seen as non-bearers of class tradition and as such were contrasted with the proletariat that existed before the great wave of internal migration, particularly before 1930. At that time, during the early stages of Brazilian industrialization, the working class was primarily composed of European immigrants, who brought class experience from their countries of origin and quickly organized a radical and militant resistance to the bosses and to the state.[22] In this analysis, the supposed persistence of traditional forms of conduct by migrants implied an absence of patterns of collective action and class solidarity. Unions and other class-based organizations would thus be alien to the experience of these workers or, at best, would be understood on an individual basis and as organs for welfare assistance. The new migrant workers, considered politically passive and apathetic, originated in an agrarian environment of paternalistic domination that "brought with it an attitude of submission by persons belonging to the lower layers in the presence of members of the upper strata, in which humility and respect are the characteristic feature."[23] They could, therefore, be easily manipulated by the discourse and action of charismatic populist politicians.

This view was widely shared. During the peak moment of urban and rural worker mobilizations in the period before the military coup of 1964, for example, a communist activist wrote that there would surely be "a natural relaxation of the class struggle" because the working class in São Paulo had "received in its ranks men and women coming from the most backward regions and the most deprived sectors, such as the countryside."[24]

This binary approach to modernization theory, which opposed a traditional subsistence sector to a modern industrial one, came under heavy criticism when internal migration became a widely studied subject in government institutions and universities in the late 1960s and 1970s, but further research and systematization is still needed to analyze how the formation of the Brazilian working class was influenced by the migration process.[25] Although studies by labor sociologists of the 1950s and 1960s have been rightly criticized for several of their theoretical assumptions and conclusions, they have the undeniable merit of trying to understand the impact of migration and the supposed cultural traditions of migrants on the proletariat of São Paulo, something rarely mentioned in subsequent studies.

In his sophisticated analysis of populism, Francisco Weffort sought to overcome the limitations of structurally oriented explanations for social and political relations in the period 1945–64, emphasizing instead the role of political actors. According to Weffort, the "endorsement of populist movements by the popular classes . . . cannot be explained by the 'absence' of urban experience or of class, but precisely by a particular kind of experience rooted in the very conditions of social formation of these [Latin American] countries."[26] Although such a statement suggests a privileging of the young working class of the period as having agency in the social and political process, and although Weffort even states that populism was the result of an alliance of classes, he does not make sufficient inquiry in this direction, as Angela de Castro Gomes has pointed out.[27]

Although Weffort's proposed interpretative model for the populist period at times affirms the ambiguity of the "manipulation" of workers by populist leaders, it in fact emphasizes the prospect of their co-optation by the state.[28] Weffort's study inspired a number of works in the 1970s and 1980s that, despite his observations on working-class action and self-organization, tended to incorporate the master narratives of a manipulative state and demagogic leaders co-opting the working masses as an explanatory paradigm of social life and national politics between 1930 and 1964. This widely disseminated explanation turned the period itself into an adjective; many began to call it the "populist era" or "populist republic."

This perspective began to be heavily criticized in the mid-1980s, as newer studies rejected the notions of workers' political passivity and of manipulation and co-optation by an all-powerful state and sought instead to emphasize an active role for workers and to overcome the widely disseminated dichotomy of autonomy versus heteronomy. Understanding workers as historical actors who make choices within a given field of pressures and counter-pressures has been one of the central objectives of historians looking into the social history of the working class between 1930 and 1964.[29]

Within this field, approaches and focuses have been developed that offer a reasonably diversified vision. John French, for example, seeks to deepen the brief Weffortian insight of a poly-classist alliance as an explanatory axis for relations among workers, state, middle classes, and bourgeoisie during that period. Although such alliances were made among unequal actors in terms of socio-political weight, they could not exist without a constantly shifting balance of negotiations and reciprocities. For French, there existed a composite "populist political system that influenced the behavior of all participants."[30]

Other historians, however, have repeatedly rejected populism as an operational concept for the analysis of social and political relations in Brazil during that period.[31] These scholars highlight the conceptual imprecision and pejorative tone that stuck to the notion of populism, making the term "elastic and somewhat ahistorical, so that it now explains everything—and as happens in these cases, it explains very little." More important, they argue that the term "populism" should be rejected, along with its "obscuring effect," because it is permeated by notions of massive state control over, and manipulation of, the "masses" and by a notion of co-optation that excludes any possibility of reciprocal relationship and thus empties its historical subjects.[32]

With differences of emphasis, Gomes, Jorge Ferreira, and Daniel Aarão Reis Filho propose the notion of *trabalhismo* (laborism) as a way to think about relations between the state and the working class during that period. Gomes speaks of a "laborist pact," which sought "to emphasize the relation between unequal actors, but in which there is not an all-powerful State." Ferreira affirms the importance of a "laborist project," whose institutional expression was the Brazilian Workers' Party (Partido Trabalhista Brasileiro; PTB), "the most popular organization during the post-'45 democratic experience, which in 1964 became the largest labor group in the country's political spectrum." Based on a relationship in which the state and the working class "identified common interests," the laborist project "expressed a class-consciousness" on the part of the workers and collaborated primarily for the establishment of a "collective identity" among them.[33] In addition, Reis considers populism to be a political and academic "invention" that, after the coup of 1964, served to hide the "laborist tradition," which was characterized by a "program that was nationalist, statist, and popular."[34]

This current debate expresses great dissatisfaction with the paradigm of populism as formulated by Weffort and his followers and seeks instead a new conceptual framework that will take into account the complex political and social dynamics of Brazilian workers' experiences during most of the twentieth century. It seems to me insufficient to replace concepts of populism with those of laborism in any of their versions. As Alexandre Fortes observed in a recent work, "Apart from the risk of replacing the stigma with the apology when we change 'populism' for 'laborism,' we might be keeping, or even deepening, the mistake of trying to explain different elements of the same historical moment in a single word."[35] An isolated emphasis on the laborist aspect of political and social relations obscures other core dimensions of workers' experience during that period, repositioning class analysis as exclusively focused on labor relations and unions. However, the urban dimension was a vital aspect of workers' lives, particularly in cities with large industrial expansion, and it seems to me impossible to understand the political relationships of the time without taking it into account and connecting it to essential questions of labor and union relations.

The political life of São Paulo—the most industrialized state in the country, with the largest working class—is incomprehensible using laborism as an absolute explanatory key. The most popular political leaders, Adhemar de Barros and Jânio Quadros, built their careers outside laborism, although they flirted with it. Especially in the case of Quadros, their recognition of the problems of rapid urban growth was central to their careers; the highly unequal distribution of the fruit of the city's intense development stimulated a host of popular demands that served as a platform for these politicians' emergence and consolidation as leaders. (Moreover, in spite of the popularity of Getúlio Vargas among the working class, his PTB was weak in São Paulo and extremely divided.) Apart from labor rights and labor relations, which were always present in the political and social agenda of São Paulo, an analysis of political relations from the 1930s through the 1960s needs to consider workers' demands for better living conditions, respectability, dignity, and the right to "progress," as understood by workers at that time.

Hence, in this book I am interested in exploring social networks created by workers both during the migration process and subsequently in their workplaces and homes in São Miguel and in understanding how these same workers acted on the process of urbanization to become key political actors in the life of the city. Moreover, such research will also bring forward elements important to understanding key aspects of working-class culture. In this way, my aim is to contribute to a more multifaceted understanding of the political and social experience of the working class in those years.

Sources and Chapters

This book was drawn from a wide range of sources. My previous research had already provided access to a series of business documents from Nitro Química—in particular, the complete collection of *Nitro Journal*, the company newsletter of the 1950s. In addition, the archives of the social and political police, the Departamento de Ordem Político e Social (DOPS), and of the Chemical Workers Union of São Paulo had an important role in this research, along with interviews with former union leaders and Nitro workers.[36]

The enormous DOPS collection at the Public Archive of the State of São Paulo has continued to be one of the principal references for this study. The investigative zeal of governors, businessmen, and political police bequeathed us an impressive array of documents about the most varied aspects of the workers' life. Obviously, many of these documents discuss political and union organizations and protests, demonstrations, and strikes, but it is also possible to extract from them a rich collection of material about the daily life of the neighborhoods and the factory, as well as about community and cultural organizations.[37]

In the library of the Municipal Council of São Paulo, I consulted the minutes of the council meetings, which gave me valuable access to the speeches and debates of the councilmen, and examined books, newspapers, and documents of the *prefeitura* (Mayor's Office) about city neighborhoods. Neighborhood newspapers, union bulletins, party organs, and "mainstream" press were all fundamental for this work, and were principally consulted at the São Paulo state archivel at the Arquivo Edgard Leuenroth (Edgard Leuenroth Archive; AEL) at the State University of Campinas (Universidade Estadual de Campinas; UNICAMP), at the Mário de Andrade Library in São Paulo; the National Library in Rio de Janeiro; and at the Documentation Center Archive (Centro de Documentação e Memória; CEDEM) at São Paulo State University (Universidade Estadual Paulista; UNESP).

In addition to the newspapers, I was able to find in the CEDEM collection interesting documents from the Brazilian Communist Party and the collection of the researcher Fabio Munhoz, a rich source for those interested in the strikes and union actions of the late 1950s and early 1960s, particularly the so-called Strike of 400,000 in 1957.[38]

At the São Paulo Regional Electoral Court I had access to electoral bulletins from the 1940s through the 1960s, which allowed a more accurate assessment of voting trends in São Miguel. I consulted the speeches of state legislators in the library and in the São Paulo State Legislative Assembly Documentation Center.

In the United Kingdom and the United States, I worked in the archives of the Public Record Office in London and in the National Archives in Washington, DC, respectively, which gave me access to reports on politics, the labor movement, and the social and economic transformation of Brazil as seen by diplomats and foreign travelers.

An extensive bibliography served as a base for the writing of this work. The UNICAMP, University of São Paulo (Universidade São Paulo; USP), Mário de Andrade, National, Roberto Simonsen (Federação das Indústrias do Estado de São Paulo), and University of Manchester libraries were essential and allowed me access to an extensive range of books and journals.[39] Also important was the library of the Center for Migration Studies (Centro Estudos de Migration; CEM), where I examined the most comprehensive collection of works on internal migration in the country.

The goodwill and kindness of many people allowed me access to personal collections and to institutions without which the fundamental documentation for this work would not have been possible. Osvaldo Pires de Holanda gave me extensive material about the Autonomist Movement in São Miguel Paulista. José Caldini Filho made it possible for me to have copies of an incredible collection of photographs, newspapers, and documents about São Miguel. Photographs were also provided to me by Nelson Bernardo, Nair Cecchini, and Helena Oliveira Silveira. Pastor Jonas of the Baptist Church of São Miguel Paulista expedited my access to the old documents and acts of that institution. At the Diogo de Faria, Carlos Gomes, and D. Pedro schools, I consulted old registers and material about students, including some schoolwork and essays. Finally, at the History Laboratory of the University of Cruzeiro do Sul I surveyed an important collection of documents, including various photographs and a very important collection of fifty-three interviews realized in 2000 by students in the history program with former residents.

I carried out forty-two oral history interviews.[40] From a network of contacts created around the Association of Retired Chemical Workers, I had the opportunity to interview several former Nitro Química workers, residents, and political activists in the neighborhood. Together with the local impact of the publication of *Trabalhadores e cidadãos*, the contacts that appeared through this network opened the way for new interviews with other residents of São Miguel who were not directly related to the trade union or political world, allowing me to assemble a rich, diverse collection of testimony.[41]

Chapter 1 of this book seeks to highlight the general importance of internal migration to the formation of the working class in São Paulo after the Second World War. In dialogue with specialized literature and primary sources, I analyze the internal migration of workers from the countryside in the context of São Paulo's accelerated industrialization of the 1950s and 1960s, when companies had an intense need for manual labor. However, in addition to economic and demographic factors, I highlight the agency of, and the strategies chosen by, the migrants in this process, as well as how gender relations influenced different experiences of migration between men and women. Finally, I seek to demonstrate how the presence and the action of migrants were basic to the debate of the "Northeastern question" and to the creation of a political and cultural imagination about the Brazilian Northeast and about northeasterners in São Paulo.

Chapter 2 approaches the neighborhood history of São Miguel Paulista in the context of São Paulo's rapid industrialization and urbanization. São Miguel was transformed by the establishment of Companhia Nitro Química Brasileira there in 1935 and had become the city's fastest-growing area by the 1950s. Although immersed in the peripheral pattern of urban growth dominant in São Paulo during this period, São Miguel was different from other suburbs that were widely considered bedroom communities. This chapter explores how the presence of a large industrial company employing most of the local workforce created unusual conditions for the formation of a working-class community.

In chapter 3, the workers' own actions toward the structuring of their urban setting is a point of analysis, as is the process of class formation beyond the factory space. Aspects of leisure and workers' culture are discussed, noting both elements of homogeneity and traces of heterogeneity within the workers' community, seeking in this way to demonstrate the complexity of the workers' set of experiences. The chapter also aims to investigate processes of building relationships of solidarity, as well as those of antagonism, among local residents. Differences of ethnicity, generation, gender, and levels of social aspiration are highlighted and analyzed. The neighborhood's infrastructure needs in relation to migrants' expectations of "progress" are treated as important issues in creating a strong sense of community. Finally, the chapter seeks to explain how the formation of a Northeastern identity among migrant workers overlapped with ideals of work and worker.

Starting from a critical dialogue with the specialized literature and focusing on the case of São Miguel Paulista, chapters 4 and 5 seek to provide an alternative and more complex view of the relationship among politics, social movements, and migrant workers during the so-called populist era (1945–64). Chapter 4 analyzes the political parties in São Miguel, with particular emphasis on the PCB and on the movements that were forged around Adhemar de Barros and Jânio Quadros. The chapter's themes include the structuring of political parties in the area; how and in what circumstances partisan options were defined; the role of elections; and the relationship at election time between neighborhood-based micro-questions and statewide and national issues. I seek to go beyond understanding relationships between "populist" politicians and the working class as focused only on labor and unions or as simply a relation between "charismatic" leaders and an "amorphous" mass. By considering the neighborhood and taking social and political relationships as the object of analysis, I hope to achieve a more sophisticated understanding of the political system of the period.

Chapter 5 looks at São Paulo's neighborhood organizations. In examining their weight within the political conjunctures, their relationships with union organizations, and their engagement in the broader struggles of workers in that period, I seek to overcome the dichotomy, all too common in the literature, between "resident" and "worker." In addition, the chapter discusses attempts by separatist movements in São Miguel Paulista to secede from the city of São Paulo. Feeling abandoned by the government, these movements believed that the transformation of the bairro into an autonomous city could bring less unequal development and make possible the construction of an urban infrastructure to improve the quality of life for the population. These autonomous movements had three strong moments (1953, 1958, and 1962–63), but they were defeated every time. I analyze the characteristics, motivations, and dilemmas of these autonomy movements and their relationship with other social movements in the neighborhood. Finally, the chapter discusses the political conjuncture before the coup in 1964, with emphasis on the action of the Chemical Workers Union in São Miguel, as well as on the local consequences of militarization and the first moments of the dictatorship. The final section studies the mass dismissals of Nitro Química employees in 1966, which symbolized the end of an era for the community of São Miguel.

A Cardboard Suitcase and a Backpack

Northeastern Migrations to São Paulo in the 1950s

In the interior of Bahia, in the county of Jacobina, in the town of Vilarejo de Caem, an anxious Artur Pinto de Oliveira said goodbye to his family one day in December 1947, leaving behind the home where he had lived his first seventeen years.

Hopeful for a better life, with "that dream of studying" in his head, he had caught the "fever of the time": São Paulo. "At that time, every northeasterner dreamed of going to São Paulo," he recalled more than fifty years later. "São Paulo became heaven; it was our paradise." His older brother had left for the capital city some months before and was already working at Nitro Química Brasileira. Their father had not wanted Artur to follow in his footsteps, but the older brother's insistent letters home wore his resistance down.

Artur's journey to São Paulo was exhausting. From Jacobina he took a train to Juazeiro, where he crossed the Rio São Francisco to Petrolina, in the state of Pernambuco. There he bought the cheapest ticket for the steamboat descending the river to the mining town of Pirapora. The drought in the northeastern interior required the boat to go slowly so it would not run aground on the sandbanks, and the voyage took fifteen days.

Along with hundreds of other migrants, Artur squeezed below deck into the second-class section of the boat. He compared it to "a ship for African slaves. You saw nothing. Full of people, promiscuous misbehavior, darkness, a bad smell." The trip would have been worse yet had not Artur, a good conversationalist, made friends with "a man from Goiás, an educated man, and communicative" and passed the days discussing "why the Northeast was so poor and why its people all migrated to other regions." Even so young, Artur already had some ideas about "why the case of the Northeast does not get solved"; he proposed taking advantage of the São Francisco and Amazon Rivers to make a large irrigation system in the region.

Probably charmed by the boy's curiosity, the man from Goiás took a liking to Artur and invited him regularly to have lunch in the first-class restaurant on the boat. Arriving at Pirapora, one bound for Goiás and the other for his new life farther south, they said goodbye. From Pirapora to São Paulo took three more days by train, then Artur stepped onto the platform of the Estação do Norte, in the São Paulo bairro of Brás, in early January 1948. From there, he took yet another train to his final destination: São Miguel Paulista, where "there was not one paved street." Artur worked there for more than forty years and has lived there all his life since.[1]

That same year, 1948, Augusto Ferreira Lima decided it was time to leave the drought-plagued area of Alagoinhas, in the state of Bahia, to try his luck in the south. Augusto had worked since childhood in the family orange groves, and by the time he was sixteen he was employed by the Ferrovia Leste Brasileiro (Eastern Brazilian Railroad). For the first two years, he divided his time between planting and laying railroad ties. Then he learned surveying, and for seven more years he continued to work both in the fields and on the railroad.

Going to São Paulo was his longtime desire, periodically reinforced when friends came back to Bahia for family visits. Augusto remembers that it was an event to see "a *baiano* arrive . . . wearing a nice suit and tie," attracting the girls' attention. "Meanwhile we, [who lived] there, had to go out in our humble clothing. That made a lot of people decide to go to São Paulo." The return visitors told seductive tales of the city's grandiosity, its abundant jobs, its leisure options. Many years later, Augusto recalled how his friend Evelino had described the beautiful train trip though the Serra do Mar and his excursions to Santos on the coast. The first time Augusto took a vacation, living in São Paulo, he took the train to Santos, repeating Evelino's journey.

With money saved from his railroad salary, Augusto bought a ticket for São Paulo. For eleven days he traveled on a truck, a *pau-de-arara*,[2] so crowded that three planks were tied outside the vehicle to accommodate the overflow. Taking the Rio-São Paulo highway, the only route between the two cities at the time, the first stop the pau-da-arara made in São Paulo was at the church of São Miguel Paulista, the bairro where an old acquaintance of Augusto's lived.

As Augusto clutched his cardboard suitcase, threw down his backpack, and got off the truck, he stepped for the first time onto the ground of the neighborhood where he has lived ever since. In the distance, he saw the chimneys of the factory where he would work for the next thirty-seven years: Nitro Química.

The trajectories of Artur and Augusto were not uncommon. Indeed, they are paradigmatic accounts of one of the most striking facts of Brazilian social history in the second half of the twentieth century: the great migration of millions of workers from the rural regions to the cities.

The largest number of migrants came from the Northeast, while the principal receiver of migrants was the greater metropolitan area of the southern city of São Paulo.[3] In some years, more migrants came to São Paulo from the geographically intermediate state of Minas Gerais than from the Northeast, and many migrants also came from the interior of the state of São Paulo; meanwhile, other places besides São Paulo received northeasterners: Brasília, Rio de Janeiro, Belo Horizonte, Salvador, Recife, Fortaleza, Volta Redonda, the north of Paraná, and the Amazonian basin.[4] But as the industrial metropolis of São Paulo transformed itself into a home and a workplace for millions of migrants, it was the worker from the Northeast, coming to escape hunger, misery, and, periodically, drought, who became the grand symbol of migration in the Brazilian social imagination.

The Fever of the Time

While the internal migration of workers from other Brazilian states to São Paulo was an old phenomenon,[5] it picked up in the 1930s, when it began to be officially encouraged. A sharp decrease in foreign immigration, aggravated by nationalist government policies that placed restrictions on foreign labor,[6] made it hard for coffee planters to find manual laborers. The problem expanded geographically as new coffee plantations in the distant interior of São Paulo state and in the north of Paraná, along with expanded cotton acreage in the state of São Paulo, demanded a larger number of "hands for labor." In response, the old policy of subsidizing immigration was repurposed to relocate "national workers." In 1935, the governor of São Paulo, Armando Salles de Oliveira, began negotiations to contract with private companies that were starting to operate in the northern part of the state of Minas Gerais and in the Brazilian Northeast, promoting and facilitating the migration of rural workers.

In 1939, when the Inspectorate of National Workers (Inspetoria de Trabalhadores Nacionais; ITN) was created as an agency attached to the Department of Immigration and Colonization (Departamento de Imigração e Colonização; DIC), the state assumed the responsibility for hiring and transferring workers. The ITN was superseded by specialized companies that recruited manual labor in the Brazilian interior, some of which became well known, including the Companhia Itauquerê, the F. Sodré Filho, and the Compahia de Agricultura, Imigração e Colonização.[7]

In the north of Minas Gerais, ITN offices were established in Montes Claros and Pirapora, both of which were terminal cities for the Estrada de Ferro Central railroad. In both cities, arriving migrants underwent a selection process and received tickets to go to São Paulo, where they were lodged at the Immigrant Reception Center before being sent to plantations in the interior of the state. Humberto Dantas, an employee of the Secretary of Agriculture, Industry, and Commerce in São Paulo, observed in 1941, "Generally, there converge on Pirapora those who flow from the São Francisco, on boats or on foot, following the axis of the river . . . with individual migrants coming [from] Piauí, Ceará, Pernambuco, Sergipe and Alagoas." In addition to "those who lived in the north of Minas," Montes Claros, the principal point of concentration of those who were looking to get to the south of the country, was already attracting "workers coming from a vast central region of Bahia."[8]

Sixteen-year-old Geraldo Rodrigues de Freitas set out for Montes Claros in February 1939. Several of his cousins had left the small village of Salinas in Minas Gerais, almost on the border with Bahia, to work on plantations in São Paulo state. On visits back home, they impressed the young Geraldo. "When they came back," he recalls, they had "their mouths all full of gold. They laughed, and you saw the gold flashing." For him, that was the proof that São Paulo was a "wonder" that left him "eager to go." Freitas persuaded his parents, and aided and accompanied by his cousins, "who had already been in the interior [of São Paulo], in Pompéia," he left on a truck for Montes Claros, where he slept outside the station, because we had no money to pay [for a room]. . . . When it was morning, we went to give our names and catch the *migração* [subsidized train to São Paulo], but they said that we couldn't go on the migração because Minas still wasn't allowed, only Bahians. . . . Since my cousin had already made this trip to São Paulo, he was no fool. [He decided they should leave and return later.] Since no one knew us, when we returned, they asked us, "Where are you from?" and my cousin said, "We're from Caculé, in Bahia.' . . . That's how we got them to give us a pass. . . . Early the next day we caught the train and arrived in Brás, here [in São Paulo].

That Geraldo Freitas's cousin gave the name of the Bahian city of Caculé when he lied to the ITN officials was no accident. According to data from the Immigrant Reception Center in São Paulo, 12,774 residents of that locality went to the capital city between 1936 and 1939, which represents a staggering 53 percent of the local population. In 1952, the county of Caculé would continue to be one of the principal regions of origin for Bahian migrants; that year alone, 8,096 people left the city.[9]

The Bahian Jorge Gonçalves Lula had already "caught the migração" in Pirapora, having made the trip in January 1937, at thirteen, along with his father, mother, and six siblings. His father, along with some uncles, had already gone to São Paulo for work five times and decided that it was time to transfer the whole family. Jorge Lula remembers that all of the family's belongings were sold very cheap, that the debilitating trip to Pirapora took ten days on the steamboat *São Francisco*. When the family arrived, they received "a little sack of flour and some pieces of brown sugar" and embarked for the interior of the state of São Paulo, where Jorge would work on a cotton plantation for almost twenty years. Jorge and his family were sent, as Geraldo and his cousin would later be, to the Immigrant Reception Center in the São Paulo neighborhood of Brás. Formerly a reception center for foreign immigrants, the hostel was now given over principally to domestic migrants, who were moving in large numbers toward the plantations in the interior of São Paulo state. Between 1935 and 1939, 96.3 percent of the 285,304 workers entering the hostel were Brazilians, and only 3.7 percent were foreigners. Of those 274,579 migrants, 130,063 (47.4 percent) came from Bahia, and 68,131 (24.8 percent) came from Minas Gerais.[10]

The Second World War unleashed a new boom in Amazonian rubber production that channeled migration to the north of Brazil, especially from the Northeast; almost 100,000 northeasterners migrated to the north in the first half of the 1940s, which was a little less than the total number of migrants from other states to São Paulo.[11] But despite that, the migratory flow to the south generally remained high and swelled enormously after 1946.

Migration into the expanding agricultural regions of western São Paulo state and the north of Paraná continued at an elevated level during the whole period. The majority of the nearly 1.6 million workers who passed through the Immigrant Reception Center in Brás between 1946 and 1960 were headed for these rural zones as a destination, at least initially.[12] "In 1950, for example," notes the researcher José Francisco de Camargo, "of the 100,123 national workers arriving to São Paulo, 97,757 were en route [via the Immigrant Reception Center] for the plantation, with the others remaining in the capital."[13] Even so, the Immigrant Reception Center registers do not measure the total flow of migrants to São Paulo, since the growing number whose trips were taken "on their own account" through personal contacts were not registered by the official structures of the Immigration Service.

Nevertheless, despite the heavy flow of migrants to rural areas, the mass-migration to urban areas was one of the great social and demographic phenomena of postwar Brazil. Between 1950 and 1980, an estimated 38 million people left the countryside, profoundly altering the nation's socioeconomic profile.[14]

The speed of the process was striking. While the city of São Paulo tripled in size from 1950 to 1970, its population of northeastern origin grew by a factor of ten. The 1970 census showed that of the country's nine major metropolitan regions, greater São Paulo had the greatest concentration of migrants, and reported that almost 70 percent of the city's economically active population had gone through some kind of migratory experience.[15]

The impact of internal migration was most sharply felt in the 1950s, when the number of migrants to the city of São Paulo from other Brazilian states surpassed the number of migrants from the interior of the state of São Paulo. By the end of the decade, seven out of every ten people who arrived in the capital were from outside the state of São Paulo.[16] The city received almost a million new inhabitants during the 1950s, representing approximately 60 percent of the county's growth.[17] The great majority of these migrants were from the northeastern states, who were massively employed in the booming metropolitan region.

Indeed, greater São Paulo in the 1950s was the setting for an accelerated, diversified process of industrialization and urbanization. The region was principally responsible for Brazil's elevated rate of growth in industrial production. Between 1945 and 1960, in one of the fastest processes of industrialization anywhere in the world at that time, the country's secondary sector grew an average of 9.5 percent a year. By 1959, almost 50 percent of all Brazilian factory employment was concentrated in the state of São Paulo.[18] Additionally, this industrial growth stimulated a great expansion of the region's service sector, increasing even more the availability of jobs and possible opportunities.

With those incentives on offer, São Paulo and the other factory cities attracted millions of northeastern workers. As described earlier by the Bahian laborer Artur Pinto de Oliveira, São Paulo became the "fever of the time," a "Mecca par excellence for migrants."[19] This prestige was strongly associated with the relative ease of finding work there, as well as with the significant difference in pay between the northeastern countryside and the great southwestern industrial cities. The asymmetry was described by Luís Fernando Maria Teixeira of the National Immigration Department in a study for the Worker Mobilization Service in Rio de Janeiro in 1949: "In the Northeast, J.B.S., in agricultural activity as a rural journeyman, receives 10 cruzeiros for a day, sunup to sundown, in the open air. From Rio, a letter arrives from a bachelor friend, revealing the following: a mason's assistant . . . earns 43 cruzeiros, working from 7 A.M. to 4 P.M., with an hour for lunch."[20]

In addition to better wages, migrants expected to enjoy rights as workers that they did not have as rural laborers. A Bahian worker interviewed in the early 1950s summed up the differences between work in his birthplace and in São Paulo: "Working for others [in Bahia] is no good, because we have no guarantee like we do [in São Paulo]. Here the pay is better, and the employer complies with his obligations."[21]

For many migrants on their way to the big industrial cities of south-central Brazil, the prospect of acquiring workers' rights meant escaping the relations of domination and exploitation to which they had been subjected in the countryside. In this sense, migration had the clear role of "eroding the powers of the great rural proprietors" of the Northeast.[22]

Finally, migrants associated the city with a range of urban benefits, particularly in the areas of education and health. "In Bahia," remembered a mother interviewed in the early 1950s, "you can't give your children a good education. The school is a long way away. Here [in São Paulo] there are more facilities."[23] Statistics confirm this aspect of workers' experience. In 1950, when there were only 1,790 hospital beds in the entire interior of Bahia, the city of São Paulo had more than 12,300.[24]

Employment, higher wages, labor rights, and better hospital and educational infrastructure made for an attractive scenario. Gradually, the idea gained momentum that life in São Paulo would be "easier," especially compared with the great difficulties that the agricultural Northeast faced after the Second World War. The northeastern agrarian structure, which for centuries had been based on the *latifúndio* (large estate), gave signs of exhaustion; its low level of productivity was clearly incapable of keeping up with the development of the country's south-central region. A crisis of traditional systems of rent and partnership, together with an increasing concentration of landownership, made survival more difficult for millions of landless rural workers. "There's no land to rent; the sugar mill takes it all," argued a northeastern migrant, interviewed in São Paulo at the beginning of the 1950s, who, justifying his move to the capital city, concluded, "How is a man going to provide for his family?"[25]

Not surprisingly, the image of the rural Northeast among intellectuals and political forces at this time was one of "backwardness" and of being an obstacle to national development. Overcoming underdevelopment therefore entailed resolving this issue. In this context, various proposals about agrarian reform were notably present in the political debate of the 1950s and 1960s.[26]

In the Northeast, the forms of land use, the work regimes, the agrarian structure, and an inert growth rate made for strong population pressures and were certainly powerful stimuli for migration.[27] Two major droughts that ravaged the northeastern *sertão* (back country) in 1951–52 and in 1958 constituted an additional incentive; not coincidentally, these were the peak moments for northeastern migration to São Paulo. The possibility of drought was strongly taken into consideration by many northeastern workers in making their decision to migrate, particularly in the region known as the "Drought Polygon," comprising the states of "Piauí, Ceará, Rio Grande do Norte, Paraíba, Pernambuco; 50 percent of Alagoas, Sergipe and Bahia, and part of Minas Gerais."[28] That the largest concentration of migrations happened between March and August (the "winter" in the Northeast) can thus be explained by the northeastern rural worker's expectations of rain until mid-March, as in the case of a recently arrived migrant in São Paulo who explained in April 1951 that in his region, if the rainy season did not arrive before March 19, there would be no "winter" that year, and drought was certain.[29]

For much of this *sertaneja* population, migration was not a new phenomenon. Seasonal migrations from the rugged sertão to the sugar mills of the nearby Zona da Mata coastal plain (where the workers were known as *corumbas*) were observed prior to the 1930s for harvesting, cutting, and grinding cane. While temporary or permanent transfers to small and medium-size cities from the countryside within the Northeast were relatively common even for industrial areas, even long-distance migrations were not completely unfamiliar to many northeastern families. At the end of the nineteenth century and the beginning of the twentieth century, and again during the Second World War, millions of northeastern workers moved to the rubber plantations in the Amazon region, where they worked in the extraction of latex.[30] Referring to a supposed "northeastern nomadism," the intellectual Souza Barros recalled the northeasterners' reputation: "The northeasterners, principally from Ceará and Pernambuco, gained fame . . . as a migratory, restless people, called the Jews of Brazil by many, especially early on."[31]

"I Suffered, but I Arrived"

The opening of the Rio-Bahia highway in 1949 greatly reduced the old difficulties of travel between the Northeast and the South. In the 1950s, the improvement of the highway system, especially in the freight routes, had significant importance for migratory growth, as the highways gradually became the most widely used means of migration.[32] Only 12 percent of migrants came to São Paulo by highway in 1950, but two years later, 38 percent of them did.[33]

Nevertheless, rail transport from the northern terminals of Minas Gerais continued to be widely used for migration. The arrival of the famous "Bahian train" disgorging hundreds of migrants became an ordinary scene in the Estação do Norte at Brás. A cinematographer from TV Tupi captured one of these arrivals in 1960: men, women, and children disembarking from a very crowded train, carrying their characteristic bags and cardboard suitcases. Journalists from the São Paulo daily Última Hora who traveled along on one of the "Bahian train" journeys in 1958 found terrible conditions on a journey of several days' duration: dirty cars jammed with more than double the number of passengers officially permitted, food poisoning, contraband traffic, dying children.[34]

Meanwhile, in becoming the symbol of northeastern worker transport, the trucks known as paus-de-arara ultimately gave their nickname to the migrants themselves. These trucks, which carried merchandise from São Paulo and Rio to the northern states, returned south dangerously overloaded with people. Sitting on boards placed across the body of the vehicle, the travelers crossed thousands of kilometers for days at a time in an uncomfortable and dangerous situation. Analyzing the journeys of paus-de-arara during that period, the journalist Marcos Vinicios Vilaça reported the migrants' bitter experiences:

The hygienic conditions of these crossings are extremely precarious, and with two days of travel the stench becomes unbearable with the stink of the children's shit and piss. The adults attend to their physical needs [by] "going into the bushes" at rest stops and at the service stations. . . . When they "go into the bushes," the men by convention go to the left side of the road and the women to the right. About fifty people travel together, although abusive drivers go as far as to put a hundred people as ballast on the body, where they eat cassava flour, biscuits, and molasses. Outside of that, those who have a little more money go exploring in the roadside taverns.[35]

The precariousness of the traveling conditions increased the risk from accidents, which were widely reported in the newspapers at the time. Reporting on the "spectacular" overturning of a "truck loaded to capacity that was going down the Via Dutra, transporting about forty northeasterners," the São Paulo morning paper *A Hora* noted that such accidents were common because the paus-de-arara were "unfit vehicles for those long journeys" and "generally turn[ed] over on the road, aggravating the situation of those poor people who had the misfortune to be born in the northeastern desert."[36] But despite their difficulties, including their prohibition by the legislature, the paus-de-arara proliferated. Data about the movement of migrants on the Rio-Bahia road in 1954, for example, show that almost 60 percent of north-south passenger transport was by truck.[37]

The owners of paus-de-arara played a central role in recruiting workers. Touting the job markets in the southeastern industrial cities, or in rural São Paulo and Paraná, they carried many workers directly to plantation owners, companies, or specialized recruiting agencies in São Paulo, some of which directly contracted trucks for migrant transport.

From the cities of the northeastern interior, passing through the entrepôts of Montes Claros and Pirapora, and arriving at São Paulo's Estação do Norte (officially renamed Estação Roosevelt in 1945) and in its surroundings, an army of recruiters tried to seduce and, typically, take advantage of the rural migrant laborers. Stories about the "insatiable gang" of recruiters who "deceive and exploit the northeasterners" proliferated in the São Paulo press during the 1950s. In 1952, for example, the São Paulo State Department of Political and Social Order (DOPS) opened an investigation into "the unscrupulous actions of recruiters in this capital who bring constant waves of northeastern workers dislodged from their homes with promises of betterment, contributing in this way to the scarcity of laborers in those states."[38]

Representatives worried over the question in the Legislative Assembly. Deputy Carlos Kherlakian, reporting the case of Francisco Pires Praciano, a recruiter who "with proposals for work and living conditions lured 119 northeasterners to endure the march South, traveling on the now notorious paus-de-arara," was offended by the "shameful details that surround the traffic in northeasterners."[39]

The comparison to slave voyages made by Artur Pinto de Oliveira ("It was like a ship for African slaves") was not only a re-elaboration of his memory. The awful conditions of the journey and the action of the agents made for such comparisons at the time. Deputy Kherlakian stated in 1959 that "our northeastern brothers are reliving today the sad history of slavery times." Renato Gonçalves Martins, director of the Division of Lands and Colonization for the Ministry of Agriculture, remembered in 1952 that beginning with the departures for Amazonia at the beginning of the century, the northeasterners traveled in "real 'slave ships.'" A reporter for the newspaper *A Hora*, commenting on the increased flow of paus-de-arara to São Paulo in 1956, referred to the northeasterners as a "new caste of slaves." In some circumstances, the migrants also saw themselves as being in a situation of slavery. Interviewed during their return trip to the northeastern back country, Gilberto José Santana, who had worked on farms in the interior of the state of São Paulo, said, "In the South we were treated like white slaves, with a work regime that we had never imagined could exist."[40]

Even allowing for some exaggeration in the comparisons, when it came to the suffering and difficulties common to the situations, the association between northeastern migration and slavery was one of the most heavily disseminated images of that period. In "A triste partida" (The Sad Departure), his *toada* about northeastern workers migrating to São Paulo,[41] the famous poet Patativa do Assaré reinforced that vision while building on its similarity to the situation of northeasterners in their homeland:

It's a shame how the northerner
so strong and so brave
lives like a slave
in the north and in the south.[42]

The awful conditions of transport and travel endured by most northeastern migrants helped create this notion. Packed trains, paus-de-arara, days-long journeys in dangerous circumstances—all of these factors created a dramatic image of the migrant in search of the "promised land" of São Paulo.

For earlier foreign immigrants, the transatlantic voyage to Brazil constituted a defining moment in their lives, with the journey often narrated in great detail many years later.[43] In the same way, for the Brazilian migrant the hard trip of several days and thousands of kilometers to São Paulo was of great importance and was commonly recalled in detail by those who experienced it. But not only the dangers and difficulties of the journey were remembered. The trip was also a site of interaction with other migrants. In such adverse circumstances, the back of a pau-de-arara or a railroad car could be a space of sociability, mutual aid, and exchange of information about the new reality to come. Marcos Vilaça, observing travelers' behavior on the paus-de-arara, called attention to how, over the duration of the journey, they stopped separating "their bags of food, with the provisions becoming communal." The pau-de-arara constituted a space for play and the creation of friendships, as seen when the migrant played a game called *jegue* (donkey), in which the winning group, on the right or on the left, counted the most donkeys on one or the other side of the road. Vilaça, however, also noted the emergence of disagreements, fights, and, in extreme cases, even deaths resulting from the "theft of small objects from someone's '*matolão*' [travel bag]."[44]

Migrants and Their Networks

Much of the literature about the migration of rural northeasterners emphasizes their economic motivation. Misery in the countryside, land concentration, and increasing dominance by the landlord over small proprietors—along with changes in labor relations, high rates of demographic growth in the Northeast, and periodic droughts—all were factors that made migration the rural worker's last resort. Attracted by employment and greater income and by the possibility of access to social and labor rights denied in the countryside, as well as by greater opportunities for education and health care, the migrants became proletarian, filling the demand for manual labor created by industrialization.[45]

There is no doubt about the importance of that socioeconomic picture as a backdrop for the migratory process and for the development of Brazilian capitalism. Nevertheless, in a significant number of these analyses, the over-valorizing of economic factors ends up belittling the role of the migrants themselves as agents in the process. In many studies, migrants are seen only as ciphers in a workforce transferred passively from less developed to more developed regions. Rural northeastern migrants were not only a reflection of externally determined economic forces, although they were immersed in them. They were also agents of their own movement and in this form, through diverse strategies, they contributed to the shaping of the migratory process.[46]

Placing an emphasis on the migrants redeems the value of their experience and memory.[47] The testimony of workers in São Miguel Paulista reveals the existence of a connected social network for effecting migration, in which determinant factors were the family, friends, and the home community. Dona Zezé Santos de Oliveira, a postmistress in São Miguel for more than thirty years beginning in the 1940s, noted that, among the hundreds of people disembarking every day from the paus-de-arara in front of the post office, "no one came without contacts. They came because a friend was [living in the neighborhood]." Augusto Lima, telling the story of his own arrival in São Miguel Paulista, recalled that "anyone who knew someone here [in São Miguel] came down and looked for his friend's house."

The frequent journalistic vision of migration as a disorderly, "irrational" movement does not correspond to the experience of most migrants.[48] The move, decisive for the lives of those involved, most of the time was meticulously thought through and prepared in the best way possible, in both the family and the community.

Information—about São Paulo, its opportunities for employment, and its possibilities for housing—was fundamental in the decision to migrate. The establishment of a network of communication between migrants and their places of origin frequently guided the migratory process. Correspondence, photographs, and postcards played an important role in furnishing data and in creating a "cultural imaginary of the destination."[49] Luiz Cava Netto, a technician for the São Paulo Health Secretariat, stressed in 1962 the importance of the "propaganda exercised by relatives and friends who spoke of the 'marvels' of the new land."[50] In an article published in 1957 about methods for attracting European immigrants, Teixeira Neto wrote that "a letter written in pencil is worth more than a book of many pages," an observation that could also apply to the northeastern migrants.[51]

As noted earlier, migratory movements were not new to a large contingent of northeastern families. However, even when a move to São Paulo was viewed as provisional, the distance and the size of the commitment it implied required careful coordination and preparation. A migrant's family and social relations in his or her community of origin were central to this process. Moving often meant a temporary rupture of family unity. The risk involved in migration, particularly over long distance, required a strategy of displacement parceled out among migrant families.[52] In general, young bachelors initiated the process, which was frequently anchored in their contacts with friends, contemporaries, or distant relatives.

The possibility of migration to smaller cities or to agricultural regions before an eventual move to São Paulo was almost always taken into account. This seems to have been common in different migratory waves between the 1940s and 1970s. Analyzing the census of 1970, Manoel Tosta Berlinck and Daniel J. Hogan concluded that "a growing proportion of migrants are indirect, having had other urban experiences before arriving in São Paulo." Using data from the same census for the so-called ABC region,[53] Antônio de Almeida stated that "of the 109,000 northeasterners resident in the ABC towns at the time of enumeration, 49,000 declared as their previous domicile places not in the Northeast." For the workers, such a "stage" in the migratory process was considered one more alternative to the risk and insecurity of a direct arrival in the city.[54]

As we have seen, northeastern families had long considered temporary migration a strategy for obtaining resources.[55] The first generations of migrants to São Paulo were highly mobile; for many, probably most, the move was seen as temporary, part of a plan of survival and social ascent. Rates of return to the Northeast were high throughout the 1950s. Partial indicators of the movement along the Rio-Bahia highway show about a 39 percent rate of return for the first half of 1953. At the end of the decade, it was believed that about half of northeastern migrants returned to their region of origin. Some scholars, however, have questioned that figure, believing it to be low.[56]

Northeasterners' mobility attracted the attention of contemporaries. Plantation owners in the interior of São Paulo state complained of the short time that a significant portion of their workers had been in residence. The historian Cliff Welch points to the high turnover of the northeasterners on the plantations of São Paulo state—due partly to farmers' inability to control them and partly to prejudice against Brazilian workers, who were regarded as less stable, motivated, and ambitious than Europeans—as the reason that large São Paulo landholders' complained about migrant workers from the Northeast.[57] The São Paulo DIC calculated that about 60 percent of immigrants to rural areas "did not stay there; they continued in constant displacements to various zones of the country, or returned to their homeland."[58] The constant comings and goings (the famous *vai-e-vem*) of northeastern migrants to São Paulo are revealing. In his research for DIC at the beginning of the 1960s, Antônio Jordão Netto was astonished by "hundreds of cases of people who came for the fourth, fifth, sixth, and even eighth time to São Paulo, over a period that varied from two to ten years."[59] Ten years before, Celeste Souza Andrade had also noted the comings and goings of migrants, describing what seemed to be a typical case:

Interviewee number 3...came from Bahia, having made the trip to Monte Azul by truck and from there to São Paulo by train. He is middle-aged, married, with five children. He came alone; it is the fifth time he has come to São Paulo. He wants to work for a year and go back [to Bahia]. There was a drought in the region where he lives in Bahia. There is no work. He has come to work to send money to the family. He has already done this at other times.... There is not enough money to bring his family. The trip is very uncomfortable, with much sacrifice; just now, on this latest trip, there was an accident.[60]

While interpreted by many as a sign of northeastern migrants' inability to adapt to "the modern urban environment," this heavy spatial displacement can also be understood as part of a rational strategy by workers and their families for survival and to minimize the risks and difficulties of migration. Family cohesion and the support of people in the home region were important elements of this strategy. Thus, whenever possible, the maintenance of a small piece of land back home was seen as essential "insurance"; migration often could be framed as a way to obtain resources for a small capitalization and investment. A survey of factory workers in the São Paulo metropolitan region of Santo André taken in 1971 found that 72 percent of the northeastern migrants had left some property at their place of origin, and 72.5 percent had family living in the home region. Among those from other regions of the country, these indices were 24 percent and 45 percent, respectively.[61]

Nevertheless, the difficulties of maintaining a small piece of property in the Northeast during the 1950s, together with the opportunities in the southeastern job market during its accelerated process of industrialization, reduced the likelihood that migrants return to their home regions. Constant, multiple "comings and goings" can be explained in that context: as opposed to a single, unidirectional flow that expelled a population from "backward" regions to "places of progress," the migratory process had a complex dynamic that consisted of continual, circular displacement between rural and urban areas.

For many workers, migration assumed a permanent nature; according to testimony, some delayed years or even decades to make a simple visit back to their native land. A migrant's permanence or lack thereof was determined by various factors, including ownership of property at the place of origin and the conditions for its maintenance to provide a livelihood for the family group; the type of strategy for the family's relocation (usually in stages); and the ease of entry into job markets in receptive regions. In any case, social networks based on family and on ties of friendship and community were fundamental. They were responsible for sending the migrants to cities and neighborhoods, and often sent them directly to work for specific companies.[62]

Several studies have highlighted the importance of the family as a fundamental characteristic of this process.[63] The decision to migrate and the strategy of migration were established within the family in most cases. Moreover, migrants' routes and destinations often depended on a network of relatives, friends, and community members that made the migratory process viable. Humberto Dantas, an official with the São Paulo Department of Agriculture who accompanied truckloads of sertanejos on the way to the railway trunk lines that offered access to São Paulo at the beginning of the 1940s, was surprised by their level of organization and by their "solidarity cemented by days and days of shared trials. . . . The trips are communal projects, both with regard to those who emigrate in families and to those who travel alone. Anyone who travels the roads of the zones of high emigration will see, for example, numerous groups moving to the South, coming from the same locality. These truck journeys in common give those who participate in them a lively sense of solidarity . . . . Among those who travel in groups, there is frequent interchange of service and help. . . . Thus they travel as brothers united on the way to São Paulo."[64] Although entire families moved occasionally,[65] this does not seem to have been as common as the dismemberment of the migrant family, which could occur because of the risk of failure involved in the process and because of the provisional character frequently attributed to moving. Particularly during the early stages of mass-migration, the migrants tended to be young bachelors; recently married, childless couples; and fathers of families.[66] The migratory process altered gender ratios. Women were rarely the first movers; they more commonly moved together with their families or when parents or friends were already well established.

When conditions required a permanent move, the transfer of all or a significant part of a family became an important objective for many migrants. By the beginning of the 1950s, observers had already noted the relevance of family relations to migration. As one scholar emphasized, relatives who were already established there were a principal attraction of São Paulo. "A father, who came ahead 'to see if it would pay off,' . . . after one, two, or three years brings the family; a bachelor son . . . convince[s] his parents to let him go [to São Paulo]; or cousins, uncles, godchildren, and so on." In the words of a woman from Minas Gerais who was interviewed in 1960, "The children were getting married and decided to come to São Paulo. They came here because they knew people here, and they had listened to the stories of others. I came later, to stay with the children. They sent for me. They insisted, [and] I came."[67]

The need for family reunification, even after many years of separation, is captured in literary form in Roniwalter Jatobá's chronicle *Brilho no Vazio* (Light in the Emptiness). Based on the history of a family Jatobá knew, it tells the story of the northeasterner Sebastiana Lira da Silva (known as "Tiana"), whose oldest son, Teodoro, visits her "after a long absence." He tries to persuade his mother to go to live with him in São Paulo, promising her new dentures if she does. After some fear and hesitation, Tiana, a midwife, gives in and goes to live with Teodoro and his wife in "a little house in the back yard of the main house . . . in São Miguel Paulista."[68]

The goal of some migrants, however, was to escape the family environment. For women, migration could be a refuge from patriarchal domination by fathers and husbands. Abandoned wives, unmarried mothers, or simply young women dissatisfied with their family situation could find in the migratory flow a longed-for flight from an oppressor at home. Such a search for autonomy emerges in the testimony of Maria da Cruz, resident of the city of Carapicuiba, in the metropolitan region of São Paulo, who told the sociologist Dulce Baptista that she had fled to free herself from the "shadow of her parents." A similar logic, though probably with less potential for family conflict, guided the migratory process of a number of young men. Beyond economic betterment, migration offered a "change of life, liberating oneself from parental influence. Emigration then transforms itself into an adventure, into a personal liberation." In the words of a young Pernambucan who had recently arrived in São Paulo at the beginning of the 1950s, "We need to know the world and see things while we're young, before we get married."[69]

But in these cases, too, migration was mainly oriented around previous contacts. Invariably, the places of destination were areas where friends, contemporaries, or relatives already lived. Research carried out in some industrial cities of southeastern Brazil in 1959 demonstrated that the great majority of migrants had a friend or relative living in the city to which they had moved. In São Paulo, 77 percent of male and 81 percent of female migrants who were interviewed had some person already established as a contact in the city.[70]

As we shall see in the case of São Miguel Paulista, such social networks were not only of great importance for the realization of spatial displacement. They would also continue to play a fundamental role in organizing migrants' lives in the big city.

Migration and the Job Market

The thousands of migrants from the Northeast, Minas Gerais, and the interior of the state of São Paulo who flocked to the capital city of São Paulo entered an expanding, highly dynamic job market. Metropolitan São Paulo's accelerated industrial development demanded a growing number of workers: industrial jobs in the region grew by an average of 4.1 percent annually during the decade 1947–56. By 1956, the total industrial workforce in the state of São Paulo was calculated at approximately 900,000, with 500,000 of them in the capital city.[71] But it was not only manufacturing that demanded manual labor; industrialization and urban expansion generated demand in the service sector, which grew significantly.

São Paulo's job market was a great attraction. "The opportunities to work here are much better," said a migrant from Sergipe who arrived in the city in the early 1950s. Because of the availability of work and the relatively ease with which one could acquire land and build a home, many migrants consider this period the golden age of migration, when "São Paulo was good."[72]

Since migrants generally arrived with meager resources and counted on the aid of relatives and friends to get started, it was essential to enter the labor market as quickly as possible. São Paulo offered that possibility: a survey taken in 1959 showed that 86 percent of men and 74 percent of women who migrated to São Paulo found work within a month of arrival.[73] However, the availability of jobs varied greatly during the 1950s, with important differences according to the sector of the economy. Despite a general tendency toward economic growth and industrial expansion, there were sporadic bursts of unemployment, the principal casualties of which tended to be rural migrants with little experience of factory work.

"In our state, the problem of unemployment is practically nonexistent," boasted a São Paulo newspaper in 1956, basing its report on information provided by the State Labor Department and further stating that "all the waves of workers who come to our state are absorbed." But the U.S. Consulate noted less than a year later that there were "a little more than 100,000 unemployed in the industries of the city of São Paulo, which was almost 7 percent of the total workforce and, therefore, a reason for concern." Assessing the state employment agencies in January 1959, the newspaper *Última Hora* noted that there was insufficient employment for unskilled workers.[74] Mariano de Oliveira, who had come from Propriá in Sergipe, was one of them. After spending all morning in line at the State Labor Placement Service, he was informed around noon that the window was closed. In an interview with a reporter, he declared, "It's always like this—many people and few vacancies. You arrive early, but already there's an endless line. I'll come back tomorrow. God willing, we'll get jobs."[75]

This situation seems to have been more the exception than the rule during the 1950s, however. Despite the scarcity of precise data on unemployment during that period, most estimates point to reasonably low rates of unemployment, and except in specific situations such as that of 1957, unemployment was not a principal concern on political and union agendas. In any case, the availability of employment in general, and particularly for migrants of rural origin, was very uneven. In part, that reflected the heterogeneity of the labor market, especially in industry.

The 1950s witnessed a major shift in the industrial structure of São Paulo, with the rise of the metallurgical sector as the largest and most important employer, accounting for about 30 percent of all manual labor in the state by the end of the decade. Contributing to this expansion was the growth of the automobile manufacturing sector in the ABC municipalities during the second half of the decade. Sectors such as chemicals and pharmaceuticals and paper and cardboard grew significantly during this period, as well, while other long-established industries lost ground. The textile sector, previously São Paulo's largest industrial employer, declined from almost 40 percent of manual labor employed in manufacturing in 1939 to around 20 percent twenty years later. The food, glass, and graphics industries also suffered a significant decline over the decade.[76]

Significant changes also occurred in production processes. In general, the availability of jobs grew in professions that required few or average skills but decreased for skilled workers—notably, in the textile sector between 1955 and 1960, when the percentage of workers considered skilled declined from 38 percent to 7 percent. Although much less dramatic, the expanding metallurgical industry also suffered a decrease in skilled jobs.[77]

Beginning in the mid-1940s, with the creation of the National Service of Industrial Instruction (Serviço Nacional de Aprendizagem Industrial; SENAI), the industrialists aspired not only to control the content, rhythm, and general characteristics of professional training, but also to define the very concept of the skilled worker.[78] The accelerated industrial growth of the 1950s brought further challenges in this area for industrialists.

Much of São Paulo's industry only required a relatively small number of highly specialized workers. For some sectors, however, the scarcity of skilled workers was a serious problem, to which employers and the state attempted to respond with policies designed to attract specialized workers from Europe and with the increasing activity of SENAI. Despite the difficulties the Brazilian government encountered in attracting European migrants during this period, the number of foreign workers in some sectors of higher-skilled industry remained relatively high.

For the majority of workers, however, the chances of getting professional training were slim. Most learned their jobs in the workplace, and few other opportunities of apprenticeship were effectively offered.[79] An intense flow of low-skilled workers was thus one of the characteristics of the São Paulo job market in the 1950s.

Industrial transformation brought direct consequences in terms of the jobs available to northeastern migrants, whose previous professional experience was overwhelmingly agricultural fieldwork. A survey conducted in the early 1960s of northeasterners at the Immigrant Reception Center in São Paulo indicated that more than 80 percent had come from occupations in the agricultural sector. Of these, about 40 percent had been small landholders. Among non-landowners, the number of *parceiros* (a type of sharecropper) is striking, particularly in the state of Bahia. In Pernambuco and other states with a strong presence of sugar mills, rural salaried workers were of some importance. Thirty percent of Pernambucans interviewed and 30 percent of respondents from Alagoas, for example, had been salaried workers.[80]

Besides their almost nonexistent industrial experience, the postwar generation of migrants had very low levels of formal education. A survey of workers who had moved to São Paulo taken in 1962 found an illiteracy rate higher than 60 percent.[81] Faced with an industrial and urban world undergoing rapid change, these workers occupied various spaces in the 1950s labor market.

The construction sector, which was expanding sharply in the "city that couldn't stop," was one of the fastest in absorbing male migrant laborers. Armando Corrêa da Silva noted the large presence of professions linked to construction in his sample when he analyzed approximately 7,000 records with detailed information about some 40,000 workers in São Paulo between 1959 and 1964 (of whom only 30.4 percent were outside the city in São Paulo state). For example, 20.6 percent said they were bricklayers' assistants; 7.9 percent were bricklayers; and 7.9 percent were construction laborers.[82] Several structural features of this type of industry seem to have facilitated the presence of northeastern migrants there. As the sociologist José Albertino Rodrigues emphasized in 1958, experience in construction served as a "kind of probationary stage" for migrants before employment in other areas. A survey of the labor market in the city of São Paulo taken in the early 1970s found that the longer the duration of residence of migrants, the lower their rate of employment in construction and the greater their participation in other industries, which seems to reinforce the idea of a transference from that sector to the others.[83]

Metallurgy was not only one of the fastest growing industrial sectors of that period in São Paulo, but also one of the largest employers of migrants. Reflecting on the growing participation of migrants, leaders of the metalworkers' union asked in a preparatory document for the Second Congress of Metalworkers in 1960, "The life of Brazilian workers . . . is a true mirror of the country's industrial development. How many of us metalworkers did not start out life toiling in the fields? How many of us got to the cities without having any industrial skill? How many of us worked in construction or learned our profession of metalworking in small workshops?"[84]

The auto industry, established in the ABC region during the second half of the 1950s, began to absorb great waves of former rural workers. A scholar of Brazilian migration wrote in 1959, "What emerges . . . quite clearly is the high proportion of [northeastern migrants of rural origin] among the personnel of the newest industry, the automotive." The Automotive Industry Executive Group developed a plan in the late 1950s to construct a pilot training center for workers in Ceará. Although the center was never established, the proposal clearly demonstrated industry executives' strong interest in "mobilizing the Northeast where, notoriously, there are large reserves of manpower that are not fully utilized."[85]

Migrant women's options in the labor market were much more restricted. The textile industry had been the largest employer of the female workforce, but it declined as the industrial profile of São Paulo changed, diminishing the possibility of factory employment for women. Manual labor in the booming metallurgical sector was traditionally male; throughout the decade, women never exceeded 10 percent.[86] Women's employment was also scarce in construction, where many male migrants were employed.

Women represented about 30 percent of migrants who arrived in São Paulo between 1952 and 1961. Although they came into an expanding job market, industrial activities registered a decline in women's participation in the workforce, a phenomenon that extended to the entire national secondary sector in the 1950s and 1960s.[87] The service sector—in particular, domestic employment—became the main economic sector absorbing migrant women.[88] However, despite the relative decrease, the availability of industrial work in some sectors and private factories was still sufficient to absorb a considerable number of women, especially those who were young and single, including many migrants.

In addition to the intrinsic difficulties of a labor market in the process of transformation, job-seeking migrants confronted explicit prejudice and exclusion. A series of reports in *Última Hora* in 1955 revealed, for example, that several factories in the metropolitan region of São Paulo refused to employ northeastern and black workers. Even in the construction industry, some companies apparently avoided hiring northeasterners. In an interview, the union member Vicente Britelli explained that many "employers have 'something' against [the northeasterners because] they have a reputation of being tough guys." Moreover, he said, "They are always the first to be fired."[89]

The *Última Hora* reports had great repercussions: several complaints about mistreatment, harassment, and labor market discrimination against northeasterners became public. The impact of the issue was such that northeastern representatives in the Federal Congress proposed the formation of a Parliamentary Commission of Inquiry on exploitation and discrimination against northeasterners in São Paulo. *A Hora* immediately printed an outraged headline, "There Is No Discrimination against Anyone on the Soil of São Paulo."[90] In the State Legislature, several representatives vehemently protested what they considered a "great injury" and a "demagogic and irresponsible" proposal; affirming the "immense degree of hospitality of the people of São Paulo," they rejected as absurd any complaint of discrimination. As summarized by the irritated representative Derville Alegretti, "Whoever knows the heart of São Paulo . . . knows that the Paulista opens his arms to all who come here: foreigners from all corners of the world, Brazilians from all regions of the country. São Paulo receives them and gives them the opportunity to have a dignified, perfect life, through the work of each individual. It is inconceivable that there are Brazilians . . . who can imagine that unequal treatment is practiced in São Paulo between Paulistas and children of other states, with respect to the northeasterners."[91]

Faced with this reaction, the commission was never formed. Complaints continued to pop up about employers' prejudice against northeasterners and blacks, however. In 1958, for example, Councilman Irineu Silva of the industrial city of São Bernardo do Campo denounced the firm Martini and Rossi for refusing to employ northeastern workers presented by the mayor. According to Silva, a partner at Martini and Rossi said that the firm "would not accept elements of the black race, or northeasterners, claiming that these elements are useless." Councilman Rio Branco Paranhos, a well-known lawyer for various labor unions in São Paulo, told the Municipal Council in 1960 about a visit he had made to the Benevolent Cultural Progress Association in Mauá, where several northeastern speakers had complained about being victims of prejudice. "The factories are closed to them because they are northeastern," the councilman shouted, "and they open up immediately when the candidates are of a different origin."[92]

Cases such as these reveal that the incorporation of northeasterners into the São Paulo labor market was much more complex and problematic than is generally supposed. Migration was not a simple, linear transfer of manual labor from less developed regions to the nerve center of Brazilian industrial capitalism. Rather, it was a contradictory process in which prejudices and deep divergences were often awakened and exacerbated. In the labor market, such discrimination existed not only on the part of some employers against workers. As we shall see, cleavages and prejudices also lurked throughout society, even among the workers themselves.

"Bahians" in São Paulo

The speed of urbanization and the intensity of migration to São Paulo in the 1950s had important repercussions for the local and national political debate. The large and growing presence of migrants of rural northeastern origin took Paulistas by surprise and created tensions between the resident population and the newcomers. Prejudice against northeasterners was relatively common, as was hostility between northeasterners and other workers. The sociologist Juarez Brandão Lopes, for example, found "a latent animosity that exists against workers from the Northeast, among other [workers]" at the factory where he carried out his research in the 1950s.[93]

Migrants experienced this animosity in their everyday experience. Augusto Lima, who worked at Nitro Química, recalled that "São Paulo . . . in those times had a terrible division." Teasing and banter about one's accent, behavior, and customs were frequent. Lima often heard the phrase "that northern race" used pejoratively. In a working-class district, it could even be difficult for a northeasterner to date the daughter of a non-northeastern worker. "I remember a Bahian, a decent guy," Lima said. "There was this Italian girl, the daughter of an Italian woman and Mr. Manoel. She liked the Bahian, but [he] couldn't even pass by her front door because of her father. 'Blue blood' did not accept northern blood."

Lima's mockery of the pretensions to nobility by those who did not have "northern blood" was clearly a response to the prejudice that his generation of migrants experienced daily. A good indication of the difficulties of social integration can be seen in a survey of university students in São Paulo conducted in 1949, assessing their degree of acceptance of different ethnic, national, and regional groups. About a third of the respondents said they would not accept marriages with "Bahians" or "northerners." Carolina Martescelli, the study's author, added, "Eight nationalities are more accepted as kin by marriage than the groups of 'Bahian' and 'northerner.'"[94]

Despite their similar migration experiences, the differences among northeastern migrants were considerable. "Northeast," "sertão," "North," and "Bahia" were generic categories that referred to different places of origin. In addition to different states of the Brazilian federation, the northeastern interior consists of macro-regions (sertão, zona da mata, and agreste) and various subregions, with their own, peculiar socioeconomic and cultural characteristics. Moreover, most migrants came from a broad, differentiated range of professions and activities in the countryside and small towns.

When they arrived in São Paulo, however, the differences among the various migrants from the Northeast and Minas Gerais tended to be homogenized, and they were generically called "Bahians." As one facetious adage circulating in the city held, "From Minas on up, it's all Bahia." The generalization reflected the large presence of Bahians among the contingent of migrants to São Paulo: between 1952 and 1961, approximately 330,000 Bahian workers were counted by São Paulo clearinghouses for migration control, making the Bahians the largest migrant group of the period, constituting about 30 percent of the total.

A racial component was implicit in the designation "Bahian." After 1950, São Paulo "was becoming a very big city," notes the historian John French, "with all these mixed and dark-skinned people who 'are not like us.'"[95] According to a survey conducted in early 1962, about 60 percent of migrants who entered the state of São Paulo in the 1950s were pardos ou negros (mixed or black), with a notable presence of Bahians among them. As the authors of the study pointed out, "We even believe that we can derive from the fact that there exist . . . a large number of mixed Bahian migrants bound for the state of São Paulo, the custom of believing any mixed individual to be 'Bahian,' or even of identifying any dark-complexioned migrant as being 'Bahian,' regardless of his state of origin, a custom that endures to this day."[96]

The generalization expressed in being called "Bahian" was taken badly by most migrants and often gave rise to disputes. Many arguments were rooted in regional rivalries among migrant workers. Lima said that he once "had a fight because of it: the guy was from another state and didn't like people to call him Bahian." "We noticed a certain parochialism," recalled Artur Pinto de Oliveira. Afonso José da Silva emphasized that "the Bahians [often] didn't mingle with the Sergipans, and the Sergipans didn't mingle with the Pernambucans." In a migration process marked by family and community relations, newcomers' first bonds of friendship and relationship in the new city predictably were restricted to people from the same region of origin, and any "mistaken" identification of those groups would cause problems.

Juarez Brandão Lopes also found that migrant workers resented such treatment. When he saw Lopes talking to a production worker at the factory where he was carrying out his research, a skilled employee asked in an ironic tone whether the "Bahian" was going to be interviewed. Lopes reported that the worker, "who [was] from Minas Gerais, muttered in a resentful tone: 'I'm not from Bahia.'"[97]

Although they emphasized their differences, the migrants clearly perceived that the rest of society tended to homogenize them. "Anytime something went wrong," said Artur Oliveira—say, a Cearan killed a Pernambucan—"everyone said, 'The Bahian stuck him with his *pexeira*. Everyone was [said to be] Bahian, when in reality [there were migrants] from all the states."[98] Afonso José da Silva said that when there was a serious fight in the neighborhood where he lived, the newspapers always printed, "A Bahian killed so-and-so," even when the perpetrator was not Bahian. The neighborhood of São Miguel Paulista "had the reputation [of being] the second Bahia," Silva said. "Most Bahians came here. Because one brought the other. Here there were Bahians, Pernambucans, Sergipans, Paraíbans. . . . There were all of them, but the Bahians had the reputation."

Another sore point between locals and newcomers was the stream of jokes and mockery directed at migrants. Francisco Weffort points to the 1950s as the moment of the emergence of "Bahian jokes," the first popular reaction to the arrival of the large northeastern contingent.[99] In October 1956, Councilman Agenor Mônaco commented on a recent wave of "jokes and humorous sayings [about] our brothers from the north." In the same period, the newspaper *O Dia* tackled this phenomenon by observing that "in the last few months, the joking spirit of the southern people . . . turned against our good brothers of Bahia, who are being endlessly talked about and mocked." The paper also noted that the jokes irritated migrants, stating, "'You know what the Bahian is . . . ?' The question is invariably heard in all parts of the city, accompanied by a punchline. But it offends the pride of the good sons of the 'good land' and puts them in a fighting mood."

As an example of the enthusiasm for jokes about "northerners," *O Dia* reported one case at a street market in the Mooca neighborhood: "A group of boys were having fun telling jokes about Bahians. Each one had a better joke than the other, and their laughter echoed, attracting the attention of passers-by, who stopped to listen and laughed merrily along." Irritated by the jokes, José Epaminondas Freire, a Pernambucan, approached the group and asked, "Do you know what a Bahian fishwife's sheath is?" Drawing a knife, he lunged at the group, shouting, "The belly of a Paulista!" He gravely wounded four people.[100] The newspaper did not say so, but it is likely that Epaminondas already knew the group of joking boys and that his anger had roots in previous disagreements. In any case, although he was Pernambucan by birth, the newspaper used him as an example of "Bahians'" irritation with jokes.

Many Paulistas saw the growing presence of northeasterners in the city as a major problem. São Paulo's rapid growth through industrialization was accompanied by a sharp increase in problems of urban infrastructure, so that transportation difficulties, lack of housing, and intensification of urban crime and misery went hand in hand with progress and development, becoming part of everyday life in metropolitan São Paulo. Far from considering northeasterners partners in development, many sectors of São Paulo society scapegoated them as responsible for the city's growth-related ills.

A series of stereotypes about migrants was created and reinforced throughout this period. Considered "naive and primitive," they were portrayed as so viscerally accustomed to misery and deprivation that, even when placed in a supposedly developed environment such as São Paulo and the other major cities, they had trouble breaking with the past and opening themselves to modernity and to "civilization."

Thus, if migration itself was "one of the great national problems," the migrants were regarded as reflecting the "low cultural and technical level of the country's population." Observing newly arrived northeastern workers in Rio de Janeiro in the late 1940s, an official from the National Immigration Department described them as having a "depressing physical aspect . . . and with social and family life conditions so inferior that it made them economically null." Francisco Barbosa Leite struck a similar tone in analyzing the situation of drought victims and the pau-de-arara journeys that carried them to São Paulo and other industrial cities: "The lack of hygiene, the misery, and the indifference of the public authorities contribute to the moral and organic dissolution of the *primitive minds* that the roads carry to these destinations."[101]

This negative view of the migrants was exemplified by an extensive report in *A Hora* in 1956, in which the presence of northeasterners in the city takes on the air of a frightening invasion of "contrary individuals . . . personas non gratas who come trying to sabotage the constructive, decent and elevated work of the *bandeirantes*."[102] Victims of an "irresistible fascination" for São Paulo, the migrants were seen as "impoverished, sick, full of children afflicted with worms. The picture presented by the northeastern family can be compared with the most backward peoples of the world. Ignoring the most elementary notions of hygiene and nutrition, even if they get work in São Paulo, as many of them do, they never abandon their modus vivendi."[103]

The image of the migrants as pauperized fugitives from the depleted sertão was reinforced by a sequence of droughts that devastated the Northeast in the 1950s.[104] Commenting on the need for measures to curb the "indiscriminate coming [of northeasterners] to São Paulo" due to the great drought of 1958, a São Paulo state deputy pleaded for the creation of a "Northerners' House" to give aid and assistance to those who inevitably would disembark in the state capital. Two years earlier, Carlos Kherlakian, another deputy in the São Paulo Legislative Assembly, demanded action against the pau-de-arara owners who, taking advantage of the "poor, working [northeasterners'] good faith" increased the numbers of "the ragged hungry . . . , poor misfits, who roam with their families in the center of the city, seeking to live off the charity of others, suffering hunger, cold, diseases of all kinds, offering a sad and humiliating spectacle for a metropolis like São Paulo."[105]

In the face of the intensity and speed of migration, rumors began to circulate about the possibility of preventing the entry of workers into São Paulo. Occasionally, journalists and parliamentarians were reminded of the unconstitutionality and impracticality of such a proposal. In March 1959, for example, Councilman José Aranha warned his colleagues that the federal government could not prevent immigration to São Paulo from the north, "because all these people are, of course, within the federal Constitution: freedom of movement." An article in A Hora, taking a similar line of argument, stated, "It is impossible and unacceptable to ban the entry of northeasterners into São Paulo. The Constitution guarantees freedom of movement."[106]

For others, however, the need for government action to control and discipline northeastern migration, on the one hand, and to extend protection and assistance to migrants in São Paulo, on the other, seemed obvious and urgent. Concerned about the situation, João Cleofas, the minister of agriculture of the Vargas government, proposed in 1952 "to dam this stream of refugees along the Rio-Bahia highway with the establishment of agricultural colonies assisted by the government on expropriated vacant land along the banks of rivers that cut through the road."[107] The idea never caught on, and there were constant complaints over the following years about the government's inability to deal with migration.

Ten years after Cleofas's proposal, Luis Cava Netto, a technical expert with the state government analyzing the rural exodus and northeastern migration, continued to demand action from the federal government. Recognizing "internal population movements" as a "necessary evil," Netto proposed a "sanitary and health selection [process] in regions of immigration." He stressed, "It is not about taking coercive attitudes aimed at preventing Brazilians from moving around in their own country . . . , but simply to make conditions for migration to develop within a certain discipline." Since the majority of migrants were "absolutely incapable of adjusting to the new environment," he argued, the proposed selection process could identify "those individuals for whom displacement would be inconvenient . . . , including the near-impossibility of adjusting, owing to the characteristics of the labor market in large cities." The "biggest beneficiaries," he said, "would be the migrants themselves."[108]

Besides the views of government experts, journalists, scholars, and parliamentarians, the figure of the migrant that prevailed in the social imaginary of the period was that of a miserable, hungry person, impelled by the economic and ecological conditions of the northeastern sertão to flee in desperation and without organization—although, as we have seen, this profile corresponds to only a small portion of the workers who moved to the capitals of the Southern and Central regions of Brazil.

The intensification of internal migration after the Second World War was essential for the consolidation of a long process of configuration and institutionalization of the Northeast. Since the mid-nineteenth century, the differences between northern Brazil and the rest of the country had been emphasized, becoming an object of discourse among politicians and scholars. The great northeastern drought of 1877 and the Canudos War of the 1890s were key moments in the construction of a vision of a region of "rude" people who were marked by the harshness of their environment.[109] Moreover, influenced by naturalistic theories that were much in vogue in the period, analysts such as Nina Rodrigues highlighted the presence of black and mixed-race people in the north who, with their "inertia and indolence," provided a counterpoint to the ever more dominant and purportedly more enterprising whites in the country's south. In this account, natural and racial differentiation would condemn the backward north to a lack of civilization.[110]

In the context of the consolidation of artistic and literary avant-gardes in the 1920s and 1930s, northeastern regionalist discourse became stronger, assuming a central role in forming an image of the Northeast as having homogeneous historical, cultural, and economic characteristics. Counterpoised to São Paulo's advancement, progress, and development, the Northeast was constructed as the space of everything opposed to "modernity"—agrarianism, the vicissitudes of drought, the sertão, traditionalism, religious fanaticism, banditry, and violence. Gilberto Freyre, José Lins do Rego, and other intellectuals and artists sought, in different ways, to valorize some of these characteristics, focusing on the creation of a common cultural identity—so-called northeastern Brazilianness. For many, the Northeast was the bastion of true national culture. Far from the European influences that dominated southern Brazil in general, and São Paulo in particular, the Northeast was seen as the authentically Brazilian region.[111]

Some modernist intellectuals of the 1920s also emphasized a regionalist discourse localized in São Paulo, the city that was the nucleus of the country's economic and social progress, as well as the symbol of modernity and Brazilianness.[112] As Barbara Weinstein has shown, the supposed superiority of São Paulo proclaimed by that regionalist discourse was also progressively "racialized," implying an association of "Paulista identity" with a white population, in clear contrast to the mixed-race and black populations of the North and the Northeast. The so-called Constitutional Revolution of 1932, a brief armed conflict between the state of São Paulo and the rest of the country, Weinstein argues, was a decisive moment for the construction of this identity.[113]

Thus, despite the influence of the idea of the Northeast as a bastion of pure national "spirit," the capitalist development of Brazil, with its increasingly deep economic differentiation among the country's regions, consolidated these images—that is, São Paulo was associated with progress and dynamism, and the Northeast was associated with backwardness and stagnation. Beginning in the mid-1940s, the large northeastern migrant presence in the south and center of the country brought together people from various regions of the country who otherwise barely communicated with one another. At the same time, it defined and was defined by existing social constructions about the Northeast and about São Paulo.[114]

Regional differentiation overlay the distinctions between the countryside, which was strongly associated with the Northeast, and the city, whose great symbol was São Paulo. In their analysis of the new forms of sociability that arose with the development of capitalism in twentieth-century Brazil, Fernando Novais and João Manuel Cardoso de Mello emphasize that "city life attracts and holds because it offers better opportunities and promises a future of individual progress, but also because it is considered a superior form of existence." City dwellers see themselves as "modern people, 'superior,'" in contrast to the men and women of the countryside, who are regarded as "backward" and "inferior." In 1950, according to the scholars, "the 10 million urbanites" very probably regarded the vast majority of the 41 million Brazilians who lived in rural areas as "bumpkins, hicks, and rubes."[115] In the following years, the adjective "Bahian" was added to those pejoratives, at least in São Paulo.

The vast majority of rural migrants expected to be incorporated into the ideal of "progress" represented by the big city. In their daily lives, the best translation of "progress" was a good job, labor rights, good living conditions, health and education for themselves and their families, and access, albeit modest, to the consumer goods that the development of Brazilian capitalism was beginning to generate. They hoped to find all this in the big city of São Paulo, whose reality was different from the "backwardness" of the Northeast. The testimony of a northeastern worker in *Viramundo*, a documentary film about internal migration in Brazil directed by Geraldo Sarno in 1965, illustrates this view: "In my house I have a TV, I have a refrigerator . . . I like São Paulo a lot, I adore its forward-looking people. I don't consider myself a Northerner but a Paulista, and I intend to die here. . . . I'm not going to return to the north, because to go back there would be turning back. I'm in São Paulo, and I want to move ahead."[116] In making *Viramundo*, Sarno relied on the advice and research of Octavio Ianni, Juarez Brandão Lopes, and Cândido Procópio, three leading intellectuals who in the late 1950s dedicated themselves to the study of the industrialization and urbanization process that Brazilian society was undergoing. Not coincidentally, the film reproduces in cinematic language some of the main theses of that intellectual generation about migrants and their integration into the industrial world of the great cities.

Not only academics and intellectuals were concerned with the growing presence of migrants at the heart of the working class in the 1950s. Trade union and left-wing militants and activists sought to win the sympathy of these workers, as well, and began to direct their discourse specifically, although tentatively, to this new contingent of laborers. The so-called Strike of 400,000 in 1957 was an important moment for the aspirations of these unionists and leftist militants. Looking to rally the mass of new laborers to strike, the communist daily *Notícias de Hoje* praised strikes and mass demonstrations as weapons to which workers would have to resort to "assert their rights and win their demands. . . . The grandparents of the grandparents of the descendants of Italian immigrants, Spanish, German, etc., went through this experience several times. The children of peasants who came to São Paulo have also realized this."[117]

In fact, young laborers from the Northeast and Minas Gerais appear to have participated in these actions at rates similar to those for other segments of workers. Companies with a large proportion of migrants, such as Nitro

Química, saw their activities paralyzed. In a euphoric account of the work stoppage at the Wheathon do Brasil glassworks, a journalist sympathetic to the strike wrote, "They are all northeasterners. They did not come to São Paulo to strike. But they began to learn that unity, struggle, and organization of workers are necessary if they are to obtain that for which they left their homes and the cities in which they were born."[118]

Reflecting an increasing political interest in the issue of northeastern migration, different political sectors, including the Brazilian Communist Party (PCB), the Progressive Social Party of Adhemar de Barros, and the Brazilian Workers' Party stimulated the creation of organizations to provide aid and assistance to northeasterners. In 1957, for example, the Paulista Association of Friends of Men of the North and Northeast appeared, with the PCB's support. With centers in different neighborhoods of the metropolitan area, the association apparently was predominantly concerned with providing assistance to northeastern migrants. Although such associations might be considered a space for political inclusion and for the construction of a northeastern identity, they do not seem to have attracted much support among migrants. Often less formal organizations, such as soccer teams and dance clubs, attracted more migrants from certain regions and cities than did the "northeastern associations."

Confronting the traditionally negative image of these social sectors as politically and culturally backward, a positive vision of the peasant and the migrant took shape among the Brazilian left during the late and early 1960s, particularly in intellectual, student, and artistic circles. Part of a phenomenon that has been termed "revolutionary romanticism" by the sociologist Marcelo Ridenti, paeans to the man of the countryside sought to rescue "a community inspired by the *man of the people,* whose essence would be found in the spirit of the peasant and the migrant slum dweller who works in the cities." For various leftist political sectors from immediately before 1964 through the end of the decade, these peasants and migrants were the real agents of social transformation. Alipio Freire, a political activist at that time, described this feeling in testimony to Ridenti by saying, "The basic subject, the agent of transformations in the national-popular, was the northeastern peasant; preferably the migrant. . . . It was assumed that the alliance between migrants and slum dwellers would be the great motivator of History. . . . Nor was this only the [idea of the] staff of the [Popular Culture Center]. It existed in the social fabric. It was part of the social conjuncture. These themes invaded all of art, all of culture."[119] Whether rural migrants were seen as archaic, backward elements or idealized as agents of transformation who would open the doors to the future, their active presence in the context of the immense, high-speed changes brought by industrialization and urbanization was one of the most consequential social phenomena in Brazil during the 1950s–1970s.

In the 1950s, the migrant presence in the industrial cities played an essential role in the emergence of agrarian reform and regional disparity as central themes in the political and social debate of the country. Thousands of migrants demanded urgent reconsideration of the northeastern agrarian structure, which increasingly came to be seen by different social actors and theorists of national development as the main cause of "backwardness" and of the immense migratory wave. Thus, in a press release issued when he took office in June 1954 as president of the National Institute of Immigration and Colonization, Francisco de Toledo Piza discussed "the remarkable social anomaly of this agrarian country in which only one farmer out of five works on his own land. It has been shown . . . that in this fact lies the main cause of the exodus of the rural populations, more serious and more active than even the northeastern drought as a determining factor in mass flight."[120]

Even *O Observador Econômico e Financeiro*, a business magazine, emphasized in 1952 that it was not just the "so-called natural factors" that caused the "flow of the human masses from the Northeast." The migrations, which were cause for "serious concerns about the political future that awaits us," according to an editorial, ought to be addressed in the context of the "recovery of the Brazilian Northeast," which could be effectively achieved only if it was supported by the "fixing of people to the land through *basic reform of the system of possession and exploitation of land.*"[121] While the social struggles that emerged among the rural northeastern workers with the coming of the Ligas Camponesas (Peasant Leagues) put the land issue at the center of the political agenda, the presence in the big cities of migrants newly decamped from the countryside catalyzed a debate on the harmful effects to the nation of the power of the large latifúndio.

The migrant presence in southeastern Brazil also contributed to the debate, fairly common from the 1950s on, about regional inequality. For intellectuals such as the economist Celso Furtado, who were concerned with the issue of national development, the migrations were seen as forceful proof of the archaism and underdevelopment of the northeastern economy and propelled a need for state intervention that would aim to overcome inequalities among regions and promote progress. In the context of this debate, various specific government organizations were created to address the "northeastern question." In 1952, the Banco do Nordeste do Brasil (Bank of the Brazilian Northeast) was created; in 1956, during the government of President Juscelino

Kubitschek (1956–61), the Work Group for Northeastern Development was instituted, culminating in the founding in 1959 of SUDENE (the Superintendency of Northeastern Development), a federal agency dedicated to promoting the social and economic development of the Northeast, with Celso Furtado, one of the principal theoreticians of national development, as its principal inspiration.[122]

The next chapters explore the relationships among the migrants' experiences, the establishment of a common migrant identity, and the process of working-class formation, particularly in the 1950s, thus providing elements for the analysis of the influence of migration on the experience of workers in São Paulo and in the entire country.

CHAPTER TWO

Land of the Northeasterners
Migration, Urbanization, and Factory Work
in São Miguel Paulista

When Mário da Natividade Valladão arrived with his family in São Miguel Paulista on the first day of 1946, his first impression of the neighborhood was not a good one. "São Miguel," he wrote in his brief memoir, "was an enormous place, some very old and ugly houses, with only one way into the city: a train that left in the morning and came back at night."

Valladão, who had been sent by the Baptist Church to found a house of worship in the rapidly growing community, was alarmed by what he found there. He did not like the neighborhood, but even worse was his feeling toward the flock he was supposed to conquer for his faith. "The people were angry and bad," he wrote. Nitro Química, the factory that dominated the town's landscape, "still functioned precariously." By road, "trucks arrived from the North and the Northeast . . . full of aimless men, without documents, who were dumped here. These were the so-called paus-de-arara."

The physiognomy of Valladão's "young and beloved wife" said it all, stamped as it was with "sorrow and grief." But there was no choice. Despite the discouragement, "we had to stay," he reported many years later.

Quickly, though, Valladão found "a virtue" in the people. It was true that "they lived in groups, like Indians," but "they loved each other, and they united with each other, too." The "spirit of cooperation that existed among them" drew the clergyman's attention. He gave a concrete example: when the factory blew "three shrill whistles . . . outside the usual hours," indicating fire in the factory, it sent "all of São Miguel . . . into action . . . men, women and children, old people and young people with cans, buckets, they organized a huge effort trying to help put out the fire." He felt that he was "privileged" to be there; God had placed him in a "promising field, with much privation" but also "with many souls to be won." Valladão founded the Baptist Church of São Miguel and was its principal pastor for forty years.[1]

The celebrated Brazilian novelist Jorge Amado had a very different impression when he visited São Miguel for the first time in 1945. Excited about the legalization and growth of the Communist Party following the end of the Second World War, Amado, who was then an important communist leader, decided to visit "the largest cell of the party in São Paulo, . . . that of Nitro Química." Forgetting to mention the female comrades, Amado recalled that the organization was made up of "a thousand-odd men, quickly approaching two thousand."

Amado enjoyed his visit. He liked the "festive spirit" that reigned at the neighborhood party headquarters. Enthusiastically, he wrote, "Nowhere have I felt so much that the party was the home of the proletariat and of the people as in the district headquarters of São Miguel." He was enchanted by the lively, informal atmosphere among the workers, whose "northern manner" included the custom of putting benches in front of the houses "where people sit and talk." Another happy memory was the choir, led by maestro Emilio Alves, "a laughing, modest, black man . . . , a factory worker and party militant." Accompanied by an orchestra of guitars, *cuícas* (friction drums), and *pandeiros* (frame drums), Alves's choir had received a visit from the singer-composer Dorival Caymmi, who "came to hear and applaud the marches of the maestro."[2]

There are no records of subsequent visits by Amado to the neighborhood, but as with the recollections of Pastor Valladão, Amado's brief report contains striking references to the presence and customs of migrants in São Miguel. In the following pages I analyze how São Miguel developed in the context of twentieth-century São Paulo's rapid urbanization and industrialization and how it became a living and working space for thousands of migrants, particularly from the Northeast.

São Miguel, the Northeast in São Paulo

The history of São Miguel was dramatically altered in the 1930s, when the Companhia Nitro Química Brasileira set up its factory there. Although São Miguel was one of the oldest neighborhoods in the city, it had barely developed since its time as an Indian village and Jesuit mission in the sixteenth century and seventeenth century, remaining a small settlement at the far eastern end of the municipality.[3]

As part of São Paulo's growth in the first decades of the twentieth century, Portuguese and Japanese immigrants settled in rural areas in the district of São Miguel, such as Itaquera and Lajeado (present-day Guaianazes), and came to have great importance in the production and supply of vegetables, legumes, fruit, and flowers for the people of the entire city. The development caused by such activities extended even to the autonomy of the regions as independent districts in 1920 and 1929, respectively. Brickworks and tile works flourished in São Miguel, supplying growing demand in the capital city. The nearby Tietê River served as a source of raw materials and as a means of transport.

Despite the growth created by its brick and tile workshops, São Miguel remained a small, isolated village on the outskirts of the city, with a population (including Itaquera and Lajeado) of 4,702 in 1920.[4] Its residents faced immense difficulties going to other regions and to the city center. This isolation was eased by the irregular Penha-São Miguel bus line, which began operating in 1930, and especially by the construction of a Brazilian Central Railroad branch line and the opening of a railway station in the neighborhood in 1932. It was, however, the arrival of Nitro Química that would forever change the face of São Miguel.

Seduced by the low cost of land, the proximity of the train station, and the Tietê River's great reservoirs of water, the entrepreneurs José Ermírio de Moraes and Horácio Lafer saw in the neighborhood the ideal location for the large chemical factory they had just acquired in the United States. With generous support from the government of President Getúlio Vargas, more than eighteen tons of equipment and machinery were moved from the original factory site in Hopewell, Virginia, to São Miguel. In 1937, after two years of construction and facilities, the factory went into operation.

The Second World War brought major growth for the company, driven by its manufacture of rayon, an artificial fiber widely used in the textile industry at the time. By the war's end, Nitro had outgrown its competitors and become the largest producer of rayon in Brazil. With various factories inside the same industrial plant, the company also produced sulfuric acid, hydrochloric acid, paint, sodium sulfate, and other chemicals. For years it provided the raw material for the manufacture of explosives by the army, which meant that it was considered a company of strategic importance. In 1946, with more than four thousand male and female workers, the company was one of the largest in São Paulo and one of the most profitable in Brazil.[5]

The company's directors developed an ambitious plan of economic expansion, with the goal of making the company into the great national supplier of chemical raw materials to other economic sectors—the "CSN of the chemical sector," in the words of the company's management, referring to the National Steel Company (Companhia Siderúrgica Nacional; CSN), owner of the country's main steel plant, created in the early 1940s by the Vargas government in the city of Volta Redonda.[6] The 1950s were marked, then, by Nitro Química's large investments in production and in the expansion of its social services, which provided assistance to workers and their dependents in health, housing, food, and leisure and were regarded by many as exemplary in the country. This project failed, however, and in the late 1950s the company began a long process of economic decay.[7]

The presence from the late 1930s on of a plant on such a scale transformed São Miguel into one of the principal industrial suburbs of the São Paulo metropolitan region precisely when the city was experiencing one of the most accelerated processes of urbanization and densification ever. São Paulo was the most obvious case of the dizzying rhythm of urbanization that Brazil as a whole experienced after the end of the Second World War. Between 1940 and 1960, the city's population growth rate reached the highest levels of the century. São Paulo became the country's largest city, with about 3.7 million inhabitants in 1960. The jingoistic slogan that the city was the "fastest growing in the world" was repeated to exhaustion. In the same period, the urban sprawl of the metropolitan area grew by a factor of about five, increasing from 200 square kilometers to approximately 1,000 square kilometers.[8]

Several scholars have called attention to the segregated character of the urbanization process in São Paulo, with its intense, continuous expulsion of the working classes from city center to periphery. This "peripheral pattern of urban growth" marked the development of the city from the 1940s through the 1980s.[9]

Until the 1930s, it was possible to see a relative concentration of workers' housing near factories and workplaces. Industrial neighborhoods such as Brás, Mooca, and Lapa, among others, were also living spaces for most of workers. Residing in workers' villages (whether or not they were built by the industrialists) or renting small houses or tenement rooms, the workers had remained close to their jobs and were not too distant from the residences of the middle and upper social classes. In this sense, the degree of segregation of the city's social space was less pronounced.[10]

By the mid-1940s, however, housing had become a major problem for workers in general and particularly for newcomers to São Paulo. The Tenancy Act, decreed in 1942 during the Estado Novo dictatorship (1937–45), froze rents for a two-year period that was successively extended until 1964. During this period, only two rent adjustments were allowed, and they resulted in values that were well below inflation. Nevertheless, some of the effects of the law were perverse for those with the lowest income. The private-initiative investment in building rental homes at popular prices fell drastically and was not even remotely compensated for by public investment, exacerbating housing shortages in cities that were experiencing intense population growth from internal migration. Even for the population sector that was already housed and therefore benefited from the freezing of rents, there were problems. The owners used numerous ploys to try to enlarge their income by charging "extra" fees and threatening tenants or even selling their houses. The number of evictions increased dramatically, because once the residents were dislodged, the owners could readjust the rents for new tenants.

Housing in postwar São Paulo thus took on the dimensions of a public problem. Nabil Bonduki estimates that between 1945 and 1948 the number of evictions may have reached 15 percent of the city's population.[11] Tenements and collective houses were particularly affected. Conflicts between residents and landlords increased enormously, and collective, organized tenant movements emerged with active participation and mobilization.[12]

For most workers, the possibility of living in the central regions and the old industrial neighborhoods of the city became increasingly slim. The growing scarcity of residences and the increase in the price of rental houses available in these regions forced many to settle in increasingly remote districts with few resources, which attenuated and altered the character of the city's housing crisis in the 1940s.

The great migratory influx of the 1950s thus accelerated the creation of districts and neighborhoods on the outskirts of the city, as São Paulo underwent a continuous consolidation of its periphery as a place of residence of the poor.

The previous standard density of workers—in which, as a rule, residence and workplace were in proximity—quickly destabilized. As workers scattered to various far-flung neighborhoods of São Paulo and neighboring cities— distant, in most cases, from their workplaces—an acute decentralization of workers' housing occurred.

A process of land speculation took over the city. Tracts on the city's outskirts were opened, laid out in streets, and sold in many parts of the suburbs of São Paulo, making old rural property immensely valuable. A specialist writing about the phenomenon in the late 1950s noted that the subdivided areas "equal[ed], if not surpass[ed], the effectively occupied stretches" of the city.[13]

This process was led by the private sector, with almost no regulation or interference by municipal governments. The precariousness of most of the subdivisions in terms of services and urban infrastructure implied an eventual transfer of responsibilities and costs to the town's city hall and public bodies, causing gigantic urban planning problems. Maintaining empty stretches between subdivisions and in regions closest to the downtown areas, for example, was a relatively common speculative strategy that damaged the organization of the city's space; in addition to impeding access to such areas for much of the population, it created sections that, given the price of land, could be acquired only by those with the greatest purchasing power.[14]

For workers, however, displacement to the periphery could mean the chance to stop paying rent and to acquire or build a "dream home." Some analysts have characterized the great value employees attached to homeownership as "a strong desire for property [that is] characteristic of Brazilian society."[15] From the workers' point of view, however, homeownership seemed to signify security, providing stability in the highly insecure and volatile environment of the big city. Moreover, with high rents and low wages, homeownership not only signifies a concrete investment and capital; it can guarantee family shelter in any situation. In some cases, as Armando Corrêa da Silva notes, landownership allowed a small crop to be planted in a home garden.[16] In his research, Silva reports on the case of a family of migrants who bought "land on the outskirts of the capital, one of the numerous existing new subdivisions, [and] maintained itself via the small incomes from what the head [of the family] planted in the *rocinha* [small farm] where they lived."

A housing survey conducted among textile workers in 1948 indicated a trend that would prevail in the following decades: of the one hundred workers interviewed who lived near the factory where they worked, only ten owned their own homes, while among the one hundred who lived far from the company, thirty-two were homeowners. The peripheralization of the working class in São Paulo was accompanied by the expansion of residential property. Between 1940 and 1970, the percentage of households paying rent versus the total number of housing units in the municipality of São Paulo fell from 75 percent to 38 percent.[17]

For most workers, homeownership in São Paulo could only be accomplished through self-constructing a home on a peripheral lot acquired with a loan. Since these lots were devoid of infrastructure, the construction was slow and piecemeal, carried out with the new landowners' own meager resources and help from family and friends, on weekends and during slack times. In 1980, it was estimated that 63 percent of the dwellings of São Paulo and surrounding cities had been built through the process of self-construction, with about half of the homes in the city having been built this way.[18]

The development of the city's transportation system favored this peripheral pattern of urbanization. While the suburban railway stations were fundamental to the expansion of the urban network until mid-century, by the postwar period the delay of rail transport in accommodating the city's growing demand was already evident. While the number of trains increased by 130 percent in the period between 1940 and 1965, the population of the regions they reached grew approximately six times more (by 734 percent).[19] The more common means of transport in the process of urban expansion was the bus, which was considered more versatile and quicker than trains or trolleys and was considered essential to the formation of new subdivisions, so that the city's expansion was accompanied by the demand for new and expanded bus lines. Over the 1950s and 1960s, buses gradually became the main means of transport of the metropolis, connecting the neighborhoods of the periphery to the center and subcenters of the city.

Thus, the accelerated urban growth of São Paulo that began in the late 1940s, motivated by intense industrial development, took on social forms that were quite segregated. In stark contrast to the opulence of the central regions and the rich neighborhoods of the city, an enormous, deprived periphery appeared. This is where the majority of workers, especially the huge waves of new immigrants, would live. Greater distance between home and work, increasing reliance on road transport based on buses, and the phenomenon of owner-built homes in peripheral subdivisions were striking features of the everyday working-class experience in this new era. The expansion of São Miguel Paulista occurred precisely in this context.

São Miguel was one of the main areas of the city that experienced this kind of growth. Numerous subdivisions transformed into districts and villages with little or no urban infrastructure in which residences were built, in most cases, by the residents themselves. "Farms and barns give way to workers' villages. . . . Thousands of small lots [are] sold on long terms, on which modest homes go up that are always unfinished," noted a historian of the neighborhood.[20]

The expansion of São Miguel and the eastern region as a whole was impressive. Between 1950 and 1960, São Miguel Paulista (including Ermelino Matarazzo, which became an autonomous district in 1959) had an average annual population growth rate of 13.4 percent, the highest in the county of São Paulo, which in the same period grew by an average of 5.6 percent each year. The region remained among the fastest growing in the city during the following decades, while São Miguel grew from about 7,000 residents in 1940 to 40,000 in 1950 and to 140,000 ten years later. In 1980, the census counted 320,000 inhabitants. Adding the population of the entire region, which includes former subdistricts of São Miguel Paulista such as Ermelino Matarazzo, Itaim, Itaquera, and Guaianazes, the total exceeded 1.2 million people.[21]

Certainly, the astonishing growth of the neighborhood cannot be attributed solely to Nitro Química. As in some other industrial suburbs of the city, the opening of the factory in São Miguel preceded population growth. The ample supply of land and the intense process of subdivision in the region enabled many workers, especially migrants, to have relatively easy access to cheap housing that they could own.

In 1945, a scholar called attention to the "contrast between the residential character and modern look of the *vilas* (literally, 'villas,' but referring to a subdivision) versus the vestiges of a distant past" in São Miguel. On the one hand, he saw the neighborhood's antiquity and bucolic air, with its seventeenth-century church and nineteenth-century houses; on the other, he saw

another "city." . . . The new neighborhoods . . . have an active life, which can be seen in their high number of commercial houses and in the movement of the streets. Not far from the station is Vila Nitro Química, which is extended to the south by the Vila Americana. Across the railroad tracks, in the floodplain of the Tietê, is the so-called Cidade Nitro Química for the working population, which continues to the east at Parque Paulistano, still in formation . . . Other "villages" also exist: Cidade Nitro Operária and Vila Curuçá.[22]

The subdivision of the neighborhood and the emergence of new vilas and settlements accelerated in an unprecedented way over the course of the 1950s. Analyzing the growth of the neighborhood, in 1958 a journalist highlighted the "phenomenon of the vilas . . . where houses pop up like mushrooms" and related it to the process of "ownership of homes built on Sundays and holidays in a collective mobilization, on land paid for in interminable installments."[23]

"Here's your opportunity: Magnificent lots in São Miguel Paulista at Vila Itaim!" shouted an advertisement in *A Hora*, a daily with strong circulation among the city's poorest. Enumerating the advantages of the business, it continued, "Ninety monthly installments—interest free—monthly payments from 500 cruzeiros. . . . Information is available from the brokers: at the final stop of bus 202 (São Miguel), in front of São Miguel Paulista Station." Another ad encouraged self-construction; "general workers" who acquired "land for construction of their own house [for] only 500 cruzeiros a month . . . in the Jardim Centenário, in the heart of São Miguel Paulista—the neighborhood with the greatest industrial progress in São Paulo," were offered a "gift . . . : five thousand bricks, a door and a window."[24]

The purchase of land was not always a safe business, however. The *grilagem* of lands, as the practice of falsification of public documents for the purpose of land speculation became known, was an increasingly common phenomenon.[25] A crime in Vila Rio Branco in São Miguel in December 1954 called attention to the problem: "São Miguel Paulista [is] a city within the capital. While much of the neighborhood is highly populated, there are lands of incalculable dimensions. As always happens in such circumstances there is confusion surrounding the ownership of land and marking of boundaries. . . . A multitude of *grileiros* taking advantage of this situation . . . do not shrink from even the most barbarian methods to ensure unauthorized possession of land. As a result, much blood has been spilled on the soil of São Miguel."[26]

Beginning in the 1940s, the development and growth of São Miguel Paulista were marked by the proliferation of subdivisions, some of them referred to as *vilas* and *jardins* ("gardens"), that were true mini-neighborhoods. São Miguel, typically seen as an example of an industrial region in the eastern suburbs of the city, gradually assumed the role of bedroom community, with its residents increasingly distant from their places of work and dependent on long commutes.[27] This relatively long process, however, was consolidated only in the mid-1960s.

Between the late 1930s and the 1960s, Nitro Química remained the largest provider of jobs in the region, and its influence gave distinct characteristics to the district and its population. Other regions adjacent to the city of São Paulo were also characterized by proximity between housing and workplaces, with the ABC cities being the most prominent example; also important were the cities of Osasco and Guarulhos, as well as the new industrial districts rising in the vicinity of São Paulo's Santo Amaro neighborhood during the mid-1950s. São Miguel's heavy dependence on a single company was a peculiarity, however, with few similar cases in the metropolitan area. Unlike other outlying bedroom communities, particularly in the eastern part of the city, São Miguel during this period maintained the characteristics of a true industrial city within the municipality of São Paulo.

Attempting to calculate the number of residents employed by local industries, a survey conducted in December 1962 evaluated different areas around metropolitan São Paulo. São Miguel Paulista had one of the highest levels, even though it was then at an advanced stage of transformation into a mostly residential neighborhood. Of the 79,777 inhabitants of São Miguel at that time, 7,704, or 9.6 percent, worked at the five companies in the neighborhood, with 75 percent of these at Nitro Química.[28] By comparison, in 1950 approximately 25 percent of the population of the district of São Miguel was working at the neighborhood company of Nitro Química.[29] Adding commercial workers and other local activities would show a greater percentage, even given that some of the Nitro workers did not live in the neighborhood.

Many workers saw the proximity of the workplace as a major draw for residence in São Miguel. Working near home was a big advantage, as it allowed workers to avoid one of their main problems in São Paulo of the 1950s: long commutes on public transportation. Explaining why he decided to settle in the neighborhood, Artur Pinto de Oliveira said, "Public transportation has always been bad here . . . and I saw my friends suffering. . . . One guy who has to be at work at 7 A.M. in Brás leaves here at 4 A.M. [I thought], I won't have to take the bus. I can go [to work] on foot."[30]

The continuous growth of the residential population and the decline of industry changed the neighborhood's status as a factory town. Beginning in the mid-1960s, Nitro Química's role in the neighborhood's economy and in job creation diminished, though it still possessed great symbolic and historical importance to the region. São Miguel Paulista, however, continued to experience high rates of population growth, becoming known in the following decades as one of the city's major bedroom communities. Although workers made up most of the neighborhood's economically active population in the 1970s (a survey in March 1973 indicated that among the heads of families in São Miguel, 19 percent were skilled workers, and 39 percent were unskilled), they had to leave the neighborhood to work, with the regions of Mooca, Sé, and Penha their main destinations. By the second half of the 1980s, it was estimated, less than 2 percent of the neighborhood's population was employed in the area.[31]

Nitro Química's past grandeur and power are repeatedly highlighted in testimony and local-history accounts. "São Miguel depended on Nitro Química," said José Caldini Filho, whose family moved to the neighborhood when the factory was still being assembled in the 1930s. Antônio Xavier dos Santos, who went to live in the neighborhood in the early 1950s, summed up a common sentiment among the locals: "Nitro Química is the mother of São Miguel."

Particularly in the context of the company's relatively low importance today, former residents and workers tended to emphasize the weight that the company once had in the life of the neighborhood and its inhabitants. Artur Pinto de Oliveira, for example, lamented that "Nitro Química company represents nothing anymore.... [T]he life of São Miguel was Nitro Química.... Nitro had full influence in São Miguel. It dominated everything and everybody." Afonso José da Silva also compared the power of the past with the present reality: "São Miguel grew a lot through Nitro Química. Nitro Química took this place forward. In 1948, when you came up to the front gate, you saw a lot of people. I had never seen so many people. "

The factory as grand provider of jobs in São Miguel is always highlighted in the interviews as a demonstration of its power. "For me, everyone [in São Miguel] worked at Nitro," said the union leader Adelço de Almeida. "Here in São Miguel practically all the families [had someone who] worked at Nitro Química," recalled Milton Furlan, a mechanic at the company between 1960 and 1990 whose family counted three generations of Nitro workers.

Discipline and the control of schedules that the factory work imposed on workers and their families are remembered as influences in the daily life of the neighborhood as a whole. "People's lives revolved around what happened at Nitro Química" recalled Maria Pureza de Mendonça. "At eleven o'clock, my aunt [would say], 'It's lunchtime. The Nitro Química whistle blew.'"[32] Artur Pinto de Oliveira also recalled how the factory whistles regulated the lives of residents:

> Sundays, ... São Miguel in ... '53, '54, '55. The famous Rua da Fábrica [Factory Street] was not yet paved. It was red clay. And the lights, those lights.... They hung bulbs, stretched out wires in the street like that, and at night the street was lit with these incandescent bulbs. The boys hung out in the street, me and my friends, and the girls passed by. Out of that came romances, marriages.... When the whistle blew, Nitro Química whistled at 6:30 A.M., 6:45, 6:55, 11 A.M., 11:45, and 11:55—those were the times of the Nitro Química whistle. On Sundays, the factory

whistled at 9:30 at night. . . . Before the whistle, the street was packed, girls strolling, boys hanging out . . . When it was 9:35, if you looked for someone in the street of São Miguel, you found not a soul. It turned into a desert. Everyone went to sleep, because almost everyone worked at Nitro Química. Those who didn't obeyed, as well. Nitro Química in São Miguel was everything. Everything!

Although the presence and importance of Nitro Química is striking, São Miguel Paulista's fundamental identity was marked by being a neighborhood of migrants, something repeatedly remembered and highlighted both by its residents and by those seeking to characterize it. Every September, for example, the anniversary celebrations of São Miguel's founding furnished occasions for the migrant presence in the neighborhood to be evoked at parties and in parades and speeches. The northeasterners were especially highlighted, as in this speech delivered at the festivities celebrating the 353rd anniversary of the neighborhood in 1975: "São Miguel Paulista, divine protection allied with labor on earth, is today a neighborhood that looks more like a city within a city. We could never . . . speak in São Miguel Paulista without mentioning the northeastern people who were the foundation of struggle, love, and sacrifice to sustain with their work what São Miguel Paulista is today."[33]

Known as "new Bahia" (a reference to the large number of migrants from the state of Bahia in the Northeast), the region established itself as one of the main places of concentration of dwellings of northeasterners in the city. Despite the large presence of migrants from other regions of the country, particularly from Minas Gerais, the association between São Miguel and northeastern migration became common in the city and even in other parts of the country from the mid-1940s on. Writing about the benefits offered workers through the company's "social service," a journalist from the business magazine *O Observador Econômico e Financeiro* who had visited the neighborhood and Nitro Química in late 1943 noted the large number of "northern workers" at the company and in the region.[34] The Igels, a family of Polish Jews who arrived in Brazil in 1937, saw the flourishing labor district as an opportunity to expand their small household items business. They moved to São Miguel in 1945 and were impressed by the large presence of northeasterners. "There were only northeasterners; no Paulistas—not one. It was just us, the northeasterners, and one Italian family" was Salomé Lúcia Igel's somewhat exaggerated recollection of the neighborhood at that time.

During the 1950s and 1960s, references to the presence of northeasterners in São Miguel multiplied, consolidating the idea that the neighborhood was "the land of the northeasterners" in São Paulo, the place "where people from Bahia, Pernambuco, Alagoas, Sergipe, Maranhão, Rio Grande do Norte, Paraíba, Ceará, in short, northerners and northeasterners, . . . live and work." A representative recalled that for that reason "it was even said . . . that São Miguel Paulista was the largest city in northeastern Brazil."[35] Regions of the neighborhood, such as the Vila Nitro Operária, site of the first concentrations of northeasterners, became famous strongholds of migrants. "The increased flow [of northeasterners] was in Vila Nitro Operária, a village . . . that had a lot of Northerners," the Paraíban Josué Pereira da Silva noted. Helena de Oliveira da Fonseca, who moved to São Miguel in 1949, recalled the large number of "pau-de-arara trucks arriving full, . . . and they came down straight to Nitro Operária. That was the place they knew best up north."

The characterization of São Miguel as a neighborhood of northeasterners marked the trajectory of the region in the second half of the twentieth century. In an article about the history of the neighborhood published in the mid-1980s, a journalist reported that "a visitor walking in certain points of São Miguel feels as if he were in the Northeast." "The 'northern houses' [small store-bar combinations typical of the Northeast that sold products, usually food] proliferate," the reporter continued, and "you can still see groups playing *forró* [northeastern dance music] in bars and barbershops." São Miguel Paulista "is a true northeastern capital," he concluded, noting that, according to the clerk of the neighborhood's Civil Registry Office, 80 percent of the residents had come from the Northeast or were the children of northeasterners.[36]

Cradle of Northeasterners

Nitro Química needed a large contingent of workers to function. During its first years of existence, its main recruiting strategy for manual labor was to attract workers from the interior of São Paulo, Minas Gerais, and the Northeast. To meet part of the demand for skilled workers and managerial positions, Nitro's co-founder José Ermírio de Moraes provided incentives for the recruitment of workers from textile companies in Sorocaba, in the interior of São Paulo. José Caldini Filho remembers from his boyhood how Ermírio de Moraes personally invited his father to come to São Miguel and "began to select from the Votorantim factory [in Sorocaba] personnel who would come to Nitro Química to be section heads, skilled workers, and managers."

Given the numerical insufficiency of the workforce already present in and around São Miguel, Nitro's management found the direct recruitment of workers from the interior of the country to be a way to fill out the ranks. By

1936, for example, "an employee of Nitro had gone to [Araçatuba, a city in the state of São Paulo] recruiting people to work in São Miguel." Among others, he eventually hired Catarina de Jesus Crusato Cano's father, who became a guard at the new company and whose wife "sewed for the clinic. She made gowns for doctors and nurses, and covers for couches."[37] During the second half of the 1930s, with the presence of Minieros and northeasterners already becoming prominent, many of the workers in construction and in the assembly plant were hired through recruiters.

Artur Pinto de Oliveira recalled that Nitro Química "went looking for people. . . . It had recruiters and trucks to bring the northeasterners." José Damasceno de Souza emphasized that the company "sent for [workers] in the Northeast. The company hired them there to get them to work here." Reinforcing the idea of a prior recruitment at the source itself, Bartolomeu de Araújo pointed out that "many people . . . of the Northeast went directly to Nitro Química." Following the route of migration, Nitro hired recruiters— "cats," they were called—to wait in the main railway stations. That is how a recruiter from Nitro Química persuaded Aurelino de Andrade, who had come from Guanambi in the interior of Bahia, to go to São Miguel when he arrived at the railway junction of Montes Claros in January 1940. Júlio de Souza Nery and Luís Gerônimo Ferreira remembered that at Estação do Norte in Brás, agents convinced newly arrived migrants to go to São Miguel.

Direct recruitment was constantly recalled in interviews with the oldest workers. Associated with the past power of the company, recruitment was, for many, at the root of the large presence of northeastern migrants in the region. After the late 1940s, however, this practice was not so common; instead, workers' contacts with relatives, friends, and countrymen came to play a decisive role in building the company's workforce.[38] Augusto Ferreira Lima, who arrived in São Miguel Paulista in 1948, remembered that while Nitro Química "sent trucks looking for people in the northeastern sertão," after a certain point, "there was no longer a need for that," because people had begun to come "all on their own." Oscar Alonso de Souza, employed at Nitro from 1954 until 1993 and one of the heads of the Personnel Department for much of that time, explained the large northeastern presence in the neighborhood by saying, "How did the northeasterner get here? . . . [He] got a position at Nitro Química because someone sent him. In turn, he sought to bring a relative, father, mother, brother, friend, whatever. . . . And that's how the northeastern community grew here."

An extensive network of contacts with home among workers already at Nitro Química ensured a heavy flow of industrial manpower. Much of the workers' testimony highlighted the prior presence of acquaintances and family members in the company as an essential factor in migrating and getting hired. "When I came from the North," recalled Luís Gerônimo Ferreira, "I immediately went straight . . . to the house of a friend I knew from a young age back in the state of Pernambuco. He was a guard at Nitro Química." Osvaldo Pires de Holanda, who arrived in São Miguel from Ceará in January 1945, also had the help of an old friend. Besides getting him a place to stay at a boarding house in the neighborhood, Holanda's friend "recommended him to the boys—almost all of them from Ceará—who lived there [in the boarding house]. He asked them to get him a good position at Nitro Química, and they arranged it in the section spinning silk thread." The Bahian migrant Antônio Xavier dos Santos summarized how much easier it was to get a job at Nitro if one had a contact there: "When one of your relatives came and said, 'Get me a place to work there' . . . you went and [asked]: 'Got a job for an unemployed relative of mine?' . . . They fixed it right then."

Migrants' correspondence served as a basic medium for exchanging information, invitations, and preparations for eventual migration. Dona Zezé de Oliveira, head of the São Miguel post office from the 1940s to the 1970s, recalled that due to the immense demand and the illiteracy of most migrants, it was necessary to hire a "girl with a typewriter" to address their envelopes and often even to write their letters. The migrants wrote about the "greatness and marvels of São Paulo . . . and São Miguel . . . , inviting the family to come because it was a good place to live."

These letters home, accompanied by photos, postcards, and, often, money, provoked excitement and the construction of an image that was, in general, very positive about São Paulo and São Miguel. For the migrants, it was important to reassure relatives and friends about their situation in São Paulo, which they commonly portrayed as a land of opportunities, better living conditions, and plenty of jobs. Irene Ramalho, who was an adolescent in Minas Gerais, dreamed day and night of São Paulo because, she said, her brothers were "living in São Miguel, and they wrote letters to us." Joaquim Anselmo dos Santos was in a dire financial situation when frost destroyed the crops on thirty-five acres of land that his family had acquired in northern Paraná, after having migrated from Ceará in the early 1950s. He decided to change his life and go to São Miguel Paulista after receiving a letter from a cousin who was already living there, who wrote, "It's very good here. You arrive one day, and the next day you already have a job." Augusto Lima noted, "I always had some friend who wrote [for a job] and found it."

Besides intensifying the desire to migrate among younger people and those who had stayed behind, migrants' return visits to the Northeast provided an important opportunity to exchange experiences with relatives and friends and possibly plan new migrations. Festivals—São João (in June), Christmastime, or even the *festa* of the local patron saint—were preferred occasions for return visits and thus were privileged moments for these contacts. Roniwalter Jatobá recalls when, in the mid-1960s, his future co-worker Everaldo, already working at Nitro Química, took advantage of the period of the festivities of Santa Efigênia, celebrated by Afro-descendants in Bananeiras (Bahia), to present his eighteen-month-old daughter to relatives and friends. While there, Everaldo persuaded Jatobá to move to São Miguel. Artur Pinto de Oliveira was impressed by the workers who came back from São Paulo to visit friends and relatives. He said, "[They] arrived so elegant. They bought sweaters here—green, yellow, black and red. . . . They arrived there, the people saw them all in suits, at the bar, drinking beer. . . . They arrived with a doctor's air, although the doctors there didn't dress like that."

Presenting an image of success and upward mobility by means of clothes, new habits, and behavior was a goal, in most cases achieved, of migrants visiting their communities of origin. "That influenced the other guys," Oliveira said, and the visits became a particularly conducive moment for furnishing information (Nitro Química, Oliveira recalled, was already "widely spoken of in the Northeast" in the 1940s), for offering invitations, and for preparing for travel and the recruitment of relatives, friends, and acquaintances. Such was the case of Afonso José da Silva, who went to São Miguel Paulista in 1948 at twenty, accompanied by his Uncle Fernando, a guard at Nitro Química; his cousin Zacaria, who also worked at the factory; and twelve of his countrymen from Senhor do Bonfim, Bahia.

Hiring relatives and accepting referrals by employees was not formal company policy, but it was encouraged. In addition to ensuring a constant supply of workers, it contributed to the creation of bonds of trust and responsibility, reinforcing the paternalist discourse of the formation of a "big Nitro family."[39] The company relied on the influence that family and friends exerted over one another to resolve workplace clashes and conflicts.[40] The hiring of relatives, friends, and countrymen, however, could also mean maintaining and deepening loyalties and general solidarity that existed prior to employment at Nitro Química. Such relationships often clashed with the interests and desires of management throughout the company's history.

In the end, having the image of a company that helped northeastern migrants who consequently became affluent workers was essential for a company that had a great need for manual labor and that, at the same time, had high rates of employment turnover. In 1939, for example, the company had an impressive annual labor turnover of about 200 percent. In 1957, that rate had fallen to 20 percent, which is still quite high.[41] Nitro Química's reputation as a company that was "good at giving jobs" and that provided a range of social benefits certainly made it attractive to migrants. The vast majority of testimony emphasized the ease of getting work and the speed of hiring. Augusto Lima remembered that "you only had to go down there and pass through the front gate. I arrived, leaned on the gate, and within five minutes the guys said, 'Hey, buddy, . . . you want to work? Come here!" At that time, . . . you went [straight] into the production area."

This picture of abundant work is often explicitly contrasted in workers' testimony with the company's present decay and the lack of jobs. The idea that the company benefited migrants, particularly northeasterners, at the moment of hiring is often remembered by older residents and former workers of the company. For some, the fact that the company's owners were from the Northeast explained the employment of so many of workers from that region. "Nitro relied on migration so much because [the owners] are Pernambucans . . . and they went looking for their staff there," said Artur Pires, a resident of São Miguel since 1945.

Indeed, the participation of northeastern workers was always notable at Nitro Química. In 1940, the year the company officially opened, northeasterners already made up about 15 percent of the total workforce. Ten years later, they represented more than 30 percent of the employees, and in 1960, more than half of the Nitro workers had migrated from the Northeast. Other migrant groups also had great importance in the composition of the company's workforce: besides Paulistas (whose numbers fell from 50 percent of the workforce in 1940 to about 30 percent), it is worth noting that Mineiros represented 10–15 percent of the company's employees in the same period.[42]

In the context of the large internal migrations beginning in the mid-1940s, Nitro Química established itself as one of the companies in São Paulo that most widely used migrant labor, particularly from the Northeast. Despite the large number of Mineiros and Paulistas among company workers, the image and memories of the company remain intrinsically associated with northeastern migrants. In the opinion of the Sebastião Adriano Mesquita, who arrived in São Miguel from Minas Gerais in 1953, "The workers who came from the north all went to Nitro Química." Upon completing his medical examination prior to being hired in 1948, Augusto Lima was told by the company doctor, "You can enter. You're going to work. We want Bahians like you—new, hot-blooded." Nitro Química "was a cradle for northeasterners," Afonso José da Silva confirmed.

An Explosive Factory

Once hired, the newly admitted workers were put to the not always simple task of learning the job. For management that meant, in most cases, having to transform former rural workers into factory workers. During the 1950s, only 20 percent of the Nitro staff had any previous experience working in industry.[43] A small sample of their previous occupations can be gleaned from lists of employees hired in April–May 1948. Of the 287 people admitted, 186 (approximately 65 percent) came directly from agricultural work, and 35 (12 percent) listed a previous position at Nitro Química as their last job.[44]

Nitro Química had an intricate production process, with more than sixty departments and an extensive line of products, but it did not need a large number of skilled workers to function. Indeed, some sections of the company did without skilled labor. In order to guarantee day-to-day production, it was necessary to have some engineers and skilled workers, together with a larger number of workers who had "learned by doing" and an even larger contingent of men and women with little education. During the 1950s, section heads, supervisors, and foremen made up 4 percent of the company's total workforce, while laborers represented 80–85 percent of Nitro Química employees.[45]

One learned to be a worker by working, as in the case of Antônio Xavier dos Santos, a newcomer from the Bahian interior who had little idea of what industrial work was when he was hired in January 1951. When asked what he knew how to do on his first day at Nitro Química, he answered, "What I know to do is run behind oxen and take care of animals. That's what I know how to do. A factory—I don't even know what that is." Aided by a co-worker and by the section head, he quickly adapted to the handling of valves and the vacuum treatment that was required in the viscose plant where he worked. "I didn't know how to do anything—nothing—[but] I learned as I went along. [I learned] so much that I worked in that service for eight years," he recalled. The staff "had the will to learn," said Augusto Lima. Learning a job could mean the possibility of leaving the most burdensome and unhealthiest sections of the company where the beginners' positions generally were located and moving to positions with better wages, working conditions, and professional recognition.

The apprenticeship of most workers occurred within the production process, in the presence of managers, technicians, and other workers. For a long time, learning through practice was extolled in official company discourse, and it also found a space in the cultural universe of the former peasants, whose life story had always been one of learning through hard everyday practice.[46] In addition, the idea that practice should be considered more important than theory seems to be a common element in the culture of various groups of workers.[47]

In the eyes of the worker, the positive emphasis on the ability to learn by doing could mean a stimulating element of self-esteem and dignity. Belarmino Duarte recalled that after working at Nitro for a while, he "already understood things, working among the engineers and chemists. I understood it not theoretically, but practically." He proudly recounts that when his boss sent his calculations to be confirmed in the laboratory, the chemist in charge said, "Belarmino did this? If [it was] Belarmino who did it, it's good," and quietly signed the report, approving the work.

While learning by practice opened the possibility of promotion and of better wages and living conditions, it could also serve as a space for resistance and for the expansion of solidarity relations on the shop floor. By exchanging experiences with a fellow worker, one learned not only how to do tasks, but also how to make a mockery of factory supervision and how to produce informal strategies of individual or collective resistance in pursuit of more control over the rate of production. After being placed in charge of his section, José Cecílio Irmão noticed that "the laborers would become tricky [once they learned a task]. They would fake it, talk instead of work, cheat at the task. . . . They slacked off." Antônio Xavier dos Santos recalled that "many people were productive during the first three months, then, from the fourth month on, they started to slack."

Despite the importance of practical learning for the company's workers, some essential functions within the industry required skills that could not be obtained solely in the day-to-day operation of the factory. The National Service of Industrial Instruction (SENAI), created in the early 1940s with the strong support and enthusiasm of various São Paulo companies, became the largest Brazilian organization of professional education for factory workers. Nitro Química was one of six companies in the state of São Paulo, and the only one in the capital city, authorized by SENAI to organize a school on its premises.[48] However, the percentage of the company workforce trained at

Nitro's SENAI school was always low. Of the approximately 260 graduates of the school between 1951 and 1960, only twenty-one were still working for the company by 1960.[49]

It therefore fell to section heads, supervisors, and foremen to teach the work to the vast majority of new workers, alongside their supervising duties. During this learning process there was no lack of references to the workers' places of origin. Frederico, who headed the unhealthy spinning section, for example, said that when he got a novice worker, he summoned the foreman and jokingly said, "Bahian, teach this Bahian the Bahians' job." Likewise, the person responsible for hiring the Bahian Antônio Xavier dos Santos decided to put him under the supervision of a Bahian boss, saying, "I'm sure you'll listen to him. . . . I'm sure you'll get along because he's Bahian."

An interview conducted by Nitro's information officer in the 1950s with Victor Garcia Cabalero, a company employee since the 1930s who had been a supervisor in various industrial sectors, highlighted the supervisors' central role in training workers who were largely inexperienced in the urban world of the factory. "Most of today's officers were trained under my guidance," Cabalero said. "Employees were hired without having any notion of the factory, and little by little they learned the handling of the machines. To give you an idea of the level of culture of some of them, I'll just say that on one occasion a newcomer, seeing a clock on the wall, asked me what it was."[50]

The section heads played a strategic role in the functioning of the factory. The importance that the upper echelons of the company conferred on section heads is demonstrated by the testimony of the chemical engineer Fábio Ravaglia, an official at Nitro since the 1950s and chief executive of the company during the 1960s:

> They were the men who really made things happen. They obeyed the technical guidelines of a few engineers and chemists, but they were the ones who could actually make the factory move. There were just over sixty of them, but they were distinguished by a very strong personality, in the sense of leadership. All of them had working-class backgrounds and had a very low level of technical training. They learned almost everything on the job. They were what I and other engineers called "technician-practitioners." . . . But they had extraordinary loyalty to the company.

The section heads' strategic role in the factory gave them considerable power. They made most of the decisions about workers' professional lives. Promotions, demotions, punishments, and transfers were determined primarily by their opinion. However, this managerial power was often perceived by the workers as discretionary and unfair. In their interviews, they repeatedly referred to the bosses' authoritarianism and arbitrariness. For example, Benedito Miguel worked at the factory for thirty-three years and believed that the company chose heads and foremen who would serve as "executioners, to stay on top of the worker." The heads were "terribly ignorant," said Gerolino Costa Jacobina, who worked for Nitro from 1955 until the 1980s. Osvaldo Lino, who worked in the company for twenty-eight years, remembered workers who were fired without cause "simply because the boss didn't like the guy's face." One section head, Paulo Bertine, became famous among workers for his authoritarianism and harshness. According to Ravaglia, however, Bertine "was not a slave driver, but he knew how to give orders." Despite numerous complaints, the ability to command and the detailed knowledge of the production process were guarantees of stability and power to bosses such as Bertine. Ravaglia also recalled that Bertine "was not a technician but was a guy who understood the job sufficiently. He came up within it . . . Because of this, headquarters didn't send him [away]. . . . Even though headquarters got complaints, he remained, because he understood how things worked. Sometimes a customer complained . . . about defective products, whatever. They sent the technician there or even the engineer [and they] couldn't fix it. Paulo Bertine went and got into the machines, figured it out, and made it work with the product."

The section head's authority derived not only from the power that the company conferred on him but also from having the image of a successful worker who had managed to move up in the company on the strength of his personal merits. In that sense, he was an example for the other workers. Section heads, supervisors, foremen, and assistant foremen were almost always controversial figures in the workers' imagination. But even though they were associated with authoritarianism and injustice, their jobs were coveted because they represented upward social mobility and greater benefits, including low-rent company houses in Vila Nitro Química. "That business of the houses was only for the bosses, some supervisors," said Gerolino Costa Jacobina. It was the offer of a "really good house" that motived Carlo Cecchini, the Italian husband of Dona Nair and a mechanic by profession, to leave his job at Indústrias Matarazzo in the neighboring city of São Caetano do Sul and transfer with his wife to São Miguel in February 1939. Carlo worked at Nitro as the supervisor of thread spooling for forty-four years, during which time he lived in a house furnished almost free by the company.

Section heads were also subject to the influence of workers' social networks established in the company and in the neighborhood. An authoritarian boss or supervisor who periodically transgressed the workers' limits of tolerance could suffer sanctions, sometimes violent ones. José Cecílio Irmão remembers that because of persecutions and injustice, "There were always fights with bosses. . . . There was barely a week without a hassle at the front gate." According to José Ferreira da Silva, a worker at the company from 1948 to 1966, "Many times someone waited for the boss at the gate. There was always some fight going on."

At times, the price section heads paid for arbitrary behavior was not only violence but also rejection by the workers' community. Augusto Lima, supervisor of the spinning sector for twenty-one years, prided himself on always having "mixed with the crew," despite the company's rules against it. He preferred to be a "friend of my friends and not a friend of industry. We're going to work in the industry, but we have to have friends, because tomorrow you'll be out [of a job], and your friends will be out, too, and you're going to need a friend in the street." Lima said he also knew section heads who preferred to be "friends of industry." One had to "go in a car to get his haircut outside the neighborhood, because he knew ten thousand [workers] lived there. He was management, and [everybody] was angry at him."

Within the production process, the workers created forms of boycotting and of demoralizing section heads who were considered too hard and authoritarian. While this was difficult to do with a supervisor or section head who was prestigious and considered essential by the company, as in the case of Paulo Bertine, it could happen with relative frequency with a supervisor or foreman responsible for a shift within a section. "It's no use taking sixty men to work and . . . not knowing how to appeal to them," said Augusto Lima. "It's no use picking them up by the heels. You have to be easygoing. That's how you get production." Lima cited the case of a supervisor named Pedrinho: "The more he pushed the floor, the more the floor was ready for him. They went crazy. They criticized him. They gave him hell." The shift for which Pedrinho was responsible almost never paid attention to production targets, and now and then someone would tie a "knot in [a machinery belt] and stop everything. The machine would remain permanently shut down."

Upward mobility for the workers within the enterprise invariably passed through being a section supervisor, but those possibilities were practically closed to women. Even at the hiring stage, women had considerably fewer employment opportunities. Between 1940 and 1960, only 20 percent of the jobs at Nitro Química were filled by female workers, but even in principally female sections, only a small number of women occupied supervisory positions.[51] Catarina de Jesus Crusato Cano, who worked at Nitro for forty-six years, said that "there was a certain discrimination [in the factory] in relation to women, who besides earning less had fewer chances for professional growth."[52]

In a factory the size of Nitro Química, the absolute number of employed women was large, although the female workers were concentrated in certain sections. Despite the restrictions, and given the precariousness of the alternatives, however, "Working at Nitro Química gave you status," as Maria Pureza de Mendonça noted. Darci Xavier Ribeiro, who began working at the factory in 1951 at fourteen, good-humoredly summarized women's options in São Miguel Paulista: "In those days, women went to primary school only up to the fourth grade. They chose cooking or sewing or they joined the circus or they worked at Nitro."

Women's factory work was generally seen by men as secondary and temporary. Marriage ideally would mark the end of it, as women moved along to assume the tasks of housekeeping and child rearing, leaving the role of provider to the men. Irene Ramalho, who worked in the company's cooperative, said that she became "despondent" when her boyfriend gave her an ultimatum: "Look, if you keep working [at Nitro], I'm not going to marry you." Maria Degersília Aragão, who began working in the thread-winding machines section of Nitro Química in 1954, at fifteen, got married in June 1959 and left her job less than two months later.

But financial conditions did not always allow women to stop working immediately after marriage. Augusto Lima's wife was still working eight years after their marriage when he said, "Now you're going to leave Nitro, and I'll keep working. You're going to take care of the children." Such decisions, however, were frequently the focus of major conflicts for working couples. Many women saw their jobs as offering autonomy and satisfying the longings that had motivated their move to the city. Even after marriage some women kept working. Celina Garcia, who worked at the factory for fifteen years, remembered that the "majority [of women] married and kept on working," at least for a while. In any case, families in which the women worked were generally seen as more "needy." Only financial difficulty justified women's employment, which was seen as "help" to balance the family's budget.[53]

But women's work was also seen as supplemental within the factory. For section heads and laborers alike, it was common to associate "real work" with manual labor that required force and resistance, characteristics that were considered masculine. Skill was also commonly considered a masculine attribute. Women were associated with "light" tasks, done with greater ease and less danger. "I want you to go to work [in the spinning section] because that's where women work," was the advice Artur Pinto de Oliveira received from his brother. "Since you're just beginning, it's not so [heavy]. . . . It's good there. Even women work there." When asked whether women worked in his section, the mechanical workshop, Júlio de Souza Nery answered, "No! There were only professionals there, only men. The mechanical workshop is pretty heavy, no? Women didn't work [in that kind of section]. The girls worked in rayon, in silk." Female workers, nevertheless, could read this division of labor differently. Maria José Santos Oliveira said that only women worked in her section because classifying silk was "a task that depended on attention and even a little on the operator's intelligence" to be done well.

The attribution of feminine and masculine characteristics to work at Nitro implied great gender segregation in the workplace. Dona Zezé remembered that the Nitro factory "was very separated. . . . Torsion was only men; dyeing was only men; spinning was men and women. The section where I worked was all women, so there was a division there."[54]

Workers and neighborhood residents remembered dangerous working conditions. "When I got here in 1949, Nitro Química already existed, and it was much talked about because of the deaths," said Benedita de Souza. "Some [fell] in a tank of acid; others [were] poisoned. There was a lot of death." Working at Nitro "was not a soft job," complained one of the workers fired in the great wave of layoffs that swept the company in 1966. "I gave twenty years of my life to working with poisonous material."[55] "It was the great company of the peripheral neighborhood," said Councilman Rio Branco Paranhos in 1960. "I know plenty about it, because I was the lawyer who brought the largest number of workers' complaints to court against that company. And the grand majority of the complaints were about the unhealthy working conditions."[56] A police investigator sent to the company to determine the reasons for a partial stoppage by workers demanding a Christmas bonus in December 1948 reported, "The working conditions of operators in the [spinning and rolling sections] are the most difficult, since they work with acids all night. . . . They're young workers, mostly northerners, who never become permanent, since the nature of the job involves the progressive loss of health."[57]

Even some interviewees who praised the enterprise and its benefits also mentioned the dangers and health problems caused by working in the factory. Helena de Oliveira da Fonseca, whose husband was chosen by the company to preside over the Internal Commission for Accident Prevention (CIPA) for eleven years, said that the "company gave the conditions for a person to work but failed on the human side. . . . A factory that works with chemicals is dangerous, [and] at times accidents would happen." José Venâncio, a resident of

São Miguel since 1953, said that Nitro Química in those days was "very good," but he also recognized that "it had that problem of gas emissions, [and the workers] coughed violently." The company's bad reputation crossed borders. When some migrants who had gone "mad" returned to the interior of Bahia, said Venâncio, people commented that it was because they had worked at Nitro Química.

The number of accidents was, in fact, quite high. The minutes of the monthly meeting of CIPA at Nitro in July 1958 calculated 320 accidents in the previous month, 52 of which required the removal of the injured worker.[58] In effect acknowledging the danger, the company conducted internal campaigns in the late 1940s aimed at accident prevention. The principal target was the "new employee . . . who does not have a defined profession. . . . He is not, then, familiar with the handling of the tools and the functioning of the machinery, and is ignorant of the risk of various operations and tasks. It falls to the foreman, to the supervisor, to the section head, to receive the new employee, and to make the necessary recommendations for work safety."

It is not unreasonable to assume that, heedless of such recommendations and pressed by production deadlines, many section heads paid little attention to safety instruction and effective supervision on safety issues. In any case, Nitro Química was repeatedly associated with accidents and unhealthy conditions. Protests and struggles against the work environment were constant from the time of the company's founding. Only two months before a visit by President Getúlio Vargas in celebration of the official inauguration of Nitro Química in April 1940, at the height of the Estado Novo dictatorship, pamphlets were distributed in São Miguel calling for a union of workers against "this terrible place: unhealthy, morbid, and the cause of premature deaths."[59] Ten years later, a bulletin distributed in São Miguel recalled the visit by the communist leader Luís Carlos Prestes to the neighborhood in 1947 and how he was "visibly shocked by the conditions of life and work of those workers and their families, where the infamous Nitro Química with such a terrible reputation . . . exploits, annihilates, and kills workers . . . , where the workers are bathed in deadly gas and leave the factory tottering from hunger, dizziness, and fatigue."[60]

Demands to improve Nitro Química's unhealthy working conditions were common in workers' movements at the company. Despite Nitro's increased investment in the field of industrial safety and a significant decrease in accident rates over fifty years, it remained one of the most dangerous and unhealthy factories in the city. Workers of different generations point to accidents, mutilations, and deaths as their worst memories. The spinning section, where rayon thread was produced, was notorious for its toxicity and became a kind of symbol of the dangerous character of the plant. The ventilation system was inadequate to disperse the toxic gases formed in the process of manufacture of the thread and contaminated the workers. It was to that section that the majority of the newly hired workers were sent. "Worst section of the factory," remembered José Cecílio Irmão. The laborer "worked two, three days. His face got full of gas, and he went to the infirmary. Your eyes got red. You went crazy. . . . You couldn't stand it. You used eye drops or potatoes . . . to alleviate it." Roniwalter Jatobá, who lived in São Miguel Paulista in the early 1970s, also noted the use of potatoes to combat gas toxicity when he reported on the unhappiness of a worker in the spinning sector of Nitro Química: "Second shift of the night, the factory: section F-5 [rayon spinning], Nitro Química, the gas attacking the eyes, entering into a teary vista, blindness. The voice of the overseer pressing [him to work]. . . . The pain in the eyes. . . . On the way home, fumbling through the streets, arriving, and then the balm of raw potato on the eyes, sucking out the gas, the vegetable turning black."[61]

The factory's dangers were well known in São Miguel. After a reactor in the explosives sector blew up in June 1947, killing nine workers, the event was memorialized in neighborhood streets and bars by guitarists and *cordel* poets, who sang about the "terrible explosion that rocked Nitro Química Brasileira" supposedly because of the "handling of too much acid."[62] The newspaper *A Gazeta Esportiva* reported that "there was an instant of panic, despite there having been frequent explosions of lesser size" at Nitro.[63]

Fear of explosions and of sometimes fatal accidents were part of daily life for workers and residents. When the factory "blew those short whistles," a neighborhood resident recalled in an interview at the end of the 1970s, "we already knew there was a fire. Then everybody was afraid, because people used to say that if Nitro Química exploded, . . . the whole city would go up along with the factory . . . . Then everybody was frightened."[64]

But it was not only fear of explosions that made the residents of São Miguel uncomfortable. Nitro Química's infamous gases escaped the factory to pollute the neighborhood as a whole, causing a series of environmental and public health problems. Complaints by inhabitants of São Miguel about pollution from Nitro were common in the 1940s. "The gas that leaked out was so terrible that people on the way to the [train] station [next to the factory] had to keep kerchiefs over their noses to catch a train," recalled Antônio Xavier dos Santos. "That was a horror," said Salomé Lúcia Igel. "People's clothes were permeated with the smell of the smoke, the smell of acid." The region's rivers, particularly the Tietê, were polluted by the company. Maria Fernanda dos Santos Gomes, a Portuguese woman who arrived in São Miguel with her family in 1951, recalled that once "the Tietê was very clean. [We] cooked with water from the Tietê."

In its most critical phases, the pollution produced by Nitro Química motivated neighborhood residents to move. A longtime resident, Waldomiro Macedo, said that "the chlorine smoke and the gas that leaked out" made sections of the neighborhood "unlivable." That was the case for the Igel family, who lived in the same street as the station, next to the factory's chimneys, and suffered constantly from the gases. "[We] couldn't stand it," said Moisés Igel. "There was acid, smoke. . . . People were coughing even in the neighborhood of Penha." Worried for their children's health, the Igels decided to move to the Bom Retiro neighborhood, although they continued operating their small store in São Miguel.

The situation became even worse in the late 1950s when a caustic soda factory opened at Nitro Química. This added considerably to the company's emission of pollutants into the neighborhood. Pressured by the residents' protests, some councilmen demanded measures from the public authorities. In April 1959, for example, Councilman Tarcílio Bernardo declared the air of São Miguel Paulista to be "completely polluted by the strong chlorine gases expelled by the big factory. . . . The chlorine expelled . . . is so strong that it dries up plantations and damages metal objects." A year later, Councilman Aurelino de Andrade sued for an investigation by the Secretary of Health into Nitro Química, which he described as a company "that for many years has been threatening, with the poison gases it exhales, the public health of the people of São Miguel Paulista, a threat that has increased in the last two years, after the installation of a factory of caustic soda where the exhalation of other gases has contributed to the high index of infant mortality in that district."[65]

Inspections and fines notwithstanding, the pollution problem persisted for a few more years. In May 1967, State Representative Fausto Tomás de Lima demanded that the Paulista health authorities act against the "super-powerful financial group" of Nitro Química, which, "without exaggeration, [was] responsible for 90% of the tuberculosis cases in São Miguel Paulista and surrounding villages."[66] The problem was effectively mitigated only in the 1970s, when a new wave of residents' protests, combined with more efficient state monitoring, finally forced Nitro to install filters in its chimneys.

Despite Nitro Química's social service, its benefits, and its power and influence in the region, many workers felt that working conditions there demonstrated how disposable they were to the company. A former union leader noted that the company had "a very good medical staff," but "health was terrible inside" the factory. Artur Pinto de Oliveira felt that "one worked in an inhumane way. . . . The health of the man [who worked] was not taken into account. Simply because it was a chemical plant [does not mean] that there was no recourse. There was no interest. It was much easier for [the company] to consider the man to be of less value than the machines."

In January 1959, the communist newspaper *Noticias de Hoje* made a similar argument, comparing working conditions at Nitro to the drought conditions through which its northeastern workers had lived:

Does not [the northeastern migrant] in São Miguel live the drama that he once knew in the rugged sertão? For here, as there, the northern man goes through the same suffering. There it is the inclemency of nature that dries everything out, that exhausts the last hopes of man. Here—or, more accurately, at Nitro Química—it is the injustice of the bosses in turning man into an instrument of production. In return, the worker leaves the industry in failing health for the rest of his life, taking with him the mark of the plant's gases and acids that make his life fade away as surely as the drought of the sertão does.[67]

The terrible working conditions in Nitro Química's worst sections may also have been responsible for a large number of workers' abandoning their jobs. Many workers stayed at Nitro long enough to acquire some industrial experience, then left to try their luck in the heated, expanding job market of São Paulo of the 1950s, although many of them continued to live in São Miguel. Amauri da Cunha, for example, who worked at the company in 1957–59, recalled that he "did not adapt to the unhealthy chemicals" and went to work at a shoe factory in Bela Vista. Antônio Xavier dos Santos said that he lasted forty-one years at Nitro Química only because he was lucky: "If I had fallen into one of those positions [e.g., begun by working in the rayon-spinning sector], I wouldn't have lasted six months." His brother, by contrast, was hired to work in the infamous F-5 section. He "went in at 7 A.M., and by 11 he left and [said], 'I'm not going ever back there.'" In the 1970s, the company's declining importance and the weakening of its benefits policy, combined with its "bad reputation," meant that workers were no longer looking at Nitro. "Those who had more experience were already looking for another company."[68]

For the many who remained, the ability to withstand the work environment depended in large measure on the creation of norms of sociability that mitigated the factory's daily grind. The informality of relations among workers via pranks and games while production was going on played a decisive role in a "creative reinvention" of work.[69]

Pranks are common in factory floor culture, and they were probably not uncommon in the agricultural work environment from which many of the workers came. José Cecílio Irmão remembered that "there were a lot of pranks [at Nitro Química]. If the worker wasn't in the mood, he could find an opening for anything. He teased his comrades, poked, hit, played at boxing." A foreman said that as soon as he left his section, the workers would begin to play with the broom: "They would stop the job . . . and hit each other with the broom." Even though it signaled an environment of informality and relaxation among the workers, such play was not always well received. The factory environment was not only one of solidarity and camaraderie. Rivalries, disputes, and conflicts among workers were as common as games, and at times they could spark real violence. Artur Pinto de Oliveira's brother did not like pranks, for instance, but "in the section [where he worked], the staff liked to play them. One day, a man from Ceará, grabbed a hose . . . and sprayed him with cold water, as a joke. . . . [My brother] slugged the guy in the face. The man from Ceará went down, bleeding from his nose and mouth."

Frequent references to pranks in the *Nitro Jornal* and in the company's regulations provide evidence of how common they were on the factory floor. For company management, not tolerating pranks was an issue of authority, of maintaining a work environment that was focused on production. One of the functions of CIPA, for example, was "to maintain discipline, combating pranks." Associating pranks with danger and insecurity was a common strategy used to persuade the workers. One story in the Nitro's internal bulletin in the 1950s recalled that "a worker accustomed to humming and shouting on the job was the victim of an electrical shock a few days ago. . . . He became a 'prisoner' of the current, and everybody heard him yelling. But since he was always yelling, his comrades paid him no mind, and if an outsider had not shut off the switch, the accident would have been fatal. Useless shouting and pranks are always harmful to the security of people who are working."[70]

At times, nevertheless, pranks were perceived as normal and even important for putting up with Nitro's intense work rhythm and could be tolerated by some bosses and foremen. Even though he was a supervisor and despite management guidelines, Augusto Lima said, he liked to play pranks on the workers in his sector, "smacking, kicking one or the other" when they exited the plant.

Nicknames were also common on the factory floor. According to José Ferreira da Silva, a company employee from 1948 to 1966, there were 140 workers in his section, and "almost all of them had nicknames, even the section heads." While in some cases the nicknames were offensive, provoking fights and misunderstandings, mostly they were code for approaching and forming relationships. Waldomiro Macedo, who came to Nitro from the interior of São Paulo in the late 1950s, recalls that he had no trouble relating to his colleagues in the factory: "I made friends, because within Nitro Química, what you found was northeastern personnel, and I made friends with everybody. I put nicknames on the guys; the guys put nicknames on me. I never had a problem fitting in."

Informal relationships, which were basic to various practices of solidarity and mutual aid among rural fieldworkers and migrants, continued to be fundamental for workers at Nitro Química. The network of coexistence and sociability among workers in São Miguel Paulista in the 1940s and 1950s was made possible by a combination of ties of family and friendship; origins in the same interior regions of the Northeast; residential concentration in the same neighborhood; and the common conditions of migration and learning the new city and the new job, all experienced under the same strenuous circumstances.

Within the factory, social networks could be consolidated and amplified. A worker recalled that "there was good, sound friendship [at Nitro]. They were all friends . . . each one with his nickname." These friendships continued outside the plant's gates. According to the worker, if someone in the workplace said he was going to kill a pig: "when our shift ended, we would go along . . . . The cost of the pig was taken out of his next paycheck. We went to his house and ate. There was a lot of that."

Scholars studying the first generations of migrants who became laborers in São Paulo have questioned the existence of collective action within the industrial companies. While noting the existence of friendships expressed in "conversation, mockery, pranks . . . and at times a get-together outside the factory," they consider that such friendships were based on coexistence, on ties of kinship, or on the fact of coming from the same city or region and that they occurred because of the workers' rural origin, "where opportunity to participate in collective action is based on ties of kinship and neighborhood."[71] Following this line of thought, the persistence of such values in the urban environment hindered the development of organized action, because the workers united through an "affective and personal form of solidarity, and not the feeling of belonging to the same class."[72]

But for the workers of Nitro Química in São Miguel Paulista, the complex of social relations formed in the places of origin and expanded in the factory and neighborhood were frequently the basis for cohesion and solidarity and were essential for the formation of a class identity. While personal relations strengthened the paternalist discourse that diluted internal conflicts and fostered the idea of the factory space as a "big family," they also opened a space to question the company's unjust policies and actions and were central elements in the creation of collective action in the workplace and at home. José Ferreira da Silva, who was a union leader from the late 1950s to 1964, emphasized the importance of those relations for organizing workers:

> In those days, we knew where our colleagues at work lived. If the colleague got sick, [we went to] visit .... Three, four colleagues would go to see how the comrade was doing. There was solidarity. When one colleague was punished . . . another would try to find out what had happened. [It was there] that I began to assume [my role as a trade unionist]. That friendship that we all had among ourselves led us to exchange ideas. Then that union grew, that friendship, and when it was time to make a claim about something, we [began] to form a commission.

Leaders were formed by being part of the social networks developed in the factory and the neighborhood and by sharing cultural references and experiences. This camaraderie made the construction of legitimacy for union action in the area possible. According to Adelço de Almeida, a worker at Nitro and the president of the Chemical Workers Union from 1956 to 1964, his "northeastern origin [gave him] access to that mass of Bahians. . . . They believed in me because I also drank *cachaça*, danced *forró*, raised hell."

CHAPTER THREE

Worker Community and Everyday Life
"Becoming Northeastern" in São Paulo

Boardinghouses, Homeownership, and Collective Effort

Beyond the factory gates, the bairro was the fundamental space for social networks and the sharing of workers' experiences. As a place of residence, leisure, and work, it was the site of a range of personal relationships among family members, friends, and contemporaries who helped urbanize migrants with essential knowledge and everyday contacts. In the neighborhood and in the vilas, bars, boardinghouses, and streets, the workers of São Miguel Paulista kept alive family ties and friendships brought from the Northeast and other regions, created new connections, and deepened contacts made at the factory. The neighborhood was thus the decisive space for the resocialization of migrants in the city and for exchanging experiences and "cultural production."[1]

Since the migration process was based on networks of contacts and personal relationships, it stimulated the proximity of housing between people of the same families and regions. Sociological surveys conducted during the

1970s show that the proximity of family housing was an important feature for workers who had come to São Paulo in previous decades. According to one such survey, nearly 70 percent of low-income workers in the city had relatives living in the same neighborhood or on the same block.[2] Certainly, this was the case in São Miguel Paulista, where many streets and blocks were almost completely inhabited by people from the same cities and regions of the Northeast.[3]

Particularly during the 1940s and early 1950s, boardinghouses played an important role in strengthening and expanding contacts for newly arrived migrants, who were mostly young single men. São Miguel had a huge number of boardinghouses, which by far were the accommodation most frequently used by newcomers; a report published in the newspaper *Correio Paulistano* in 1948 that linked the neighborhood to the migration of northeasterners noted "the singular phenomenon of [São Miguel] being one of the few suburbs where there are boardinghouses and hotels, beds for rent, etc., the way there are in the city center."[4]

In his memoir, Pastor Mário da Natividade Valladão highlighted the presence of collective housing in São Miguel in the late 1940s. When in 1946–47 his Baptist church decided to start a "door-to-door evangelization campaign" in the neighborhood, Valladão found that there were "few families [but] many hostels where numerous young men were thrown together."[5] Lídia Castelani, who owned a bar in the center of São Miguel in the late 1940s, decided to set up a small *pousada* (inn) after noting the intense demand for such accommodations. "Every day, people showed up looking for a place," she said. Augusto Lima, who lived in various boardinghouses in the neighborhood before he got married, remembered that São Miguel was known as "the land of the boardinghouse in São Paulo."[6]

An idea of what this kind of lodging was like can be gleaned from a complaint registered in 1951 with the São Paulo Department of Political and Social Order (DOPS) against "the excessive rent" charged by Ambrozina Teixeira, the proprietor of a boardinghouse at "6 Beraldo Marcondes Street in São Miguel Paulista": "Said lady . . . rents five rooms to young men, with three to five beds in each. There are eighteen young men . . . , mostly laborers. . . . There also exists a front room [that] upon information and belief is occupied by people of her family."[7] Besides providing shelter, these boardinghouses or *pensões* (pensions) generally served food, thus providing basic security for newcomers. At that time, "São Miguel had no restaurants," said Lídia Castelani. "It had only little boardinghouses. So people who had an extra room would serve food and turn their home into a boardinghouse." In the late 1930s and 1940s, the

Bernardo family's boardinghouse served "an average of 88 meals for boarders and . . . another 130 to various people."

Moreover, the boardinghouses were points of reference for people in search of relatives, friends, and contemporaries. For example, João Freitas Lírio said that people "came down from the [São Miguel railroad] station looking for the nearest boardinghouse, . . . and they went along asking, 'Do you know so-and-so?'" The net of contacts between the migrants and their communities of origin was a sophisticated one. Augusto Lima remembered constantly being "sought out by the people from my homeland, by more than a hundred-some people. [They arrived] at the boardinghouse where I lived and looked for me by name. Everybody knew I was there. At night, people were sitting there waiting when I got home."

Some boardinghouses even transformed themselves into points of arrival for entire communities. Nelson Bernardo said that many pau-de-arara drivers "came already oriented and . . . the *baianada* [Bahian multitude] got off the trucks . . . right in front of the boardinghouses." Nelson Bernardo's was the first boardinghouse at which Augusto Lima stayed. It always "had a crew of northeasterners from the back country of Piauí," he said. When in a stroke of luck Dona Zezé's brother won a prize in the federal lottery in the early 1940s, her family decided to use the money to start a boardinghouse that, because of its clientele, came to be known as the "Mineiros' boardinghouse."

In tight quarters, in chats during coffee breaks and lunch, or between beers after dinner, newcomers to the city struck up the first contacts of their new reality, exchanging information and experiences.[8] The main priority was to find employment, in which both longtime and newly established contacts were essential. As soon as Augusto Lima arrived at the Bernardos' boardinghouse, he spent "the night talking with a group" who gave him information about how to get a job at Nitro Química. "The next day, when the Nitro Química whistle blew at 7 A.M. . . . . I was already at the factory gate," he said.

The boardinghouses therefore were a key space for workers' socialization in São Miguel Paulista. "The boardinghouse was great for friendship. It was through the boardinghouse that people became friendly, where people got together and liked each other. They threw parties and went out on the train sightseeing, all together. . . . That was how I got to know São Miguel Paulista—you can believe it—in the boardinghouses of São Miguel." Antônio Xavier dos Santos had similar memories of his time living in boardinghouses. "The environment of the boardinghouse was plenty friendly," he said. "I made friends with people at the boardinghouse. We went to parties. We went to the park on Sunday." Extended stays in the boardinghouses were common. Santos, who came to São Miguel in 1950 from Babaçu, Bahia, lived in a boardinghouse for eight years, until the arrival of his mother and other family members prompted him to rent a house where they could all live together. João Freitas Lírio, originally from Camponoso, Bahia, spent six years in a boardinghouse before he got married. Boardinghouses provided a temporary perch for young migrants while they decided where to stay permanently in the new city. In general, marriage or the arrival of other family members made moving necessary; many, in their recollections, associated the boardinghouses with youth and with the "hell-raising" of unmarried men.

While the importance of migrants' social networks was evident in the environment of the boardinghouses, those networks continued to be decisive in the process of settling down in the neighborhood. Beyond the attraction of Nitro Química's great demand for labor, São Miguel Paulista, as we have seen, was particularly popular with migrants because it offered relatively inexpensive lots for purchase. "A patch of land [in São Miguel] was cheap," recalled Amauri da Cunha, a resident of the neighborhood since 1954. Henriqueta Lopes Fernandes said that "people started coming here because [São Miguel] was the cheapest neighborhood to buy land." Fernandes herself moved from the Brás neighborhood to São Miguel in the 1960s when it became possible for her to build a house there. In the early 1960s, Lucilene Sanchez Guimarães's newly married parents left the Vila Maria neighborhood, where they shared a property with Lucilene's grandmother, and "bought a plot [in São Miguel] because it was cheaper." In addition to the low price, the possibility of buying land on an installment plan made this viable for many workers. Lídia Castelani, who with her husband purchased a site in São Miguel's Jardim Helena neighborhood in the mid-1940s to open a small store that sold grain, recalled that it was "easy and cheap" to buy a piece of ground and that "low monthly payments" made it possible for them to buy. This was also the case for Jorge Gonçalves Lula, who ten years later bought a lot in Jardim São Vicente, another of the numerous subdistricts of São Miguel. Gonçalves Lula said that he paid "the same amount [until] the last installment, without interest, with a non-adjustable rate . . . . I paid 700 cruzeiros down, [and the] installment payment was 700 cruzeiros [per month]. I made the minimum wage . . . at Nitro Química: 3,000 cruzeiros [per month]."

Even houses built by real estate companies could be acquired in São Miguel more easily than those in São Paulo's more central areas. An advertisement for the São Miguel company S.A. Vila Curuçá published in the *Folha de São Miguel* in 1954 urged readers to stop "paying rent," offering for sale a "house with a 10 [meter] x 30 [meter] lot," with the following payment terms:

"When making a reservation, 500 cruzeiros: within 30 days, upon signing the contract and handing over of keys, 4,500 cruzeiros; the remainder in 91 monthly installments of 600 cruzeiros without interest from the following month. There are also contract and registration expenses of 560 cruzeiros. We still have lots of land for sale, without fees or interest."[9]

One might suppose that payment terms were reasonably favorable for many workers, such as those at Nitro Química, taking into account the wages paid by the company. Although figures for 1954 are not available, in 1956 the lowest-paid positions in the plant, such as that of *servente* (unskilled worker), paid about 3,700 cruzeiros a month.[10] In São Miguel, therefore, the possibility of acquiring a house near the workplace was very attractive both for newly arrived migrants and for older residents who had no home elsewhere in the city. Purchasing one's own home meant no longer paying rent, of course, which represented a great savings in a working family's budget.

Besides the capital asset it provided, a house had great cultural value. The configuration of the space and the security it gave the family as a basic guarantee against the uncertainties of the labor market were values directly related to workers' attainment of homeownership. In addition, a house was a financial asset that often meant extra income, given the widespread practice of subleasing and renting out rooms and of building smaller houses on the grounds. Owning one's own home thus acquired increasing importance in the minds of the workers of greater São Paulo from the late 1940s onward.[11]

For many workers, male and female, the purchase of a lot to construct a house occurred soon after marriage. Augusto Lima recalled that after he and his friends married, "We all bought land, and we all built houses." The abundance of land in São Miguel Paulista made the neighborhood into one of the busiest locales for the sale of property at low prices. There were many "land salesmen," he recalled. "They were on the street by the station; they were here on the square. Everywhere there were parked cars of people selling land to . . . the working class, especially to those who worked at Nitro." The Portuguese migrant Manuel Caçador, newly arrived in São Paulo in 1952, also remembered that once while he was visiting a cousin in the neighborhood of Penha, he saw "the Plaza 8 de Setembro . . . all full of signs: 'Lots for sale. Vila Parque Paulistano—São Miguel Paulista.'" He got into a broker's car right then and there, and after seeing various lots that he considered "bad, even stinky," he ended up buying a back lot.

Land purchases were obviously driven by price, but the choice of a plot also took into account the proximity of relatives, friends, and acquaintances, who in turn helped maintain and expand the migrants' networks of cooperation and mutual aid. This criterion was also decisive in the process of self-construction of housing, which required the organization and help of the greatest number of people possible, as *mutirões*—joint efforts for the construction, expansion, and improvement of workers' homes—became a common practice in São Paulo's peripheral areas.

The sociologist Juarez Brandão Lopes attributed the supposed low level of solidarity among the workers of rural origin in São Paulo to the absence of most forms of cooperation within the Brazilian countryside. "Even the *mutirão* has disappeared or is disappearing in most of the national territory," he noted.[12] Other scholars also observed the decline of the mutirão in the Brazilian countryside during the 1950s.[13] However, migration to cities may have brought about a revival of neighborly and mutual aid practices of rural origin, including the mutirão. As readapted in the urban environment, the mutirão largely would be used by the workers who were constructing their own homes.

Home-building mutirões, based on networks of personal relationships, were common in São Miguel Paulista. A survey conducted at the end of the 1970s showed that "building through the mutirão predominate[d]" among those who built their own houses, but the practice was already common by the 1950s.[14] Gerolino Costa Jacobina, for example, said he built his house through the mutirão. "There was a lot of that," he added. "I helped others to make their homes, and others helped me make mine. It was like that . . . on Sundays and holidays." In general, the mutirão was arranged in the workplace, but "people who did not work in the factory" also joined in. Nitro even listed among the "benefits" offered to its workers a facility for the purchase of construction materials. Geraldo Lopes recalled that "many workers . . . built their homes with stuff from Nitro Química. We received a discount, which was taken out of our paychecks." According to an extensive report about Nitro Química published in the newspaper *O Dia* in September 1956, the creation of a "Department for Home Construction" was among the advantages the company offered. According to the former laborer Benedito Miguel, "If you worked at Nitro Química, the company provided the cement. It sold it to you cheaper and took a deduction from your paycheck. [The company] sold tiles; it sold . . . a lot of things. The company provided [materials] for you if you had the land."[15] But despite Nitro's help with the materials and the goodwill of the mutirão, the quality of most housing left a lot to be desired. A study conducted in São Paulo in the late 1940s found that only 15 percent of São Miguel's houses met its criteria to be considered satisfactory.[16] In any case, the typical festive environment of the rural mutirões was reproduced on Sundays in the periphery of São Paulo. It was generally the hosts' responsibility to supply food and drink, and often the mutirão was followed by a *roda* of song and dance.[17] It was an important space for socialization in working life and in the consolidation of social networks in the neighborhood. When one worker in the spinning sector died tragically after being hit by a car on his way out of the factory, the foreman in charge of maintenance for the area was informed that the worker "lived in a rented house but had a plot of land." He immediately decided to coordinate "a group to build a house for the widow," remembered Fábio Ravaglia. Certainly, the self-construction of a home, which implied great sacrifices and hardships for the workers, should not be romanticized. Several scholars have drawn attention to how construction of one's own home can be seen as an important example of "urban dispossession," using a concept described by the Brazilian sociologist Lucius Kowarick. The Brazilian social scientist Francisco de Oliveira argues that home construction by mutirão contributed to a higher level of exploitation of the workforce and to keeping wages down. The urbanist Ermínia Maricato argues in the same vein, subordinating the spontaneity and solidarity supposedly expressed in urban self-construction. Although correct in noting the uneconomical nature of self-construction, such analyses overlook how, in the words of Nabil Bonduki, "Obtaining a home effectively represented for workers an improved outlook on life." Such analyses also do not give due weight to the actions of the workers themselves in this process. Similarly, the anthropologist James Holston considers self-construction an arena of symbolic and political mobilizations that generate "an expansion of the political field" toward the dimensions "of everyday life, of personal life and of urban space."[18]

Informality was as essential to the network of neighborhood social relations as it was in the factory. Based on these relationships, residents organized themselves, created spaces for mutual aid, and, as we shall see, demanded improvements from public authorities. Leisure and cultural activities were important to the maintenance and expansion of social networks among workers, as discussed later. Soccer teams, dance clubs, and theater and music groups, among others, were formed through informal ties in the community and at the factory, often in the process of creating associations and movements that made demands for improvements.[19]

Soccer, Cinema, Dances, and Bars

In the principally working-class community of São Miguel between 1940 and 1960, patterns of leisure were clearly conditioned by poverty, by limited cultural and entertainment offerings, and by the marked presence of Nitro

Química and other companies that concerned themselves with the "free time" of their laborers. A more detailed analysis, however, reveals that neighborhood residents took advantage of existing spaces and options in the area, creating for themselves a relatively wide range of amusements for their moments away from work. As we will see, such recreation frequently assumed different forms for men and women.

Despite the industrial predominance of Nitro, São Miguel was officially considered a rural area of the city of São Paulo in the 1940s and into the 1950s. Its rivers, lakes, and vast green areas were widely used as spaces for leisure and walking by locals, as well as by people from other parts of the city. The predominantly young residents of the neighborhood, however, preferred to take their weekend walks through Campos Salles, the main square of São Miguel. There and on the adjoining Rua da Fábrica, young men and women walked nonchalantly as late afternoon turned to evening on Saturday and Sunday. Maria José Ferreira Jensen said that in the 1950s and 1960s, "Our fun was . . . wandering around the square." Maria Pureza de Mendonça also recalled that "after people left Mass they stayed [in the square]. . . . Then the boys stood on one side of the square, and the girls walked around the square to be flirted with. If the boy saw you and was interested [*laughs*], he'd find a way to talk to you." José Caldini Filho's testimony reinforced the notion of the square as a space for meet-ups and romance during those weekend strolls in the center of town. "[It was in the Rua da Fábrica] that you found your footing in São Miguel," he said, "where [we] went to meet the girls, and where I met my wife."

During Carnival, which was celebrated intensively in São Miguel, the neighborhood's streets and public areas became an important space of leisure and entertainment. Laurentina do Carmo Geraldo, a resident of the neighborhood in the mid-1950s, recalled that "there was a group . . . of our friends who went through the streets having fun during Carnival." Regina Igel remembered when, in the late 1940s, her father, a Jewish immigrant who was unaccustomed to Carnival celebrations, became profoundly irritated when he saw girls "costumed as odalisques" and men "coming down the Rua da Fábrica shouting" and making noise.

Nevertheless, as in other spheres of São Miguel's social life, residents' leisure patterns were mainly dictated by Nitro Química. The Regatta Club of Nitro Química, created by the company in 1939, for decades was the most important reference point for leisure and entertainment in the neighborhood. Established to provide a range of services and benefits, promote social peace, and win the loyalty of Nitro workers, the club was an important part of the welfare complex assembled by the factory in the 1940s. Such was the confidence of the company's directors in its social services and the range of benefits provided to its workers that, according to Barbara Weinstein, "The company that most insisted it had no need of SESI [Industrial Social Service] was Nitro Química. . . . José Ermírio [and other owners of traditional companies] apparently thought that assistance and services directly offered by their administrations were more effective in promoting social peace than the programs developed by SESI. [They] also . . . believed that they would have better results by focusing on improving relations with their own laborers than by cultivating good relations with the working class as a whole."[20]

An article published in the newspaper *O Dia* in 1956 described in detail the facilities and comforts the company club offered:

> With reference to the workers' social lives, it is worth mentioning here that the Companhia Nitro Química Brasileira has built its own social center for the club, in a beautiful two-story building, with a gymnasium for volleyball, basketball, soccer, and other sports; a large dancehall; and on the upper floor a restaurant that serves four hundred meals a day to members. In addition, it has reading rooms and a library, music rooms with pianos, various games, television, and so on. Besides the social pavilion . . . , Nitro Química dedicated a considerable area to its sports court, which we can testify is one of the largest and most complete in the capital, rivaling the principal clubs. We saw there, among other facilities, the football field, the volleyball court, a well-built bar, three swimming pools of official dimensions, and a shed for dancing, because there's plenty of room. With all that, it has become the most favorable environment for the socialization of the workers.[21]

In a poor neighborhood such as São Miguel, a club of such size necessarily occupied a central role in the social life of workers and residents. For many older residents, it was their principal reference when they were asked about workers' leisure before the 1970s. "The leisure that we had here in São Miguel was the Nitro club, it was the only leisure there was at that time," recalled Antônio Xavier dos Santos. Maria das Graças Lins Cacian, a migrant from Minas Gerais and a resident of São Miguel since 1948, said, "The club is what I most remember from my childhood. . . . On Saturday and Sunday everybody went to the Nitro club."

Sporting activities were one of the club's strong points. Its soccer team, one of the best known and most powerful in the region, went as far as to professionalize and play in the third division of the Paulista championship in the early 1960s.[22] Boxing was equally popular, and beginning in the 1940s, Regatta Club boxers participated in amateur competitions promoted by the newspaper *A Gazeta Esportiva* (The Sporting Gazette).[23] They took third place in the Workers' Boxing Championship of 1950 (Social Peace Cup) and were champions in SESI's Boxing Championships of 1951 and 1952 and in the Third Workers' Tournament in 1953. With the rising popularity of the sport and the existence of various competitions, the club's Boxing Department became more highly structured with the hiring of the well-known coach Attilio Bianchi in 1955; it sent representatives to the Pan American Games in 1959 and produced several professionals.[24]

Club membership was compulsory, and the workers were strongly encouraged to practice sports. According to an elderly worker at the company, "Every employee was obligated to be a member of the Regatta Club, and [the monthly membership fee] was taken out of your paycheck."[25] Because membership was not restricted to factory employees, many area residents used and enjoyed the club's services. Maria Pureza de Mendonça recalled that "the chic thing was to have a little Nitro club purse [*laughs*]. That place was hot. It was where everything happened."

The club's dances became major social events in the neighborhood, attracting hundreds of locals every weekend. Its Carnival celebrations spilled beyond the borders of the region and were famous throughout the city. In addition, the club presented famous singers and artists in São Miguel. In January 1957, for instance, the *Nitro Jornal* mentioned the "auspicious presentation of [the singer] Ângela Maria in the social center of the Nitro Química Regatta Club."[26]

Nitro's Regatta Club carried a great deal of weight in the neighborhood's culture and leisure practices, but there were other activities. Religious festivals, for example, had a long tradition in the neighborhoods that preceded industrialization. The testimony of former residents collected in the late 1970s and early 1980s emphasized the importance of these festivals before the 1930s. "There was festivity here in the old days," said one of former resident, adding they would go on for "fifteen days, eating and drinking all the time. . . . There was the festival of Santa Cruz [and the festival of] São Gonçalo." Another former resident remembered that "the festivals were made by the residents. All of the houses had a cross, and wherever there was a cross, the whole gang would stop there, dance, pray, have coffee, things like that."[27]

The celebration of these older festivals was diluted by the arrival of Nitro Química and the great population growth it brought. Moreover, the permanent presence of priests in the parish after the 1930s diminished the autonomous and spontaneous character by which these religious festivals had been organized. At the end of the 1940s, as another resident noted, "There were no more of [the festivals] because by then the priests had come in . . . and they took charge of the events."[28] Participation by the faithful was still great, however, and the increased presence of northeasterners added more religious festivals to the calendar of those traditionally celebrated in the neighborhood. Lucilene Sanches Guimarães said that in the vila in which she lived as a child, there were "traditional festivals that were brought from the north: Three Kings, São João, and many whose names I don't remember. I remember many processions, lots of praying, and everyone attending. For the São João festival, all of the neighbors got together and built bonfires. There was more human contact among us."

Soccer (*futebol*) was an important part of workers' leisure activities. Antônio Xavier dos Santos, who arrived in São Miguel from Bahia in 1950 at twenty-one, said that the residents' main entertainment on Sundays was "to play or watch soccer." Jorge Gonçalves Lula, a neighborhood resident from 1956 on, also called soccer the principal "entertainment in São Miguel."

Nitro Química provided incentives for its workers to participate in the highly popular sport. The Regatta Club team became legendary in the region and, as we have seen, competed in the lower divisions of professional championships, acquiring a great following among neighborhood residents. Nelson Bernardo assiduously attended the Regatta Club games and recalled one occasion when the team went into playoffs against the "Sampaio Moreira at the Parque São Jorge [the stadium of the Corinthians, the most popular professional club in São Paulo] . . . and there were fifteen trucks packed full [of fans attending the game]." Important games were retransmitted over loudspeakers in the Praça Getúlio Vargas near the Rua da Estação. Participation in competitions and friendly matches with teams from other factories and neighborhoods were frequent, attracting small crowds and rousing great interest in São Miguel, as in the friendly match between Nitro and the Democrático do Tucuruvi in October 1954. "Even playing without the full team," Nitro beat its opponent by a score of 4–3, "thanks to the great performance by Edgar, who scored three spectacular goals on that inspired afternoon."[29]

Soccer teams existed at various companies. Savóia (Savoy), the team of the textile factory in Votorantim, next to the city of Sorocaba, was named in the 1920s in homage to the heavy presence of Italians working for the company; the team gained prominence in championships in the country's interior and in friendly matches with clubs in the capital, accumulating a large legion of fans.[30] For the owners of Nitro, the tradition of promoting soccer was an integral part of the policy of creating a "family" environment at the company that would bring together employees and employers.[31]

In addition to encouraging the formation of teams that represented the company as a whole, the company organized regular intramural championships as part of its social policy. In December 1955, for example, the team representing the rayon and mechanical sections, "confirming all predictions . . . , took first place in the domestic soccer league, promoted by the Nitro Química Regatta Club between the departments of the factory."[32]

Soccer in São Miguel, however, was not restricted to the factory. Although amateur soccer was an old phenomenon, it enjoyed an enormous expansion in São Paulo throughout the 1940s and 1950s. As São Miguel's various districts witnessed an explosion of amateur teams, it was impossible for the Nitro club to accommodate all of the workers who wanted to play; in addition to opening preferential space for company employees, the club, especially in its professional period, sought to enlist only those considered the best among the area's various teams. The ever increasing distance to the new residential areas from the center of São Miguel, where the Nitro club was, stimulated the creation of teams by informal groups who organized matches in their own vilas and streets, thereby opening a space of autonomy in relation to management and control of workers' leisure by Nitro and other businesses.

The spread of *futebol de várzea* (amateur soccer) during the 1950s was a matter of concern for companies and organizations such as SESI. Weinstein tells of attempts by SESI to "discipline" amateur soccer, "organizing and legalizing soccer clubs connected with factories or workers' neighborhoods." Offering technical and financial aid, these clubs sought to inspire in the players "an air of comradeship, friendship, and good relations with company management," taking care to avoid "excessive enthusiasm," which it considered "a negative aspect of amateur sports."[33]

The large number of soccer fields built in the neighborhood in those years attests to the spread of the sport. "In that piece [of ground] where I live . . . seven soccer fields came into existence, one after another," recalled José Venâncio. Jorge Gonçalves Lula said that when he moved to São Miguel in the mid-1950s, "The lots were already divided up, [including] the soccer field." Afonso José da Silva agreed: "Every new residential district . . . had to leave an open area, and that area was to be the soccer field."

More striking than the number of fields was the enormous number of teams. According to José Caldini Filho, in the mid-1940s "Esporte Clube São Miguel, . . . which had a soccer field belonging to the Lapenna family, . . . was the only soccer team here in São Miguel." But in the following years there was such a proliferation of amateur teams that they became a neighborhood trademark. A survey taken at the end of the 1980s pointed to the existence of "about 160...local amateur soccer clubs...that were traditional in the region."[34]

In each new neighborhood that was formed, fields were built, and dozens of teams were started, constituting a fundamental feature of workers' leisure in the city of São Paulo. Popular newspapers such as *A Gazeta Esportiva, Última Hora* (The Latest), and *A Hora* (The Time), among others, devoted special sections, sometimes with multiple pages, to covering the amateurs. In the 1960s, a researcher looking into Paulista workers' entertainment options reported that "soccer obviously is the type of recreation, entertainment, or leisure most accessible to the Brazilian people and also to the people of São Paulo."[35]

Playing in or attending soccer matches therefore was among the principal weekend leisure options for workers and residents of São Miguel. "Back then, going to the [sport] clubs to play soccer, to go for the championship, that was our entertainment here," said Afonso José da Silva. There were festivals, as they were called, during which the various neighborhood teams could play against one another. In October 1954, for example, a neighborhood Workers' Circle organized a festival with various matches between regional teams. A local newspaper reported, "To finish the festival, there was a match between the greatest teams of the area: E.C. São Miguel and Workers' Circle. This was undoubtedly a great opportunity for both teams to show off their best players to the large public that showed up at the neighborhood playing field. From the beginning to the end of the competition, there were sensational and even some rough plays. After the match ended in a draw, there was a penalty decision, and São Miguel won, 3–2." The creation and maintenance of amateur teams was strongly associated with informal groups that, in general, got together in neighborhood locales. Practically every area with a name also had its own amateur club. "There was not a vila that didn't have a team," said José Gonçalves Lula. "Every little place had a [soccer] club," said Nelson Bernardo. Bartolomeu Araújo remembered that in Vila Curuça, "There was a field [for] two teams.... Curuça, which played on Saturdays, and Avante, [which played] on Sundays."

The amateur teams were important in the affirmation of identity for residents of vilas. Living in a group of dwellings, often newly built and precarious in various ways, the inhabitants often saw the teams as a representation of their "piece," or their "area," where they lived and shared hardships and solidarities with neighbors and friends.[36] The rivalry between teams from different vilas was such that scenes of violence and fighting between players and fans were not uncommon. Joaquim Serafim da Silva, a resident of São Miguel from 1960 on and an enthusiastic player with (and, later, fan of) Guarani da Vila Rosário, said that it was unusual to see "a player from one vila go to play on the team of another, . . . and when it happened, many people got into fights."[37] The great participation and enthusiasm of fans in various local festivals and championships was not surprising. When, for example, União Esportiva Paulista, another team from Vila Curuçá, went into the regional playoffs against Santa Cruz de Guaianazes, said Maria José Jensen, "Trucks went out . . . filled with fans."

In addition to mirroring the identities of the vilas and their residents, teams could represent migrant groups, as in the case of the Bahia team from the Vila Nitro Operária. Antonio Xavier dos Santos says that the club was named Bahia in "homage to the northeasterner . . . because the vila [Nitro Operária] had many Bahians." Josué Pereira da Silva, another Bahian and the founder of Esporte Clube Bahia, explains that the club was "created by us [Bahians] in Vila Nitro Operária." Although the team was founded by Bahians, participation in it was not reserved for a specific migrant group. Neighborly relations and friendship seem to have guided the association with a team more than other criteria, expanding the integration among the various residents of a particular locality. Thus, for example, a resident of the same vila as the team, the Paulista nephew of the Mineira Helena Oliveira da Fonseca, had no problem playing for Bahia in the 1960s. According to Joaquim Serafim da Silva, there were other, less explicit examples of the relationship between clubs and migrant communities. "Vila Curuçá was the team of the Mineiros, while in the Guarani, Bahians and Paulistas played," he said. Connecting so many local networks and relationships, the soccer teams provided a fertile field for political oratory and vote getting.

Although soccer was a masculine entertainment, women also found space for leisure in the local teams. Playing the sport was restricted to men, but some women followed the teams from match to match. Often a soccer match was family recreation, with some fields serving a kind of picnic, with lunch and drinks included. Beyond that, teams often produced entertainment and leisure events in the vilas, promoting dances, festivals (at the headquarters of Guarani da Vila Rosário a forró was held every weekend, according to Joaquim Serafim da Silva), and "elections of queens and princesses." Maria Fernanda dos Santos Gomes said she liked attending "Olaria soccer games," and in 1963, at fifteen, was elected "queen of that club." Esporte Clube Bahia equally promoted regular "queen and princess" contests. In one of these selections, the daughter of Helena de Oliveira da Fonseca was chosen "spring queen" of the team.[38]

While soccer was limited as a leisure option for women, the same cannot be said of movies—"The second most popular and important source of recreation and leisure in the state of São Paulo," according to J. V. Freitas Marcondes.[39] The testimony repeatedly contains references, from both women and men, to the neighborhood cinemas' cultural importance during the 1940s and 1950s.

The first movie house in the region, in the early 1940s, was in an outbuilding of Nitro Química. "It was a small cinema called V-8," José Caldino Filho recalled. Few residents, however, remembered that room. Most remember the Cine São Miguel, founded in the mid-1940s, as the first movie theater in the neighborhood. "When the cinema came to São Miguel . . . more or less in 1945 . . . it was a great joy," recalled Vilma Garcia Matos, a neighborhood resident from 1938 on. "We went to the movies almost every day; every time they changed the film, we were there." The peak of cinema as popular entertainment in São Miguel, however, occurred after 1952, with the grand opening of the bigger, more modern Cine Lapenna. After that, the Cine São Miguel, the more popular and inexpensive option, became known as the "old theater."

Once again, São Miguel exemplifies a phenomenon that occurred in other neighborhoods and industrial areas of the region. Throughout the 1940s and 1950s, going to the movies, considered an "urban, modern activity," became common among all social sectors in the different areas of the capital city. Inspired by the movie palaces of the United States, grandiose theaters opened in different neighborhoods, while in the downtown area a circuit of grand cinemas made up the sophisticated "Cinelândia" of São Paulo.[40] In 1950, São Paulo had 119 cinemas and about 35 million spectators; between 1955 and 1965, the "188 [movie] establishments in existence had . . . a growing viewership."[41]

The Cine Lapenna, located in front São Miguel's main square, became associated with weekend strolls, becoming a space for friends and acquaintances to meet, as well as a privileged space for flirting and romance. "You couldn't kiss a woman in the middle of the street," recalled Antônio Xavier dos Santos, "but you could at the movies." Even for more religious people, the movies were an important place of leisure and meet-ups. "Our hobby was the square and the cinema," said Maria José Ferreira Jensen. On Sundays, "It was sacred to go to church and afterward to the movies."

In a time of expanding influence for U.S. cultural productions in Brazil and globally, U.S. serials were highly successful on the screens of the São Miguel and Lapenna theaters. "In the 1940s and 1950s," attests Bartolomeu Araújo, "the cinema offered many serials, which were like a television series today with different episodes. . . . If you liked a film that was in twenty parts, it took twenty weeks to see it. And people went to see it!" In the late 1950s, at the age of "seven, eight years," Benedito Carlos Vieira already was a regular customer of the Cine Lapenna "to see those serials . . . . Every Sunday I had to buy a ticket there [to see] Batman." Despite the success of American serials, however, São Miguel's most popular cinematic attraction featured themes that were not far removed from the moviegoers' reality. Mazzaropi, a character created by Amácio Mazzaropi, was a comical caricature of a *caipira* (hick) from the countryside who triumphs in the capital with his simplicity and truthfulness. His films attracted multitudes and were always great successes at the neighborhood box offices. The movie critic Jean-Claude Bernardet explains that Mazzaropi was popular "because his movies tackled concrete, real problems, which were vivid for the immense public that went to see his films," but despite that, "the key to the dramaturgy of 'Mazza' and of his success [was] identifying problems while avoiding any critical attitude toward them." Another film scholar, Paulo Emílio Salles Gomes, writes that the secret of Mazzaropi's permanence "is his antiquity. He touches the archaic foundations of Brazilian society and in each one of us. The best thing about his films is [Mazzaropi] himself."[42] In an interview in the early 1980s, the owner of the Cine Lapenna, José Lapenna, said that "Mazzaropi [was] the only actor in those days" who filled his theater.[43] Valdemir Lopes da Silva was one of those who never missed one of the comedian's films. "When there was a Mazzaropi movie, I [went to the Cine] Lapenna," he recalled.

Besides cinema, neighborhood dances brought women and men together. For years, the most popular dances were held at the Nitro Química club. "We would go to the movies, and afterward . . . we dropped into the [Nitro] club to dance a little. . . . In the afternoons, they had a dance matinee with the orchestra of Toninho, who was an employee [of the factory] and lived in Vila Nitro Química . . . In those days, Toninho [and his orchestra] made our afternoons happy," recalled Maria das Graças Lins Cacian. "Every Sunday afternoon there was a dance called 'matinee' at the [Nitro] club," commented José Amaro Sobrinho. Carnival dances were particularly well attended. "Many people came from far away just to have fun" at the club's Carnival, Alderi Campos Aragão confirmed.

Besides offering entertainment possibilities for women and men together, the club's dances seem to have been moments of camaraderie among the neighborhood's various social sectors, frequented as they were by workers, bosses, businessmen, and residents of São Miguel. Some, such as Regina Aparecida Mateus, saw such integration as a very good thing. "It was beautiful. [At the club's dances,] the cream and the scum got together; no one was turned away. Rich and poor shared the same space," she said. Others, however, were made uncomfortable by so much "social mixing." Palmira Bernardo, the sister-in-law of Councilman Tarcílio Bernardo, commented that "the club of Nitro Química used to be good, it was like family . . . it had that agreeable ambience. Then it got to be a mess, so I didn't go there anymore." As we will see, the founding of the 200 Club, the famous space for dance festivals in the neighborhood during the 1950s and 1960s, was an attempt to create a "differentiated" space for the wealthiest families and sectors of the neighborhood.

Dances were not limited, however, to the Nitro Química club and the 200 Club. They were also held in various parts of the neighborhood. Josué Pereira da Silva remembered that "when there was a holiday, we 'fell down dead' at the dance. We danced two, three days. That was our greatest entertainment. Everyone who lived in that area held dances. In any bar you could find someone playing an accordion."

Cícero Antônio Pereira said that besides the "cinema, the entertainment in those days . . . was dance. A *batucada* with a *pandeiro*, something like that."[44] He remembered in detail the "dances they had every Saturday in the subdistrict of Jardim Camargo, in São Miguel. . . . They called it the banana tree festival [because] it was in a house full of banana trees." Lídia Castelani helped start a dance club in Jardim Helena, the area of São Miguel where she lived. It "was common," she recalled, for people to "create clubs for leisure, for Carnival."

Before the 1960s, one of the most famous dancehalls in São Miguel was Clube Fubá (Club Cornmeal). Located in the center of the neighborhood, it was more accessible than the neighboring 200 Club. "It was a lower-class place," said Geraldo Rodrigues de Freitas. "Anybody could [come in] and dance." Aurelino de Andrade, who was a councilman at the time, reinforced the comparison: "The Fubá was a dance club for the poorer population. It was the lower people, folks from the North. The 200 Club was elite, and the Fubá was the mass." The Fubá dancehall "was a more liberated ball" frequented by the workers of Nitro. "The families [of the neighborhood 'elite'] didn't let their daughters" attend, added Nelson Bernardo. "They put out paraffin and cornmeal (*fubá*) on the floor. That was good for dancing, [and] the name Fubá stuck."

For many, the heavy presence of northeasterners in the neighborhood explains the proliferation of dances and parties. The Mineiro Amauri da Cunha attributes the great number of forrós in São Miguel to the presence of the northeasterners. "Here [in São Miguel it was] all northerners, and there was no shortage of forró.... There was dancing everywhere." Nelson Bernardo comments that his family was uncomfortable with the "noise" made by the "Bahians" who lived in the boardinghouse in front of his mother-in-law's home. "They talked loud, shouted, and sang. They had batuque [drumming] all night long." According to Josué Pereira da Silva, "The greater flow of [dances and parties] was in Vila Nitro Operária" because it was where the northeasterners were most concentrated. There, Silva adds, "they had forrós and more forrós, which [is what] they called the northerners' dance."

The singer and composer Edvaldo Santana, whose father came from Piauí and whose mother came from Pernambuco, was born in 1955 in Vila Nitro Operária. Remembering his childhood, he says that he was "raised in a house that always had a circle of music. The northeasterner likes parties and fun. My father played guitar and he always brought lots of people to party in our house. Most of the laborers who came from the Northeast were single.... Lots of forrós and bars.... And I was brought up in the middle of that, dancing a lot."[45]

Unlike the dancehalls and clubs, where men and women socialized, the bars and taverns were masculine areas. As one of the oldest, most permanent spaces of entertainment for workers,[46] taverns were of great importance for popular leisure and were, along with small stores, the most common commercial establishments in São Miguel. For that matter, the difference between stores and bars was often hard to discern. Some grocery stores served alcoholic beverages. Amauri da Cunha said that in the late 1950s, for example, on a corner near his house on Parque Paulistano, there was a little shop called André's that sold pinga, a sugarcane spirit also known as cachaça. André's, Rufino's, and Baranguzinho's were where "the guys drank on Saturdays and Sundays."

Bars were the perfect locale for conversation, for small talk among friends and acquaintances, for exchange of information, and formation of opinions. It was in the bar that many sought to relax after long work days, with cards, dominoes, and billiards providing distraction from daily problems. Not coincidentally, as already noted, the network of informal relationships formed around the taverns "tends to be very stable." The sense of harmony and companionship provided by the act of drinking together reinforced a sense of community and friendship among the bar's patrons.[47]

In São Miguel, the northeastern presence seems to have stimulated a strong musical tradition in the neighborhood bars. There is testimony about the presence of musicians and singers in local taverns. Salomé Igel remembered that at the family's store there was great demand for "guitars, *pandeiros* and *cavaquinhos*. This was their fun."[48] Josué Pereira da Silva recalled:

I remember well Gonzaga's bar [in Vila Nitro Operária], much frequented by northeasterners. There was always northeastern music, music of the north. They had a guitar player called João Piloto . . . who passed the professional test on the now disappeared Radio Piratininga. . . . [There were] lots of *chorinho* groups [who] got together in bars. . . . [They were formed] by three or four *pandeiro* players, *cavaquinho*, guitar. They went from there to the dances. They'd stop in, play two or three numbers. The bar owner would give them beer, and the players would try to get people to move around in the bar.[49]

The neighborhood's strong musical and cultural presence was felt in the political world. Rallies in the area, for example, were almost always accompanied by presentations of local musicians and bands. In the period of the Communist Party's great popularity in the region, right after the Second World War, local residents composed *marchinhas* (little marches) and *chorinhos* in homage to the party or its leader, Luís Carlos Prestes. Emídio Alves Freire, a resident of São Miguel and a frequent visitor to the area's bars, directed a musical group that presented itself at various PCB rallies in the city, playing marches he composed.[50] Decades later, in the late 1970s, the anthropologist Antonio Augusto Arantes was astonished by the vitality of the "informal networks, where day after day culture is produced" in the neighborhood. Rooted in those networks, the Popular Art Movement of São Miguel Paulista emerged in that same period, founded by residents who with music, poetry, painting, and other artistic expressions formed one of the most expressive cultural movements in the periphery of São Paulo.[51]

However, the bars and their northeastern customers were also frequently associated with tension and fighting. Lídia Castelani, owner of a bar for decades in São Miguel, believed that the northeasterners were "nervous" and that "the least little thing would set them off." Alcohol, however, was the principal reason for the violence, which at times could end with dead and injured. "They just had to drink two or three . . . and, at times, a little disorder became a big one," she added. Augusto Lima explained, "Fights also got started from playing games. At that time they played a lot of snooker. In São Miguel, the bars had four, five snooker tables. [The people] drank beer, cognac, cachaça. When it got to be midnight, things were on fire. Any little thing—someone steps on someone's foot—there's a fight, somebody gets cut with a knife."

Problems related to alcohol consumption went beyond the space of the bar, as suggested by various articles published in the internal Nitro Química journal about the risks of alcoholism.[52] In addition to alcohol, the "ill repute" of some bars was related to prostitution. In November 1954, for example, in an indignant speech in the Municipal Council, Tarcílio Bernardo denounced "the women of easy means who assault our bars and taverns and who spend their time late into the night in orgies and bacchanals incited and stimulated by alcohol." About a year later, Bernardo continued his moral crusade against the "lack of shame reigning" in São Miguel that, he said, had become "the general barracks for the decadent of São Paulo."[53]

In certain periods of the 1950s, repression of prostitution in the center of São Paulo provoked a migration of sex workers to less policed areas of the city, such as São Miguel. The councilman's irate speeches corresponded at that moment to the greatest visibility of the phenomenon in the neighborhood. Nevertheless, prostitution was an ancient practice in the area. Proximity to the factory and the large number of single men stimulated the growth of brothels. During a certain period, Rua 4, for example, was notorious for the intense demand for prostitutes on Nitro's payday. In spite of that, information about prostitution was rarely furnished in interviews. The matter eventually came up in informal conversations, but the greater part of those interviewed asked that the recorder be turned off if there was a question about the topic.

Where Crime Was at Home

In their remembrances, many old-time residents and workers of São Miguel Paulista tend to minimize the level of urban violence and the indices of criminality in the neighborhood in the 1940s and 1950s. Violence, for them, was confined to fights and drunken assaults in bars and taverns. São Miguel is generally remembered as a calm, tranquil place, where robberies and assaults were only sporadic occurrences. For Augusto Lima, the neighborhood

> had no thieves, no one robbed you, there wasn't this business of killing in order to rob, there was none of that. . . . São Miguel was silent, it was marvelous. It was no different sleeping in your house from sleeping leaned up against a wall or in the doorway of a bar—the same thing, nobody messed with anybody. Back then there was no problem of killing, robbing, doing evil to the daughters of others, none of that. Nobody even knew what the word "rape" meant. [The year] 1948 in São Miguel was a time of happiness, believe me.

José Venâncio, an area resident since 1953, said that he "could go out at any hour to the movies or to a bar. It seemed like crime didn't exist." There was also more security for women, according to Vilma Garcia Matos, a neighborhood resident since 1938. "There was no violence," she said. "São Miguel had no light—it was dark—[but] you could walk tranquilly at night." Lídia Castelani, who moved to São Miguel in 1943, agreed that in those years there were no "robberies or assaults in the neighborhood."

Although such memories reflect residents' experience of daily life at the time, they are surely conditioned by the comparisons with the neighborhood's contemporary situation. Present-day São Miguel has one of the highest crime rates in the city of São Paulo, and its population is traumatized by urban violence. In light of that, the idealization of the past is perceptible in the memories of old residents. The comparison of current reality with everyday life in the 1940s and 1950s no doubt reinforces the image of a quiet, crime-free neighborhood. It is no wonder that when asked about crime in São Miguel in that period, the majority of those interviewed made comparisons with the present.

But despite respondents' characterization of São Miguel in the 1940s and 1950s as devoid of crime, many contemporary records disprove that, or at least relativize the notion. São Miguel's councilmen frequently made speeches in the Municipal Council demanding better policing and security for the neighborhood. In March 1955, Councilman Tarcílio Bernardo described a "São Miguel Paulista, the major workers' center of the capital, . . . totally unpoliced, at the mercy of robbers and the lowlifes, and given over to the practice of various crimes, in broad daylight." Two months later, Bernardo warned about the growing number of muggings occurring in São Miguel, affirming that such "acts have been happening here, with a certain constancy, for some time in the absence of policing" in the neighborhood. The police, he added, "are not enough to confront the elevated number of outlaws that proliferate in this dense region of the county." In March 1956, Aurelino de Andrade, São Miguel's other councilman, also took to the podium of the Municipal Council to say, in an alarmed tone, that there had "occurred in São Miguel, in these [recent] days, more than twenty muggings with a deadly weapon. Defenseless citizens are being mugged and wounded in their own homes."[54]

When prompted, longtime residents remember the existence of crimes and violence in the neighborhood. Although Salomé Igel emphasized that when she lived in the neighborhood in the mid-1940s, "People were peaceful, and no one was thinking about mugging anyone," her store was robbed. Joaquim Anselmo said that in the 1950s there were "many daring bandits in

São Miguel," but the majority were *"malandros*, . . . cardsharps." Among them, nevertheless, "there was a guy called Juarez who robbed people's residences." João Freitas Lírio also remembered Juarez as "a bandit who had robbed all the houses in the area."

Juarez became notorious in the neighborhood. In September 1957, after he was killed by the police in his hideout following intensive searches, the newspaper *O Estado de São Paulo* described police efforts to find the swag from his last robberies, "a television set that he had taken in Jardim São Vicente, in São Miguel Paulista. From that residence also two radios were stolen, still not recovered." Other recent victims of Juarez in São Miguel, continued the report, had lost "objects worth 30,000 cruzeiros." Commenting on the death of the "terrible bandit known as Juarez," Councilman Bernardo said that "when he was only nineteen, [Juarez] was already known by the police as a daring bandit who defied everyone and everything and terrified the populations [of the region] of Central do Brasil. . . . Juarez was so audacious and criminal that he robbed people in broad daylight. He was so resistant that he never surrendered to the police, and out of his resistance came his death."[55]

The press, particularly the sensationalist organs, gave plenty of space to crime in São Miguel. Artur Pinto de Oliveira remembered that "the tabloid *A Hora* only ran stories about misfortune and crime." Everywhere in the neighborhood, he remembered, there was always "a young man or a boy [selling the paper and shouting], 'Look at *A Hora*! Look at *A Hora*! Crime in Vila Nitro Operária! He went from house to house, and people bought it. It was a very popular paper." Augusto Ferreira Lima also remembered that *A Hora* "was a paper that everybody bought early in the morning to see the miseries that had happened in São Paulo."

"São Miguel Paulista: A Den of Thieves," shouted *A Hora*'s headline on May 11, 1956. The article denounced the absence of police and of resources to combat criminality in the neighborhood. Reporting on the absence of a telephone at the police station, the journalist wrote, "When the police at the station need to communicate with their superiors, they have to go to Nitro Química and ask permission to use the telephone." The report even affirmed that there were "seventy thieves known to the police, who catch them today and the laws turn them loose tomorrow. Rare is the day in which a house— business or residential—is not robbed by the most audacious means."[56]

In the same spirit of describing São Miguel as a criminal hellhole, another popular newspaper, *O Dia*, recalled in 1956 that the neighborhood "came up constantly on the police blotter as one of the areas of the capital where crime is most at home. Not a week passes without tragic details of bloody occurrences unfolding there." Even the sober *O Estado de São Paulo* did not fail to notice crime in the neighborhood, with the crimes being even crueler, in the vision of the paper, for having happened there.[57] The paper reported on a home invasion in which Teodoro de Matias, a resident of the Parque Paulistano in São Miguel, received "a violent beating. Meanwhile, in the face of the resistance they encountered . . . after going through [the house], the [robbers] burned it. The firemen could not get to the site of the blaze because of the terrible condition of the streets."[58]

The construction of the image of São Miguel Paulista as "the home of crime" in the city had a basis in reality. Poverty, privation, and rapid, disorderly urban growth certainly created conditions for steadily growing rates of crime and urban violence beginning in the 1950s. Nevertheless, there was evident exaggeration and, as we will see, an increasing tendency among journalists to associate the northeasterners and poor people who were the majority of neighborhood's residents with a supposed irrationality and propensity toward violence.

"São Miguel Was All Mata*": Urban Privations and "Progress"*

When at thirteen Helena de Oliveira da Fonseca saw São Miguel Paulista for the first time, she had "a very ugly impression." She had come with her parents to join her brothers, who were working at Nitro Química after leaving the south of Minas Gerais years before. Contrary to her expectations for the neighborhood, there was still "much *mata* [brush]" in 1948. Many years later, she recalled that São Miguel "had no asphalted street. . . . Only the São Paulo–Rio highway had cobblestones. The rest was all dirt." Benedito Miguel, who migrated to the neighborhood in 1946, two years before Oliveira da Fonseca, also recalled that "in those days, São Miguel was all mata."

Despite the accelerated process of industrialization and urbanization between 1940 and 1960, longtime residents of São Miguel recalled the absence of urban infrastructure during that time, typically explaining that the neighborhood consisted of a factory, a central square and its surrounding area, and the "rest was all mata." Celina Garcia, who came to live in São Miguel in the early 1940s, said that she would go shopping with her older sisters in Penha, and on the way back, the bus fare collector would always make the same joke coming into São Miguel: "Who's going down into that mata?" Speaking of some of the neighborhood's best-known districts, Amauri da Cunha said that when she arrived in the mid-1950s, "Vila Rosário was all mata, all mud. [Vila] Curuça was nothing. . . . Jardim Helena had a half-dozen [*sic*] houses."

Although the most central areas of the neighborhood were already quite urbanized in the 1950s, even those who arrived in the early 1960s emphasize the undeveloped character of São Miguel. Juraci Pereira de Cavalho, who arrived from Bahia in 1961, said that "in those days . . . there practically existed only the center [of the neighborhood]." There were "few streets," and "São Miguel was nothing but mata."

Undoubtedly, this testimony is strongly marked by comparison with the present-day neighborhood, intensely urbanized, with an enormous population density, and practically without any green areas remaining—a transformation that the old-time residents witnessed. Their testimony thus tends to emphasize this difference and the character of São Miguel as "mata" in the old days. Nevertheless, the idea that the neighborhood "was only mata" not only is present in the memory of a low level of urbanization and of the great number of green areas that existed in the past, but also represents the difficulties and privations that the residents confronted. Although São Miguel was part of the capital, it was not what many migrants had supposed the capital to be. Instead of "progress" in "the world's fastest-growing" city, in the boastful slogan of the local elite, they found an absence of resources and infrastructure. In spite of the image of development associated with the great factory Nitro Química, the neighborhood conditions reinforced the description of São Miguel as "very backward in those days," in the words of José Pedro, who moved to the neighborhood in the late 1950s. In addition, the geographic distance of the area from downtown São Paulo contributed to a sense of isolation and of difference in relation to the capital.

A report published in the daily *Correio Paulistano* in April 1948 as part of a series titled "Neighborhood Focus," dedicated to discussing the problems of various districts of the city, contrasted the neighborhood's industrial development with its lack of services and urban infrastructure. "Baquirivú, ex-São Miguel," said the article, "is a great nucleus of workers. In their two factories [Nitro Química and Celosul] nearly ten thousand operators of both sexes work. They contribute large sums to the municipality of the capital, but in spite of that, Baquirivú has no better luck than the other neighborhoods or suburbs of São Paulo. Its urban problems drag on unresolved . . . and it goes on leading the life it has always led: half rural, half progressive, a satellite village of the capital."[59]

The idea of São Miguel as "backward" was associated with the absence of paved roads. Even in the late 1950s, Amauri da Cunha recalled, São Miguel "was all dirt streets. There were no gutters, no drains, nothing!" José Venâncio, who lived in the neighborhood from 1953 on, remembered that "the streets were not asphalted," which turned São Miguel into a very "isolated" place.

On rainy days, the situation became worse. José Damasceno de Souza, who arrived in São Miguel in the late 1950s at eighteen, remembered that "the streets were all dirt, and in the rainy season it was hard to get home, because everything was covered with mud." Amauri da Cunha also remembered that sometimes it was necessary "to roll your pants up to your knees" to get to work. He also said, "I carried a pair of [extra] shoes to put on at Nitro." João Freitas Lírio said that "everybody brought a wipe cloth [because] the mud was a foot deep." Not by chance, paving the streets was considered a clear indicator by the residents of urban improvement and "progress."

Besides getting the residents muddy, the rainy season brought floods, some of which had terrible consequences. Maria Pureza de Mendonça recalled that when she was a girl in the 1950s, "It was a great suffering when it started to rain and the street began filling up with water. That caused great agony." Recalling a sad memory of her childhood in the late 1950s and 1960s, Elza Alcântra de Araújo said that "floods . . . always happened in São Miguel." Some children would go out to play in the floodwaters, and "there was a boy who lived on Rua 13, carried away by the water, and it took three days to find him."

Adjacent to the Tietê River and cut by various tributary streams, São Miguel was a site of swamps, marshes, and ponds, and many of its subdivisions and vilas were constructed over areas that flooded easily. In August 1957, Councilman Bernardo stepped up to the podium in the Municipal Council of São Paulo to denounce the Companhia Mirante, which had "subdivided the Parque Real in São Miguel Paulista. The area that made up the Parque was a real pond . . . however, the company caused ditches to be opened in that area so that the water would drain and the land be presented as habitable. The lots were sold one by one . . . counting on the drought and the carefully opened ditches to be able to deceive the poor workers."

Days after the pronouncement, a heavy rain struck the neighborhood, and the "population of Parque Real, in order not to drown, were forced to abandon the locale in the rain and look for shelter somewhere else."[60]

The constant flooding made evident the grave problems of sanitation that tormented the neighborhood's population. The article from *Correio Paulistano* in 1948 cited earlier observed that one of the principal complaints of the area was the "terrible water quality" that provoked "serious gastric disturbances, principally among children." The problem, still unresolved five years later, was scrutinized in a report by the daily *A Hora* that was reprinted in a local newspaper. "In Vila Nitro Operária," said the article, the best way not to get lost is to follow the creek that runs down every street. It seems a creek from far away, but it is really just an open-air sewer. The conditions of the densely populated neighborhood would terrify anyone. In front of number 27, where Joaquim Alves da Silva lives, the pit cannot contain the organic remains in fermentation. It begins to drain out to the street, forming a creek of putrid black mud, the most fetid possible. That filters into the permeable land, reaching water level a little more than a meter down. Contamination is the immediate consequence.[61]

The installation of a water and sewage network, one of the principal demands of the neighborhood's population, was only beginning to be addressed in the late 1950s. Even in June 1956, Councilman Aurelino de Andrade remembered that "since 1951 there has been a tremendous struggle by the people of São Miguel Paulista to get that district's water and sewage installed."[62]

The neighborhood's unsanitary conditions directly affected the health of the population. Outbreaks of diphtheria and typhoid were frequent, and infant mortality rates were quite high. In 1948, six of the twelve monthly obituaries registered in the neighborhood were for "children affected by gastroenteritis." In 1953, A Hora announced that the "proletarian neighborhood delivers to the cemetery six, seven, or eight children a week." Even the conservative newspaper O Estado de São Paulo, in a report about the neighborhood in 1955, sounded a tone of melancholy: "[The] local cemetery is overflowing. More than half its area is full of little sepulchers, four hand spans long.... Most are without a cross, just a stake with a number, no flowers, like mounds of earth symmetrically aligned within the high walls. The population of São Miguel has grown in all expressions of life and death."[63]

Nor did the neighborhood's growth bring street lights. In the early 1940s, when Maria José Santos Oliveira arrived in São Miguel, illumination came from "small lamps, [principally] in the square of São Miguel." Little had changed twenty years later, when, reading a petition he was sent by residents, Representative José Maria Costas Neves complained in the Legislative Assembly that "São Miguel Paulista, a populous manufacturing bairro, still does not have public illumination."[64] In the vilas, the situation was even worse. Darci Ribeiro, for example, commented that in the 1950s, "The houses in Vila Rosário had no electricity; it was all well water, without asphalt, all mata. We'd get home, and everything was dark."

The neighborhood's telephone service was minimal. The nurse Cícero Antônio Pereira, who resided in São Miguel from 1946 on, said that for a long time "the telephone here was only at the post office and at Nitro Química; no one had their own telephone." In November 1954, Councilman Bernardo, also responding to the appeals of petitions from residents, complained about "the near-nonexistence of [telephones] in São Miguel Paulista, a district of São Paulo with more than sixty thousand inhabitants, [that] has only two telephones."[65]

The demand for education in São Miguel was quite high. For the local population, mostly composed of migrants with little schooling, moving to the city was intended to improve access to instruction. The availability of schools was considered an attraction of São Paulo by many recently arrived youth. That was the case for Artur Pinto de Oliveira, who "dreamed of studying" and so was motivated to go the capital because in his "village . . . and in the towns of the interior of Bahia," the schools were few. Even when migrants were frustrated in their own aspirations, the prospect of securing a better education for their children was seductive.

Unfortunately, the availability of public schools in São Miguel fell well short of residents' needs. The only primary school, the Grupo Escolar de São Miguel Paulista (later renamed Grupo Escolar de Baquirivú and finally Grupo Escolar Carlos Gomes), founded in 1938, was clearly insufficient for the large number of students in the area. Moreover, the geographical expansion of the neighborhood was an obstacle to the transport of the students from various vilas to the local school. In 1954, commenting on the difficulties of the various regions of São Miguel, a councilman stated that "in these vilas everything is lacking. Right now there are 1,500 school-age children unenrolled." A year and half later, the complaint continued, "Jardim Popular, in São Miguel Paulista, has 700 school-age children who can't enroll for lack of openings . . . in the same district, [in] Burgos Paulista, there are nearly 200 children without school. . . . Innumerable other localities situated in that zone of São Paulo . . . are without openings for the large number of school-age children."[66]

Under pressure, the public education authorities created provisional schools housed in wooden sheds. José Venâncio remembers that for a long time in Vila Sinhá, where he lived in the 1950s and 1960s, "the municipal school was a little wooden shed, all made of boards." Besides being insufficient to handle the demand, the sheds were often "terribly built." In 1950, for example, the shed in Vila Sinhá "was totally destroyed by a windstorm." Two years later, sixty children ran in "panic [when] there was a strong wind in São Miguel Paulista and the shed of Vila Jacuí fell to the ground."[67]

In the mid-1950s, the growing number of students completing primary school forced the realization of one of the residents' principal demands:

the establishment of the Professor Francisco Roswell Freire State School, a middle secondary school. In 1959, a dedicated building opened for the D. Pedro I Municipal School.[68] Despite having twenty-two rooms and holding classes in three shifts, the new school was incapable from the beginning of absorbing the growing demand. In February 1960, "842 candidates competed for 400 openings" in its admission exams. On that occasion, the director of the new educational institute, Neusa Amaral, declared to the press "that she expected a large turnout, owing to the lack of public high schools."[69] In 1966, official data continued to demonstrate the lack of educational establishments in the neighborhoods. São Miguel possessed that year only three middle schools, one high school, and one for preparation of primary school teachers.[70]

The neighborhood's rapid growth in the 1950s intensified an old problem of the region: transportation.[71] The internal expansion of São Miguel, its distance from downtown, and the lack of effective motor transportation made the problem of mobility strongly felt in the neighborhood, even as more of its residents began to work in other parts of the city. Considering the lack of transport, the travel time, and the high costs, many of those who worked at Nitro Química saw the proximity between home and workplace as a great additional advantage. So when in 1963 a director of the factory proposed a financial agreement for the union delegate Valdevino Raimundo da Silva if he would resign, da Silva readily responded, "That doesn't interest me. First, this is so close to my house that I can eat hot food in my own home. If I leave here, I'm going to have to carry a lunchbox."

"I lived five minutes from the factory," said Joaquim Anselmo dos Santos, emphasizing the nearness of Nitro as an advantage. Milton Furlan, who walked to work at the factory every day, recalls that "it was good; I never depended on rides." Irene Ramalho, who worked in a cooperative of the company in the 1940s, said that when one of her bosses left his job, he invited her to work with him downtown. "But I didn't want to," she said, "because I wasn't going to leave [São Miguel] to go traveling."

"Traveling" within the same city became a daily experience for many. Cícero Antônio Pereira, who like most residents of São Miguel commuted via the Central do Brasil rail line, remembered that he always took the "second . . . Maria Fumaça [traditional steam locomotive] that left [from the São Miguel station] at 4:30 [A.M.]" for Mooca and "got to work at seven." The trains were so crowded that there were even "people on top of the cars." The always full Maria Fumaça was also a memory for Amauri da Cunha. "You couldn't get on [the train] because there were already too many people," he said, "so you got on where the baggage went. . . . Just like an ox, right? When the train was full, it was like a bunch of oxen." In one of his speeches to the Municipal Council, Councilman Bernardo made a similar comparison to criticize the area's rail service: "That railway provides the residents of that locale truly revolting [conditions] from the customary irregularities it presents. The schedules are not obeyed, the trains are really pigsties from the lack of hygiene, and the transportation of the population is done as if it were a new kind of livestock: human livestock."[72]

In addition to cars crammed full, terrible traveling conditions, and daily delays, accidents were relatively common on the São Paulo railways. One of the worst accidents in the history of the city happened in June 1959 on the line that connected São Miguel to the neighborhood of Brás, when a collision near the Engenheiro Goulart station left forty-eight people dead and more than a hundred injured. Elvira Souza de Alcântra was "very impressed by [the accident]. . . . It was a terrible thing . . . a pile of people, all dead." Amauri da Cunha, who was on the train, was left profoundly affected by the experience. "That was the most horrific thing I ever saw in my life," he said. "That crash was so strong that no one remained standing up. . . . one person went falling over the other."

During the 1950s, rail gradually lost its status as the principal means of transport for São Miguel Paulista and the metropolitan region, with road transportation progressively preferred. The geographer Juergen Langenbuch shows that between 1940 and 1965 the number of daily trains in the metropolitan area grew by 130 percent, "while the population grew almost six times more." In that period, "an ever larger and more important participation of road travel in the transportation system [occurred]. . . . The railroad could not keep up with the rhythm of suburban development it generated."[73] But neither did the buses meet suburban demand. São Miguel "was terrible for driving," recalled Henriqueta Lopes Fernandes, summing up a common memory of old-time neighborhood residents.

The first regular bus line established in São Miguel linked it with Penha. It was initially owned by a realtor in the region, "the Hungarian Geny, . . . [who] in 1945 already had three buses and a garage"; the line was then acquired by Antônio Marqui da Silva, who created the Auto-Ônibus Penha-São Miguel, which operated a local line between São Miguel and Penha, as well as an inter-municipal line between Praça Clóvis Bevilacqua (in downtown São Paulo) and the Bairro dos Pimentas (a neighboring district, but in the county of Guarulhos). In 1952, the municipal transportation company CMTC (Companhia Municipal de Transporte Coletivo) began operating line 202, "which left Rua da Estação opposite number 30 for Parque D. Pedro II," downtown. In addition, in the 1950s there were bus lines that connected São Miguel with the nearby bairros of Itaim Paulista, Ermelino Matarazzo, and Itaquera.[74]

Complaints about the bus lines were constant. "The Penha-São Miguel bus company [had] two long Chevrolet buses," recalled Valdemir Lopes da Silva, originally from Rio Grande do Norte, who worked in downtown São Paulo during that period. "One came, and the other went. It took more than two hours to get from here to Penha." The week after the Mineiro José Amaro Sobrinho arrived in São Miguel in August 1954, he had to go downtown to "get a professional license." He was shocked by the distance and the travel time. "I spent two hours getting from São Miguel to Penha," he said, "and from Penha we took a streetcar to Praça da Sé."

Buses were not only scarce and slow. They were also expensive. "Besides being deficient," said Councilman Bernardo in 1956, "the private companies charge exorbitant rates—8, 9, and 17 cruzeiros—that most people in São Miguel can't afford. . . . For its part, the CMTC, which offers the same transportation at an accessible price, is cutting the number of cars on its line daily. The workers lose days on the job for lack of transport, decreasing their meager earnings."[75]

Like the trains, the bus services were subject to accidents. In the Municipal Council, another councilman from the neighborhood asked in January 1957 for support for the transit service to avoid the "customary disasters that occur [in São Miguel]."[76] Henriqueta Lopes Fernandes remembered "customary" bus accidents at the "curve of death [near] Nitro Química. When it approached the curve, everybody made the sign of the cross." News of collisions and rundowns in São Miguel appeared with some frequency in the São Paulo newspapers. O Estado de São Paulo, for example, reported in August 1952 on the "disaster in the Estrada de São Miguel . . . near the curve of death." As early as 1948, it reported on an accident "with bus number 43.965," which also occurred "on the road to São Miguel. Three people were injured in the disaster."[77]

This general picture of privations reinforced an image of São Miguel as isolated and abandoned. Geographically distant from downtown São Paulo and reputed to be one of the city's poorest areas, São Miguel was frequently seen as a counterpoint to the affluence and opulence of the capital. At times, it was regarded as belonging to another, neighboring city or as an autonomous municipality. In April 1960, for example, Councilman Andrade reprimanded the director of the municipal transit service for "the absurdity of saying that São Miguel Paulista was a municipality that did not belong to São Paulo."[78] In the imagination of the city's residents, São Miguel was a poor neighborhood, distant and deprived of "everything," that was sought out by the humble and destitute and especially by migrants.

Significantly, it was in São Miguel that Leni, Geni, Darci, and Ailton were born in 1954, in the middle of the commemorations of the city's fourth centenary that were celebrated that year. They were thus nicknamed the "centennial quadruplets" by the press. Five years later, *Última Hora* reported that the "four little black children had gained fame and nothing more"; children lived in the "poor residence of their parents in Vila Rosário in São Miguel Paulista." Their father, the bricklayer João Romualdo da Costa,

> breaks his back, as the expression goes, to provide for them, along with his other three children. Dona Josefina da Costa, their mother, washes clothes, cooks, and offers cleaning services in order to help out. But they live with tremendous frustrations. The famous quadruplets, ragamuffins, poorly nourished, posed for photographers. Now they are merely the children of the stonemason João and the washerwoman Josefina. Nor do they belong any longer to the city, which after adopting them for its festival, abandoned them definitively to poverty.[79]

For the rest of São Paulo, São Miguel was characterized in large measure by the poverty of its inhabitants, its inadequate urban infrastructure, and its supposedly high index of violence and criminality. Irene Ramalho, an area resident since the 1940s, remembered that the neighborhood "had a bad reputation. When people spoke of São Miguel, it was with fear."

While such "fame" accented a certain image of "segregation" and stigmatization among the neighborhood residents, it also reinforced the construction of the idea of a specific community with a common identity. Prominent among the self-ascribed characteristics of this identity was the idea of São Miguel as a workers' neighborhood. Unsurprisingly, speeches and pronouncements by São Miguel's representatives in the Municipal Council invariably referred to it as a place of residence for poor workers. In one of his first speeches in the parliamentary tribune, Bernardo presented São Miguel as a place "exclusively inhabited by humble workers, people who live from their work."[80] Augusto Ferreira Lima reinforced that characterization. "In those days," he said, "there were few really rich people, the elite of São Miguel. The rest were all workers at Nitro."

For São Miguel's residents, these notions of isolation and abandonment were part of the image of the neighborhood. It was a "remote, totally abandoned neighborhood," said Antônio Nilton de Lima. "There was great negligence by the authorities," recalled José Caldini Filho. "Nobody took care of São Miguel." The neighborhood's councilmen echoed these complaints. "It is saddening," said Bernardo in 1957, "the abandonment to which the district of São Miguel Paulista has been relegated." Andrade sang the same tune, complaining that for the authorities, "peripheral municipalities seem not to be part of the capital."[81] As early as 1948, a report in *Correio Paulistano* emphasized the lack of attention to neighborhood problems on the part of municipal authorities, but it also praised the residents' autonomy and initiative. According to the paper, when the neighborhood wanted "to repair its potholed streets, it [went] to one of the factories and solicit[ed] material aid, completed afterward by the goodwill of the laboring population, which quickly and spontaneously [went] to work to get the job done. Thanks to that capacity for taking care of itself, the historic suburb [could] survive."[82]

As we will see, these notions of abandonment and isolation had important political consequences, one of which was to strengthen the idea that the district ought to constitute an autonomous city in relation to the municipality of São Paulo. Osvaldo Pires de Holanda, one of the leaders of the São Miguel autonomy movement of the early 1960s, said that the fact of the neighborhood's being "completely abandoned" was his principal argument for separating it from the capital. According to Osvaldo, "Our following was large because we said, 'São Miguel has nothing. It has no public illumination, no asphalt, no water, no drains.'"

In any case, the neighborhood's condition formed no part of the migrants' expectation of "progress" associated with São Paulo, an image strongly encouraged by the discourse of administrators and entrepreneurs. The proud São Paulo press drummed out its slogans—"The World's Fastest-Growing City," "São Paulo Can't Stop"—but the migrants' São Paulo went undescribed by the jingoistic local media. The residents of poor areas quickly perceived the differences among the various "cities" that existed in São Paulo and saw that the "progress" they desired did not come to them automatically when they arrived in the capital. It had to be demanded, and its conquest would have to be the object of mobilizations and struggles.

Migrants, "Elite," and "Mixture"

Neighborly relations, friendships, mutual aid, and solidarity are elements strongly present in the collective memory of São Miguel Paulista's longtime residents. For them, São Miguel kept its sense of community—it was a place where "everybody knew everybody," said Maria das Graças Lins Cacian, who moved to São Miguel in 1948—as it confronted growth and transformation from the 1940s into the mid-1960s. "It was like a city in the interior of the country," said Helena de Oliveira da Fonseca, also a neighborhood resident since the 1940s. "We were friendly." Vilma Garcia Matos emphasized mutual acquaintanceship and relations between neighbors during her childhood in the 1940s:

In the street where I lived there was a very nice, big house. That was the house where we went to live. At one side, there was a vila of thirteen houses [of the type] living room-bedroom-kitchen. With everything. Then we met our neighbors there, everybody was our friend. In addition, when electricity came to São Miguel, my father was the only person who could buy a radio at that time. My father was a supervisor [at Nitro Química], so he made more money and he could buy a radio. That meant that my house was a party. Every day at seven my house filled up with people to hear the *novela* [soap opera].

After Osvaldo Pires de Holanda left his job at Nitro Química in 1947, he worked at a bank and lived in a rooming house downtown, but he went back to São Miguel every weekend "because I had already made friends there. At that point, I arranged to take a house in São Miguel, and I brought my parents here." The importance of friendships and of neighborly relations was also recurrent in Waldomiro Macedo's memories of São Miguel in the late 1950s and early 1960s. "At that time, there was more friendship," he said. When someone had a health problem, for example, "the closest neighbor helped the person at any time of night or day. If you needed a neighbor, someone was there for you. People volunteered to help." Roniwalter Jatobá sees this mutual aid as related to migration. "People suffered. They had a hard time coming here," he explained, "so they were [mutually supportive]; they tried to help. A guy would divide his plate of food with you, especially if you were from the same place as him."

There is, obviously, a selective nature to these memories. The emphasis on the richness and extensiveness of personal relations in the neighborhood of those days is clearly contrasted, in the testimony, with the difficulty of maintaining these same relational standards today. In the vision of the old-timers, the enormous growth of São Miguel and, especially, the daily violence that afflicts the area have done much to dilute the relations between neighbors and the solidarity that reigned among them. Accordingly, there is a tendency in their testimony to idealize a kind of "golden age," in which friendship and mutual aid are emphasized and exaggerated. Despite that disclaimer, the testimony describes the construction of effective networks and ties of group solidarity in São Miguel during that time. These networks and ties were basic to the process of socialization of the migrants in the new city, as emphasized by various scholars of the migratory process.[83]

In this sense, living near relatives, contemporaries, and people one already knew was an important facilitating element in the life of the migrants. Jatobá told the story of his friend Everaldo, who from the beginning of the 1960s, "little by little, brought everyone [from Bananeiras, Bahia, his village of origin] here." Taking advantage of the low prices, they bought a lot in São Miguel, where family members and friends "constructed their houses [in] mutirões. On Sundays everyone [lent] a hand to lay a slab or raise a wall." The houses of Everaldo and his relatives, who came "from a little dead-end village," became, from then on, a "point of reference" for those coming from Bananeiras. "There were always thirty, forty people on weekends. People [went] there to meet up," said Jatobá. People from Piauí, in particular, became famous in the neighborhood for living near their countrymen. "The people of Piauí are very united," explained Antônio Pereira da Mata, who was himself from Piauí. "That means we adapt better. This thing of one helping the other. . . . Solidarity."

Migrants' homes were frequent points of encounter for relatives and friends. "There was this thing of going to a friend's house for a visit. . . . You'd go out to visit someone's house or they'd come to our house," remembered Waldomiro Macedo. But the greatest nostalgia in the testimony is reserved for unasked-for aid in times of need (particularly health problems), often contrasted with a supposed impersonality and absence of solidarity in present times. When in 1957 Carlos Cecchini "crushed his leg" in an accident at Nitro Química, he "received great support from the families" of São Miguel, his wife, Nair, recalled. "In those days, it was normal for one family to help another in its hour of need." Helena de Oliveira da Fonseca also recalled that, in the late 1950s "in the vila [where] our house [was], my brother-in-law had a car . . . at a time when it was difficult to have a car, [and] he took everyone to the hospital, to the clinic, . . . to the closest emergency room." It was not unusual for activists from class, community, and party associations to involve themselves in such solidarity actions, as illustrated by a small note published in the communist newspaper *Hoje* in 1950: "The workers and the people of São Miguel are engaged in an active work of solidarity with Dona Rosária Pais, widow of the worker Benedito Pais, who died poisoned in the hell of Nitro Química as a consequence of the miserable working conditions there. To help Dona Rosária a commission was constituted in which Fraternidade Lopes, a young worker, and Mrs. Trindade Gonçalves are participating, with the aim of collecting donations for the widow."[84]

The neighborhood's conversion into an industrial area dependent on a single, powerful company; the shared migratory experiences of the immense majority of its residents, many of whom even came from the same areas and cities, bringing with them traditions of mutual aid; the complex of difficulties that such migrants confronted in getting established and in their daily lives in São Paulo—all of these factors help explain the climate of camaraderie and solidarity expressed in the testimony.

The relative social homogeneity of São Miguel Paulista is perceptible in a survey of the neighborhood's professions taken in 1948 by the Regional Electoral Tribunal of São Paulo among the 4,082 voters registered in the district of Baquirivú (the official name of São Miguel between 1945 and 1948),[85] which corresponded to about 19 percent of the 21,039 inhabitants. For the city of São Paulo as a whole, registered voters represented about 27 percent of the population; the large number of recently arrived migrants presumably reduced the proportion of registered voters in São Miguel compared with the city as a whole, and the greater presence of illiterate people who did not have the right to vote probably also lowered the proportion of voters (see Table 3.1).

The number of industrial workers is striking. "Industrial employees" and "laborers" (both terms related to factory employment) made up 73 percent of the neighborhood's economically active population. If one considers other salaried professions (railroad workers, commercial employees, etc.), the number is above 80 percent, demonstrating an enormous concentration in a few types of positions. Also striking is the absence of middle-class professionals such as lawyers, doctors, and dentists. Unfortunately, similar surveys do not exist for the 1950s and 1960s, when there would surely have been greater diversification, both in the number of the professions and in their distribution among the population of São Miguel. However, as we saw earlier, the majoritarian presence of industrial workers and manual professions in the neighborhood was maintained.

While the formation of a wide social network in São Miguel Paulista is evident, we should not exaggerate the extent of relations of solidarity among the workers of the neighborhood. Having a high concentration of industrial workers indicated a reasonable sharing of experiences, but it did not by itself create solidarity and communitarian sentiments.[86] Although São Miguel was quite homogeneous by the standards of the city of São Paulo, there were internal differences that periodically resulted in tension and disputes.

TABLE 3.1. Professional Occupations in São Miguel Paulista, 1948

Profession	Total
Lawyer	0
Farmer	69
Banker	1
Shop owner	44
Commercial employee	113
Dentist	5
Engineer	2
Pharmacist	3
Railroad worker	42
Industrial owner	10
Industrial employee	2,171
Doctor	1
Military personnel	6
Laborer	807
Domestic worker	419
Teacher	23
Public employee	55
Transport worker (except railroads)	60
Various professions (employer)	9
Various professions (employee)	232
Other	11

In a community so strongly marked by the presence of a factory as was São Miguel between 1930 and 1960, it was predictable that the workplace division between section heads, specialized technicians, and general workers would have repercussions in the life of the neighborhood. The most visible of these distinctions was the location of the various workers' residences.

Two residential nuclei were constructed by the company almost simultaneously with the installation of the Companhia Nitro Química in the late 1930s, expanding São Miguel immediately beyond the existing colonial town centered on the old church from Jesuit times and the grand plaza around it.[87] The first of these nuclei was principally for the technicians and engineers from the United States who participated in the building of the company and in its first phase of production from 1936 to the beginning of the 1940s. For this reason, it was known as Vila Americana. The second residential complex, called Vila Nitro Química, was intended for the company's workers, particularly supervisors, section heads, guards, and other employees with strategic functions in the company.

Nitro Química used the houses in these vilas to attract skilled manual laborers and others who were essential for production. But with the great influx of workers that began in the 1940s and, simultaneously, with very high turnover of much of its manual labor, the company was not interested in providing universal access to housing for all its employees. By the beginning of the 1940s, Vila Nitro Operária, Parque Paulistano, and Vila Curuçá, among other new housing nuclei, began a process of accelerated expansion with the arrival of migrants and new residents. As we saw, the new subdivisions expanded the geographic area of São Miguel even more, with the appearance of numerous districts in the neighborhood. In Vila Nitro Química, however, access to housing remained available only to a restricted group of workers at the company, whom many considered privileged. The small Vila Americana, which was considered a stronghold of the highest company employees even after the departure of the North Americans, continued to be considered an area for the "nobility" of São Miguel.

José Caldini Filho viewed Vila Americana as the vila of the "elite" of São Miguel, inhabited by "the engineers and . . . those businessmen who were a little better off." The storekeeper Salomé Igel repeated that "the engineers . . . , the bosses of Nitro Química lived there in Vila Americana." Nair Cecchini, who lived in Vila Nitro Química, drew a distinction between her neighbors and the residents of Vila Americana. In the former, where "the bosses lived," many had their "noses in the air" and were not in the habit of helping their neighbors. A similar image was used by Ana Maria Silvério Rachid to refer to the section heads of Nitro Química and their families. For her, many of them had "their noses in their feet, . . . like they were going around with a king in their belly."[88]

The geographical separation of neighborhood housing into different areas did not merely follow the social differences between bosses and laborers. As we have seen, many streets and vilas had concentrations of residents who had come from the same region. Vila Nitro Operária, for example, was considered the main stronghold of the northeasterners, particularly those from Bahia and Piauí. Many Mineiros were concentrated in Vila Eiras, whose street names "recalled for the residents the memory of their cities of origin: Estiva, Camanducaia, Cambuí, Extrema, Praça Pouso Alegre, among others."[89] In any case, the formation of a social elite in São Miguel is perceptible throughout this period. This elite, which tried to differentiate itself from the great majority of poor workers and manual laborers, consisted of section heads and the few engineers and liberal professionals in the neighborhood, as well as some shop owners and the so-called traditional families of São Miguel. The

Lapennas, established in São Miguel since well before the presence of Nitro Química, is a good example of one of the neighborhood's more "reputable" families. With the intense growth of São Miguel in the 1940s and 1950s, the Lapennas expanded their brickworks business in the area to sell tiles and construction materials, and in 1953 they opened the Cine Lapenna on the neighborhood's central plaza. Meanwhile, the Miragaias, who got rich selling property during the period of sharpest expansion, became one of the best-known families in the area.[90] Cícero Antônio de Almeida, a migrant from Rio Grande do Norte and a resident of São Miguel since 1946, summed it up: the "Miragaia [family] sold the lots, and the Lapennas sold the tiles with which the northeasterners built São Miguel."

These social distinctions had a great influence on community and political life. In the 1940s, for example, the members of the Esporte Clube São Miguel, whose families were considered traditional in the neighborhood, made club membership difficult to achieve. "In those days," explained Nelson Bernardo, "people came from everywhere, and the clique did not allow mixing." Years later, discontented with "the great amount of mixing" in the Nitro Química club, a "group of São Miguel families, including some of the bosses, thought they ought to have a more exclusive club." In the mid-1950s, they founded the 200 Club, with the clear intention of "providing São Miguel society with a more closed, selective club." Similar ideals were at the root of the creation of the so-called service clubs, such as the Lions and the Rotary, in the 1960s.[91]

Osvaldo Pires de Holanda became a member of the 200 Club. "It was a rec-reational society," he recalled. "There were a lot of dances, and it lasted a long time." Holanda also remembered the social distinctions operative in the club: "After those dances got popular, the more distinguished people stayed away until it closed." For him there was a clear social division in São Miguel. "The traditional [families] of the neighborhood never mixed. The Lapennas, the Miraguaias, the Rachids, the bosses of Nitro Química, they didn't mix. A boss was a boss. They lived in Vila Americana. . . . Those people were the elite."

Certainly, the level of coexistence between the various social sectors of São Miguel was relatively high compared with that in the rest of the city, but the self-ascribed necessity of the so-called elite of the neighborhood to create exclusive, reserved spaces is an indicator that there was more "mixing" than they wanted. Ana Maria Silvério Rachid, who was a grade-school teacher in the neighborhood from the 1940s to the 1970s and who had married into a family of traditional shop owners in the area, was proud to have been "every-one's teacher in São Miguel." In her classroom, there were "children of bosses and of laborers," she said. "My husband wanted to take our son out . . . and put him in th[e] Salesian college in São Paulo. I said, 'No, sir! He's going to stay in this group to live with everyone, poor, rich."

In the 1940s and 1950s, the neighborhood's social divisions corresponded strongly with the distinctions between those with commanding positions at Nitro Química and families considered traditional versus the migrants in general. It is interesting to note this strong distinction between "established" and "outsiders" in São Miguel, a migrant community where the immense majority could be considered "outsiders" by some measure.[92]

Access to the most influential positions in community life was restricted for the first generation of northeastern migrants, although they subsequently altered their situation through participation in politics and social movements. In any case, the majority of northeasterners remained associated with industrial work and excluded from any notion of the area's "elite." For others, meanwhile, commercial activities were seen as a ladder to a position considered "superior" in the social scale of the neighborhood, even though few succeeded by this method.

Throughout this period, petty commerce was one of the most developed activities in the area, but even so, São Miguel's growth was not accompanied by a proportional growth in stores to serve the varied needs of the population. Describing life in São Miguel in 1945, a longtime resident said:

> You could count on your fingers the commercial businesses, for example: the Companhia Nitro Química Brasileira pharmacy, under the direction of the pharmacist Armando Cridey Righetti; the bakery of Sr. José Caldini; stores: Casa São José of Sr. José Badra; A Econômica do Povo of Sr. Henrique Piateka; Casa Para Todos of Sr. Herman Koshitz, who sold it to Sr. Nestor de Oliveira. There was only one restaurant, and despite its pompous name—Restaurante Internacional—it was unsanitary, and the food was terrible, but it was where the engineers and bosses of Nitro Química had their meals from Monday through Friday.[93]

Even in succeeding decades, the neighborhood's commercial offerings were insufficient. Elza Alcântra de Araújo, born in São Miguel in 1954, remembered that her father "went to buy bread on his bicycle, it was so far away. . . . [The] businesses were all far away. We went shopping over in Brás. . . . Everything we were going to buy was right downtown." Elvira Souza de Alcântra, a Bahian migrant and resident of the neighborhood since 1952, also recalled the scarcity of commerce in the area and the necessity of long travel to consume: "Here [in São Miguel] there was nothing, nothing. . . . If you wanted to buy clothes you had to go downtown."

The area's small markets and stores gradually became the most common commercial establishments. They sought to overcome residents' difficulties, particularly in the new subdivisions and vilas, in getting food and basic necessities. Nitro Química's co-op, the principal supply center of the neighborhood in the 1950s, was insufficient to handle the enormous demand. Only company employees had a right to the co-op's services and, moreover, it was located in the center of São Miguel, so that its customers who lived in the more remote vilas were forced to take long trips to shop.

Empórios (small general stores), which usually also functioned as bars or taverns, filled this supply gap. "There were lots of empórios in every [part] of the neighborhood," said José Venâncio, resident in São Miguel since 1953. Many workers saw in the creation of an empório the possibility of a supplement to their Nitro Química wages. After working at the company for three years, Jorge Gonçalves Lula decided in 1959 to construct a room in front of his house to serve as a store in the Jardim São Vicente, where there were no businesses at that time. He worked in his store for five years, during his time off from the factory. It was relatively successful, and he resigned from Nitro in 1964. In 1947, Lídia Castelani also took advantage of an existing room in her father-in-law's house and, with her husband, opened a small "tavern" near the Rua da Fábrica. "I worked at Nitro, and I had the bar," she said. "I covered the bar in the morning while [my husband] slept. After that I went to Nitro. At 5:30, I went to the factory, and my husband stayed home. Sometimes dawn came, and there would still be a customer in the bar." Irene Ramalho, a young employee of the Cooperativa da Nitro Química in the 1940s who had acquired some experience in business, said she realized "that working only at the company wasn't going to do it." After marrying, she and her husband opened a small grocery in Vila Nitro Operária, where they lived. Others, who had no possibility of investing in a bar or store, saw ambulatory commerce as an option. That was the case with the Alagoan Oscar Pereira da Costa, who after working as a machine assistant at Nitro became a "walking vendor (*camelô*), working on my free days" in São Paulo.[94]

When a business prospered, its proprietors invariably abandoned their factory jobs. In addition to the greater revenues, working in sales allowed them to escape the various difficulties and dangers of factory work. Moreover, the location of the business, generally in their own residences or very near them, was seen as a great advantage, especially for women who could reconcile such activities with their domestic chores and child raising. Mercantile activity also permitted the participation of children and other family members in amassing household income. However, it was not so easy to open a store, even a precarious one. Besides the lack of capital—inaccessible for most workers and neighborhood residents—administering a business required dedication and experience, and these small ventures frequently failed.

One of the few businesses that expanded to allow its owners to become large-scale businessmen was that of the Rachid family, Syrian-Lebanese migrants with experience in commerce. The father, who had a fabric store in the interior of São Paulo state, had accumulated some capital that greatly helped his children in São Miguel, where Wilson Rachid "was a spinner of nylon thread at Nitro. He left to start the first service station and automobile electrical repair shop [in São Miguel]." The Rachids set up their own businesses and became one of the neighborhood's most successful families.[95]

The participation of northeastern migrants in local commerce was evidently important in the traditional *casas do norte*, or restaurants specializing in northeastern delicacies. According to José Amaro Sobrinho, a Mineiro who moved to São Miguel in 1954, "casa do norte was what there mostly was in São Miguel." Antônio Pereira da Mata also remembered that when he arrived in the neighborhood in 1952, there were "some restaurants here with northern-style food." In spite of that, it was common for residents to associate local commerce with foreign migrants in their memories. When they spoke about food wholesalers, the "Japanese market" in the center of the neighborhood was remembered; when they spoke about buying fabric, clothes, or furniture, they referred to the "Turks." Elza Jardelina dos Santos, for example, said that business in São Miguel consisted of "small shops of the Turks. That was what there mostly was." Cícero Antônio Pereira recalled that in the 1950s, in the Rua da Estação, there were "some clothing and furniture stores that belonged to the Turks."

It is unlikely that people from Turkey were active in business in São Miguel in the 1950s. Besides the traditional confusion with Syrian-Lebanese, who generically were called "Turks" in the city, it is possible that the name covered other nationalities. The Igels were Polish Jews who for many years sold clothes, fabric, and shoes and boots at a store near the station. "At first," Salomé Igel remembered, "we had buckets, plates, aluminum cookware, household utensils, umbrellas, guitars, hats. Farther up front my husband put furniture." But for a long time the store's best seller was the flashlight. "There was no illumination," Salomé explained. People "got off the train in the dark, stumbling. So we sold a lot of flashlights at that time. [It was] like a baker selling bread; we sold flashlights. People came down from the train—twenty, thirty [people]—and bought flashlights. Our daily bread was the flashlight."

As did other spheres of social life in São Miguel, business revolved around Nitro Química, relying heavily on revenue provided by the company. The relationship was such that in the 1940s purchases could be made on credit at neighborhood stores and deducted from company paychecks, according to Salomé Igel. "It was a guarantee," she added, "because the people were migrants and they couldn't pay [otherwise]." The company's connection with the shop owners reinforced even more the image of its power, as can be seen from a story told by Artur Pinto de Oliveira: "Nitro Química was everything in São Miguel. The shop owners, all the shop owners who sold things, gave credit. . . . 'Ah? You're a Nitro Química employee?' You had credit in the stores of São Miguel."

Even in the 1950s, when the possibilities of purchasing had increased and the practice of deducting from paychecks had ceased, Nitro continued influencing the local commerce enormously. During the strike of 1957, for example, Councilman Andrade "proposed that the workers go back to work, so that the company, after forty-eight hours, could study the bases of an agreement: 10–15 percent over current wages, noting that *local trade, in consequence of the movement, has practically closed its doors*."[96] Only beginning in the mid-1970s, with the decline of the company and the opening of branches of popular chain stores, was the relationship between Nitro and local commerce definitively altered.

Baianos, Northeasterners, and Workers

An irrational propensity to violence, associated with poverty and ignorance, was commonly attributed to male northeastern migrants as a kind of legacy of the hostile, aggressive environment of the Northeast, especially the sertão. Beginning in the 1950s, such a representation was exhaustively explored by the sensationalist press and became almost a common sentiment among city dwellers. Popular bars, alcohol, and arguments over relationships were the most frequent components of the fights and even assaults involving northeasterners in São Paulo, where people in a wide range of social sectors typically characterized northeastern men as gross and rude. A Lithuanian immigrant remembered, for example, that in the textile factory in the neighborhood of Mooca where he worked, "People didn't like [the northeasterners] because they were crude. They came from a crude environment, where they were treated like beasts. . . . For any little thing, someone would pull a knife. But that's because of the way of life they lived there [in the Northeast]."[97]

At that time, the stereotype of the *cangaceiro* was easily associated with the migrants involved in brawls or crimes.[98] The "fishwife" was another important component of the association of migrants with violence. When brought to the cities, it earned an explicit significance as a weapon, becoming a symbol of migrants' aggression in repeated news references to "Bahians" committing crimes with "fishwives." The assassin of João Rodrigues Neto, nicknamed the "bully of São Miguel" by the daily *A Hora*, did not content himself with shooting him but also gave him "a hard blow of the 'fishwife,'" leaving the dead man with "his guts on display." Even when the weapon used by a criminal northeasterner was a simple jackknife, as in this case, the newspaper headline transformed the blade into the more dangerous fishwife. Reinforcing the association between the migrants and the fishwife, the reporters and cameramen of TV Tupi, noting the arrival of another wave of northeasterners in Estação do Norte in December 1961, asked them to show the viewers their burlap sacks, their cardboard suitcases, and their fishwives.[99]

With its high concentration of northeasterners, São Miguel Paulista acquired "a terrible reputation" as a dangerous place. While affirming that there was practically no criminality in the neighborhood during that period, many old-time residents emphasized that there were many fights and much violence among northeasterners. "In those days," said the Paulista João Caldini Filho, "it was wonderful. There was no violence, in spite of the northeasterners. . . . They're temperamental, they fight over anything." That opinion was shared by the Mineira Helena de Oliveira da Fonseca. In her opinion, "the nature [of the northeasterners] is kind of violent. They have . . . a short fuse. They fight over anything." Nair Cecchini also remembered that there was not much crime in São Miguel, only bar fights, "because the northerners are high-strung." São Miguel "was a place where they fought over little things," said the Bahian Augusto Lima. In the opinion of Benedito Miguel, a Mineiro, this happened because "the northeasterner doesn't put up with insults."

Besides considering violence as a natural characteristic of northeasterners, many attributed the migrants' supposed propensity for conflict and disagreement to their origins. The "backwardness" of the Northeast and the rustic life of the majority of its inhabitants served as the explanation for the aggressive behavior of those who moved to São Paulo. For Lídia Castelani, the fact that "people of the north" came from the mata explained their being "kind of brutish." Nelson Bernardo also said that the northeasterners "came [to São Miguel] accustomed to the northern way. In the north, something happens, you pull a knife." Most northeasterners came from "there in the mata, in the interior," said José Caldini Filho. "They're products of their environment. They were raised that way. It's not their fault that their lives were like that; they learned to live that way, with those habits."

Many northeasterners remember that kind of violence in the neighborhood, even when they emphasized that only a few migrants were involved in fights. On life in São Miguel in the 1950s, the Sergipana Maria Pureza de Mendonça commented, "In those days there was violence, all the more because the northeasterner carried a fishwife." Augusto Ferreira Lima believed that São Miguel's "bad reputation" started with trouble at the dances and bars. Artur Pinto de Oliveira recalled that the principal entertainment in São Miguel was "the bar. And the bars had drink." People "argued, fought, and a fight never ended with one person [merely] smacking the other." Another Bahian, Jorge Gonçalves Lula, said that when he arrived in the neighborhood in the mid-1950s, "There were no muggings, but there was plenty of fighting. The northern crowd fought . . . because of cachaça, women, and games." Augusto Lima even localized the focus of violence among the northeasterners of São Miguel mainly among the Piauienses, noting that conflicts were motivated by "drink" and by the

> ignorance . . . of that mistaken way of thinking from there [the Northeast]. There, the life of a *caboclo* is only to get on his horse [and go] running behind the livestock [with] the shotgun on his back and the machete hanging at his side. Drinking cachaça, he gets drunk, hitting other people, that crazy life. He gets here, he wants to do the same thing, he wants to play the bully. But later . . . he also starts getting civilized, starts getting straightened out, and he's not the same man he was before.[100]

Vila Nitro Operária, the area most inhabited by northeasterners, was considered the most dangerous part of São Miguel. "There, the bar was kind of heavy," said José Caldini Filho, using a contemporary expression. "I remember that on one occasion the deputy police chief, Orlando Gomes, who was also an employee of Nitro Química, made a raid in Nitro Operária that filled up a sack—one of those big ones—with knives." Helena de Oliveira da Fonseca also said that many fights ended in "knifings. There was a lot of that, especially in Nitro Operária."

São Miguel's bad reputation gave rise to discrimination in other areas of the city. Shopping outside the neighborhood could be complicated, because while the simple fact of working at Nitro Química was reason enough for getting credit in São Miguel, this was not true in other places. When Augusto

Lima finished filling out the credit form to buy "a watch at the Mazzei store" in downtown São Paulo, he learned, to his displeasure, that credit was not available for residents of São Miguel Paulista. They "ripped up the form on the spot," he recalled. Many shop owners held the opinion that "northeasterners didn't pay, because they say that the northeasterners . . . fought with everybody. They made trouble, ran away to the north, and didn't pay."

The available data suggest that the number of northeasterners who left the city and ran out on their debts must have been relatively small. Between 1935 and 1984, for example, only 5,770 employees (5.74 percent of the total number of workers at the company during the period) left their jobs at Nitro Química. Of those who left, only 28 percent (approximately 1,460 employees) were northeasterners.[101] Even so, there were enough stories of those who fled the capital after fights and crimes to frighten away merchants and other potential creditors.

That was the case of the older brother of Artur Pinto de Oliveira, who was "forced to return" to Bahia after a fight at work (described in chapter 2). He "fled, jumped over the wall, disappeared, and never returned." In March 1955, *A Hora* reported the story of Herculano Isidoro de Barros, a resident of São Miguel who "was murdered by knife blows when he tried to separate three individuals who were fighting" in front of an area bar. Since "everyone who was at the place disappeared," the police worked for more than a year trying to identify those involved in the fight, reporting that the probable killer, David de Sousa, "is in Bahia, hiding out at a relative's home."[102]

In the second half of the 1960s, as crime rates grew, responsibility for the violence continued to be attributed to northeasterners. Vicente Lopes, the district spokesman for the police, explained the violence this way: "São Miguel is a violent neighborhood because the majority of its population are northeastern migrants, who are deprived, violent people." Decades later, another police chief continued to sing the old song about the residents of São Miguel. "Justice here is done with a fishwife," he said.[103]

Most migrants condemned violence as a sign of "backwardness," a legacy of the "uncivilized" Northeast that was generally associated with alcoholism, games of chance, and amorous relations. Bravery, however, was respected by northeasterners in São Paulo, who saw it as essential to a deeply rooted sense of masculinity. In spite of this, the space for legitimizing violence that was tolerated for such an identity seems to have been significantly smaller than in other professional categories, such as the dockworkers at the port of Santos or Chilean copper miners. E. P. Thompson's observation about "villages or streets that acquire the reputation for being 'rough'" would seem to apply to the neighborhood: since communities "have reputations to maintain," residents will rebuke those who have the reputation of being "rough," but "such a community may meet any enquiry from outsiders with extreme reticence, protecting its 'own.'"[104]

Many migrant men cultivated the image of the *cabro-macho* who does not "put up with an insult" and thus commands respect among his peers.[105] The caricature of the cangaceiro, in turn, was frequently reappropriated by northeasterners as a symbol of courage and strength. The correct use of the fishwife, the knife typically used by the cangaceiros as an instrument of defense, denoted bravura, because, unlike with firearms, it required physical contact in a fight. The Pernambucan singer Luiz Gonzaga, nationally popular in the 1940s and 1950s, included in his wardrobe items attributed to the northeastern cangaceiros,[106] playing an important role in the diffusion of—and, in a sense, the connection among—*cangaço* (banditry), bravery, and northeasterners.[107]

In a scene from the film *O Homem Que Virou Suco* (The Man Who Turned into Juice), directed by João Batista de Andrade, the protagonist, a northeastern migrant in São Paulo during the 1970s, looks for work doing subway construction. In the process of being hired, he is forced to watch an animated cartoon in which a cangaceiro migrating to São Paulo ends up a failure despised by his colleagues, including other migrants, because of his behavior.[108] The film offers an interesting scenario of how the image of the cangaceiro might represent the backwardness and violence supposedly inherent in the northeasterner and, at the same time, function for the migrant as a symbol of courage.

For various northeastern migrants, any supposed aggression could be considered a question of honor calling for violent response, marking an increase of self-esteem and identity in relation to the "southerners." According to José Caldini Filho, the behavior of the northeasterners "created the prejudice against them." Caldini witnessed various fights in the neighborhood in which "the subject with a knife in his hand" explained the reasons for the conflict by saying, "It's because *I'm Bahian!*" Antônio Mendes Corrêa also remembered clearly what happened when, in the mid-1950s, he published a small item about the niece of the Paraibano Fausto Tomás de Lima in his tiny local newspaper, *Folha de São Miguel*. Lima "didn't like what had gone out in the paper," Corrêa said, and resolved to attack him. "He said: 'Give me the knife, and I'll kill this cowardly Paulista.'"

This valorization of bravery partly explains the frequent violent reactions against the authority of the section heads and supervisors at Nitro Química. To "impose themselves" on the workers, many section heads tried to show that they were braver than their subordinates.[109] But this sense of masculinity did not only open a space for resistance to the power of management. In collective movements such as strikes, many used violence or threats to intimidate reticent workers or even bosses. The Mineiro José Ferreira da Silva, leader of the Chemical Workers Union of São Paulo, noted that the Nitro strike in 1957 was successful partly because the strikers "were northeasterners. . . . These damned northerners are regionalists. One day I was talking at the gate [of the factory], and I saw people hitting each other. I went there, and [the comrade] said, 'That guy was talking shit about you, Ferreira. I smacked him!'" Evaluating incidents during the Strike of 400,000 in São Paulo, a chief of pickets from the glassworkers union explained, "You know how it is. There's a lot of 'flatheads' [northeasterners], and each one has his fishwife. When the boss said no [to something], some of them said, 'I came here to stop [the factory]. Let's smash the door down, break things.' But that was not with the intention of provocation but because they'd had it with the boss."[110]

Fights and violent incidents were also common in the political life of the neighborhood during the 1950s. In this case, as well, many connected the conflicts to the presence of northeasterners. In 1955, a police report on Aurelino de Andrade, newly elected as councilman from the Progressive Social Party (PSP), stated that "[Andrade] is friends with Aurelino Constatino de Araújo. Both, together with Mardiqueu or Mardukei [sic: Mardoqueu] Pereira Schmidt, Severino Barbosa de Souza (health inspector) and innumerable others, the majority northeasterners, live perpetually armed, causing disorder constantly, without any motive in many cases."[111]

There are many reports of disturbances and trouble at rallies. "São Miguel was a living war," remembered the Janista Nelson Bernardo.[112] "One time," he said, "I held a rally for Jânio Quadros in the Praça Getúlio Vargas Filho [and saw] two guys on the asphalt with knives." When Bernardo asked them what they wanted, they answered, "We're sharpening our knives, because they say there's going to be a rally here, and we're going to make sure there won't be." Nelson responded, "I'm going to be the presenter of the rally. I'll have my revolver under my belt. If you want to get tough with me, come right up to the front of the podium and threaten me with your knives and see what happens." Particularly, as we will see in the next chapter, the rivalry between Janistas and Adhemaristas (followers of Adhemar de Barros) frequently brought their supporters to the point of blows. The Adhemarista Aurelino de Andrade, for example, remembered a rally that Quadros and Porfírio da Paz tried to hold in his base of Vila Nitro Operária at which there was so much trouble that "Jânio hurried away, and Porfírio wrote in the newspaper *A Hora* the next day . . . that the cangaceiro here [Andrade was referring ironically to himself] hit Geraldo Lessa." In 1954, *A Hora* reproduced a speech by Councilman Cantídio Sampaio of the PSP warning that "blood [would] run in São Miguel!" because "disgusting individuals, brought in as partisans of Sr. Jânio Quadros, are coming into dusty São Miguel Paulista, provoking, inciting, and confronting laborers." Sampaio asked for police reinforcements, because he had "knowledge that a considerable group is being organized . . . to lead this disorderly horde."[113]

As we saw earlier, the presence of fights and arguments reveals internal differences among the northeasterners. Various interviewees emphasized that most problems happened because of regional rivalries among the workers. Artur Pinto de Oliveira remembered people brawling "because one was from Piauí and the other was from Bahia, and the one didn't like the other for that reason. . . . They got to arguing because one was from Piauí, another was from Paraíba, another was from Ceará, another was from Bahia." According to Antônio Xavier dos Santos, of Vila Nitro Operária, "In those days there was a rivalry between Bahians and people from Piauí. They didn't get along, [but it was] pure ignorance. They fought at festivals. There was always fighting, and when you went to find out [the reasons], it was because of the feud between Bahia and Piauí." The indiscriminate use of the name "baianos," principally by Paulistas, to refer to northeasterners was a cause of irritation and, at times, even of fighting. Augusto Ferreira Lima remembered many disagreements "because somebody was from one state and he didn't want to be called a baiano. 'I'm a Pernambucan. Don't call me baiano.'"

Such shows of respect to the state of origin, particularly in reaction to the generic designation "baiano," however, did not signify the absence of a sense of commonality among "northerners" or "northeasterners." On the contrary: the generalized way in which they were treated favored the construction of such an identity. Although they did not lose sight of their various internal differences, and in some cases even reinforced them, the migrants also presumed a homogenization, and they rapidly identified and expressed themselves as "northeasterners." As in other processes of identity construction, the "northeastern identity" assumed multiple forms, often contradictory, the signifiers and symbols of which were in constant flux.[114]

Qualities generally stigmatized by Paulistas were attributed to northeasterners, affecting how they were perceived in São Paulo. The historians Edson Penha de Jesus and Adriano Duarte have shown how in the neighborhoods of Penha and Mooca old-time residents associated the arrival of the northeasterners with the supposed decline of the neighborhood, implying a redefinition of the identity of those areas of the city.[115] But the concept of the "Paulista" was also multiple and wide and could include, besides natives, the wide range of different nationalities present in the capital. Many interviewees noted the difficulty of integration among northeastern migrants. When Antônio Xavier dos Santos arrived in São Miguel in 1950, he found it hard to relate to the Paulistas. "In those days," he recalled, "there was not much mixing. . . . . The Paulista didn't talk much to the northeasterner. You had to try to get to know people to be able to converse." Nelson Bernardo, a Paulista with Portuguese parents, found the customs of the northeasterners very different from his, which made closer relations hard. "That bunch from the north came," he said, "and at times you had one or two to be your friends, but the rest of them you stayed away from [because] it was cachaça, fighting, and confusion." But, Bernardo continued, "The same way we were prejudiced against them, they were prejudiced against us."

The Bahian Augusto Ferreira Lima also perceived a "terrible division" in São Miguel of the 1940s and 1950s. In addition to customs and habits, speech was a noticeable mark of differentiation. Lima talked about how impressed he was by the local pronunciation. "In those days, the Paulista 'language' was the legitimate one," he said. "They'd say [imitating a Paulista accent], 'Listen, senhorrr, I opened the porrta [door] and took a smack at the cachôrrra [dog], I beat the cachôrrro, the cachôrrro.' We were sure that the true language of the Paulista was like that."

Lima recalled that it was nearly impossible for a young migrant man to date a Paulista in São Miguel. João Freitas Lírio had a similar memory, saying, "When he went to a dance, the [Paulista] girls wouldn't want to dance with the guy because he was Bahian." When the Bahian Antônio Xavier dos Santos married the daughter of Italians in the 1950s, it was "against the wishes of the family, who didn't want it that way," Xavier recalls. "They said, 'A daughter of Italians with a northeasterner? Never! Northeasterners are ignorant.'"

Certainly, racial differences were an important factor in reinforcing prejudice in relation to the northeasterners. As we saw in chapter 1, the traditional elitist vision that associated nonwhites and poor people in general with backwardness and ignorance was quickly projected onto northeastern migrants. Such a perspective was quite present in the popular imagination of a multiethnic city such as São Paulo in the 1950s.[116] Lidia Castelani, a descendant of Italians and resident of São Miguel since the 1940s, said that "in getting married, Italians and Japanese were always kind of racist." In those days, she said, Italian and Japanese parents would not let their daughters date northeasterners because "they're meio preto [half-black]."

Countering the theme of violence, many migrants preferred to emphasize hospitality, solidarity, and readiness to give aid as northeastern characteristics. Afonso José da Silva, for example, rejected the reputation of northeasterners as aggressive and violent. Reinforcing the importance of social networks and the migrants' readiness to come to one another's aid, he insisted,

> The northerner had the reputation [of being a tough guy], but it wasn't like that. . . . I think of him as hospitable—so much so that when some-one would arrive at the Estação do Norte who didn't know where his family was, he went to the front gate of Nitro. Then, when the people came out, the chief of the guard would say, "So-and-so, do you know so-and-so? Can you take this so-and-so to his house?" . . . The people com-ing out from work would take [the newcomer] where he needed to go.

This was precisely the experience of Antônio Xavier dos Santos from Babaçu, Bahia. When he arrived at the Estação do Norte in Brás, he could not find his brother. Completely lost and with no other reference in the city, he was informed by station workers that there were many northeasterners in São Miguel. He decided then to go to the neighborhood and, indeed, "it had many northeasterners," who helped him get set up in a rooming house, "clean up his documents," and get hired at Nitro Química. Based on his experience, Santos thought that "the northeasterners were very involved with one another." The Cearense Osvaldo Pires de Holanda summed this up in a phrase: "The north-easterners are very given to solidarity."

Far from being a completely homogeneous, harmonious community, the workers of São Miguel Paulista were a diversified, complex group. Nevertheless, elaborate social networks and common experiences of migration, work, and life in the neighborhood and in the city created bases for common languages and identities. Throughout the 1950s, when the Northeast became a "national question," many migrants reappropriated for themselves the idea of "north-easternness" and articulated their regional identity as workers.

Prejudice, discrimination, and daily difficulties were responded to with the assertion and valorization of migrants' capacity for work. "When the northeasterner gets work, he goes to work," said Afonso José da Silva proudly. Augusto Ferreira Lima believed that "the northeasterner brought . . . the courage to work" to São Paulo. The large presence of migrants in civil con-struction at the moment of unprecedented urban expansion is emphasized as one more demonstration of northeasterners' readiness to work and of their essential role in the city's development. "The northeasterners are a race of working people," said Antônio Xavier dos Santos. "As a matter of fact, São Paulo should be grateful to the Northeast for the buildings it has everywhere today, because only northeasterners worked on those projects doing the heavy things. . . . The guys from here aren't strong enough."

The same logic is invoked to explain the large number of migrants at Nitro Química. According to Antônio Xavier dos Santos, "Many northeasterners were hired there because they [the owners and company heads] knew that [the northeasterner] was a hard worker." In his analysis of the influence of what was called "traditional standards and values" of workers of rural origin in São Paulo industry in the 1950s, Juarez Brandão Lopes also detected a strong "valorization of the 'traditional working man'" on the part of the migrants.[117]

The association of the northeasterner with the idea of "working people" characterized by their solidarity and disposition to work recurs in the testimony of migrants in São Miguel. It is also evident in this verse of *poesia de cordel*:

You never saw a northerner
Speak of weakness
All for one, one for all
That's how they are
They even say that fear is laziness
And people who sneer at working are no good.[118]

Barbara Weinstein demonstrates how in the 1940s and 1950s many executives, managers, and technicians of business institutions such as SESI and SENAI shared a fundamentally negative view of the Brazilian worker. Seen as immature and culturally deficient, the workers were regarded as a "problem" and even, in some discourses, an "obstacle" to the capitalist development of Brazil. In particular, as part of "the tendency to consider the urban labor force" maladjusted, the young working class of recently arrived migrants was tagged as "inexperienced and 'ignorant' of the exigencies of modern industrial life."[119] Such a vision, as we have seen, found an echo in numerous sectors of society, including among academics.

In a way, northeasterners' discourse that emphasized their capacity for work and their identity as workers was a response to this assertion of their imagined deficiencies. They struck back at the many who considered them ignorant or simpletons by affirming their importance to the development of the country, appropriating the idea of progress, and emphasizing their role in the city's history, as in this testimony by Augusto Lima:

In those days . . . the Paulista wanted shade and cool water. He didn't want to work in three shifts: "Let the Bahians work." That was how they talked. So progress was created by the man from the north, who came in under the sun, in the chill, in the rain, in everything. He fell down, he died, but he didn't slack. He was there [at work]. He brought progress to São Paulo. I don't mean only the northeastern man, no, because the Mineiro was [also] that kind. . . . São Paulo in the last fifty years was raised up and held its head high because of the hands of the northeasterners.

The traditional argument that the early rural migrants to Sao Paulo did not adapt to industrial work implied that these workers did not identify with their condition as laborers.[120] Although the workers' situation was sometimes undesirable—terrible working conditions, authoritarian bosses, a strenuous pace of production—and although other employment options were available in the labor market, the migrants' common experience of the big city, their shared cultural values, and their networks of social relations reinforced their identity as workers. And it was as workers that the northeasterners in São Paulo shared a language of class that reinforced their role as dignified producers of wealth, constructors of development, and citizens with rights.

CHAPTER FOUR

The Right to Practice Politics
Parties and Political Leadership in São Miguel Paulista

The Pride of the PCB

Brazil was the only Latin American country to send troops to Europe during the Second World War. Despite the strong presence of fascist sympathizers in the executive elite, including in the high ranks of the army, the dictatorial government of Getúlio Vargas was pressed by the United States and by mobilized, pro-Allied sectors of Brazilian society to declare war on Germany in 1942. As of July 1944, an expeditionary force of nearly twenty-five thousand Brazilians was sent to the final battles of the war, especially in Italy. The relationship between the United States and Brazil became much closer during this period. Brazil's participation in the war was crucial to its economic development in those years and led to the end of the Estado Novo dictatorship after hostilities ceased.[1]

The residents of São Paulo hailed the end of the war with unprecedented enthusiasm. It was no different in São Miguel, where news about the conflict was followed with enormous interest. Some local youths had even been drafted and found themselves fighting in Europe as "expeditionaries." So when the Allied victory was announced, the population took to the streets to celebrate.

The rejoicing, however, had a strong political connotation. The Bahian Aurelino de Andrade, who worked at Nitro Química throughout the war, was one of the millions who cheered Brazil's entry into the conflict. According to Andrade, a "grand march" took place in the neighborhood when the war ended. The people shouted "*Vivas*" to "Roosevelt, Stalin, Churchill, to Marshal Tito," he recalled. "Then in the middle of it, I saw someone shout "*Viva* Comrade Prestes!" (The reference is to Luís Carlos Prestes, the principal leader of the Communist Party of Brazil.) José Caldini Filho, then eighteen years old, also was caught up in the "euphoria of the end of the war" and remembered "a very great march that went through all of São Miguel" to commemorate the Nazis' defeat. Taking advantage of the excitement, many workers rose up during the demonstrations and smashed "the four cars that the heads of Nitro Química had [in São Miguel]," Andrade said.[2]

There was a link between the explosion of joy and the rage directed against the bosses' cars. Many laborers attributed the dangerous working conditions and the authoritarianism that reigned in the factory, especially during war, to the bosses' supposed Nazi-fascist tendencies.[3] During the so-called state of war, initiated in 1942, various industries were covered by the War Effort Law, which in practice nullified most labor rights, prohibited strikes, militarized work, and gave autocratic powers to industry in relation to its employees. For many workers during that period, excessive control and discretionary practices by section heads and supervisors in the companies were frequently associated with Nazism.[4]

In addition, Nitro Química, the largest chemical factory in the capital and supplier of explosives to the army, was one of the first to be designated of "national interest." As Andrade noted, "A lot of people came to see [Nitro Química] as the Axis—first, because we had no social rights, no law, not even galoshes, no overalls, no schedule." Moreover, he said, "The high-level bosses were foreigners . . . , and in those patriotic times, that led us to believe that they were from the Axis." Denunciations of foreign industrialists' supposed Nazi-fascist sympathies were frequent during wartime. Many workers took advantage of the opportunity war provided to denounce authoritarian section heads as "fifth columns" and Axis supporters in letters sent to the President Vargas.[5]

In the case of Nitro, the laborers' distrust had a basis in reality. Conscious of the company's strategic importance, the Brazilian political police, the Agency for Social and Political Order (Departamento de Ordem Política e Social; DOPS), kept a watchful eye on it during the war. For about sixty years (1924–82), DOPS investigated all sorts of political activities in the country. Known for their brutality, DOPS officials spied on and arrested important social actors, political parties, clubs, and individuals. Even during the democratic rule of 1945–64, the level of surveillance of political parties, trade unions, individuals, ethnic communities, social clubs, and women's and racial associations, and the observation of everyday life in factories and working-class neighborhoods, remained impressive.[6]

The common police practice of infiltrating agents into factories was widely deployed at Nitro Química. Especially during the war, the industrial zone was controlled and kept under surveillance. When the state of war was decreed, Japanese migrants and their descendants in the area were forbidden to approach Nitro Química. In São Miguel, according to a police investigator in 1943, the Japanese "were ordered to move away from near the factory . . . . Also prohibited was the passage of Japanese and Germans on the street bordering Nitro Química, . . . [which] implies that to come to São Paulo they will have to make a detour of about twenty kilometers, but that will save Nitro from any eventual criminality such persons might possess."[7]

However, as the police quickly realized, fascist sympathizers were easier to find inside the factory. A DOPS investigator working at the company reported the presence of Axis partisans there, concentrated especially among the company's section heads; after Brazil entered the war, the investigator noted, they generally did not show their sympathies openly because they were "afraid of losing their jobs. . . . If there were sabotage [at Nitro], it would come from these elements, and not from the laborers, who are mostly sons of the North, humble working people who get involved only in issues of work and schedule." The report presented a list of twelve employees, most of them section heads, who were sympathetic to the Axis but who did not show their sympathies "in the presence of people who do not belong to their circle."

Some, however, were not so discreet. In the same investigation, the investigator observed that "various Integralist elements [who worked at Nitro], many of them Axis sympathizers, . . . express themselves publicly, not only in the factory, but in the nearby bars and shops of the neighborhood. . . . Dr. Hipólito, one of the directors, is an Integralist who has corresponded with Dr. Plínio Salgado."[8] Hipólito was explicit in his preferences. "His writing objects were all green: pencil, pen, and inkstand. He even went to the factory in a green shirt and later wore it underneath. Today he has gone out several times with a green jacket. Besides this one, [there are] other elements already known to the police."[9]

In an observation parallel to his report, the DOPS investigator noted "persecutions" by section heads and foremen against the "poor laborers." Although there were no news reports of sabotage at the company, it was not hard for many laborers to generalize about the arbitrary treatment they received at the hands of certain bosses as representing Nazi-fascist sympathies. "There was a section head at Nitro Química who was part of the fascists, part of the Integralist movement here," José Caldini Filho recalled. With the end of the war and of fascism, many workers believed humiliation and persecution within the company would be a thing of the past.

Indeed, as pressure for democracy widened, a new era of participation and political mobilization among Brazilian workers began. Political amnesty in April freed hundreds of political prisoners (including Prestes, the leader of the PCB), while growing demands for general elections and a new constitution shook the political world. Afraid of President Vargas's manipulations to remain in power and of his undeniable support in the popular media, the military, many of them tied to the regime, deposed him in a coup on October 29, 1945. As Vargas retired to his farm in the state of Rio Grande do Sul in a kind of "internal exile," the presidency was handed over to José Linhares, president of the Supreme Court, who, despite the military coup, continued a process of political inclusion and kept to the electoral calendar.

New political parties were created in 1945. The Democratic National Union (União Democrática Nacional; UDN) principally combined the anti-Vargas vote of the liberal opposition with strong support among some of the oligarchic and middle-class sectors. Vargas meanwhile supported the creation of two parties: the Social Democratic Party (Partido Social Democrático; PSD), which was anchored in the dominant rural oligarchies of the states and in parts of the federal bureaucracy; and the Brazilian Workers' Party (Partido Trabalhista Brasileiro; PTB), which was based in the Ministry of Labor and the unions that were connected with the regime. The PTB tried to oppose the growing popularity of the PCB, which had been legalized (although in 1947 the PCB would return to illegality and clandestine activities). The PSD, PTB, and UDN were the principal parties on the national political scene in the period between the redemocratization of 1945 and the civil-military coup of 1964.[10]

Paradoxically, the three parties were relatively weak in the country's most industrialized and economically powerful state. In São Paulo, as we will see, the Progressive Social Party (Partido Social Progresista; PSP), created and led by Adhemar de Barros (elected governor of the state in 1947, mayor of the city in 1957, and governor again in 1963) and the political forces tied to Jânio da Silva Quadros (elected, successively, mayor of São Paulo in 1953, governor of the state in 1953, and president of the republic in 1960) dominated the local political scene during that period.

The workers celebrated the end of the war and the arrival of democracy, but after years of dictatorship, they also demanded what they considered their rights. In São Paulo, 1945 and 1946 were marked by an intensification of strikes in various factories of the capital and in other industrial cities in the state and by collective protest movements in several working-class neighborhoods. Although the PCB took an ambiguous position toward this movement, particularly regarding the value of the strikes, it turned out to be the party most identified with the aspirations of the workers and gained huge popularity, especially in working-class districts.[11]

In São Miguel, the end of the Estado Novo marked the beginning of a period in which politics became part of workers' daily life. Many workers were enthusiastic about the possibility of effectively influencing the country's political game. Most young migrants had barely had contact with the political world in their states of origin; the postwar political opening meant that arrival in São Paulo brought new possibilities for political participation. Augusto Lima, who arrived in São Miguel in 1948, compared political life in Bahia, where he came from, with that of São Paulo:

> [In Bahia] they had politics just for voting, but we had no right to practice politics from the inside, and here we have it. There in Bahia I was a voter from 1945 to 1948 . . . and I cast my vote directly for the party of Getúlio Vargas, which was called the PTB. But I had no right to take part, had no right to go to a meeting. We had the right only to vote. Here in São Paulo [when elections were held], I had already received my card from the PSP. . . . Adhemar de Barros, he was the candidate, and our committee was here. So now I had entered inside. Now I had the right. Now I helped [the campaign]. . . . That means that [here in São Paulo] we were part of it, and there [in Bahia] they gave us only the vote, just the vote, and we were gone.

Many workers in the neighborhood shared this enthusiasm for political participation. The great repository for the hope and enthusiasm of working men and women in postwar São Miguel was the PCB. São Miguel's Augusto Pinto cell, founded by local communists in tribute to the militant killed in 1937 at the Maria Zélia prison, became "the pride of the PCB" within a few months. With more than a thousand affiliated workers, the Augusto Pinto cell was the party's largest grassroots organization in São Paulo.[12]

At the height of the war, party leaders, attempting to put down roots in what was becoming one of the largest areas of workers in the city, moved Ramiro José de Souza (nicknamed "Portuguezinho" for his Portuguese descent) to the region, and he began recruiting while working at Nitro Química. His successful structuring of the PCB in São Miguel earned him an entire chapter in the book *Homens e coisas do Partido Comunista* (Men and Matters of the Communist Party), written by the novelist and PCB member Jorge Amado in 1946. "I look with wonder at the smiling face of this young worker of twenty-three years," wrote Amado, "and then I understand the exact meaning of the word 'communist.'"[13] Andrade, whom Ramiro recruited to the PCB, considered him an exceptional cadre: "He had solidarity, he was brave . . . , a tremendous organizer, very competent. . . . He made the connection between the party" in the neighborhood and the governing bodies.

An important party nucleus structured itself around Ramiro. In addition to Nitro workers such as Severino Barbosa, Eurídes de Oliveira, Januário Cavalcanti, João Vichino Vazquez, and Joaquim Martins da Silva, other social sectors of the neighborhood came to the group, including the realtor Mardoqueu Schmidt and the businessman Mário Hachid. When the war ended, their work provided the foundation for the enormous support that the PCB received in São Miguel in 1945, when PCB members became part of the directorate of the Chemical Workers Union of São Paulo. Andrade, a worker at Nitro Química and a recent convert to communism, became secretary-general of the organization. The union's branch in São Miguel, opened in 1943, became the main center of political discussion and mobilization in the region.

With the growth of the PCB, several leading party figures came to visit the distant neighborhood. Writers and artists supported the PCB enthusiastically; in addition to Jorge Amado, the writer Graciliano Ramos and the composer Dorival Caymmi visited São Miguel, among other communist intellectual figures of the period. Andrade remembered that "banned books began to appear: the 'Life of St. Louis' [*laughs*]; it was a biography of Prestes, written by Jorge Amado. Then we started reading those books: Marx, then came Lenin, Gorky . . . The Augusto Pinto cell [established] a library." Prestes himself did not delay in visiting the promising communist nucleus. On the holiday morning of September 7, 1945, Prestes went to the neighborhood for the first time to attend a rally. He was greeted by about four hundred people waiting for him outside the "small, narrow house" that was the communist headquarters, and Joaquim Martins da Silva, a member of the local committee, invited Prestes to lunch at the Nitro Química restaurant. A "group of girls accompanied by some musicians, whose instruments were guitar, *cavaquinho*, and *cuíca*, sang the national anthem," wrote Jeremiah Franco de Oliveira, the DOPS officer who accompanied the visit, who continued in his report, "Arriving there when workers usually have lunch, various organizers of the rally posted themselves in front of the factory, shouting, 'We want six lunches,' reducing [their demand] thereafter to only one lunch, and they remained there for forty minutes, until their demand was met. This happened because the organizers did not remember, of course, to obtain the necessary authorization from management to offer lunch to Prestes."

The visit continued with the staging of a rally in which Prestes told everyone about the need to register for the elections "in order to send their representatives to the Constituent Assembly so that a constitutional charter [could] be written ensuring the rights of the people."[14] But it was Prestes's fast lunch in the company restaurant that remained in the memory of various residents of São Miguel, even many who did not live in the neighborhood at the time. Artur Pinto de Oliveira, for example, knew about the lunch even though he did not arrive in São Miguel until 1948 because "the people said, 'Prestes had lunch with us here at the table! Luiz Carlos Prestes, he came in, got in line, took a tray and ate lunch with the people.'"[15]

The years 1945 and 1946 saw a wave of communist-organized rallies and neighborhood activities. While elections and debates in the Constituent Assembly dominated the more general speeches of leaders and parliamentarians who came to the neighborhood, at a local level it was the struggle for rights and better wages at Nitro Química, as well as for better living conditions in the neighborhood, that drew the attention of the audience of militants and party sympathizers. Two days before Prestes's visit, Rafael Valério, the deputy police chief from São Miguel (which was then called Baquirivú), who was also responsible for Nitro Química's firemen, addressed a letter to his superior requesting instructions because "the elements belonging to the local Communist Party are carrying out a series of rallies, in many of which political order is completely distorted in order to launch criticisms and personal attacks aimed at provoking disturbances and riots." Valério even stated that two months earlier he had been "obliged to intervene to prevent a rally from being held that was called minutes before under the name 'Proletarian Protest Rally,' where . . . they wanted to go public with past mundane and internal matters in a local factory."[16]

On September 14, 1945, just over a week after Valério sent his complaint, the communists were again "gathering two hundred people, more or less," in Santa Isabel Street, in São Miguel. The following week, another rally in front of the Chemical Workers Union with the "presence of 250 people" called for a Constituent Assembly. On October 8, the "use of a loudspeaker" was necessary so that the orators could be heard by the large crowd. The adoption of the "rally hearing" in which a parliamentary member or a party leader was questioned by those present permitted greater participation by the public and was a great success. On April 14, 1946, for example, Carlos Marighella, a communist deputy in the Constituent Assembly, took questions at a rally held "in the Largo da Estação in Baquirivú . . . with about four hundred people in attendance." In addition to "explaining details of the Constituent Assembly," he "attacked the administration of [Companhia] Nitro Química, saying that the company sucked up the sweat of its laborers by making irregular deductions from their salaries."[17]

São Miguel's communist activists and sympathizers were also excited by the strong showing they made in the major demonstrations held by the PCB. When the PCB promoted a large public meeting in the central area of Vale do Anhangabaú on September 23, 1945, to require the convening of a Constituent Assembly, they "took part in the performance of the choro 'Luís Carlos Prestes,' composed by workers of São Miguel. The worker Emílio Alves Freire, also from São Miguel, sang various songs, among them . . . 'Liberdade,' 'Sentimento,' and 'O Careca.'" At the main rally in São Paulo for the campaign of Yedo Fiúza, the PCB's candidate for the presidency in 1945, which was also held in Anhangabaú in November, "The first cell to attend and to receive a tremendous ovation was the Augusto Pinto cell of Baquirivú [São Miguel]." During the famous "São Paulo Prestes" rally at Pacaembu Stadium, one of the biggest banners read, "PCB—Workers of Nitro Química."[18] "That rally was serious business," said Andrade. "We filled up two old trucks [in São Miguel] with people we packed in." So many people wanted to go that it was necessary for the vehicles "to make more than one trip." In his book PC linha leste (C[ommunist] P[arty] Eastern Line), Antônio Carlos Felix Nunes provides a fictional narrative of his experiences as a PCB member in the eastern part of São Paulo during the 1950s, describing an episode involving a character named Ramón who lived "in the distant neighborhood of São Miguel Paulista." Ramón loved to tell his daughters, "With the enthusiasm of someone discovering the beauty of life, about the rally . . . when Prestes emerged from the jails of the Estado Novo into the arms of the people."[19]

The communists' capacity for mobilization in São Miguel was impressive. During the period in which the PCB was legal, its members occupied themselves insistently and energetically with the tasks of political proselytizing, mobilization, and popular debate. This attracted the attention of the local population and garnered their sympathy, even from those who did not consider themselves partisans of such ideas. The Bahian and former Nitro worker Cícero dos Santos described how he saw the party during this period: "The communists were quite united. It was a pleasure to see them parading in marches in the streets of the neighborhood. . . . They were trying to aid the unfortunate."[20]

The communists' behavior in São Miguel was shaped by Nitro Química's dominant presence there. The vast majority of militants and party sympathizers were obviously workers in the factory, and the local political agenda was heavily influenced by the large number of problems relating to the company. Not incidentally, when PCB directors came to São Miguel, they necessarily spoke about the demands and complaints of Nitro workers, and the neighborhood's problems also received the communists' attention. The party's journal, *Hoje* (Today), carried reports about the unfortunates of the city, along with residents' complaints.[21] Even simple problems might be highlighted in the *Hoje* if they were not being addressed by the authorities. The "Voice of the Streets" section of the issue dated November 22, 1946, for example, reported that "Baquirivú demands supervision of hygiene," because fishmongers in the open-air market held "on the principal public thoroughfare [on Fridays] leave remains in the street, exuding a bad smell and creating a serious threat to the health of the population."[22]

With the entry of militants and communist sympathizers into the Chemical Workers Union in 1945, the PCB took a more active role in affairs. Its directors became involved in union organization around the Workers' Unification Movement (Movimiento Unificador dos Trabalhadores; MUT) and at various congresses and meetings. Assemblies for that category of worker also became more constant, with much greater and more active participation, in particular by workers from Nitro.[23]

In March 1946, amid a new wave of strikes in the city, a large-scale, although partial, shutdown reached Nitro Química. For thirteen days hundreds of workers refused to work, pressing their long-standing demands for wage increases and better safety conditions at the plant. Police repression, together with several layoffs implemented by company management, ended up defeating the movement.[24] The failure, however, does not seem to have affected the PCB's local reputation. With the closing of the company restaurant as retaliation for the strike, the party and the Chemical Workers Union initiated the "Hunger Campaign." Marches and rallies took over São Miguel, denouncing the company, publicizing the workers' situation, and building solidarity among the local population. A community kitchen was installed at the union's local office, and many residents helped distribute food to workers.[25]

Although surprised and fairly intimidated by the growing communist influence in São Miguel, Nitro Química's management tried to fight the PCB throughout its period of legality by pressuring and laying off communist workers and sympathizers. One of the most insistent questions asked of the Deputy Milton Caires de Brito of the PCB when he participated in a picnic organized by the party's district committee in São Miguel in January 1946 was, "What should be the position of the employees of a large company who face the expulsion of comrades because of their affiliation with the workers' party?"—a clear reference to the repressive policy of Nitro.[26] In December 1946, Gregory Tripak, who was in charge of the factory shift, accused the company of persecuting him for political reasons. During that month, he had been suspended for five days for having advised management in advance that he would be absent "for reasons" and despite having provided a substitute. The suspension cost him a year-end bonus that was paid to all workers, reported Tripak, "except those who, for whatever reason, have been suspended during the year."

"They always see me at Communist Party meetings," said Tripak, "and they decide that I can't belong to a legally registered party. . . . They don't like me because twenty or so days ago I asked for a wage increase for all workers, [and the head of service] told me to watch out for my life, that he had no control over the others."[27] The company worked closely with DOPS to identify "suspect" workers. Thus, in May 1945, when the police agency warned Nitro Química's management that Ramiro José de Souza, along with Eurídes de Oliveira and Joaquim Morais, were "again agitating the workers of the company," management "decided to dismiss the agitator Eurídes de Oliveira."[28]

Despite the PCB's impact in São Miguel, Vargas still had enough popularity and influence to persuade most workers to vote for his former minister General Eurico Dutra, who was Vargas's choice in the presidential elections of late 1945. To Andrade's surprise, many workers, even PCB supporters, voted not for the PCB's presidential candidate, Yedo Fiúza, but "for Dutra, because at the last minute Getúlio told them how to vote." Even so, he said, "Fiúza had a good vote" in the neighborhood.

TABLE 4.1. Electoral results in São Miguel for the legislative election of January 19, 1947

Party	Number of votes (% of the total for the neighborhood)
Brazilian Communist Party (PCB)	947 (35.8)
Brazilian Workers' Party (PTB)	790 (29.9)
Social Progressive Party (PSP)	477 (18)
Social Democratic Party (PSD)	139 (5.2)
Democratic National Union (UDN)	93 (3.5)
Others	194 (7.05)
Total	2,640

Source: *Boletim eleitoral do Tribunal Regional Eleitoral de São Paulo*, no. 10, October 15, 1947, 128.

On December 2 of that year, General Dutra, who had supported the Estado Novo dictatorship, was elected president of the republic with nearly 56 percent of the vote. Dutra, who was the PSD's candidate, had the support of the PTB and, decisively, the support of Vargas, who on the eve of the election openly asked people to vote for his former collaborator. Another military man, Brigadier-General Eduardo Gomes of the UDN, received a disappointing 35 percent percent of the vote. The PCB's "symbolic" candidate for president, the unknown Yeda Fiúza, got almost 10 percent percent of the national vote. In the same election, the PCB elected a surprising slate of fourteen federal deputies, the fourth largest in the National Congress. Prestes was the second most voted for senator in the country (behind only Vargas). With heavy electoral support in various industrial districts and port cities, the communists considered the result an evident triumph. In the case of São Miguel, however, the results of the PCB's activity in the neighborhood at that time would be much more visible in the elections for São Paulo state's Legislative Assembly, held on January 19, 1947 (see Table 4.1).

In supplementary elections to Congress on the same day, the PCB's candidates, in a coalition with those of the PSP, gained 1,393 votes (52.7 percent of total votes), with the Communist Pedro Pomar receiving only 944 votes. Together, the PTB candidates obtained 838 votes, with Armando Leyder receiving 553 of the total. The PSD-PR coalition gained 186 votes in the district and the UDN only 81.[29]

The numbers for this electoral victory by the PCB in São Miguel are even more impressive when compared with the party's vote in São Paulo. In the capital, the party also received the most votes, but at a lower level (25.3 percent). In the fourth electoral district (which included Baquirivú, along with other neighborhoods in the eastern zone, including Belénzinho, Penha, and Tatuapé, and in the northern zone, such as Santana) the PCB received 32.3 percent of the votes, also coming out the winner. In São Miguel, the communists got one of their largest neighborhood votes in the entire city of São Paulo.[30]

The strong vote for the PTB and PSP (23.1 percent and 19.5 percent, respectively, for the entire city) called attention to the stunning defeat of the two main national parties, the PSD and the UDN, with unimpressive votes in the neighborhood and in the principal working-class areas of the capital (9.7 percent and 9.6 percent, respectively, of the citywide vote). In the same elections, Barros was elected governor with decisive support from the communists, winning 58.7 percent of the vote in the São Miguel district. Barros's alliance with the PCB, which was critical to his victory, opened the opportunity for his party, the PSP, to begin its conquest of working-class voters and of the periphery.[31] There is no way to know how voters born in São Paulo voted compared with those who had come from other states, but given the impact of migration on the composition of the São Miguel population at that time, it seems reasonable to assume that a significant number of migrants contributed to the communists' victory in the neighborhood.

Despite the strong vote for the PTB, the election results in São Miguel serve at least to color the findings of Azis Simão in his famous 1956 article on the workers' vote in São Paulo. Analyzing the 1945 and 1947 elections, Simão observed that "the majority [of migrants] were located in the still-empty spaces of the old neighborhoods and especially in its peripheral and suburban areas." For Simão, "the voters of this population were voters for the PTB or for its leader [Vargas]. For them, especially for those from rural areas, the possibility of living in the state capital and having legal guidelines for labor and social welfare presented themselves as unexpected, immediately accepted gifts, thanks to the government led by the head of the PTB." For workers, certainly, the link between Vargas and labor legislation was quite close, although it is difficult to assert that this relationship was stronger among migrants than among those born in São Paulo. While the electoral force of this relationship can clearly be seen in the vote of 1945 (and again in 1950, when Vargas ran for president and won), the 1947 elections show that other factors could weigh decisively in the electoral choice of workers in São Paulo, including migrant workers. As we see in the case of São Miguel, the vote received by the PCB in 1947 was related to its ability to articulate the demands of workers and neighborhood residents. As Simão observed, "The PCB maintained headquarters in the neighborhoods and organized groups in the workplace, particularly in the factories. Its supporters thus had the possibility of influencing in a direct, immediate, and substantial way the direction of the industrial [workers'] vote."[32]

The sympathy the PCB attracted in industrial areas, including São Miguel, derived not only from the great enthusiasm for the return to democracy or the prestige of Prestes and the Soviet Union, but also from the appeal of a party "of the workers" that emphasized workers' dignity and importance in society in a moment of political opening and incentive to popular participation. José Caldini Filho joined the PCB as a student in mid-1945, at the time of its great growth in the neighborhood. In his opinion, the communists had a lot of support "because of the factory. Here the labor movement was strong and . . . the party was working [at Nitro] and had strength." The PTB, the other party that competed to represent the workers politically, by contrast, did not put down strong popular roots in the region, as it did in the rest of the state of São Paulo; instead, it depended excessively on the prestige and popularity of the national leadership of Vargas and some state leaders.[33]

Moreover, considering the official party line and its twists and turns, the local leaders and the bases of the PCB often sought to make visible the working masses' problems and concerns. With this, the PCB capitalized on the enthusiasm and sympathy of the workers who, mostly for the first time, could debate and complain publicly about their problems. Unsurprisingly, the streets and public squares were given over to politics during those euphoric months. The large number of rallies and demonstrations met a growing demand of the workers not only to hear, but especially to make themselves heard. The adoption by part of the PCB of "Sunday meetings" at which the speakers not only made speeches but answered questions posed by the audience was a way to understand the population's desire to manifest itself.

One of these meetings—a "confraternization picnic for the Baquirivú workers" held in January 1946 on a site in Itaim owned by a Dr. Siqueira Campos—culminated with a question-and-answer session (*sabatina*) in which the newly elected Constituent Assembly Delegate Milton Caires de Brito "was harassed with many questions from the workers about various problems," including questions about military enlistment, fighting Integralism, employer repression at the companies, women's rights, and even "what the party thought about divorce."[34]

In addition, the rallies and popular meetings had in themselves an obvious ludic aspect that remained present in the popular imagination many years later. When Elza Alcântra de Araújo was asked to talk about entertainment during her childhood and youth (the 1950s and early 1960s) in São Miguel, she did not hesitate to mention political rallies alongside movies and the amusement park.[35] In that same period, as we shall see, the young Quadros understood as few other politicians did this aspect of rallies as entertainment.

In São Miguel, as in other places, the communist militants incorporated manifestations of popular cultural into political life. Dances, parties, and music were frequent at party events. Right after sabatina with Milton Caires de Brito, "a lively 'matinee' dance began on the grass, which lasted all afternoon to the sound of the choir of São Miguel."[36] Lídia Castelani, who joined the PCB during this period, remembered "the northerners making music [that they invented] on the spot, spontaneously, . . . in the hall" that the PCB had on Rua da Fábrica. She also remembered the "dances that the party held." It was "gostoso, and it was a hit," she said.[37]

In a sense, São Miguel's communists shared in the informality of personal relationships in the neighborhood; this helps to explain the party's postwar growth and sympathy there. At the same time, the party favored and was favored by a strong sense of class and a common language that was spreading among the urban workers at that moment.

It must be emphasized, however, that the vast majority of those who adhered to communism were not what are conventionally called militant cadres. They were sympathizers who maintained a fairly tenuous relationship with the party's organization. Although the following was large and enthusiastic, the structure of the party was still in its infancy, and after the strong repression and persecution of it that began in mid-1947, its future was uncertain.

The Era of Repression

On the morning of May 12, 1947, Paulo Rangel, assistant police chief of DOPS, along with a police clerk, went to São Miguel on a mission to close the PCB's local headquarters. The five party members they found on site offered no resistance but followed the guidelines of the party's National Executive Committee, which called for calm and obedience to the "unjust" decision of the Supreme Electoral Tribunal, which five days earlier, clearly influenced by the Cold War political climate, had decided by a 3–2 vote to cancel the PCB's electoral registration, alleging that it was an organization commanded from "outside [the country]" and was at the service of international powers, which would put at risk the very survival of Brazil.[38] Dorval Svizzero, João da Cruz Rodrigues, Nelson Lisboa de Novaes, Mardoqueu Schimdt, and Álvaro de Souza Rocha were present, surely with sadness, for the closing of the place that had been the home of so much enthusiasm and that during the two previous years had agitated the political life of the neighborhood. The DOPS police chief confiscated a vast quantity of propaganda: pamphlets, posters, newsletters, banners, and booklets. A "poster advising the people of Baquirivú of the existence of a list of popular complaints" was carried off. Rangel also confiscated an "oil painting of the daughter of Senator Prestes, with the initials J. M. J.," and several panels, among them the one that had covered the façade of the headquarters "containing the inscription 'Brazilian Communist Party: District Committee of Baquirivú.'"[39] The library and the party's archives were not found, however. Concerned about possible police action, members had hid the material before DOPS agents got it.[40]

Some days later, the Chemical Workers Union was also the target of government intervention. Accused of supporting the creation of the General Confederation of Brazilian Workers (Central Geral dos Trabalhadores do Brasil; CGTB), the union's directors, along with various others in the PCB's orbit, were removed from their positions. In their place, a governing junta was appointed by the Ministry of Labor. Despite the vehement protests of João Izidro Galvão, the organization's president, and of Andrade, who had become secretary-general, all of the board members were dismissed, except Vice-President Luiz Gonzaga Braga, who was named president of the junta in an atmosphere made tense by accusations of betrayal.[41]

It was a hard blow for the communists of São Miguel. The situation worsened in the following months when several activists, led by Andrade, began to flock to Governor Adhemar de Barros's PSP. Aurelino de Andrade had played a prominent part in the communists' campaign supporting Barros's election. At the rally promoted by the PCB to introduce Barros to the population of São Miguel, Andrade was the only local leader who addressed the more than one thousand people gathered that night of Saturday, January 4, 1947. In addition to soliciting support for Barros, Andrade "asked the people to vote for the popular slate of the PCB for the good of all, attacking the management of Nitro Química for the hunger-inducing salaries [salários de fome] they paid their workers."[42]

Four months later, Andrade was removed from the directorate of the Chemical Workers Union and witnessed the criminalization of the party with which he was affiliated. Despite this, Andrade, then only twenty-five, continued what would be a long political life. Together with other militants, he joined the PSP, and he rapidly became the party's principal leader in the area. "Adhemar was popular," said José Caldini Filho. "He had political charisma and money to spend." In a short time, the Bahian Andrade became one of the most influential figures in São Miguel.

The reasons for Andrade's exit from the PCB are disputed. He said that he and the party already had differences at the time due, among other things, to the lack of internal democracy and strong hierarchical rigor of the organization. The peak of his disagreement, he said, occurred when PCB directors tried to rig a "Workers' Queen" competition promoted by the union in São Miguel in favor of the daughter of a local party member. "Look, comrade," a party boss reportedly said to Andrade, "that girl [Maria Leão, a secretary at a typing school and the leading candidate] is bourgeois. You have to throw out her votes and put the laborer in." When Andrade refused, the communists threatened to "break everything." In the face of that, he related, "I called DOPS, and then I broke with all the rules, all the levels of the Communist Party. That was my split with them, right there, because I gave it [the Workers' Queen title] to Maria Leão as an act of justice." The party members of the time, however, had a much less noble-sounding explanation for Andrade's exit from the party. Geraldo Rodrigues de Freitas, for example, said that Andrade did not leave but was expelled by the party: "He began to turn in the gang [of communist activists] at Nitro, so the party expelled him. [Then] he went over to Adhemar's side, . . . and today he's one of the richest men in São Miguel."

It is possible that, because the PCB was outlawed, some joined the PSP as a way to continue their political activism. This seems to have been the case for Severino Barbosa. "We could no longer be activists freely," Barbosa said in an interview. "We thought it would be good to join another party in order to propagate the communist cause." Since the PCB remained illegal for several decades, it is possible to suppose that various sympathizers and even some former members preferred to act legally in another party, maintaining a more tenuous relationship with the PCB party structure. According to the Geraldo Rodrigues de Freitas, that was what happened in the case of Mardoqueu Schmidt, who was "one moment with Adhemar, then another moment . . . with the Communist Party." In any case, whatever brought Andrade to the PSP, the fact is that in several industrial districts of the capital and the metropolitan region at the time, Barros was co-opting many emerging popular leaders like him for his party.[43]

The defection of Andrade and of other militants, together with the criminalization of the PCB, resulted in a clear weakening of the local party structure. In spite of that, the communists won a great victory in the municipal elections of November 1947 under the umbrella of the small Social Labor Party (Partido Social Trabalhista; PST). The "Prestes candidates," as they were known, were widely voted for in the principal industrial cities in São Paulo. In the capital city, fifteen councilmen were elected, making the PST

(PCB) the largest faction in the Municipal Council. In Sorocaba and Santos, the party also obtained the majority of seats, and in Santo André, in addition to a majority in the local council, their candidate Armando Mazzo, a worker, was elected mayor.[44] In São Miguel, Durval José Svizzero, a Mineiro who "for six years worked as a simple switchman on the Brazilian Central railroad and as a child had worked at Nitro Química as a water carrier for the workers constructing the buildings for that company," was the party's candidate. The 847 votes he received were not enough to get him elected, but they still represented a meaningful number.[45]

The offensive against the PCB, however, was already in place. At the request of several other parties, a Superior Electoral Court ruling in late 1947 invalidated the votes given to communist candidates and divided their seats in the Municipal Councils among other political groups. Amid turmoil and protests, the police prevented the communist councilmen in São Paulo and other cities from taking their seats. The city of Santo André was besieged by DOPS agents, mounted troopers from the Public Forces (police), and even army soldiers to prevent the new mayor and the councilmen who supported him from assuming their positions. In São Paulo, the PSP was the major beneficiary of the disfranchisement of the communist councilmen's mandates, receiving eight of the fifteen seats to which the PST (PCB) was entitled. In the country as a whole, 195 elected councilmen had their votes nullified.[46]

A few days later, the mandates of all communists in Parliament, including Senator Prestes, were revoked. The party was definitively declared illegal, and the government of General Dutra further tightened the repressive knot around party militants. Unable to act openly, to take public office, and to act in the unions, the communists' response was radicalization. In January 1948, the party launched a manifesto demanding the immediate overthrow of the government of General Dutra, who had come to be considered "dictatorial" and guilty of "national treason in the service of American imperialism." The manifesto also proposed the formation of a political front formed by sectors opposed to imperialism, feudalism, and capitalism and advocated installing a democratic, progressive, nationalist government. In the trade union field, the communists also trod a more radical path, proposing a total break with the union structure established during the Vargas period, which they considered an instrument of class conciliation and a basis for authoritarianism and corruption among the workers. They thus assumed the defense of union liberty and autonomy. They frontally attacked the concept of union dues, an essential tool for the functioning of official unionism, and proposed parallel unions based on workplace organizations.[47]

The experience of so-called parallel unionism would prove a failure, but even in the absence of many activists, it was adopted by most of the communist cells and groups tied to occupational categories. Even in the face of government intervention in the union, there was still widespread dissatisfaction among Nitro workers that provided a basis for communist action and leadership. The company's working conditions were still terrible, and despite its extraordinary postwar profits, it was intransigent in not granting wage increases. In December 1948, the factory was buzzing with the news that Nitro would not grant a Christmas bonus that year, and other complaints came up. On December 13, the "workers of the weaving section stopped work for a while until the late-night section collected their back wages. After the payment was made, the work continued that same night." But the "discontent of the workers" across the plant was great, and "a strike is being prepared by the same," reported a DOPS agent on December 17, 1948. "The motive," the agent continued, "is the non-payment of the Christmas bonus, which as far as we know the company will not be granting this year." Finally, he warned that "the pacific character of that strike is being undone by the communists . . . . This strike should happen before the 23rd of this month, it is almost certain that it will be on the 21st or 22nd."[48]

Indeed, the police investigator was well informed. A report dated December 22, 1948, reported that "partial stoppage occurred yesterday at [Companhia] Nitro Química Brasileira in Baquirivú. About fifteen workers from the new wiring section and approximately sixty in the rollers section stopped production, demanding that the Christmas bonus the company is paying this year on the basis of fifty hours be the same as the previous year, when it was paid on the basis of one hundred hours." The informant, a DOPS section head, seemed to concede some reason to the workers, since he added that the company that year had made "a profit of more than 50 million cruzeiros," and "working conditions of operators in the above sections are the hardest possible . . . . They are young workers, most of them northerners, who never get to become permanent, since the nature of the service involves a progressive loss of health." Perhaps because of that, the DOPS police chief did not start the repression of the movement. Instead, accompanied by other officers, he "went to the site to explain to the workers that the bonus was optional, at the will of the company." Surely intimidated by the police presence, the workers returned to work, but not for long. DOPS agents withdrew from the factory at 2 A.M., "pursuant to a declaration by Nitro management that the police presence was no longer necessary." The work groups who were supposed to take over at 5:30 A.M. and at 7 stopped work, and the strike became widespread within the company.

Most sections of the company joined the stoppage, "with the strikers refusing to withdraw from the factory, in order to get other workers at the company to join." This time, however, the police did not want dialogue and expelled the workers from the company with "forceful action." The workers, in turn, "posted themselves near the entrance gates to prevent the entry of the new shift that would take over at 1:30 P.M." Once again, the crowd was "forcefully dissolved." But the workers remained in the nearby streets, and "repeatedly until 9 P.M. the strikers tried to reach the factory gate, in a last effort to get the coming shift to join in." Faced with such resolution and persistence of workers, the police chief in the plant "thought it wise to request reinforcements." That night and the next morning, a "cavalry picket" patrolled the neighborhood, preventing demonstrations and ensuring the dissolution of the strike movement.

Representatives of the State Department of Labor and of the Chemical Workers Union of São Paulo (at that time under government intervention for more than a year and a half) initiated talks with the strikers, but they had nothing more to offer other than an allowance based on fifty hours of work, which had been the company's original proposal. With the situation having reached an impasse, Nitro management promised not to punish the strikers who returned to work by 7 A.M. on December 23, but those who did not show up for work would be immediately dismissed. Faced with the company's threats and with heavy police repression in São Miguel, most sections, "although with some missing," started running again during the following days, and DOPS promised to produce a report containing "the names of communist elements who are directing the movement."[49]

It would be neither the first nor the last time that the interveners in the union (whose core would continue directing it into the mid-1950s) would collaborate with Nitro Química and with DOPS in their search for "communist and subversive" elements that were causing "unrest" in São Miguel. Some months before the strike in 1948, for example, the union leadership was in close contact with DOPS requesting help to dissolve mobilizations of Nitro Química workers to attend a meeting to demand wage increases. In September 1948, pamphlets signed by a "Central Committee of Claims against Nitro" called on company employees to attend a meeting to fight for better wages and combat the "false friends of the union" who would be in "agreement with Nitro to betray the workers." The coordination between the union directorate and the police officers was quite effective, preventing the transport of workers from São Miguel to the assembly (which was to be held at the union headquarters in downtown São Paulo) and ensuring that "nothing abnormal be [ratified] at the meeting in question."[50]

It is quite possible that the so-called Central Committee of Claims against Nitro was the parallel communist union in embryonic form. The strong police and business repression that followed the defeat of the strike practically aborted any possibility of creating a new organization. Still, in February 1949, a report by DOPS pointed to the "recrudescence of communist activities in São Miguel Paulista," pointing to an attempt to hold a rally at the gate of Nitro Química. Aided by the "police agents that work at the company," the DOPS agent detained Durval José Berthod at the rally. Nevertheless, Berthod "was pulled out of the investigators' hands, evading them all at once." Before taking flight, however, the activists "threw newsletters among the workers going out to lunch. They are pieces of mimeographed paper." These "pieces of paper" were clear examples of the communists' attempts to fight the official union led by interveners:

> Comrades of Nitro: When in our last strike we fought for a Christmas with less hunger and misery, what did the Union do? Betrayed our movement, not taking a position, as was its duty, alongside the workers, and did the job that interested the sharks of Nitro. Now they want to deduct union dues [from workers' paychecks]. What are union dues? These dues are destined to finance the banquets and pay for the lovers of these traitorous sellouts—that is, take [food] out of the mouths of our children, mothers, and wives to feed the traitors and their lovers. We will not permit the deduction of this immoral tax. Should they insist on deducting it, we will respond with a strike. Down with the sellouts! Down with the Union Dues!"[51]

A few days later, in a new attempt to rally outside the Nitro gates, Svizzero was arrested, along with other communist activists. Because of the repressive measures that were being adopted in the country as a whole, and within companies, it became almost impossible to summon workers to any public demonstration. Reports of rallies and demonstrations are increasingly rare from this period. Still, a "manuscript pamphlet" signed by the General Workers Union, a new, clandestine communist-oriented organization, was distributed at Nitro Química in July 1950, claiming that the company's wages had not "increased since 1946." Since "during this period, prices rose alarmingly," there was "a situation of misery never before seen." The pamphlet continued:

Wages do not increase. What increase are the profits for the sharks of Nitro, which last year were [the very high sum of] 8,000 contos.[52] To aggravate the situation further, there are persecutions, suspensions, and the infamous deductions that are no more than outright theft. Sundays and holidays, which since 1946 is law [sic], are not paid. They do not furnish gloves, sleeves, shoes, appropriate visors that are essential for ensuring the health of workers. . . . What we see is that for [the bosses] . . . the laborers are animals and only serve to make profits. In short, there is only one solution to this situation: it is to demand, with everyone united and organized, the solution to these things. To do this, it is necessary to form commissions of five, six, or ten workers in each section. . . . United and organized, you will secure the victory."[53]

Frightened by the postwar growth of labor and communist militancy in the neighborhood and within the company, the management of Nitro saw in the criminalization of the PCB and intervention in the union a great opportunity to undermine leftist influence among the workers from then on. They saw the growth of social welfare measures, together with the expanding activities of the company's renowned social service, as a way to contain discontent about working conditions. It was precisely in the second half of the 1940s that this sector came to have increasing investment and to expand its activities.[54] However, management also intensified its relationship with the political police, periodically scanning the factory for possible "agitators." With some regularity, DOPS "spies" worked at Nitro, with the support of the section heads. The presence in the union of leaders who were close to company management facilitated the control and containment of the workers' discontent and demands.

From 1947 onward, as the company strengthened its ties with the political police, it routinely sent lists of potential hires to DOPS for political background checks; the aim was to prevent the hiring of "troublemakers," principally communists and their sympathizers. It was enough to have been tagged "communist" by DOPS anywhere in the country for police archivists to communicate that fact to Nitro's Personnel Department, as in the case of José Tenório da Silva. When Nitro sent a list to DOPS with his name on it in May 1953, it was returning with the warning that "in 1948, that name was reported in a list of communist elements belonging to the PCB in the state of Pará, with no address or occupation. With regard to the others, nothing to report." Raimundo Alves de Souza, who name was included on a list dated January 1952, was also "tagged . . . as a communist from Valparaíso, according to a list of names from that precinct on [March 15, 19]48, a laborer by profession."[55]

But not only alleged communists were reported. Working men and women who for some reason had attended some event contesting the companies, or even those who had protested individually in a plant, could be denounced to Nitro if their names were in the police files. Manoel José da Silva's name, for example, was on a list sent to DOPS in April 1957, which reported that "an identical name figures as a worker at the Moussalhe Brothers textile plant, located at Rua Alferes Magalhães 255, who in February 1955 was suspended for a day for endangering the production of the industry in question." José Barbosa Lima probably did not get a job at Nitro because DOPS reported that "in May 1954, when he was working in the Fábrica Nacional de Artefatos de Metal, . . . he was verified there as one of the heads of the strike."

These reports could at times be incredibly detailed. João José Rodrigues, according to information provided by police to Nitro Química in August 1948, was the name of someone "tagged in our archive . . . who, with others, signed a protest against the closing of the PCB sent by residents of the Quarta Parada [a neighborhood on the east side of São Paulo] in July 1947 to Dr. Adhemar de Barros." Benedita Santos, a "daughter of Paulo dos Santos and Olga Camargo, born in São Paulo on [February 16, 19]28," was both on a list of job seekers at Nitro Química in June 1952 and in the DOPS archives, which stated "that name appears in our file as a weaver of Rondon Knitwear and one of the signatories of a telegram addressed to the then communist Deputy José Maria Crispim demanding the payment of the Christmas bonus, as published in *Hoje* of November 26, 1946. In 1947, she was part of the union committee of said knitwear manufacturer and followed PCB guidance. She resided at the time at Rua Conselheiro Belisário, 151. As for the other names, nothing to report."[56]

This control, though intense and long-lasting, did not prevent strong movements about specific demands from developing within the company between 1940 and 1960. Nor did it completely block the admission of old and new militants into the company. Adelço de Almeida, for example, was already blacklisted as a communist by DOPS when he asked for a factory job in 1954. He remembered that the "problem of the party at that time was to get into Nitro Química." Those who managed it "did not have the conditions to act there, [since the] management [was] very rigorous, anticommunist in the extreme. The command structure inside was controlled by the police, and everything was infiltrated." Despite being tagged by the police and an arrest that had recently appeared in "a picture in the newspaper *O Globo*," Adelço was hired by Nitro and became one of the company's major labor leaders, leading the strike that shut down the factory in 1957 and serving as president of the Chemical Workers Union from 1956 until he was removed shortly after the military coup in 1964. However, despite its occasional slip-ups in combating the left and preventing demonstrations on the factory floor, the intimate relationship[57] between company management and DOPS police is a strong indicator of the permanent repression and control of workers and of the real limits of democracy in the period between 1945 and 1964.[58]

In the popular memory of São Miguel, the continued repression and persecution of militants, especially communists, caused that political current to be associated not only with struggle and combativeness, but also with suffering and fear. Thus, one thing that marked the life of the former worker Josué Pereira da Silva was witnessing the struggle of the communists of Nitro in favor of those "workers who were being trampled" in the factory in the mid-1950s. He remembered that "the firm would call the police . . . and the Communist Party was revoked by the police." Referring to the same period, Osvaldo Pires de Holanda, who never belonged to the PCB, said that he "much admired the grit of the communists." The determination and strong will of various communists were viewed sympathetically by many workers who—although they did not associate with the organization or even subscribe to its ideas—saw admirable qualities in the men and women who were persecuted by the police and by the company for their defense of workers' interests.

Although they remember the persecution by Nitro and by the police of members of the PCB in the 1940s and 1950s, the repression unleashed against the militants of the left after the coup of 1964 greatly marked the memories of former neighborhood residents. In addition to admiring the communists' courage, Osvaldo Pires de Holanda attributed the absence of police persecution against him after 1964—even though he had led the movement for neighborhood autonomy—to the fact that he had never belonged to the party. Commenting on the communists in the period immediately after the military coup, Afonso José da Silva affirmed that "many fled, they went through hell."

However, the communists and the repression they suffered also caused fear in many. The anticommunist rhetoric of the company and the local church, among others, appealed to many workers. Helena de Oliveira da Fonseca remembers that she "was very afraid of communists . . . I thought [communism] was very dangerous." Nair Cecchini, who was influenced by the Catholic Church and by her husband, the director of the São Miguel Workers' Circle, said that she "didn't even want to know about the Communist Party."

Unlike in other places, however, the association of communism with "evil" was not strong in São Miguel. Any attempt to associate the PCB only with foreigners or with an anti-national ideology was extremely fragile, since the activists had adopted a clearly nationalist discourse that became increasingly pronounced during the 1950s, and the presence of foreigners among its activists was accordingly reduced.[59] More than the fear of the party itself or of its ideas, the major factor for the withdrawal of neighborhood workers from the communists seems to have been the fear of reprisals and persecution. Artur Pinto de Oliveira reported that despite being repeatedly approached by communist friends in the factory and in the neighborhood, he never joined the party because he was afraid. "Not that I thought they were wrong," he said. "I was afraid, because I saw what the repression was like. So I never joined. The people [of São Miguel also] were afraid, because when the police discovered that someone was [a communist], they did everything they could to destroy him. They beat him in the public square. Took him off to jail. Everyone ended up knowing about it."

In any case, beginning in the late 1940s the criminalization of the PCB and its subsequent repression, along with the party's own internal divisions, opened a large space for other options and political parties in São Miguel. The rise of other political forces linked to the popular classes in São Paulo, such as Adhemarism and Janism, cannot be explained only by the decline of the PCB, but clearly they benefited greatly from the political vacuum caused by the absence of a public platform for the communists. São Miguel Paulista, as we shall see, was one of the places in São Paulo where the new discourses of Adhemarism and Janism found receptive ears among the workers.

The Catholic Church and the São Miguel Workers' Circle

The friendly relations between Nitro Química and the parish of the Catholic Church in São Miguel Paulista became even clearer following the formation of a workers' circle in the neighborhood in 1946.[60] Founded as a reaction to a strike in the factory the previous year and, more generally, to counter growing communist influence, the circle had enormous support from company management, gradually becoming an appendage of the company's social service.

The Circulista movement, seen as the best way for the Catholic Church to act within the unions (which the state made official as of the 1930s) received a boost at the end of that decade from the establishment of the Estado Novo dictatorship. At the Catholic Workers National Congress held in 1937 in Rio de Janeiro, the thirty-one delegates, representing organizations from nine states, specified as a basic goal the "founding of workers' circles in all centers of labor as a basic organization for all achievements of the Catholic program in the socioeconomic arena on the part of the working class."[61]

Inspired by the social doctrine of the church, which was based principally on the encyclicals *Rerum Novarum* (1891) and *Quadragesimo Anno* (1931), Circulism preached social harmony and collaboration between classes. An article in the *Nitro Jornal* explaining the objectives of the São Miguel Workers' Circle summarized this view by stating the organization's ultimate purpose as the need to "restore peace in the world of work through respect for mutual rights and through the reestablishment of harmonious relations between employees and employers."[62] Combating communist influence among the workers was thus considered one of the main tasks of the Circulista movement. Not by chance, the financial support of workers' circle activities by São Paulo businesses was common.

Besides actions of a clearly religious character, the circles were greatly concerned with the "free time" of the working class, so they organized recreational and educational activities and often provided medical and dental care.[63]

Opposition to communist ascendance among the workers was crucial to the foundation of the São Miguel Workers' Circle. The PCB's popularity and its influence on the protest movements at Nitro Química caused great apprehension on the part of company management and among politically conservative sectors of the neighborhood. The church and its proposed circle thus seemed an excellent antidote to the "Bolshevik threat."[64]

The communists of São Miguel saw in the circle an obvious counterweight to its growth in the neighborhood and considered it a sufficiently dangerous rival to merit a counterattack. At the ceremony mentioned earlier, a DOPS investigator reported that "the communist committee held an impromptu party in honor of the three communist leaders of Russia [*sic*]: V. I. Lenin, R. Luxemburg, and K. Liebknecht, with the intention of undermining the ceremony of the São Miguel Workers' Circle." The action seems to have been successful, since it "diverted the attention of many people who went to the Cine São Miguel to attend the ceremony that was performed there. After the party ended, communists numbering three hundred, more or less, tried to march but failed because of the immediate intervention of the [political police] who were there on duty."[65]

This open conflict between communists and Circulistas did not last long. With the illegality of the PCB in 1947 and the consequent weakening of the party in the region, the circle seems to have accentuated its characteristics as a "service-providing and leisure club," functioning almost as a department of Nitro's social service. This is how it was remembered by many former residents. When asked about the São Miguel Workers' Circle, Augusto Ferreira

Lima associated it directly with the company and the entertainment activities the company sponsored. The union's function of open combat, one of the driving forces behind its creation, seems to have been diluted over time. The intervention in the Chemical Workers Union of 1947 and the consequent exclusion of the communists, along with the advent of a new directorate close to company management, certainly contributed to a significant reduction in the circle's hostilities in relation to the union. When a new management linked to nationalist and leftist sectors regained power in the union between 1956 and 1964, the Circulista movement was much weaker nationally, and particularly in São Miguel, where it was seen as an appendage of Nitro Química.[66] For Augusto, the circle "was a place organized by Nitro Química. . . . The Nitro Química Workers' Circle was a very cool (*bacana*) building. It had the best party [on] Sundays. Children got together, and they had a soccer field. The Workers' Circle was leisure; it was playing ball, schoolchildren with their teachers. It was a leisure circle—that's what it was." When asked whether the circle was anti-union, he answered, "No, many of the members [of the circle] were also members of the union—like Miguel Brasão, who was a union member and still today is in our association [of retirees]."

Even the militant communist Geraldo Rodrigues de Freitas confused the circle with the company in his memory. The São Miguel Workers' Circle "was [part of] Nitro," he remembered, adding that the organization "was a kind of little club [that] provided medical and dental care. We paid almost nothing, and we had a doctor and dentist . . . . Everyone liked it because at that time [getting access to] a health center here was very difficult." Certainly the fact that the company deducted membership dues directly from employees' paychecks tended to reinforce the idea that the circle was linked to the structure of the company. Jorge Gonçalves Lula, a factory worker in the 1950s, said that "everyone who worked at Nitro Química was a member [of the circle]. It was taken out of our paychecks."

The São Miguel Workers' Circle had a dedicated page in the *Nitro Jornal*, in which circle and company directors affirmed the excellent relations and permanent collaboration between the two institutions. Interviewed by the *Jornal* shortly after his inauguration as president of the circle in the first months of 1957, Enry Saint'Falbo listed the "perks in the healthcare-education field" that the organization offered its members and took advantage of the "opportunity to thank publicly the management of Nitro Química Brasileira . . . for the unrestricted and permanent aid always given to the Workers' Circle, in both the moral and the material field."[67] The closeness of the circle to the company generated distrust among many workers who, pragmatically, saw in the organization a space of leisure and assistance but never used it as a way to further complaints or claims about the company.[68]

The "club-like" character that the circle gradually assumed is shown in several reports that highlight recreational activities sponsored by the organization. The São Miguel Workers' Circle "had parties and dances," recalled Antonio Mendes Corrêa. Nair Cecchini remembered that the circle "organized picnics and excursions to Santos," a popular seaside resort.

In addition to leisure activities, women especially tended to remember the circle as a space for courses and educational activities. Nair Cecchini recalled that its headquarters "had a night school, culinary arts, and sewing." Helena de Oliveira da Fonseca defined the São Miguel Workers' Circle as a "club" where she took a "course in cooking . . . and sewing" and where there were even music lessons. For Ana Maria Silvério Rachid, the circle was the place that "gave classes in sewing" in São Miguel. Significantly, such courses for women reproduced the same concepts about the role of women's instruction as educational institutions created by the industrial companies for workers in that period, such as the SESI and the SENAI. The idea that working-class women should prepare first of all for their supposed duties as wives and mothers formed the basis for offering courses such as sewing and culinary arts, while the notable presence of women in manual labor was generally slighted in the offering of vocational educational curricula and activities.[69] Although the concept behind such courses extended only to the domestic sphere and in preparing for the role of homemaker, many women took advantage of their new knowledge to seek extra revenue for the family. Fonseca, for example, seems to have taken advantage of the basics of sewing she learned in the course at the circle and began working "in a house [where] they made and sewed trunks for [soccer] players," which were sold in her sister Irene's store.

But in spite of the leisure, educational, and assistance activities it offered, the São Miguel Workers' Circle lost importance in the neighborhood's social life over the course of the 1950s. With rare exceptions, this phenomenon affected the Circulista Movement throughout Brazil. In the specific case of São Miguel, where the circle was closely connected with, and dependent on, Nitro Química, it is likely that the company's crisis in the 1960s and its consequent reduction of benefits for workers cost the circle financial resources and political support. The loss of Father Aleixo Mafra in the early 1960s certainly helped deepen the crisis and the subsequent closing of the São Miguel Workers' Circle.

The opening of a new parish church and the death of Father Aleixo in 1967 symbolized the end of an era at the church in São Miguel Paulista. Father

Aristides, one of Father Aleixo's successors in the late 1960s, was almost the antithesis of his predecessor. Known for his extroverted personality and his unconventional procedures, Father Aristides became famous in São Miguel for his impatient, innovative approach, particularly in relation to youth behavior.

In the 1970s, a more distinctly political attitude became established among São Miguel's Catholics. The neighborhood became one of the main strongholds of ecclesiastical base communities (*comunidades eclesiais de base*, CEBS) along the periphery of São Paulo and was strongly influenced by the action of clergy and laypeople connected to liberation theology. Especially after D. Angélico Sândalo's appointment as bishop of the eastern region of the capital, militant Catholics became more active. Their broad participation was decisive in the establishment and strengthening of several social movements that erupted onto the country's political scene in the second half of the decade.[70]

Adhemarism and Janism in São Miguel

After being elected governor in 1947, Adhemar de Barros skillfully used the governmental structure and public resources he controlled to assemble the Social Progressive Party (PSP), the strongest party organization in São Paulo until the 1964 coup.[71] The banning of the PCB had paved the way for the PSP to penetrate and consolidate itself in various working-class areas where the Communists had prevailed during their two short years of legal activity. In addition, the PSP greatly benefited from the internal disputes in Vargas's PTB, which never managed to capitalize fully on its leader's popularity among São Paulo's workers. Besides frequently being in conflict with national PTB leaders, the party's state leadership fragmented during the 1950s and 1960s into various currents and positions.[72] Barros allied with and co-opted several local political machines in the state, blocking much of the traditional political space of the PSD and oiling the party machinery of the PSP in the rural regions of the state as well.

With a discourse that was constantly directed to workers, Barros condemned the deep inequalities in Brazilian society and denounced what he considered the selfish and arrogant "elites," creating around himself an image of generosity and accessibility. At the same time, however, he easily allied with the most conservative sectors, and he frequently repressed strikes and demonstrations. A figure laden with ambiguities, Barros was one of the traditional politicians who most clearly perceived the new phenomenon represented by the rapidly growing presence of thousands of new voters in São Paulo's working-class neighborhoods and cities. As highlighted by John French, Barros's victory in the 1947 elections "marked the emergence of a new kind of political leader who was willing to court, albeit opportunistically, the urban and working population of the state."[73]

São Miguel was one of the working-class neighborhoods where the PSP took shape. Taking advantage of Barros's governorship, Andrade, together with other former communists whom he attracted to the ranks of social progressivism, turned the PSP into the major local political organization of the 1940s and early 1950s. A political and union leader in the neighborhood, Andrade also managed to win over several other countrymen to the party of Adhemarism. The Bahian Augusto Ferreira Lima remembers that he was excited about Barros and entered "politics along with Aurelino Soares de Andrade, who already had a committee [of the PSP] based in São Miguel." Indeed, Andrade's origin in the Northeast seems to have been an important factor in his choice by the governor as local party leader. "São Miguel is for the Bahian," said Barros when he designated Andrade president of the PSP in the neighborhood.

But it was not just Andrade's charisma and regional origin that enabled the PSP to grow in the area. The party's municipal and district directorates controlled the appointment of a number of public offices and, along with several state agencies, served as intermediaries for residents' claims and requests. Mario Beni, an important PSP politician, remembered that the party "had as its norm the establishment of zones of influence . . . the way it was done in the system of regional districts." The directorates thus acquired enormous influence in local life and in the state's machine. Justices of the peace, police chiefs, and deputy chiefs (who in turn could appoint strategic "block inspectors") were invariably chosen by the local PSP directorates, which provided, in addition to power and prestige for those appointed, a broad network of contacts and loyalty that was extremely useful for the party at election time, as well as a considerable coercive force in each area.[74]

Because of this, said Andrade, "Adhemar gave more prestige to the president of the directorate than a congressman [receives] today. I was more in charge in this region than any congressman." Indeed, Andrade remembered that even before he became a councilman, "Adhemar *gave* [me] twelve subdelegations to assemble . . . in various districts of the eastern zone of São Paulo: Vila Matilde, Itaquera, Guaianazes, Goulart, Vila Buenos Aires, Ermelino, Itaim, Burgo Paulista. So we had a cordon here." In São Miguel, for example, Andrade said that Barros chose as a subdelegate "Aurelino Constatino de Araújo, who was from Piauí, in place of Roque Mastromônico, who was Italian, and I took him out. That was the greatest victory. . . . I named a 'Bahian.'"

In addition to the party machine assembled around the government structure and the PSP, Barros developed an original and popular style of approaching voters. During his time of intervention in state government in the late 1930s and early 1940s, Barros had a radio program, much like U.S. President Franklin D. Roosevelt's "Fireside Chats" of 1933–34 but innovative in the Brazilian context, titled "Palestra ao Pé do Fogo" (Fireside Talk). On it, he communicated with a considerable portion of the population of São Paulo using simple, direct language and an invariably friendly tone.

During the campaign in 1947, Barros began visiting outlying neighborhoods of the capital, starting a practice that would be followed by several other politicians during the period. He went not only to the neighborhoods but to visit the homes of supporters and voters in general. The presence of a politician of such magnitude in humble locations, which the inhabitants considered abandoned and forgotten by the authorities, had a great impact. Even today this remains fresh in the memory of old-time residents. Nair Cecchini says that "she was always an Adhemarista" and remembers that Barros came to São Miguel frequently, "He went to Vila Nitro Química, too. He went to peoples' homes. He came, and so did Dona Leonor [Barros's wife]. They came into peoples' houses and had coffee." Augusto Ferreira Lima said that in the back of his house in Vila Nitro Química there was a school that Dona Leonor de Barros used to visit. She "came to the back of my house," Lima continued, "saw the peoples' children, and there we hugged. Barros leaned against his big car, and [we] conversed with him."

These visits to voters' homes generated a different kind of involvement between Barros and his constituents, bringing them closer and indicating to the residents that he understood their values, as well as their problems, anxieties, and needs.[75] Barros tried to approach the broad universe of informal relationships that guided the lives of workers in São Miguel Paulista, positioning himself as an authority but also as someone closer, a friend. Certainly, the visits were a source of pride and an indication of prestige for those who received them. Andrade reported proudly that during his time as governor, "Adhemar came with Dona Leonor to my house ten times. [He] gave me prestige." Augusto Ferreira Lima confirmed the esteem of the local president of the PSP: "In the house of Aurelino Soares de Andrade, on Maria Eva Street, there was a bed on the second floor for Adhemar de Barros [where he] came to rest."

These visits played a fundamental role in political campaigns. At election time, recalled Andrade, "Adhemar would come here with Dona Leonor, and we would make twenty visits on a Sunday. . . . When I got to the tenth house, [Barros said] 'I can't take any more,' but [I pressed him] because I wouldn't accept sending word to a common, simple citizen waiting at his house that we weren't coming. I never tolerated that."

Dona Leonor de Barros seemed to have greater sensitivity about the importance of direct contact with the voters' homes and families. Andrade said that when Barros seemed to be fading and wanted to stop the marathon of visits, it was Dona Leonor who convinced him to continue. "No, Adhemar! Let's go!" he recalls her saying. Besides her importance in coordinating women's work for the PSP, collaborating in the conquest of the large new electoral contingent of female workers, Leonor de Barros was central to the formation of Barros's benevolent and charismatic image.[76]

Many old-time residents of São Miguel went as far as to say that the district's voters were primarily captivated by Leonor. Joaquim Anselmo dos Santos believed that "a lot of Adhemar de Barros's vote was because of his wife. . . . All these vilas, his wife went there, bringing things, distributing that whole business, [and it] worked, because the people voted. They voted more because of his wife." The communist Antônio Pereira da Mata also attributes to Dona Leonor an essential role in Adhemarist politics. "In my understanding," said da Mata, "it was Leonor de Barros who helped Adhemar get elected. [She was] an excellent woman who did a lot for his social standing." Even in campaign speeches, Barros's references to his wife were constant. Da Mata said that he often heard Barros make campaign promises along these lines: "I came here to give you a message from Leonor. . . . Allow me to talk with you. Leonor told me to tell the mothers and fathers of this neighborhood that a maternity hospital will be built at Nitro Operária."

The alliance between the PSP and the PTB, which nominated Vargas to the presidency in 1950, consolidated the prestige of Barros and his party in São Paulo's working-class neighborhoods by associating his name with that of the most popular politician, beloved by workers. Both Vargas and the PSP's candidate for governor of São Paulo, Lucas Garcez, were elected. In addition, the PSP elected the largest slate to the Legislative Assembly, with nineteen members, making it the largest party in the state. Although the results by district for the 1950 elections are not available, it can be assumed both from accounts of former residents and by the candidates' resounding triumph in the state's major cities and industrial areas that Vargas and Garcez were largely victorious in São Miguel.[77]

The successful campaign of the Popular Front (the name of the coalition of workers and PSP members) in São Miguel appears to have been conducted almost exclusively by local PSP members. The PTB was practically nonexistent as a party structure in the neighborhood, while the PCB, now illegal, had made the decision to propose "voting blank" (i.e., abstaining), denouncing all of the candidates as bourgeois and against the interests of workers. The only DOPS report about the campaign of Vargas and Garcez in the area discusses a rally on September 7, 1950, that brought together about seven hundred people and featured several speeches, including those by "Aurelino de Andrade, president of the center Adhemar de Barros of São Miguel Paulista; Luís Cristiano, a member of said center; Severino Barbosa, secretary-general of the same; João Mendonça Falcão, candidate for state representative; and Ubirajara Kentenejian, for federal representative." The "tendency of the speeches," according to the officer who attended, was "propaganda by PSP candidates."[78]

In municipal elections the following year, Andrade and his group decided to support a local candidate for councilman. Even though it was the strongest party in the area, the neighborhood PSP, keeping the name Popular Front from the previous year's election, supported the tailor Tarcílio Bernardo, who was running on the PST ticket. According to Andrade, the support for Bernardo was rooted in his relations with the richest and most traditional families in the area, which guaranteed a greater arc of alliances to elect the neighborhood candidate. Bernardo was married to a daughter of the Miragaia family and had the sympathy of leading members of the Esporte Clube São Miguel, the club of the small local elite, including the Lapenna family. Nelson Bernardo, Tarcílio's brother, remembered that "they started looking for someone to be councilman for São Miguel, and the Esporte Clube São Miguel was influential. It was practically the club and the Lapenna family that launched my brother."

Bernardo was the director of the Esporte Clube São Miguel and a member of the staff of the PSP, including being a subdelegate in São Miguel. His experience in the PSP and his ability to garner substantial support from traditional sectors in the neighborhood must have been a factor in the decision of PSP members to embrace his candidacy. Moreover, they would have taken into account that the UDN had also decided to run a local candidate, the doctor at Nitro Química, Albano Gouveia da Rocha. Bernardo's campaign had moments of tension. At one of its rallies, in late July 1951, "the representatives João Mendonça Falcão and Ivo Pereira Smith . . . attacked the police vehemently in the person of the local deputy police chief, Valério [who was responsible for security at Nitro]." At the same meeting, "in the presence of about three hundred people . . . Severino Barbosa of the Popular Front of São Miguel; . . . Aurelino Soares de Andrade, also of the Popular Front of São Miguel; . . .

Dr. Rafael Hércules Regina, secretary of the PSP municipal directorate; and Mr. Mardoqueu Schmidt" declared themselves in favor of Bernardo's candidacy. In October, on election day,

> there was friction between elements of the Popular Front . . . , who are supporting the candidacy of Tarcílio Bernardo for councilman and the group supporting the candidacy of Dr. Albano, the doctor at Nitro Química. Aureliano Manoel Marques insulted the latter group, of which Ananias de Sousa was a part, saying that it was composed of fascists (Integralists), that nothing could be expected from them. With the intervention of third parties, tempers calmed, and each group went its own way. Later, at about 3 P.M., Ananias and Aureliano ran into each other near the city and got to arguing, to the point of blows. They were separated by the intervention of other people, with both reportedly injured.[79]

In that election, Bernardo received 1,109 votes, making him the third biggest vote getter of the PST and becoming in consequence the first substitute of the party. Two years later, he was seated as a councilman, but by then he was a member of the PTN, the party led by Councilman Emílio Carlos and one of the political organizations that would support the meteoric political career of Jânio Quadros. The doctor from Nitro Química, Albano Rocha, won 521 votes, remaining a distant twentieth alternate of the UDN.[80]

The 1951 elections were the last in which Andrade and his political group would work side by side with Bernardo, whose affiliation with the PTN marked his break with local PSP politics. Bernardo's defection to the Janistas was an obvious signal of Quadros's rapid and growing popularity in São Miguel Paulista. In the following years, the neighborhood would be consolidated as a Quadros stronghold.

Quadros began his political career in the late 1940s as a fierce opponent of Governor Barros and of the PSP while he was a councilman in São Paulo for the Christian Democratic Party (Partido Democrata Cristão; PDC). Without administrative autonomy since the Estado Novo dictatorship, which was regained only in 1953, the capital was directed at that time by officers designated by the state government. Quadros became known for his harsh criticism and denunciations of corruption and mismanagement directed at the mayors designated by Barros and his party.

By raising the outlying districts' issues and problems in the Municipal Council, Quadros became one of the best known politicians in the city. He was probably the São Paulo politician who best understood how to address the growing demand for urban improvements, goods, and services by workers in the suburbs and the poor areas of the city. With his singular style, he made their demands into his battle flag, winning huge popularity and prestige by doing so.[81]

Quadros's speeches in the Municipal Council tribunal narrated and protested many of the problems the capital's workers faced daily. Among the issues constantly and vehemently denounced by Councilman Quadros were high prices, abuses by unscrupulous businesses, and delayed trains. Light, the company that had the concession to distribute electricity in the city at the time, was a frequent target. Quadros prioritized the popular neighborhoods as the center of his activity; as he politicized the residents' difficult daily routines and demanded their rights as inhabitants of the city, he increasingly appeared to be a kind of champion of the periphery of São Paulo.

But Quadros also innovated by not restricting public debate on such matters to the council. He regularly visited the various neighborhoods of São Paulo, watched the situation up close, listened to residents' demands and complaints, and became linked with a number of local organizations. Backed by the newspaper *A Hora*, Quadros publicized each area's burning issues, exposing them in the newspaper and reporting them with his usual inflammatory verve.

These neighborhood visits were his main source of raw material for political action as a councilman. In addition, they articulated a series of relationships and support in the local clubs and associations, allowing direct contact with a large number of workers, who were unaccustomed to seeing politicians up close outside of election time. Out of these contacts, Quadros forged an image as a different kind of politician—a simple, accessible man who was interested in the life and problems of the poor residents of the periphery. In her survey of the residents of a vila of São Miguel in the early 1980s, Teresa Caldeira reported the strong memories that former residents had of Quadros, who was the best remembered of the pre-1964 politicians in the neighborhood. He "remained represented," Caldeira wrote, "not only as a head of state who did things for the people, but as someone who was of the people, . . . who had popular origins and dressed in ordinary clothes, even with a dirty jacket, and he walked the neighborhoods 'drinking *pinga* out of a glass' with his constituents."[82] In the interviews I conducted, I also found several references to the identification that residents of São Miguel Paulista felt with Quadros. Artur Pinto de Oliveira, for example, remembered that "he arrived in São Miguel and came with a black overcoat, . . . eating a sandwich, going into the bar, and drinking pinga with the workers. . . . Even though he spoke impeccable Portuguese, he didn't come to the public square with university arrogance, like a doctor, a professor. No! He was one of the people. . . . He had a spotty overcoat, which the guys said was from the dandruff that fell from his hair. That overcoat was famous! And . . . his voice, his way of talking. . . . Everyone supported him."

An orator with his own style and sense of theater, Quadros adroitly manipulated the symbols and themes that identified him with the poorest parts of the city. From the time of his campaign for councilman in 1947, he realized the importance of direct contact with the public through meetings, visits, and rallies in the peripheral neighborhoods. The PCB's political experience in previous years had demonstrated to the various politicians who courted the same labor constituencies as Quadros how these meetings could pay off in terms of popularity and electoral results. Adriano Duarte commented that during Quadros's campaign for the mayoralty in 1953, "while his opponents were renting halls and holding rallies in enclosed spaces, with the audience sitting politely, Quadros went to where his voters were [with street rallies]."[83]

In addition to the political content, Quadros understood how to exploit the ludic character that workers around the periphery attributed to the rallies. Again, the testimony of Artur Pinto de Oliveira is revealing. He said that Quadros "held a rally here on the main square, the Praça Getúlio Vargas Filho. I came with my wife—at that time, she was my girlfriend—and with friends. There were even families who came to the rallies. . . . I went because at that time politics was something attractive . . . The life of São Miguel was political; it was the rallies they held in that square. Every Sunday during election season there was a rally there, and people went. I went, my wife, her brothers and sisters, friends . . . families."

By making the popular neighborhoods' demands the axis of his political activity, Quadros went deeper than even Barros had done in forging links and creating empathy with city workers. Although Barros could be seen as a benevolent politician, for residents of the periphery he was clearly an "other," a politician of the dominant moneyed classes who, unlike most of his peers, was concerned with the poor. But Quadros took it further. He was identified with the *povão* (the masses), someone who not only understood and shared workers' problems but was also willing to fight to the end for their resolution. Andrade explained Quadros's popularity in São Miguel by saying, "Jânio was so popular because he ate lunch when he got there. He showed up saying he hadn't eaten that day and took a bologna sandwich and ate it there at the rally. 'I'm just like you' [was the message he transmitted, and] that was a problem [for Adhemaristas]. . . . He made a great speech. He was a good orator."

Moreover, emphasizing honesty and the struggle for administrative morality as political banners, Quadros widened the gap in the popular imagination between himself and Governor Barros, who was considered corrupt. (Barros's supporters, for example, were the authors of the famous expression "Steals but does.") Even a faithful Adhemarista in São Miguel such as Augusto Ferreira Lima said that "Jânio Quadros was kind of hard-nosed, but he was honest. . . . He wanted certain things. . . . He was bad, but he was honest, and when a person wants to be honest, he himself is bad [sic]." Quadros understood how to capitalize on growing popular discontent with the ethical misconduct of the PSP's state government. "There was also a revolt that he preached: the moralization of public administration," added Arthur Pinto de Oliveira. "He was very strict in his decisions, in his administrations, and in his correct use of the public money."

Thus, an image was created of Quadros as a "moral authority" (which in practice often descended into authoritarianism). Many city residents, especially the poorest, saw him as a different kind of politician—one who was ethical and concerned with their problems and demands. As one analyst commented, "He created . . . his own image of 'conscious authority' and as a dispenser of vigilante justice, in whom the weak and the wronged could take refuge. With this image, he conquered the heart of the city."[84]

Although problems in the neighborhoods and peripheral areas, along with issues relating to administrative morality, were the central themes of Quadros's parliamentary action, he did not stint in his political support for the strikes and protests of workers against those he classified as "arrogant, greedy bosses," along with criticizing the repressive measures of the Dutra government against the trade union movement. Quadros also defended the northeastern migrants in the tribunal of the Municipal Council. In his speeches, he frequently denounced the precarious working conditions at various São Paulo companies and demanded that labor legislation be complied with, attacking Nitro Química, Celosul, Cimentos Perus, and Companhia Melhoramentos, among others. The workers of the last company, located in the neighborhood of Caieiras, came to him directly to present their complaints of maltreatment and the breach of labor laws by industry.[85]

As a congressman in the early 1950s, he defended the complaints of striking railroad and bank workers. The former union leader Luiz Tenório de Lima remembered that the great bank workers' strike of 1951 brought political advantage for Quadros. "He took advantage of the strike," Lima wrote. "He went out in front of the strikers and created a phrase that became famous: 'One more piece of bread for the bank workers; one less cigar for the bankers.'"[86]

In only a few years, this kind of political activity made Quadros one of the most popular public figures in the city. In 1950, he was the most voted-for candidate for the Legislative Assembly, with 17,840 votes. On the local political scene, Quadros's profile was positioned squarely on the left. He was close to the parliamentarians of the Brazilian Socialist Party (Partido Socialista Brasileiro; PSB), and although he declared himself an anticommunist, he garnered sympathy within the PCB for having defended strikes for higher wages and the peace movement that the party launched during the Korean War. Quadros also protested the arrest of the communist weaver Elisa Branco, who had been detained for participating in a demonstration against the sending of Brazilian troops to Korea.[87] So when the city of São Paulo regained its autonomy and mayoral elections were scheduled for March 1953, Quadros emerged as a politician who not only had a vast support network in the popular neighborhoods through local organizations such as Friends of Neighborhoods Societies (Sociedades de Amigos de Bairro, or SABs, as these neighborhood associations were known from the 1950s on), but who was also able to attract support from other political groups, such as the PSB, and a large sector of the PTB, which broke with the official candidacy of Francisco Antônio Cardoso and even supported the vice-mayoral candidate on Quadros's slate: General Porfírio da Paz.

In spite of this, the political world initially received Quadros's nomination for mayor of São Paulo as an act of bravado. Francisco Antônio Cardoso, the secretary of health in the government of Lucas Garcez, seemed unbeatable. Backed by a coalition of seven parties—the PSP, PSD, UDN, PTB, PRP, PR, and PRT—that brought together the main political forces in the state, Cardoso was the overwhelming favorite of the cabinet and of the press. The PCB endorsed the candidacy of André Nunes Júnior, a former PTB councilman who had supported the communist-inspired Autonomist Alliance for Peace and against High Prices. Nunes's vice-mayoral running mate was the PST's Nelson Rustici, president of the Textile Workers Union of São Paulo.

Using the slogan "A Penny against a Million," a reference to the economic resources of Cardoso's candidacy, and the symbol of the broom, Quadros's campaign synthesized the main themes of his career so far. He brought into the public debate the demands of the residents of the periphery, preached the moralization of administration, and thrilled the population of São Paulo with noisy rallies and impassioned speeches. His victory was overwhelming. The more peripheral the area of the city, the higher the number of votes Quadros received. He was defeated only in the rich neighborhood Jardim América. Analyzing the election, the sociologist and future president (1995–2002)

Fernando Henrique Cardoso would write that with Quadros, the periphery of the city (which Quadros jokingly called the "bottom of the barrel of society") "made itself known in public life." In total, he obtained 65.8 percent of the vote, versus 26.6 percent for Cardoso and 4.3 percent percent for Nunes.[88]

In São Miguel, Quadros had 74.5 percent of the vote, one of the highest levels in the city. The elections of 1953 made the neighborhood one of the principal Janista strongholds of São Paulo. From then on, Janism and Adhemarism polarized political disputes in São Miguel, as well as in the rest of the city and state, until the coup in 1964. With Quadros's mayoral victory, Barros was weakened in the capital. Some scholars even describe a "ruralization" of Adhemarism after 1953, referring to the fact that Barros and his PSP remained as the main political force outside the state capital. In any case, Barros, despite being defeated in the neighborhood in all of his direct disputes with Quadros, remained a very strong political leader in the area.[89]

The strength of the Janistas and Adhemaristas was evident in São Miguel, where the two councilmen elected in the second half of the 1950s and the early 1960s belonged to opposing political currents: Andrade (PSP) was tied to Adhemarism, while Bernardo (PTN) was a Janista. In 1954, when Quadros and Barros both ran for state governor against Prestes Maia (PDC, PSD, UDN, PR, and PRP) and Toledo Piza (PTB), the two combined received an impressive 88.4 percent of the neighborhood vote. Quadros, once again, had a sweeping triumph, with support from 7,177 local residents (65.7 percent of the total).[90]

Quadros's management of the mayoralty and the state government maintained the prestige he had gained as an opposition figure in São Miguel. Although São Miguel was not as well known as Vila Maria, the popular neighborhood considered his main political stronghold, Quadros also considered it one of his most loyal bases. When in 1954 he decided to run for state governor and entered into a conflict that ended with his breaking from the PDC, he read his supporters a document describing his version of the crisis with the PDC. In the message, he expressed gratitude for the solidarity he had received, particularly in "some meetings I had in São Miguel Paulista and in Parque Peruche."[91]

Having been elected by the peripheral neighborhoods, Quadros sought to deepen his relationship with the Friends of Neighborhood Societies and tried to develop a program to expand street lighting and public pavement, in addition to somehow responding to the suburban population's innumerable demands for urban goods and services. São Miguel seems to have been one of the neighborhoods that benefited from some improvements during Quadros's municipal management. For example, João Freitas Lírio, a neighborhood resident from 1950, called the election of Quadros a milestone for the area. Quadros "put down the asphalt on the street from the factory to the station," Lírio said. "With him, things started to improve." His moralizing actions in the administration also remained in the memory of many older residents. The dismantling of the PSP machine was celebrated by many.

In 1957, when the Nitro Química workers went on strike and the police violently repressed the strikers and the local population as a whole, when he learned about the situation, Quadros, then the governor, replaced the commander responsible for the action and ordered the arrest of the feared Lieutenant Valério, chief of security for the company, who had assaulted several workers. In addition, the government provided groceries for the striking workers. Quadros also played a decisive role in negotiating with the company's managers, who after several days of stoppage agreed to grant a wage increase. The strike, then, was considered widely successful, and Quadros further consolidated his prestige in the region. Not coincidentally, Joaquim Anselmo dos Santos, a former Nitro worker, believed that when Quadros "was governor of the state, [he] spoke the . . . language of rights."[92]

In the late 1950s and early 1960s, after a slate led by the communists was elected to run the Chemical Workers Union, followed by the victorious strike of 1957 at Nitro Química, the PCB again began to matter in the political life of the neighborhood, although it continued to be illegal. While it did not have the same strength it had in the period 1945–47, the Communist Party again distinguished itself in the local political game, with consequences even in the electoral field. The support of communist activists in São Miguel was decisive, for example, in the election of Rio Branco Paranhos as a councilman in 1959. Paranhos, an old-time communist militant known as a lawyer for unions and workers, including those of Nitro Química, ran as a PTB candidate and won 7,363 votes, mostly in São Miguel.[93] The communist Geraldo Rodrigues de Freitas recalled that "we elected Dr. Rio Branco Paranhos councilman with three days of campaigning [because] his candidacy was only allowed by the registrar three days before the election, and here in São Miguel there was a burst [of votes]." Rodrigues was referring to an attempt to prevent Paranhos's candidacy on the grounds that he could not run because he was a communist, which was disallowed by the electoral tribunal only a few days before the election.[94]

In 1960, the PCB was the only force that campaigned in São Miguel for Marechal Teixeira Lott, a presidential candidate on the PSD ticket, in alliance with the PTB. The campaign rally held in the neighborhood in June 1960, for example, brought together "about eight hundred people" and counted Prestes and Councilman-elect Paranhos Rio Branco among its participants, along with the Chemical Workers Union leaders Manoel de Almeida Montanhani and Adelço de Almeida, who used the opportunity to shout "*Vivas* for the PCB." Vava, the president of the local amateur soccer team Olaria, "addressed the treatment provided by the Nitro Química to its laborers, who live on a miserable salary, without assistance of any kind, dying, if not from want, then from the poisonous chlorine of the products manufactured there, which . . . is also killing the residents of São Miguel Paulista."[95]

The elections of 1960, however, once again demonstrated that Quadros was the great local political force. He ran for president on the ticket of the small PTN, with the support of the UDN, which saw in his candidacy the opportunity to finally defeat the PSD and PTB candidates who had won the three previous presidential elections: Dutra (PSD) in 1945, Vargas (PTB) in 1950, and Juscelino Kubitschek (PSD) in 1955.

Quadros's final campaign rally in São Miguel seems to have been an apotheosis, demonstrating his great support in the neighborhood. According to the report of a police agent, about 2,500 people attended the rally in Praça Um. When he arrived, Quadros "was borne by the crowd to the podium." He said he was tired, because he had just arrived from Pernambuco. From the outset he declared that Brazil wanted to be neither an American nor a Soviet colony. "We are Brazilians," he stated, and "we are ready to reach out to all people because we are friends of peace."[96] Aware of the large presence of migrants at the event, he made a number of references to poverty in the North. "From Minas down, people are still breathing," he said, "but from Minas on up, nobody walks without tears in their eyes." He attacked the federal government on the issue of education. "Do you know of any great nation inhabited by illiterates?" he asked. Finally, he asked for votes for a landslide victory, which he obtained. Quadros got 9,711 votes in São Miguel, about 50.5 percent of the total, versus 4,442 for Barros, the PSP candidate (23.1 percent), and 3,695 for Lott, candidate of the PSD-PTB coalition (19.2 percent). In the vice-presidential contest in São Miguel, at that time also decided by direct vote, Quadros's running mate, Milton Campos (UDN), had a slight advantage over Marechal Lott's running mate, João Goulart (PTB), although he was defeated nationally. Campos received 7,428 votes in São Miguel (38.6 percent); Goulart received 7,158 (37.2 percent).[97]

Andrade and Bernardo

Many analyses of São Paulo politics between 1945 and 1964 highlight the populist leaders' charisma and ability to manipulate voters as reasons for their success. One should not, however, disregard the decisive role of the networks of local contacts who defended and struggled for those leaders daily and, in electoral periods, mobilized to run the candidates' local campaigns.

In São Miguel, Janism and Adhemarism established networks of contacts and well-oiled political machines. A great rivalry between the groups of Councilman Andrade (PSP) and Councilman Bernardo (PTN) reproduced at the local level the disputes between Barros and Quadros. As the only peripheral neighborhood of the city that had two councilmen representing opposing currents of São Paulo politics, São Miguel was the scene of fierce clashes and tensions motivated by the local polarization. Despite political differences, however, a more detailed analysis of the action of these councilmen and groups shows great similarity between their practices and the sharing of a language for defending the interests of workers and representing the interests of the neighborhood and its "modest and poor laborers." The very presence of two councilmen elected by the area, with speeches and actions that were almost exclusively aimed at its residents, reinforced a notion of neighborhood identity, of a specific São Miguel community.

After becoming a figure of confidence for Barros and presiding over the PSP in São Miguel, Andrade was elected councilman in 1955. So began his very long career in the Municipal Council of São Paulo, to which he was reelected for nearly forty years. In his electoral debut, he received 3,309 votes.[98] Andrade had long since moved away from the PCB, but his past as a communist militant brought DOPS, after the election result, to investigate his ideological preferences. Since the agency only found references to his participation in the Communist Party during the 1940s, the police dossier did not result in the revocation of his victory. In the same year, 1955, Governor Quadros also requested an investigation of the newly elected councilman, addressing a note to the director of DOPS that asked him "to take appropriate steps against Aurelino Soares de Andrade, to be adopted with the utmost rigor." However, after reviewing the record of the investigation, Luiz de Godoy e Vasconcelos, deputy head of police intelligence, concluded that "at present no other measure can be taken against Aurelino Soares de Andrade than to put him under police surveillance [while waiting for] an opportunity for legal procedure."[99]

A year later, in the Municipal Council, Andrade fiercely criticized the actions of DOPS, which "has not done anything other than bring the worker to despair." Mindful of the police activity, Andrade continued,

> When [DOPS] gives information, with rare exceptions it's wrong. . . . Often it sends out a police investigator, a man who knows nothing about what he is doing, and because someone says at a public rally that a laborer is starving, this investigator will tell the police chief—counting on having made a "tag"—that the worker who said it is Communist. [For DOPS] every demand for good in this land is the work of communists, because whoever defends the worker is a communist; whoever speaks of unionism is a communist; whoever disagrees with the government is a communist; whoever does not agree with those in command is a communist. . . . In this country, whoever is decent is a communist.[100]

In the 1950s, several informal networks in the neighborhood played a fundamental role in the creation of Andrade's political group and his election as councilman. Many old-time residents who claimed to have voted for Andrade in that period reported having met and been friendly with him before he was elected. Maria José Oliveira Santos remembered that they met when both were workers at Nitro Química. "At lunchtime, we entered together in the factory," she said. "He was very outgoing, very talkative. I even worked for him in his first moments as a politician." Sebastião Azaria de Souza recalled meeting Andrade during his first campaign for councilman through a brother-in-law of Andrade's who "worked at Nitro Química and took him there to present him to the workers. Through the brother-in-law . . . I ended up voting for him." Antônio Xavier dos Santos had contact with Andrade through Aurelino Araújo. "They were very close," he said. "Araújo was a gentleman who had a bar in front of where I lived, and we used to play badminton in the street."

In addition to friendships and personal contacts, being northeastern seems to have weighed favorably for Andrade in his first elections. Having Vila Nitro Operária as a political base, with a high concentration of migrants in its population, Andrade repeatedly called attention to his origin, referring to himself as sertanejo and a "Bahian." Andrade himself admits that he owed his first victories to the broad vote he had among the northeasterners of the neighborhood. Nelson Bernardo, Tarcílio's brother and a fierce opponent of Andrade, remembered that in the 1950s many people decided to vote for Andrade, saying, "He's from the same place as me, so we'll go with him." Enoque Ribeiro had migrated from Piauí and became the owner of a dry and wet goods store in Vila Nitro Operária. Ribeiro was an influential figure in the large community of Piauienses in the area. His nephew Antônio Pereira da Mata recalled that Andrade "became his close friend [*compadre*], and at the time of the electoral campaign my uncle helped him." Da Mata remembered clearly that, in his first election living in São Miguel, his uncle told him, "Look, my son, we'll do our best here to elect our compadre Aurelino."

The political use of personal and informal relations presupposed an exchange, some kind of giveback by the candidate—especially, of course, if he was elected—and Andrade understood the rules of that game. Irene Ramalho, his faithful voter, said that when one of her cousins was leaving the Nitro Química plant and crossing the rail line, "a train hit him, and he died. Andrade bought things for his wife, who had a lot of children. . . . They brought bread for them every day, and that's how [Andrade] grew in people's opinion."[101]

After successive reelections, however, Andrade was perceived as not as close and accessible as he had been. "After he was elected, he became very different," said Maria José Santos Oliveira. "Politics is something, you know? They change." In the early 1960s, a Paraiban, Fausto Tomás de Lima, ran for the office of councilman and won the votes of many northeasterners in the neighborhood, taking away the uniqueness of Andrade's regional identification. Lima's campaign style emphasized the differences between him and Andrade, who claimed that "Fausto stood at the cemetery gate during the campaign. Whoever came, he gave them a hug. Fausto's situation allowed him to do what I did not. He signed onto anything, because he had nothing. And I, who had something, couldn't [just] sign [anything]. Then his followers said bad things about me."

For many voters, however, Lima's actions were similar to Andrade's in the past, before his election victories. Lima's behavior was regarded not as electioneering, as Andrade suggested in his testimony, but as the result of his simplicity and closeness to the people of São Miguel—characteristics that, in many people's eyes, Andrade had lost. Afonso José da Silva, for example, said that "Fausto was an excellent person. . . . [When he] was elected the first time, [he went to] the pharmacy next to Nitro Química and said, 'All my salary is to give medicine to the poor, to people who need it.' And he established a house to attend to the folks here, while [Andrade] did not help them." By acting in this way, Andrade broke one of the essential links of relationship between the population and the local politicians: accessibility. Speaking about his promise to vote for Lima, Afonso José da Silva said, "I want nothing. The only thing I want is, when I do ask for something, you attend to me."

Nevertheless, for many years Andrade was known as one of the candidates who represented the neighborhood. In his speeches in the Municipal Council, both he and Bernardo clearly identified themselves and were identified as councilmen of São Miguel. Nair Cecchini said that she voted for Andrade because he "was from here; he was the neighborhood's candidate." Waldomiro Macedo also voted for and rooted for Andrade, the "neighborhood's candidate for councilman."

The idea of belonging to the neighborhood was therefore basic to Andrade's political success. It assumed that relations of exchange and reciprocity existed not only among isolated individuals, but also among the community as a whole, struggling for attention to their demands from the Municipal Council and the executive authorities. When Andrade summed up his life as a representative, he highlighted his actions to bring "progress" to the neighborhood, repeatedly citing as his achievements the building of schools and the paving of streets. "When I got here," he said, "this area did not know what paving stones were, or asphalt. Today, it has the largest school system in Latin America." His constituents also emphasized the improvements Andrade brought. "Everything we have here in São Miguel," said Antônio Xavier dos Santos, "has Aurelino's hand in it."

Andrade was not the only politician identified with the neighborhood. Bernardo, São Miguel's first elected councilman, served on the Municipal Council for more than ten years. Although a partisan of Quadros, Bernardo developed a reputation of being a likable person and a negotiator. His disputes with Andrade were always fierce and polemical, however, and he did not hesitate to involve the political machinery of city and state government, particularly in the period between 1957 and 1958, when Barros and Quadros were concurrently mayor and governor. For instance, *Última Hora* reported in August 1958 that "Governor Jânio Quadros [had] dismissed all of the employees of the Health Center of São Miguel Paulista and immediately admitted, by the same act, political friends of the councilman of that *city*, Mr. Tarcílio Bernardo."[102] On the eve of the election, Bernardo demanded from Quadros the traditional "purge" of public servants to amplify his political power in the town. Many of the dismissed, in turn, were probably officials appointed by the local PSP to previous administrations.

Despite the Janistas' heavy majority in the region as of 1953, the total for the two local candidates was always quite close (see table 4.2).[103] With the rise of Quadros, many of Andrade's voters did not necessarily vote for Barros. That was the case with Antônio Xavier dos Santos, who said that "when Aurelino started in politics, I started working with him to help." However,

TABLE 4.2. Vote totals for São Miguel Paulista in elections between
Arelino de Andrade and Tarcílio Bernardo

	Election for councilman (1955)	Election for state deputy (1957)	Election for councilman (1959)
Aurelino de Andrade	3,309 votes	7,015 votes	6,283 votes
Tarcílio Bernardo	2,879 votes	7,397 votes	6,054 votes

despite Andrade's support, Santos never voted for Barros, because he "liked Jânio Quadros. I voted for Jânio a lot." Nelson Bernardo said that Quadros's popularity made it easier for his brother, Tarcílio, to capture votes from among Andrade's supporters than for Andrade to win votes from among Bernardo's supporters.

As we have seen, Bernardo's initial entry into the world of party politics was the result of his relations with the elite sectors of the neighborhood. But it was the support of the PSP, and principally his adherence to Janism, that opened the doors for him to seek more of the popular vote. Despite the personality differences between Andrade and Bernardo—and especially among the political currents that gave them support—their practices and performance styles were similar. Like Andrade, Bernardo and his group based much of their action in informal networks and in the contacts and personal relationships they constructed.

The various amateur soccer teams in the area played a central role in Bernardo's political campaigns. As privileged spaces for socializing among local residents, the teams not only demanded facilities for the game itself but often served as a sounding board for the complaints and demands of the towns and villages in which they were located.[104] Bernardo attended games in the region, helping the teams and establishing through them a network of key contacts for election time. Explaining how the relationship with the teams worked, Nelson Bernardo said that the campaign "had to be based in friendship. We always lived in the middle of soccer. So [Tarcílio] already had a base. And a sportsman is more expansive, he conversed, he would say: 'Hey, people,' and gather everyone together and say, 'You have to help me. Go into your friends' homes . . . . Go there to lend a hand. The comrade is with Aurelino? Go there. Convince him to go with me.'"

Like Andrade, however, Bernardo needed to appear to be always available to help his constituents and the people of the neighborhood as a whole. "My brother had a car that he adapted to function as an ambulance," Nelson continued. "He visited people. And there was one thing: he had no schedule. . . . He was always there for the *turma* [group]. If he had to go out with his family on Sunday and a problem appeared for him to solve, he would settle that first." Sebastião Azaria de Souza, a former constituent of the councilman, confirmed that "he was the one people most looked to for everything."

But the demands on Bernardo were not primarily individual. Far from being based solely on charisma, manipulation, and patronage, the relationship between São Miguel residents and politicians presupposed reciprocity. Attending to popular demands, particularly in terms of services and goods for the various villages and poor regions, was essential for the continuation of support. Because they represented the neighborhood and lived in it, councilmen played a particularly vital role in moving forward and fighting for attention to the demands of the community. For a local politician, it was not enough to live in the neighborhood; it was necessary to establish a relationship of belonging, which assumed a sharing of experiences. Relations of identity based on class and regional origin could also generate or strengthen links between residents and representatives.

In any case, residents increasingly realized that in the still incipient democratic game of the time, it was not enough for people who lived in peripheral neighborhoods, far from the centers of political and economic power, to elect representatives. It was also necessary to pressure the representatives and demand their rights as workers. Residents sent a large number of petitions seeking neighborhood improvements to their councilmen and to authorities in general. In September 1956, Councilman Andrade spoke in the Municipal Council claiming to have received "a petition from the residents of various vilas of São Miguel Paulista" pleading for a change in "the schedule of the bus line of Vila Curuçá and also the places where the bus stops." In another speech, years later, Andrade commented on another "petition signed by a large number of residents of São Miguel Paulista, Itaquera, and Guainazes who are suffering the consequences of rationing by the [electrical utility] Light." In September 1960, Rio Branco Paranhos mentioned a "submission with nearly 1,500 signatures [on] forty-four signed pages" that read, in part, "The undersigned residents of São Miguel Paulista respectfully solicit the Council's . . . collaboration in solving the most agonizing problem of our neighborhood: air pollution by Nitro Química. Councilman Paranhos, here we can no longer breathe. The chlorine kills our plants, attacks our domestic animals, and poisons children, whose mortality here is simply terrifying."[105]

Residents' committees and neighborhood organizations were also common, such as the one created "with the support of the Chemical Workers Union and all the organizations of São Miguel Paulista, Itaquera, and Guaianazes" to pressure the Municipal Council to intercede, together with the Ministry of Labor, for the "creation of an [Institute of Industrial Workers' Retirement and Pensions] post in São Miguel." Another "committee of residents of several villages of São Miguel Paulista" went in the company of Councilman Tarcílio Bernardo for an audience with the governor at Palácio dos Campos Elísios, "demanding several improvements to this dense region." In the late 1950s, with the increase of residents' organizations in the local vilas, the pressure on councilmen became even more direct. As Nelson Bernardo recalled, "[When] vila organizations began to appear, they asked for some things, asked to fix the street, asking for I don't know what."[106] The next chapter examines how these "vila organizations" emerged and what their importance was in the political and social life of São Paulo—and, in particular, in the neighborhood of São Miguel.

CHAPTER FIVE

Workers and the Neighborhood
Social Movements and the Struggle for Autonomy

Neighborhood Friends

One of the most striking political phenomena of the 1950s in the peripheral areas of São Paulo was the proliferation of popular organizations. One analyst, impressed by the number of neighborhood organizations in São Paulo at that time, characterized the city as a "hotbed of social movements."[1]

The best-known neighborhood organization of the period, the Friends of Neighborhood Societies (SABs), began to take shape in the late 1940s and 1950s and gained public prominence when they played a key role in the victorious mayoral campaign of Jânio Quadros. From then on, São Paulo had to take the SABs and their demands into account.

Aware of this, Quadros's successor as mayor, Toledo Piza, who had also been supported by several SABs, sought to deepen his relations with the neighborhood organizations, probably with the intention of creating a broad political movement around his name and at the same time mitigating the impact of their demands during his term. Arguing for greater integration between the organizations and the city, Piza made district councils the official representative bodies of the neighborhoods' residents. There were already organizations called "district councils" in some areas. When he signed the new law in August 1956, Piza stated that, "with the institutionalization of the district councils, neighborhoods will have multiple benefits once their representatives are in daily contact with the mayor." But in fact, the government action sought to control the existing organizations in each area, taking away their autonomy and reducing the influence of the SABs in particular. The draft formulated by the Mayor's Office of the assembly act founding the district councils was explicit in its attempt to weaken the SABs. When referring to the debate about the name of the new association, it said, "Several names are being proposed, among them 'Society of Friends . . .', 'Union of . . .', 'District Council of . . .', etc. . . . By absolute majority the decision was made that with the name 'District Council of . . . ,' [the new organizations] would not be confused with the various existing associations and would convey the idea of a neighborhood advisory body."[2]

The reaction was immediate. Even though the mayor organized a large number of councils, most SABs were reluctant to participate in a process that, in practice, would cost them some of their autonomy. Initially, the PCB came to support the formalization of the district councils. Speaking on the day Ordinance 152 was signed, Mathilde de Carvalho, a councilwoman linked to the Communist Party, praised the councils and argued that there was no opposition between them and the SABs. "The [district councils] are not opposed but greatly collaborate with these organizations," she said. She noted the danger that the city government could try to put the district councils "into its electoral service," but nevertheless, she concluded, they "are not owned by the mayor." After Ordinance 152 was published, the PCB criticized it harshly, arguing that it gave excessive power to the mayor and hurt "the very essence of the district councils . . . , namely, their autonomy in relation to the public powers and any current political party."[3] The councils would not survive to the end of Piza's mayoralty in early 1957, and in the late 1950s the SABs became the main neighborhood organizations in São Paulo.

In his analysis, Francisco Weffort considered the PCB one of the main forces maintaining the official union structure and in the consequent harnessing of the unions by the state. Starting from a similar interpretative viewpoint, José Álvaro Moisés argues that in supporting the creation of district councils, the communists were reproducing at the local level their system of political institutionalization, which tied popular organizations into the state's apparatus. However, the reaction of the PCB to Piza's decree significantly weakens this interpretation.[4]

The year 1957 seems to have been a particularly important one for the SABS in São Paulo. The Federation of São Paulo Neighborhood Friends Societies (FESAB), which had been created in 1954,[5] became stronger and started to structure a more constant mode of joint action by several societies. In July 1957, FESAB sponsored a convention of the São Paulo SABS. In addition to coordinating common action "toward obtaining immediate general improvements, or local improvements such as transportation, housing supply, water, electricity, sewers, sidewalks, post offices, telephone, public health, education, [and] sports," the convention demanded the right to participate in the organizations of the "master planner of the city . . . and the administration of [the municipal transport company]" and the formation of a "consumers' cooperative for metropolitan São Paulo" to alleviate supply problems in the city. Furthermore, FESAB was tasked with asking "the present mayor [Adhemar de Barros] to repeal outright" Ordinance 152, which instituted the district councils. Finally, the SABS proposed a series of measures to expand neighborhood organizations in the city and to more widely disseminate their actions, using, for example, "the great spoken newspaper of [Radio] Tupi, at night or in the morning." The resolutions continued: "If need be, the federation would have meetings, rallies, visits, etc., in order to encourage residents of the visited neighborhood to found a Society of Friends."[6]

On September 8, 1957, FESAB held a rally in São Miguel aimed at combating the "increase in private [bus] companies' fares and calling for the creation of intermediate lines." The rally attracted seven hundred people, among them Councilmen João Louzada and Molina Júnior, as well as Aurelino de Andrade and Tarcílio Bernardo. All of the representatives "told those present that everything would be done to repeal the act that authorized such an increase and that governments must do what they promise, since the people demand it." As their demands grew, the neighborhood residents became strong enough to force traditionally iron-clad adversaries in local politics to be present on the same platform.[7]

The neighborhood organizational efforts showed results. Two months after that meeting, a new convention brought together SABS from the city's east side. Representatives of forty local organizations gathered in Penha for five days to debate the main problems and demands of the residents of that area of the city, and to prepare a common plan of action for area SABS.

Besides members of the societies, Councilmen João Louzada and Agenor Mônaco attended the closing rally, as did representatives of Mayor Adhemar de Barros (1957–61). Commenting on the meeting in the Municipal Council tribunal, Councilman Louzada said that "the people are already realizing that in order for [the politicians] to comply with what they promised at election time, their unity, their organization was necessary." The DOPS agent who attended the convention at Penha appeared most worried about the "almost exclusively political activity of [these] organizations, so that it has been worthwhile for the Brazilian Communist Party to infiltrate its elements into these 'societies,' where they find fertile ground for the spread of their nefarious program."[8]

It was, however, the Strike of 400,000 in October 1957 that marked a turning point toward closer relationships between neighborhood organizations and the union movement. The growth in communist influence and of various popular and nationalist political factions pointed toward a connection between unions and SABs, but it was the perception of a common language and agenda of demands, in which workers acted as city residents, that strengthened the bonds of unity among these organizations.

In early 1957, the presence of neighborhood organizations at a meeting convened by the Inter-Union Unity Pact (Pacto de Unidade Intersindical; PUI) to discuss "the increasing cost of living in São Paulo" did not escape the notice of the U.S. consul in São Paulo. The PUI was created in 1953, bringing together the majority of the more militant trade unions in São Paulo. It consolidated an alliance between trade union leaders connected to the PCB, which was then illegal but was very active in the factories and neighborhoods, and those tied to the Brazilian Workers' Party (PTB), with its Vargas-linked origins and, at that moment, increasing identification with Vice-President João Goulart. However, the presence in the PUI of labor leaders without ties to those parties or who were allied with other politicians—for example, Governor Jânio Quadros (1955–59) of São Paulo—was significant. In addition to the defense of workers' interests, the discourse that held such broad alliances together inside the PUI was permeated with nationalism and anti-imperialism.

In late 1957, the alliance between neighborhood associations and unions was strengthened. Several SABs positioned themselves in favor of the PUI program in defense of workers' rights and against high prices. In the middle of the October strike, FESAB issued a manifesto of solidarity to the working men and women, because the "SABs are made up of an absolute majority of workers of all classes and professions . . . , and the struggle for cheapening the cost of living is inherent in all people." During the strike, the neighborhoods were one of the main stages of aid and support for the stoppage, while popular participation in picket lines and demonstrations far exceeded the most optimistic forecasts.[9]

The tightening of relations between neighborhood movements and unions continued in the following years. In June 1958, a new meeting of FESAB, which by then boasted 196 popular associations, discussed not only earlier demands, such as paving the peripheral streets, but also the "formation of a united front of action, between [neighborhood] organizations, the PUI, and the State Student Union."[10] Problems of the neighborhood and demands of city residents were also discussed by the unions, as in a meeting held at the bank workers' union at which union leaders and SABs discussed "the project of Councilman Norbert Mayer Jr. about the contract renewal" of the Brazilian Telephone Company. Issues such as supply problems and cooperatives began to enter the agenda at PUI meetings.[11]

In February 1959, FESAB organized a large, statewide conference against the high cost of living, bringing together representatives of "nearly three hundred societies from São Paulo and the ABC municipalities—Santos, Guarulhos, and Mogi das Cruzes." The meeting culminated in the drafting of a "memorial on the subject" to be delivered to President Juscelino Kubitschek. In July of the same year, FESAB promoted the first Neighborhood Sports Festival. In addition to electing "queens and princesses" of sport, the festival featured trophies for "clubs and participating athletes . . . , with the silver 'João Goulart' cup going to the first-place Santa Terezinha Football Club. . . . Several elements that distinguished themselves during the campaign were also honored, among them Lourival Rodrigues Rocha, for the general organization of the festival and as a representative of Sport Club Guarani, of Itaim," in São Miguel Paulista. Councilmen of various parties were present, along with representatives of former Deputy Governor Porfírio da Paz and of Vice-President Goulart.[12]

The high cost of living was one of the themes that united neighborhood associations and unions. In the late 1950s, these organizations jointly organized several protests against inflation, the loss of purchasing power of wages, and widespread impoverishment. In June 1959, for example, the British Consulate's labor attaché reported preparations for a "hunger march" that would lead a caravan of "trade unionists, students and members of neighborhood associations" to Rio de Janeiro. This growth of FESAB and of neighborhood movements in São Paulo worried the authorities, and when the organization actively participated in the planning of a strike movement in December, the Ministry of Justice drafted a decree to close it and other SABs for ninety days, but the decree never became effective.[13]

The experience of the SABs and of the São Paulo unions in the late 1950s and early 1960s demonstrates a much greater political connection between the worlds of work and urban issues than that to which the general literature has admitted. Fernando Henrique Cardoso, Cândido Procópio, and Lúcio Kowarick emphasize that in the 1950s and 1960s, "as a rule workers were absent from political life at the level of urban demands. . . . It was not the habit of the unions . . . to put issues of urban problems into their programs, [and] it cannot be said that the Neighborhood Friends Societies were representative of the workers. They represented much more the resident, a specific social category that the city created and whose action during the metropolitaniza-tion of São Paulo mitigated, if not dissolved, their class behavior." Thus, they conclude, "Most residents of São Paulo remained politically on the margins of municipal life." José Álvaro Moisés also believes that "for a long time," the unions did not express interest "in the complaints about urban living conditions by their members."[14]

But, in fact, at various times the workers and their organizations were able to unify their demands, erasing in practice the boundaries between the struggles of the factories and those of the neighborhoods. This supposed division between worker and resident, emphasized by these scholars, was in fact often overcome by political action based on a much broader notion of class that embraced various dimensions of life of working men and women in São Paulo.

São Miguel Paulista saw an increase in the number of neighborhood associations in the late 1950s and early 1960s. As has been mentioned, mobilizations and organizations in the neighborhood already had a long history. But this strong local associativity, based on informal relationships and on various existing social networks, was not always translated into the construction of permanent organizations. An organizational discontinuity permeated the tra-jectory of various social movements of the city, although this rarely meant the absence of struggle for rights.

Leisure activities often could be the basis for protest movements. Accord-ing to Waldomiro Macedo, "Many recreational associations made protest movements." In soccer teams, as Nelson Bernardo explained, it was common for "the people to strike up [a discussion of] politics" and the problems of the neighborhood.[15] Autonomous initiatives of the residents could turn into public protests. The Friends of Jardim São Vicente Society, for example, was founded in the late 1950s out of a mutirão created to pave the neighborhood's two main streets. From there, a resident recalls, "We kept asking the city and the state for lighting, paving, a market, and school, and we got it."[16]

The Friends of São Miguel Center (CASM), the oldest neighborhood organization that we know of there, was also founded out of a recreational society, the Esporte Clube São Miguel. In August 1945, the newspaper *O Estado de São Paulo* announced, "The Friends of São Miguel Center has reopened, which aims to help the development of that suburb."[17] Nelson Bernardo remembered that the association "had dances, parties . . . , but also protested about things on behalf of São Miguel." The organization, however, had a restrictive membership policy. Probably inspired by the Friends of the City Society, an organization founded in São Paulo in 1934 by professionals and members of old Paulista families interested in "looking after the interests of the city," the CASM restricted its membership to those considered traditional neighborhood families. "The vast majority of the board of CASM," recalled José Caldino Filho, "were also employees [at management and professional levels] at Nitro Química." Thus, the CASM's cliquish character seems to have taken precedence over protest, and the organization never bothered to broaden its representation to other social sectors of São Miguel.[18]

A process of forming local residents' organizations in the various towns that appeared across the region intensified in the late 1950s. From then on, the axis of organization of residents shifted from the center of São Miguel to the surrounding vilas and jardins. No single organization could now claim to represent all of the residents of growing, diversifying São Miguel. Jorge Gonçalves Lula, for example, remembered that by 1959, shortly after he moved to Jardim São Vicente, "Some guys had already brought the idea to us, and a society came out of it. . . . The society got us water, got us electricity. . . . It organized a lot of things." Back then, he said, "every vila [in São Miguel] had a society."

Union activists and communists played a preeminent role in stimulating the organization of many of these neighborhood associations, especially after the victory in 1956 of a Chemical Workers Union leadership slate with strong communist and nationalist influence. As the main popular organization of São Miguel, the union not only provided political support but also was able to collaborate with other movements in terms of infrastructure and logistical support from its local headquarters. In addition, a majority of the union leadership was composed of activists who lived in São Miguel and often were also involved in neighborhood protests. The legitimacy gained by the union after the strike at Nitro Química in October 1957 further favored the central role of the organization in the social struggles of the region.

The Nitro stoppage is an important moment for understanding the connections between workers' social networks in the factory and those in the neighborhood. For ten days, men and women put down their tools to demand a wage increase and better working conditions. The strike was strongly repressed by the police in its early days, with various scenes of violence documented throughout the area. Nevertheless, the strike remained strong and, with the mediation of the regional labor chief and Governor Quadros, the workers won a 20 percent raise, which they considered a victory.[19] But the strike went far beyond the limits of the company. Almost the entire neighborhood was involved in the movement. With the support of most residents, pickets took over the streets of São Miguel. Informal contacts and social networks of workers played a decisive role in the formation of the pickets and in the expansion of the stoppage.[20]

The local office of the Chemical Workers Union was transformed into a headquarters, where workers and the public gathered, organized, and made decisions regarding the strike. The solidarity movement expressed itself not only by participating in pickets and meetings, but also in mutual aid, such as assembling a collective kitchen and dining hall that replaced the company restaurant during the strike. It was "damned enthusiastic," recalled Augusto Ferreira Lima. "All night, the union office was packed with people, . . . not only workers but residents of São Miguel."

Santos Bobadilha was one of the communist activists most involved in organizing neighborhood associations in the late 1950s and the 1960s. Bobadilha, the director of the Food Workers Union in São Paulo, lived in Jardim São Vicente, São Miguel, where he was one of the founders of the local society. Joaquim Anselmo dos Santos said that he and Bobadilha helped found "about thirty Neighborhood Friends Societies" around 1964. For many left-wing activists and sympathizers, these neighborhood associations became a form of possible participation after the military coup of 1964, when, despite the repression, local conditions were favorable for this type of activity. The administration of Mayor Faria Lima (1965–69), elected mainly thanks to the support of sectors politically connected to Quadros, paved the way for the foundation of, and government dialogue with, the societies and the creation of the regional administrations, a long-standing demand of the neighborhood organizations, opened up the possibility for greater communication and community pressure on municipal government.[21]

Joaquim Anselmo dos Santos recalled that, after the coup, "Most people were afraid of unions. The union was revoked and the people did not go there." For many, neighborhood associations became the best—and sometimes, the only—avenue for political action. The former communist militant Manuel Caçador remembered that in 1964, "Everything was oppressed . . . ; everything was clandestine. So I organized a society [Friends of Parque Paulistano] because there it wouldn't be so easy for them to catch me." In the vilas and around the neighborhood, people were favorably disposed to the organization, and there was enormous demand for popular power. Santos recounted how he and Bobadilha helped create the societies:

> Our people arrived in the neighborhood and already knew more or less the people who stood out there. Those who sometimes went to the regional [administration] to make some complaint about the disorder in our neighborhoods, things like open manholes, ditches, holes in the streets . . . , that kind of thing. In those days, it was good to do that. It wasn't a good time for party politics, but you could do a movement to make complaints together with the regionals. Even in our vilas, we got a lot of things . . . electricity, asphalt.

The political and social repression that was unleashed nationally in 1968, when the dictatorship became much more oppressive, had considerably slowed the organizational momentum in the neighborhoods by the beginning of the 1970s. "People were afraid to go to the discussions because there was that business that we could not assemble, so we couldn't organize anything," Santos recalled. But later in the 1970s, when new social movements spread in São Paulo, it was no accident that São Miguel once again became one of the most active, participative areas of the city. A long, subterranean organizing tradition in the neighborhood supplied material for "dialogue" with these new activists and organizations.

"Neighborhood or City?" The Struggles for Autonomy

On the afternoon of June 16, 1962, Osvaldo Pires de Holanda and ten other residents of São Miguel gathered in the center of the neighborhood to found the Popular Autonomist Movement of São Miguel Paulista (Movimento Popular Autonomista; MPA). Holanda, who chaired the meeting, explained that the movement's aim was the "separation of São Miguel Paulista from the city of São Paulo, to become an autonomous municipality," since it was not possible that the neighborhood could continue in the condition it was in, "completely forgotten by the central administration, left to its own devices." The MPA worked for a referendum among area residents on administrative autonomy for the district and to convince the majority of the population to vote for the autonomy of São Miguel. Its statutes, approved just over a month after its inception, established that the MPA would be composed of an "unlimited number of partners" whose commitment was to "fight for the autonomy of São Miguel Paulista," uniting "the neighborhood residents to take action to cooperate with future administrations of the 'city' and press for local improvements."[22] Indeed, the struggle to transform the bairro into a city excited many residents during the following months. Dozens of meetings, demonstrations, rallies, and other activities seeking autonomy were held, mobilizing the local population in a debate over the community's future.

The debate over autonomy was not new; nor was it exclusive to São Miguel. Throughout the 1950s and 1960s, a series of movements demanding the emancipation of popular districts and neighborhoods emerged in various parts of the metropolitan region of São Paulo. According to Moisés, between 1940 and 1964, there were "no fewer than 17 cases of peripheral districts that wanted to become autonomous" in São Paulo and surrounding municipalities.[23] These movements had in common the idea that their areas had been abandoned and that only with legal emancipation would it be possible to bring local power to bear on the population's real needs. The defenders of autonomy commonly believed that the distribution of public funds by the Mayor's Office was strongly unfair, favoring the rich central neighborhoods at the expense of the poor periphery.

In compliance with the Constitution of 1946, a district demanding political and administrative emancipation had to ask the Legislative Assembly to authorize a referendum; if the referendum was defeated, there was a five-year waiting period before a new popular vote could be held. However, even when autonomy was approved by a majority of local voters, political and legal resistance was common on the part of municipal mayoralties affected by secession. They tried to prevent the dismemberment of their territory and the consequent loss of contingent population and economic resources. As a result, a campaign for autonomy required large, ongoing popular mobilization, with strong legal support and political pressure.

This was the case of Osasco, probably the most successful example of an autonomous district in the state capital. After its defeat in a first referendum held in 1953, local autonomists regrouped and were victorious in a new round in 1958. The city of São Paulo appealed, and after a long legal and political battle, which resulted in an impressive popular mobilization, Osasco finally separated from the capital, becoming an autonomous city in 1962, when for the first time it elected mayor and councilmen.

The struggle of the MPA in São Miguel was not new. In 1953, a referendum over administrative autonomy for the district mobilized the community's attention. Led, among others, by Councilman Tarcílio Bernardo, who was then the sole representative of the neighborhood in the Municipal Council, the autonomists of São Miguel formed a broad alliance that included merchants, workers, Adhemarist and Janist politicians, and communist activists. *Folha de São Miguel*, the region's first newspaper, founded that same year by Antônio Mendes Correa, promptly joined the campaign for the emancipation of the neighborhood. On November 28, 1953—the eve of the referendum—the paper's front-page headline read, "Autonomy or Death to São Miguel." The paper justified its position in an editorial that affirmed the abandonment of the area by the municipal administration, noting that the area lacked "everything, starting with transportation to the capital. . . . No one can show us one accomplishment worthy of praise, where public authorities have invested one miserable cruzeiro. . . . The millions of cruzeiros that the city of São Paulo takes from here provide employment in distant neighborhoods for the furtherance of ends unknown and foreign to our people." Defending a "yes" vote for autonomy, the paper made a special call to migrants, saying, "You have a duty to the place that welcomed you and to your children who were born here."[24]

Similar arguments were repeated at the large rally organized by autonomists in downtown São Miguel on October 25. More than 1,500 people crowded into the Praça Um to attend the public act, according to the DOPS agent assigned to the event. A large banner that read "To Vote against Autonomy Is to Betray the Progress of São Miguel" graced the podium, on which were assembled politicians from various parties, including the president of the Municipal Council, Cantídio Sampaio of the Progressive Social Party (PSP). Almost all of the speeches emphasized the neglect of São Miguel. Dr. Alberto Fonseca Santana, the president of the pro-autonomy commission, for example, reminded his listeners of the absence of "schools, hospitals, and so many other things São Miguel needs." José Augusto Mutti, president of the Friends of Ermelino Matarazzo Society, said the area was "stripped of everything. . . . We don't have a sports plaza. . . . We don't have schools, hospitals. In short, we have nothing. But we will achieve all this through autonomy."

Autonomy was seen as a way to solve local problems, since tax revenue paid by residents—and especially by Nitro—would be applied to the neighborhood. Another speaker, Miguel dos Santos, hit that point. "We need autonomy," he stated, "since this is a district where more than four million cruzeiros are collected and is neglected by those who don't want to know about São Miguel. They don't spend even twenty thousand of that four million here. If we need autonomy it is so this revenue can be spent on schools, hospitals, and sanitation services so that our children and families can have what many districts that do not have this revenue already have."

Anxious to counter the anti-autonomists' arguments, the speakers at the rally denounced as "lies" the claims that if "São Miguel has autonomy, workers' wages will be reduced." The representative of the PDC, the party of Mayor Jânio Quadros, stated that the neighborhood should not fear losing Quadros as a protective friend, since he would soon be elected again, and "you will then have the freedom to deal directly with the governor through your mayor."[25]

The autonomists' concerns were reasonable. But proponents of keeping São Miguel part of the city of São Paulo were also very organized, and their range of support covered an equally broad spectrum of political parties and forces. A pamphlet calling for a "no autonomy" rally was signed by councilmen and members of various parties.[26] Their campaign based its appeal not merely on the support of politicians, but also on the supposed disadvantages and dangers that autonomy would bring, generating fear among residents of the neighborhood. Another pamphlet, signed by Pedro Monteiro, accused autonomists of "only wanting positions and government jobs" and listed reasons that one should vote against autonomy for São Miguel. In addition to arguing that the future municipality would start out in debt, Monteiro insisted that taxes would be higher, raising the prices of basic necessities, transportation, and gasoline. Making a direct appeal to the great majority of local electors who had voted for Quadros eight months earlier, he said, "The present municipal government . . . merits the people's confidence. . . . What we must do and ask for insistently is that they attend to the needs of São Miguel, applying more funds on improvements here, which in other mayoralties divorced from the population they have not done."[27]

The anti-autonomists' rally was marked by sharp conflicts with pro-autonomists. "When the speakers were talking, they were constantly booed by the large audience, in the middle of which constant fighting has been confirmed," a DOPS agent later recounted. A "group of anarchists [among them Aurelino de Andrade, president of the local PSP; Mordecai Schmidt, a former PCB member; and the dentist Cristovam Colombo Fleury] started throwing rotten eggs, potatoes, [and] corn," forcing an end to the anti-autonomy rally.[28]

The greatest damage to popular support for autonomy was caused by rumors that the municipality of São Miguel would be considered part of the "interior," and therefore the index in force for the minimum wage (which was different for the capital from that for other regions of the state) would be lowered. This issue must have resounded among the large working population, as shown by the autonomists' argument in rebuttal to the "No" campaign that wages had remained the same in São Caetano do Sul after it was emancipated in the 1940s.

In addition, Nitro Química's proactive stance against the autonomy movement seems to have been a key factor in defeating the referendum. The day after the defeat, the pro-autonomy State Deputy Rogê Ferreira of the Brazilian Socialist Party denounced to the press that "the coercion exerted by the owners of Nitro Química in São Miguel Paulista against the electorate of that district was the most disgraceful possible. They required their workers to vote 'no'; made demagogic promises; rented in advance all taxis. Plus, the polling place was on the company's premises instead of in state buildings. . . . A disgrace!"[29] Many residents attribute the defeat of the pro-autonomy forces in 1953 to the pressure exerted on workers by Nitro's management. José Caldini Filho said that Nitro's management was against autonomy because it feared a greater challenge to its power in the neighborhood. In his view, the company "gave the orders in São Miguel. The councilman was from Nitro; everything was from Nitro. It ran everything. It was afraid that if São Miguel became a municipality, the mayor and the councilmen could form a front against Nitro Química, and they stood to lose a little of their power here. So they directed a campaign against it."

Quadros also did not make any effort to bring about autonomy, contrary to his campaign promises to support autonomist movements in various parts of the city, especially in Osasco. Once in power, Quadros sought to postpone any decision that would involve territorial division and loss of revenue for São Paulo. In spite of the support for autonomy by local Janists such as Tarcílio Bernardo, Quadros tried not to get involved in the debate, and, some said, he supported the campaign against it from behind the scenes. When Councilman José Diniz of the PSP evaluated the autonomist campaign in São Miguel a few years later, he would note that "Mayor [Quadros], newly elected . . . , got operatives to work with the people of São Miguel . . . against the elevation of that district to municipality status."[30]

In any case, the autonomy debate polarized the neighborhood, reinforcing its local and community identity and bringing up the population's dissatisfaction with their poor living conditions. At the same time, it clearly showed a pressure for the extension of democracy at the local level and a popular mobilization for citizenship that went beyond the labor and trade union field.

Urban needs, then, were a magnet that brought people together in the struggle for rights.

Five years later, in 1958, when the voters of São Miguel were once again called on to decide on autonomy, the pressure in favor of autonomy seemed weaker. The impact of the autonomist wave of 1953, however, required action by the political forces of São Paulo. In those years, debates on sub-mayoralties, administrative decentralization, and ways to bring the city to the poorest neighborhoods were constantly on the agenda of discussions at the Mayor's Office and the Municipal Council. In addition, neighborhood organizations came to assume a central role in municipal politics, demanding that the periphery's needs be addressed.

In the specific case of São Miguel, the existence of two councilmen from the neighborhood after 1955 responded somewhat to autonomist demand by placing local representatives in the spheres of power and decision making and must have mitigated the drive for autonomy in the minds of many residents. The campaign of 1958 was much weaker and attracted fewer followers. The local PSP, which had supported autonomy in 1953, changed its position; Councilman Andrade led a public campaign against autonomy. On the eve of the referendum in December 1958, Mayor Adhemar de Barros opened a bus line from São Miguel to the center of São Paulo, managed by the municipal transport company (with lower rates than lines controlled by private companies), but explicitly conditioned its maintenance on the defeat of autonomy. Quadros once again stayed out of the debate, despite the continued support by his faithful political colleague Tarcílio Bernardo for the autonomist cause.

In the low-turnout referendum on December 12, 85 percent of voters (2,740 votes) were against autonomy, with 426 in favor; 23 ballots were left blank, and 20 were spoiled.[31] Two months earlier, 17,679 citizens of the district had voted in elections for governor, the Senate, the National Congress, and the Legislative Assembly. Of these, only 3,209 (about 18 percent) bothered to vote on autonomy for São Miguel. The same day as the São Miguel referendum, eight more districts of São Paulo and neighboring municipalities held autonomy referendums, and in five of them (Cajamar, Embu, Osasco, Pirapora do Bom Jesus, and Taboão da Serra), autonomy won.

The autonomy project in São Miguel did not die, however. Four years after the landslide defeat of 1958, circumstances seemed more favorable to creating a new municipality. The strong mobilization and the victory of the autonomists in Osasco served as an example and gave a strong stimulus to those who preached the emancipation of their districts in various parts of the metropolitan region of São Paulo. The new mayor of Osasco, Hirant Sanazar, and several councilmen of the newly created municipality gave their explicit support to the various autonomist movements in São Paulo and bragged about the supposed improvements and development of Osasco as demonstrations of the success of separation. At an autonomist rally in São Miguel in June 1963, Sanazar attacked those who opposed secession and reminded his listeners that

> for four years, the stepmother São Paulo did nothing for Osasco, but only took care of elegant neighborhoods. . . . Today, Osasco contributes revenue of 808 million [cruzeiros] and gets back around 30 percent. . . . Today we have thirty asphalt streets. Before we had three ambulances taken out of service by the city of São Paulo, and even school desks and tractors, which are essential to the people, were removed. In fourteen months, we bought fourteen new cars, and street cleaning is no longer done with donkey carts. We have a new emergency aid service and new ambulances. We have a cancer facility and the works and services sector reaches 70 percent of the area. . . . We constructed five kilometers of sewers. . . . Autonomy means redemption.[32]

With its underlying debate about local democracy and urban problems, autonomy seemed to relate directly to the climate of change and mobilization motivated by proposals during the government of João Goulart for *Reformas de Base* (Basic Reforms). These were a platform of grassroots and nationalist policies, such as land, educational, and constitutional tax reforms, which were intended to promote social and economic development from a left-wing perspective. So when someone requested at an MPA meeting that speakers "confine themselves only to the problem of autonomy, leaving aside other issues, such as, for example, the Basic Reforms," Geraldo Rodrigues de Freitas and José Firmino dos Reis argued against the request, apparently with the support of the majority of those present, explaining that "the Basic Reforms are tied to the problem of autonomy."[33]

The transformations that São Miguel went through, along with the residents' continued difficulties in resolving basic urban needs, motivated the autonomists to reflect on the future of the area and to consider development alternatives. Nitro Química was no longer seen as a guarantor of progress, and its domination of life in the neighborhood was called into question. In the early 1960s, when Nitro could no longer provide jobs for the neighborhood's growing population, the autonomy movement was seen by many as a way to criticize the company's monopoly in the region while opening the possibility of attracting new businesses and jobs. Speaking at an MPA rally in 1963,

Osvaldo de Souza, who had lived for many years in São Miguel, commented on "how easy new industries will find it to move into São Miguel, since taxes will be lighter, and for that it is necessary to have autonomy. With new jobs coming in the door, we'll get away from those packed trains; we'll have paved and illuminated streets." Souza concluded excitedly, "We have the freedom to become a great industrial city." At the same rally, Salomão Teixeira, another local resident, made this new vision explicit:

> Nitro Química doesn't want prosperity in São Miguel, because it's the only employer here, and everyone has to bow down to the [company]. . . . Look at São Caetano, which became an industrial park, thanks to autonomy. We'll have a mayor, and we'll make Nitro Química swallow its own gas. We'll have our mayor, and we'll have our own latifúndio, whose taxes will be spent on improvements for our beloved São Miguel. . . . The time for us to progress is coming. The hands that labor in São Paulo will labor here, reducing the cost of transportation. Food will be made not to eat cold in São Paulo but—yes!—hot in your own home, here in São Miguel. The worker will have peace of mind, because he will be close to his own. He will live in peace, without that commotion of São Paulo. For these and other principles of freedom, say "Yes"!"[34]

Similar reasoning once again motivated the local PCB to support the autonomist cause. With a much stronger presence in the life of the neighborhood than in previous campaigns, the communists had great influence on the local headquarters of the Chemical Workers Union and on various pro-autonomist associations and neighborhood organizations. Several party members were on the MPA's executive committee, which, in alliance with other forces considered leftist and with nationalists in the area, directed the outlines of the campaign. Beyond the possibilities of influencing the election of a future mayor and of electing aldermen, there was a debate among PCB members and leftist militants about the need to change the destiny of São Miguel. Antônio Pereira da Mata, director of the Chemical Workers Union and a communist militant, recalled that many supported autonomy because "we wanted to make São Miguel not a dormitory neighborhood, but an industrial city. In those days there was a lot of land, and we had a plan to give an average ten-year [tax] exemption for companies to come out here."

The autonomy campaign of 1962–63 was even larger than the one ten years before. The growth of São Miguel required a geographic change in the axis of movement and activity, and the areas adjacent to downtown had more weight. The MPA created nuclei in various areas, such as Jardim São Vicente,

Vila Jacuí, Vila Nitro Química, Vila Clara, and Itaim. Neighborhood Friends Societies, including those of Itaim, Jardim São Vicente, and São Miguel Paulista, declared their explicit support for the MPA. Concern about the support of the villages was an ongoing issue in autonomy meetings. On February 16, 1963, for example, Virgílio Gomes da Silva proposed that the MPA organize periodic visits by the "vila leaders" to the movement's headquarters so they could hear the arguments in favor of emancipation. Autonomist rallies multiplied, reaching the remotest areas of the neighborhood. Osvaldo Pires de Holanda remembered that in 1963 alone, the MPA held twenty-seven rallies in the area, not to mention the "rapid actions" organized at the front gate of Nitro and elsewhere.[35]

The movement to transform São Miguel into a municipality was also reinforced by the support of the Chemical Workers Union, and many leaders of other unions were also part of the campaign. For example, Santos Bobadilha, the leader of the São Paulo Dairy Workers Union and the Friends of Jardim São Vicente Society, was a selfless advocate of autonomy for São Miguel. It was surely through his influence that his union's newspaper, A Média, supported the initiative. In April 1963, the agency recalled that "São Miguel lives forgotten, and all the campaigns for its elevation to municipality were sabotaged by the enemies of autonomy, mainly Nitro Química, which in an independent town could not continue to exploit its employees as it presently does."[36]

In addition to criticizing Nitro, union members played an important role in convincing the workers, especially regarding the salary issue, which had been the Achilles' heel of previous autonomy campaigns. Union leaders became regular participants at movement rallies and briefing meetings. Likewise, the Chemical Workers Union began to include the issue in its meetings and events, as revealed in a letter sent from the organization to the MPA inviting it to take part "in the parade that will be held on May 1, 1963, in São Miguel Paulista."[37]

The PCB's national weekly publication Novos Rumos (New Directions) dedicated space to the autonomy struggle in São Miguel and highlighted that the movement "has the sympathy of a large part of the local population, in addition to the support of several institutions, among which the São Paulo Union of Workers in Chemical and Pharmaceutical Industries deserves special mention for its role in the campaign."[38] The active participation of communists and trade unionists in the São Miguel autonomy campaign contradicts the conclusions of Moisés, for whom the union and leftist movements were absent from the autonomy movements.[39]

Father Aleixo Mafra and the São Miguel Workers' Circle showed support for autonomy for the first time. They sought out Osvaldo Pires de Holanda, expressing reticence regarding the communist presence in the MPA. Holanda said that he refused to expel PCB members from the organization and answered, "My position is this: I'm going to make a movement, with the doors open to God and the devil. Whoever wants to support São Miguel is on my side." Despite this, Father Aleixo and circle members supported autonomy, although they did not participate directly in any separatist group.

There were divisions among the autonomists. Dissatisfied with the conduct of the campaign and with the small membership of the MPA executive committee, Dr. Gilberto Maida led a group that broke with the movement in February 1963 to form the São Miguel Paulista Autonomist Front. Months later, the entity suffered a new division when the Center of Autonomist Orientation was founded. Despite the strategic support for the Autonomist Front by Palmeira Júnior, editor-in-chief of the *Tribuna de São Miguel*, a small local newspaper created in late 1962, the MPA was always the largest, most organized movement for the administrative emancipation of the neighborhood.

Despite the divisions in its upper ranks, the autonomist campaign grew. A contest for Autonomy Queen, autonomist sports festivals in the vilas, and support by businesses were all clear signs of growing support in the neighborhood. The "rooster," a campaign symbol created by Osvaldo Pires de Holanda, became popular and a lapel pin with its image was distributed at rallies and in stores and bars. Likewise, the pompous anthem of autonomy, whose verses called for "freedom, freedom/autonomist movement/freedom, freedom/ for São Miguel Paulista/Paulista and Northeasterner/we will march hand in hand/and our unity/will construct our destiny," was intoned at meetings and movement events.[40]

So when in April 1963 the autonomists of São Miguel delivered their documents calling for the referendum to the Legislative Assembly, the popularity of their cause in the neighborhood seemed quite high. Throughout the second half of 1963, autonomist mobilization continued, preparing for the popular referendum that presumably would occur later that year. Unlike in previous campaigns, residents who were against emancipation did not demonstrate openly in the public square, which reinforced the sense that this time autonomy would win.

Surprisingly, however, the Legislative Assembly rejected the neighborhood's request for a referendum. In addition to pressure from the São Paulo municipality, the representatives tied to Quadros, fearful of widespread dismemberment of the city's territory, played a key role in rejecting the request, which was defeated by one vote. Quadros, who was considering running in the municipal elections of 1965, did not look favorably on the loss of votes from his old stronghold and thus guided the deputies who were under his influence to stop the autonomist movement. Amid widespread disappointment and demobilization, the three local separatist movements organized a joint protest and obtained a judicial suspension of the decision.

The military coup of April 1, 1964, however, put an end to any possibility of mobilization by autonomists in São Miguel. Despite that defeat, many participants in the movement believe that their struggle made the municipal administration turn a little more attention to the peripheral neighborhoods. "All the benefits that came to São Miguel were after the MPA," said Osvaldo Pires de Holanda. Antônio Pereira da Mata also said that "the struggle was not in vain. We don't consider it a loss, because we made the authorities turn their attention to São Miguel, and from that the whole east side benefited." Indeed, the creation of the regional administrations in São Paulo by Mayor Faria Lima in 1965 was a direct response to the mobilization of neighborhood organizations and the autonomist movement that developed in the city in the years before the military coup. The reasons that brought the peripheral neighborhoods to call for separation from their "stepmother" São Paulo would still require their mobilization and struggle for many years to come.

The Coup of 1964 and Dismissals of 1966

The autonomy debate was not the only issue in the political life of São Miguel during the months before the military coup of 1964. As in various other parts of the country, many residents were enthusiastic about the Basic Reforms proposed by the government of João Goulart. The mobilization of rural workers during that period and the hope of land reform that would bring development to the country, particularly the Northeast, excited sympathy among many.

The resignation of Quadros in 1961, after a solid electoral victory a year earlier, was disappointing for most of his local constituents and represented a significant blow to their prestige. "We were all very disappointed," recalled the Janista activist Nelson Bernardo. Many interpreted his departure from the government as a "coup" against the workers' interests. In order not to repeat the experience of Getúlio Vargas (who committed suicide in 1954), Quadros preferred to withdraw from power. In the memories of the people of São Miguel, some even became confused and thought that Quadros was the last president before 1964 and had been deposed by the military. As Teresa Caldeira has noted, the identification of Quadros as a popular governor is much stronger than that of Goulart, who was popularly known as "Jango."[41]

Although less well remembered, and, compared with Quadros, seen by many as a distant politician outside the daily experience of most neighborhood residents, Goulart enjoyed prestige in São Miguel. His historical links with Getúlio Vargas made people confident about him. In São Miguel, where Goulart's popularity was directly linked to Vargas's labor tradition, this relationship ensured him a landslide in the neighborhood when he ran for vice-president in 1955. Even in 1960, when he ran against Quadros's running mate Milton Campos, Goulart lost in São Miguel by fewer than three hundred votes, receiving 37.2 percent of the vote, one of the highest levels in the capital and a considerably larger percentage than he received in the city of São Paulo as a whole (31.3 percent).[42] While on one hand, the interviewees who discussed Goulart's government underscored the political instability of the period, on the other hand, they referred once again to his commitment to workers' rights. "Jango spoke the language of the people," recalled Joaquim Anselmo dos Santos, "the minimum wage, the thirteenth salary [a Christmas bonus guaranteed by law in 1962 under Goulart], right to strike: these things all happened during his government." For some, this was precisely the reason for his ouster:

> João Goulart? I still think he was very much on the side of the people, and even the promises he made, we saw that he was on the side of the people. Since he was very much on the side of the people, they took him out. At that time he made a lot of promises about agrarian reform. . . . It was just when he was starting that, we thought he was in power, and then he was out on the street.[43]

A leftward drift in local politics during the early 1960s can be measured by the behavior of Aurelino de Andrade, a faithful member of the PSP and a historical ally of Adhemar de Barros. His speeches in the Federal Chamber during the pre-coup period were increasingly critical of the conservatism that marked Barros's governance. During the episode of Quadros's resignation from the presidency in 1961, Andrade openly praised the "campaign of legality" conducted by the governor of Rio Grande do Sul, the nationalist and leftist Leonel Brizola (PTB). This successful campaign aimed to secure the position of Vice-President João Goulart against coup attempts orchestrated by conservative military and civilian sectors, which energetically rejected the possibility of Goulart's assuming power. Thanks to the posture of Brizola, Andrade said, "against some elements who wanted Brazil for a group of four or five individuals, Brazil took a decisive step on the road to emancipation and true legality." Months later, Andrade declared his support for President Goulart, "whose point of view is the same as that of most good Brazilians." Even while receiving a barrage of criticism from various colleagues, he resolved then to propose bestowing the title of São Paulo citizen on Brizola, which brought endless polemical debates in the chamber. On April 6, 1964, days after the overthrow of Goulart, a surprised Andrade still declared that he had been "for the Basic Reforms, and I will continue to think they are needed within the historic evolution of our country."[44]

Andrade's support for Goulart and his proposal to award the title of Paulista citizen to Brizola brought strong criticism from O Estado de São Paulo and threats that he would be removed from office. Nevertheless, his support of government forces after the civil-military coup and his joining of the National Renewal Alliance (Aliança Renovadora Nacional; ARENA), the party of the regime, in 1965 ensured his mandate and gave him wide political space during the dictatorial period.

From the local point of view, the first half of the 1960s saw the beginning of a sharp economic crisis at Nitro Química and the progressive de-legitimization of its central role in the community of São Miguel.[45] The truculent reaction of company management to the strike of 1957, when dozens of workers were dismissed and employees' access to the company's lauded social services became increasingly restricted, was evidently very ill received among workers and residents of the neighborhood. In his book on the company's history, Fábio Ravaglia, an engineer at Nitro at the time, says that "for the 'active' strikers . . . all benefits were cut." A secret report by DOPS prepared soon after the end of the stoppage reported that the "administration of Nitro Química is about to lay off about three hundred employees implicated in the strike movement, so that the mechanical section will almost entirely go. . . . Reported among the dismissals are employees with over twenty years of service, who in the company's thinking should not receive severance pay." The police report also said that "the orders for dismissal emanated from one of the directors (Mr. Moraes) who wanted to blame the local administration, saying that if you feed the hyena, the hyena feeds on you, making short work of you, so you take drastic measures to behead the evil."[46]

The former laborer Artur Pinto de Oliveira recalled some of these measures. After the strike, he reported, those who did not participate in the stoppage received a "little card from the factory." The holders of this document, who were mainly section heads and foremen and who became known as "crabs," continued to receive a number of benefits, while others had to pay for them. Oliveira continued:

> [The company began to] decrease the paternalism that it had for the employees. It wasn't all at once; . . . they didn't do it immediately. They started with little things, cutting. . . . But there were some things they had already started charging for. They charged for the doctor when previously the doctor had cost nothing. People picked up discount coupons at the factory. They cut those out. You could only get them if you had the card and money. . . . In other words, they started removing them from the cooperatives, the pharmacy, the butcher shop, the factory.

The company's reduction of social benefits was not just a reprisal against the strikers and the mobilization of working men and women. It was a clear reflection of the financial difficulties Nitro was experiencing. In any case, these moves caused great discontent among the employees and certainly contributed to the residents' enormous irritation at the high levels of environmental pollution caused by the company's new soda factory (an enterprise that would fail in a few years). Unable to absorb the neighborhood's intense population growth in the form of jobs, and faced with growing dissatisfaction by residents and workers, Nitro was a questionable company in a state of crisis by the time 1960 arrived.

The Chemical Workers Union gained support and legitimacy during this period. Instead of intimidating the workers, Nitro's repression of the strike of 1957 stimulated the struggle for workers' rights and mobilization in the area. After the strike, reported Artur Pinto de Oliveira, "The union remained strong. [It] remained strong and fought hand to hand with Nitro." The unionization of Nitro workers, for example, increased dramatically at the end of the 1950s and beginning of the 1960s. As early as January 1958, the communist daily *Notícias de Hoje* praised the action of the directorate of the Chemical Workers Union and proposed that one of the main results of the strike that had occurred months earlier had been the growth of "workers' confidence in its strength and organization. From six hundred members, the union wound up having four thousand [at Nitro]." José Ferreira da Silva, a Nitro Química worker and union leader during the period, said that in the factory "we had a section where only the head was not a member."

Much of the support the union received was based on one of its guidelines, which had enormous appeal among workers: to compel the company to comply with its legal obligations. "When we were elected to the union," recalled José Ferreira da Silva, director of the union's Legal Department, "we started making Nitro Química follow the law." He recalled hiring the lawyer Valter Sampaio.[47] "I read the Consolidated Labor Laws [CLT] a lot," he recalled, "and I said, 'Doctor, we're going to do everything that's in this book. Everything that's here, you'll make Nitro Química pay for.'" By early 1958, the union had already sued Nitro Química over "labor of children and women on Sundays."[48]

The effect of this new union leadership's actions on the workers was impressive. Afonso José da Silva explained that he joined the union because it demanded "nothing more, nothing less, than those rights we [already] had," with which the company did not comply. "Law of vacation, Sunday pay. . . . All of that was the union's struggle. It fought and won. That's why the union was strong. . . . There existed that security of the union being strong, everyone unionized. When they said, 'Don't go to work,' no one went." Augusto Ferreira Lima described the impact on the Nitro workers of the struggle the union developed for rights existing in law. He remembered the assemblies in the Ministry of Labor's Regional Labor Departments (Delegacia Regional do Trabalho; DRTs) to which the laborers, alongside the union leaders, went to denounce the irregularities of Nitro Química and demand their rights:

> Various times workers assembled, filling up the street in front of the station, and went to the DRT on Rua Martins Fontes. . . . Everyone had a [copy of the CLT]. Everyone got on the train with their copy, like believers going to church [carrying the Bible]. . . . The union bought [copies] and passed them out to us to distribute among the gang. There was a Portuguese guy in the factory. He went out covertly at lunchtime calling [the workers] and asking them, 'Where's your CLT? Have you read this?' He underlined everything there and sent people to read it, and people adapted to it . . . Everybody there knew what their rights were [with] the [CLT] in their hands."[49]

One of the union's largest campaigns during that period was against hazardous factory conditions. Nitro had long refused to acknowledge being an unhealthy work environment and therefore refused to pay the additional sums it would owe to the workers. In the late 1950s and early 1960s, however, the workers, individually and through the union, began to sue the company in the Labor Court. The wave of lawsuits was huge, and along with union pressure it forced management to negotiate. Finally, in February 1963, representatives of Nitro and the union signed an agreement pursuant to which the company would recognize and list all of the unhealthy sectors (most of the factory) and, obviously, pay the additional sums to all of those who worked in those sectors. Also, the agreement provided for the mediation of the Department of Occupational Health and Safety of the Ministry of Labor, "given that there are sections in the factory where there is doubt as to whether or not there is a hazard." Although this agreement did not recognize the right to health standards for all workers in the industry, it was seen as a great victory for the union.[50]

The presence of the union on the shop floor and in the community made Nitro Química one of the most labor-organized companies of São Paulo in the pre-1964 era. From the mid-1950s, there was a large investment in the training of shop stewards in each section of the company. "We have two or three union representatives in each department. In the factory as a whole we have six hundred," said José Ferreira da Silva. Even though those numbers may be exaggerated, the fact is that the union organization had spread within the company like never before. These workplace representatives had a key role in raising issues and communicating them to the union leadership. They were primarily the ones responsible for the unionization and organization of workers in the company. In times of open conflict, as in strikes, they often were the ones who led pickets and demonstrations. Valdevino Raimundo da Silva, one of those union delegates, remembered vividly a "stoppage inside the factory" he organized in 1961. While the pickets convinced the workers on one shift not to enter for work, Valdevino and other union activists recruited members inside the company. "We made a march inside the factory," he recalled. The work of convincing the workers and clarifying the issues to them, he added, did not take place only inside the company. Many delegates also participated in "Friends Societies [where they discussed] neighborhood problems, demands for public transportation, [and] housing."

This growing mobilization of Nitro workers was reflected in the Chemical Workers Union's active participation in trade union struggles. Besides acting in the Federation of Chemical Workers of the state of São Paulo, founded in 1958, the directors of the union were present at the organization of the main inter-union alliances of the period, including the PUI in the late 1950s and the General Workers Command (Comando Geral dos Trabalhadores; CGT) between 1962 and 1964. At the height of union mobilizations during the Goulart administration, the CGT and the seventy-nine-union Joint Action Pact declared a strike for a wage increase and for a guarantee to allow union representatives to act within companies, among other demands that included the approval of the Christmas bonus law by Congress. The workers of Nitro Química supported the activity in large numbers.[51]

According to the newspapers, "The first factory to go on strike in São Paulo, in obedience to the order of the CGT, was Nitro Química." The pickets once again played an essential role in the success of the stoppage. Also once again, the repression was violent. "A number of clashes have been confirmed between police and workers in the workers' neighborhoods, particularly in Mooca, Lapa, Santo Amaro and São Miguel Paulista," a newspaper sympathetic to the strike announced. In São Miguel specifically, the report continued, "The worker Virgílio Gomes da Silva was shot and received a head wound."[52]

Perhaps because of that, according to Valdevino Raimundo da Silva, the law that guaranteed a thirteenth salary (Christmas bonus) for all workers "was born in blood." In any case, the strike was largely successful at Nitro and reflected the high degree of organization that factory workers had achieved at that time. "Nitro Química: A Raise of 80% Is Approved," read the headline of the newspaper *Notícias Populares* referring to the Labor Court's judgment on the strike.[53] The union demanded a 100 percent adjustment, and the news was received with great joy by the factory workers. In addition, the mobilization brought into existence the Christmas bonus law. José Ferreira da Silva, one of the leaders of the stoppage, said that the strike in 1963 was "the best there was. . . . [I]n the assembly here, [many] workers could not even speak, they were so excited."

Such contentment, however, lasted only a short time. Five months later, the military coup, widely supported by Brazilian businessmen, had as one of its main targets the union movement and the organization of workers. In São Miguel, the initial impact of the blow fell squarely on the Nitro Química Chemical Workers Union, which was one of the first to suffer government intervention and have its directorate dismissed. Criminal cases were opened against several officers accused of subversion and corruption. Adelço de Almeida and other directors were forced to flee and hide. "The dispossession was bitter," recalled a melancholic José Ferreira da Silva. "I had nowhere to go. . . . There was only prison to look ahead to."

Not only the leadership was affected by the coup. Company directors seized the moment to once again persecute and dismiss workers considered "rebellious" and those connected with the union. At Nitro, everyone whose employment stability was not guaranteed was at risk. Joaquim Anselmo dos Santos called 1964 "a time of great persecution of leadership inside the factory." Outside Nitro, Valdevino Raimundo dos Santos was hired at the beginning of the year by Metalúrgica Cosmopoliti and remembered that, "after three months of employment, the factory sent for my file." Fortunately, another employee warned him in time to "get out of here very carefully, because things are ugly. . . . The political police are after you."

The military coup was a huge setback for social movements in São Miguel and throughout the country. However, after the first wave of repression, many people cautiously returned to militancy. As noted earlier, although conditions for open action by militant leftists in the labor movement were very difficult, the scope of repression appeared to be smaller in neighborhood organizing.

But even for the union interveners who were loyal to the new government, life was not easy. Some months after the directorate of the representative organization of Nitro workers was dismissed, a police observer reported to his superiors that "in the Chemical Workers Union, as has been happening in other unions under intervention, the interveners have had some trouble gaining members' trust, since the imposition of a new leadership by the authorities seems to them an act of restriction of union freedom."[54]

In 1965, when an election for union officers was convened, this discontent found expression. Particularly in São Miguel, the dismissed board members and activists created an opposition slate made up of names not known by the police. Waldomiro Macedo, one of the workers contacted at Nitro, said that "one day at lunch, at the factory gate, Manuel Lopes de Almeida, who worked in the Nitro paint factory," convinced him to participate. At the first meeting, in Jardim São Vicente, "a guy showed up who was appointed by the [Communist] Party to advise us . . . and that's when we started a movement." The slate was ready. The police, meanwhile, were not unaware of the movement. In October 1964, a "restricted circular" from DOPS stated that "the communist partners of the Chemical Workers Union are organizing a slate to contest the elections for its directorate. This is in São Miguel, where the largest communist concentration is located." Almost a year later, a new report warned that in the São Paulo chemical workers' elections in late September 1965, the "green" slate, competing with the "blue" slate captained by the former intervener Reinaldo dos Santos, was "organized under the auspices of the Communist Party." Although the candidates on the slate were not communists, their "ties with the Reds are evident," the report concluded. Despite the police warnings, the "green" slate won a resounding victory.[55]

The communists, however, did not have much time to exert their vaunted influence on the new unionists. Besides the dictatorial repression, ferocious infighting occupied the PCB at the time, which also left its marks on São Miguel. In the second half of 1965, the communist leader Carlos Marighella published *Por que resisti à prisão* (Why I Resisted Arrest), the first of a series of acid criticisms of the predominant positions in the Central Committee of the Communist Party, in particular of the moderates' belief in the possibility of a peaceful path to revolution, and of the "illusions" of an alliance with the national bourgeoisie. In the following months, Marighella and his comrades would deepen the tone of their criticism. Influenced by the Cuban Revolution, they founded the National Liberation Alliance (Alianca Libertadora Nacional; ALN) in late 1968, one of the largest groups of armed struggle developed by the Brazilian left during that period.[56]

Marighella's critiques resounded sharply among some of São Miguel's communist militants. Dissatisfied with the performance and the direction of the party, Virgílio Gomes da Silva, the militant who had been shot during the strike of 1963, led a dissident faction in the São Miguel PCB. Most former union leaders remained in the party, but Silva's faction attracted some membership at Nitro. Valdevino Raimundo dos Santos, a former union delegate at the company, was one of them. He said that that when others "went to train as guerrillas in Cuba," he did not go because he was married and had a family. Silva became a noted leader of the ALN and in 1969 commanded one of the most audacious and successful acts of the Brazilian armed struggle: the kidnapping of the U.S. ambassador in Rio de Janeiro, for which da Silva was pursued relentlessly, arrested months later, and killed under torture, a story recalled in the testimony of former militants and unionists of the neighborhood.[57]

But more than the divisions of the communist left—more, even, than the strong repression of the union and of political activists in general—the end of a period in the social and cultural history of São Miguel was most clearly symbolized by the wave of dismissals at Nitro Química in April 1966. In what is remembered as a tragic month in the history of the neighborhood, Nitro Química began an unprecedented reduction of its workforce. The company's financial difficulties, which had been evident for some years, were aggravated by the national economic crisis of 1965. After the breakthrough of nylon and other, more modern artificial fibers, rayon was seen as deficient and outdated. Further, the company's main industrial gamble, the soda factory, had proved a fiasco and was closed. As a result, Nitro's owners urged a heavy restructuring of the company, which included shutting down various sections and dismissing staff.

What followed had a brutal impact on the company's already battered image in the eyes of its employees and the residents of the neighborhood it had created in the 1930s. In early April 1966, the company announced the layoff of two hundred stable workers (those with more than ten years of work by the laws applicable until 1966), with only 50 percent of severance paid to those dismissed, and that in twenty-four installments.[58] The news fell like a bombshell, and not only in São Miguel. The federal government had just announced the end of the "stability" law that guaranteed employment for workers with more than ten years of service at the same company. Unions protested vehemently against the measure and had the support of the opposition party in Parliament, among them Senator José Ermírio de Moraes, who on the Senate floor criticized the government for extinguishing worker stability. Elected for the PTB as a senator from Pernambuco in 1962, Moraes had transferred into the only opposition party permitted, the Brazilian Democratic Movement (Movimento Democrático Brasileiro; MDB), created in 1965, when the pre-coup parties were extinct. However, it was precisely in the factory co-founded by the senator of the supposedly oppositionist MDB that the end of job stability was consolidated in practice.

Responding to a telegram sent by the Chemical Workers Union, Moraes proclaimed the unhappy situation of Nitro, "which had to choose between closing its doors and making 3,200 workers unemployed or reducing that number and diminishing the social impact." In any case, Moraes guaranteed that "workers' rights, as has been the standing rule of our companies, will be respected." Throughout that month, however, in an agonizing routine, more and more workers were dismissed, most of them considered stable, without guarantees that they would receive their rights. On April 20, *Jornal da Tarde* noted that 138 more workers had been sent away from Nitro, and 756 workers had already been dismissed, with compensation. On May 2, the number reached 810. In total, nearly 1,300 workers were dismissed in that period.[59]

The inexperienced new leaders of the Chemical Workers Union tried to sketch out a reaction, quickly organizing the union's Legal Department to file lawsuits in the Labor Court against Nitro. At the same time, it asked the DRT for the immediate supervision of compliance with labor laws at the company, especially in regard to the rules relating to health and safety at work. The strained negotiations between union and company management did not advance much. All they could obtain was the reduction of the number of installments for the indemnity payout from twenty-four to twelve months, a proposal that was promptly rejected by the workers' representatives.[60]

Meanwhile, the union began a campaign to aid the unemployed. Taking advantage of the public events held by the trade union movement protesting against the end of stability, the union flag was used to raise funds for those who had been dismissed. "The green flag, which flew during the stability gathering last Wednesday, received 60,000 cruzeiros. The previous Sunday, the same flag had collected 55,000 cruzeiros. It was in the public act at Cine São José do Belém." In São Miguel, the solidarity demonstrations continued.

At the same time, recalled Waldomiro Macedo, director of the union at the time, "the revolt was great" against the company. The fact that a large part of the layoffs hit workers with many years of service, some very close to retirement, amplified the outrage at the company's posture. "Nitro was a mother to the workers before. For about the past eight years, it's been a disgrace," one worker said.

A worker identified as Clementino, who had been fired after twenty-seven years at the factory, gave a statement to the *Jornal da Tarde* that was indicative of the general feeling among neighborhood workers and residents: "Why cry about it? These guys are no good. I was making the base of 120 contos a month there in the powerhouse, where the heat was. They never gave hazardous conditions pay, so that even today I have bronchitis. . . . Not just me, all my colleagues are sick, one with sinusitis and one with tuberculosis. All our life we give our blood to Nitro Química and now we get our reward."[61] Bewildered, the dismissed workers spent those April days looking for information in the union office and at the factory gate. Coordinated by the new vicar of the local church, Segundo Piotti, a campaign to collect foodstuffs was carried out in the streets of the neighborhood.

Many found in the drama of São Miguel's workers an unparalleled opportunity to strike at old rivals and political enemies. The Mesquita family, owners of the traditional and conservative newspaper group *O Estado de São Paulo*, tried to make a ferocious attack on José Ermírio de Moraes, who in the election had supported Miguel Arraes, the gubernatorial candidate whose victory was revoked by the military regime. The newspaper's editorialists accused Moraes of, among other things, having received support from the communists.

Launched in 1966 by the same group that owned *O Estado de São Paulo*, the new *Jornal da Tarde* produced a surprisingly detailed story. The dismissals of workers were directly imputed to Senator Moraes of the MDB (and formerly of the PTB, as the *Estado* and *Jornal da Tarde* journalists repeatedly recalled), and his contradictions were minutely explored. An editorial in *O Estado de São Paulo* openly solicited an action of the government "of the Revolution" against the "industrial senator." It continued, "The suspension of political rights of Mr. José de Moraes Ermírio would be a measure of simple justice—not of revolutionary justice." The newspaper attacks were so intense that Moraes was forced to defend himself on the Senate floor. In a long rebuttal that attacked the Mesquitas, he tried to justify the unjustifiable in relation to the dismissals at Nitro. Speaking about the company's crisis, he repeated the arguments that Nitro "faced a dilemma: to shut its doors, harming all the workers, or to dismiss them, with respect to the rights of each, which it never denied, only 10 or 15 percent of them." He recalled Nitro Química's strategic importance to the country and the number of its benefits and charities.[62]

Time was on Nitro's side. As a union leader recalled during the first weeks of the crisis, "The workers can handle a month or two. But once hunger starts to squeeze them, they end up accepting any deal. That's want the factory wanted: to conquer them by resistance." Indeed, over the next months, most workers eventually accepted Nitro's proposed installment plan for severance pay. Many who lived in the company's houses in the Vila Nitro Química wound up trading the severance for titles to their residences. A few years later, the handful of workers who had kept a lawsuit going ended up winning their entire severance pay and were rehired at the factory by court order.[63]

Nitro Química's management finally subdued the resistance and effected the restructuring of the plant. The number of employees was reduced substantially, and in the mid-1970s the company became profitable and competitive again. However, as the company's technical director noted at the time, "The massive dismissal of personnel damaged the company's image." The dismissals of 1966 dealt a decisive blow to the power and identity of Nitro Química as understood by the neighborhood of São Miguel, symbolizing the end of an era.

In the late 1960s and early 1970s, a team of sociologists and political scientists led by Francisco Weffort conducted a series of interviews with union leaders and activists who had been active before the coup of 1964. These oral histories served as the basis for various research projects by that group on the history of the workers' movement between 1945 and 1964.[1]

In one interview, a former union leader at the Paulista Steel Company (Companhia Siderúrgica Paulista; COSIPA) in Santos was asked whether there was "any observable difference" between the workers coming from the Northeast and the Paulistas. While considering the question a "difficult problem," the former unionist gave a very long answer. He started by saying, "Northeastern workers, in general, . . . had not been salaried agricultural workers, but peasants. So there's been a lot of argument about whether the working class of São Paulo was somehow distorted by the large influx of northeastern workers who came here. I've disagreed on some points, not because I'm a northeasterner, but because things are often not as we imagine them or would like them to be; nor are they often the way some sociologists and even psychologists understand them."

Next he explained the differences between the northeastern construction workers, "who had very little opportunity to better themselves" because they became "floating workers" who were completely subject to the fluctuations of the labor market, and the migrants in the manufacturing industry, "which evolves more rapidly, because it is integrated at a more intellectual level, with more knowledge, more fighting spirit, more tradition." He disagreed with those who thought that "the defects of the São Paulo working class comes from this flow of migrants, whether northeasterners, or Mineiros, or from the interior of the state of São Paulo." This is "not quite true," he continued. "I knew companies, even the big ones, where the concentration of northeastern workers was quite large, [and] in a short time they acquired a spirit of extraordinary struggle. [Moreover], most union leaders in São Paulo . . . in the 1960s up until 1964, were northeasterners. The overwhelming majority of leaders who stood out were northeasterners."[2]

Both the question and the response are quite revealing of the political and academic debate about the labor movement in the pre-coup period. Embedded in the question is a description of a more diffuse social order owing to the weakness of the São Paulo working class, due to its members' "rural origin." But the answer of the union man from Santos, focused on understanding the differences in the labor market and in the organizational traditions of the various professional categories, shows the greater complexity of this issue. We need not agree with his arguments—for example, his remark about the "overwhelming" predominance of northeasterners in the union leadership is probably exaggerated—but the fact is that his answer makes room for a greater understanding of the experiences lived by the northeastern migrants and how they adapted to the process of class formation. As the union man's response indicates, to understand the new working class that emerged, it was certainly necessary to understand the rural origins of the northeasterner. But it was also necessary to go beyond those origins. That is what this book has attempted to do by focusing on everyday life at work and at home, trying to connect them and understand how identities and conflicts were forged.

By analyzing densely the case of the northeastern workers in São Miguel Paulista, this book has tried to build a bridge between these local experiences and the great processes that Brazilian society underwent from the 1940s to the 1960s. Migration, urbanization, and industrialization cease to be abstract, demiurgic processes when seen from the perspective of those who experienced them and sought, within their field of possibilities, to influence them.

I have tried to show how the migration process was fundamental to understanding the action and the role of migrants in that society. Thus, particular attention was given to networks and social ties built by those workers in the migration process—ties that were maintained and expanded at work and in their urban experience. Such networks continued to be important in the formation of the social life of those migrants in the city and in the construction of their actions and political options.

The specific conditions of São Miguel Paulista, in addition to being somewhat unusual in that region, enabled the emergence of a strong sense of community that was fundamental to understanding social life and political struggles at the local level. The omnipotent presence of a large company decisively influencing the life of the area was highlighted as essential to the understanding of a community identity.

This sense of community in São Miguel became entwined with the formation by the migrants of a tense, relational northeastern identity. In the specific context of the 1950s during which the "northeastern question" took shape, migrants played a key role in this process. This "northeastern" identity, created and re-created in São Paulo, transformed in turn into an identity as workers, which paved the way for a strong class feeling among many migrants.

Such identities were also forged in the everyday life of the neighborhood. Hence, this work undertook to explore the dynamics of housing, leisure, and local culture, as well as to understand how the enormous need for urban infrastructure in São Miguel prompted an ongoing struggle for the same right to "progress" and develop as that enjoyed by the city's more affluent areas.

In that sense, this book has pointedly rejected the resident-worker dichotomy that has been widely disseminated in the literature on social struggles in the city. It has sought to understand how demands for urban improvements and rights were inserted into a context of class struggle and how popular organizations became linked in the process. Finally, it has emphasized how the workers' relationship with the political world was an active one, in which the "urban question" weighed heavily, and how, even with all of the limitations they faced, the workers of São Miguel constructed themselves as a fundamental political actor.

NOTES

FOREWORD

1 Although massive internal migration typically has been studied in the Latin American context, one could argue for analogous features in the great northward migrations of African Americans that began in a somewhat earlier period: see Kimberley L. Phillips, *Alabama North: African-American Migrants, Community and Working-Class Activism in Cleveland, 1915–1945* (Chicago: University of Illinois Press, 1999); Joe William Trotter Jr., ed., *The Great Migration in Historical Perspective: New Dimensions of Race, Class and Gender* (Bloomington: Indiana University Press, 1991).

2 Other works in this vein include Larissa Rosa Corrêa, "Trabalhadores e os doutores da lei: Direitos e justiça do trabalho na cidade de São Paulo—1953 a 1964," *Histórica*, no. 27 (November 2007); Adriano Duarte, "Cultura popular e cultura política no após-guerra: Redemocratização, populismo e desenvolvimentismo no bairro da Mooca, 1942–1973," Ph.D. diss., History Department, Instituto de Filosofia e Ciências Humanas, Universidade Estadual de Campinas, 2002; Antonio Luigi Negro, *Linhas de montagem. O industrialismo nacional-desenvolvimentista e a sindicalização dos trabalhadores* (São Paulo: Boitempo, 2004); Murilo Leal Pereira Neto, *A reinvenção da classe trabalhadora (1953–1964)* (Campinas: Editora da Unicamp, 2011).

3 Herbert Gutman, *Power and Culture: Essays on the American Working Class* (New York: New Press, 1987).

INTRODUCTION

Epigraph: Edvaldo Santana, "Ruas de São Miguel." *Edvaldo Santana.* Eldorado, 2000, CD.

1 There is a diverse bibliography about populism. For an analysis of some of the principal approaches to the subject, including perspectives that criticize the use of this concept, see Jorge Ferreira, ed., *O populismo e sua história. Debate e crítica* (Rio de Janeiro: Civilização Brasileira, 2001); John French, *The Brazilian Workers' ABC: Class Conflict and Alliances in Modern São Paulo* (Chapel Hill: University of North Carolina Press, 1992); Angela de Castro Gomes, *A invenção do trabalhismo* (São Paulo: Vértice, 1988); Francisco Weffort, *O populismo na política brasileira* (Rio de Janeiro: Paz e

Terra, 1980). See also the special issue about populism and *trabalhismo* (laborism) edited by Antonio Luigi Negro: *Cadernos* AEL 11, nos. 20–21 (2004).

2 *Translator's note: Trabalhismo getulista* is the "laborist" ideology associated with Getúlio Vargas. One of the most important and controversial political figures in Brazilian history, Vargas served as president of Brazil twice, first from 1930 to 1945, and again from 1951 until his suicide in 1954. He was first brought to power as the leader of the so-called Revolution of 1930, and in 1934 he was indirectly elected president by state representatives during the writing of a new constitution. Three years later, with military support, he led a coup that installed the Estado Novo corporatist dictatorship until 1945. Vargas favored nationalism, industrialization, centralization, social welfare, and labor rights. In 1943, he promulgated a national labor code, which regulated labor relations for many years after his death. Vargas was very popular and was elected president democratically in 1950. He was supported by nationalistic forces and by the majority of the trade unions, but his second administration was fiercely opposed by conservatives and a great part of the media, to the extent of provoking his suicide in 1954.

3 Paulo Fontes, "'Centenas de estopins acesos ao mesmo tempo.' A greve dos 400 mil, piquetes e a organização dos trabalhadores em São Paulo (1957)," in *Na luta por direitos. Estudos recentes em história social do trabalho*, ed. Alexandre Fortes, Antonio Luigi Negro, Fernando Teixeira da Silva, Hélio da Costa, and Paulo Fontes (Campinas: Editora da Unicamp, 1999); Paulo Fontes and Francisco Barbosa Macedo. "Strikes and Pickets in Brazil: Working-Class mobilization in the 'Old' and 'New' Unionism, the Strikes of 1957 and 1980," *International Labor and Working Class History* 83 (2013); Antonio Luigi Negro, *Linhas de montagem: O industrialismo nacional-desenvolvimentista e a sindicalização dos trabalhadores* (São Paulo: Boitempo, 2004); Murilo Leal Pereira Neto, *A reinvenção da classe trabalhadora (1953–1964)* (Campinas: Editora da Unicamp, 2011).

4 *Translator's note:* The political rivals Adhemar de Barros and Jânio Quadros were the two most prominent politicians in the state of São Paulo between the end of the Second World War and the military coup of 1964. Barros was the leader of the Social Progressive Party, which was very strong in São Paulo. He was elected governor of the state of São Paulo in 1947, mayor of the city of São Paulo in 1957, and governor again in 1962. Jânio Quadros had a meteoric political career. He was elected consecutively councilman (1947), member of the state Legislative Assembly (1950), mayor of São Paulo (1953), governor (1954), member of the National Congress (1958), and president of Brazil (1960). After seven months as president, Quadros resigned—a controversial political move whose cause is somewhat obscure and that began a political crisis in Brazil that led to the military coup of 1964.

5 For an interesting example of this movement in Brazilian literature, see the various essays published in Cláudio Batalha, Fernando Teixeira da Silva, and Alexandre Fortes, eds., *Culturas de classe. Identidade e diversidade na formação do operariado* (Campinas: Editora da Unicamp, 2004). For a more recent account, see Sidney Chalhoub and Fernando Teixeira da Silva, "Sujeitos no imaginário acadêmico: Escravos e trabalhadores na historiografia brasileira desde os anos 1980," *Cadernos* AEL 14, no. 26 (2009).

6 Daniel James, "O que há de novo, o que há de velho? Os parâmetros emergentes da história do trabalho latino-americana," in *Trabalho, cultura e cidadania*, ed. Angela M. C. Araújo (São Paulo: Scritta, 1997).

7 Paulo Fontes, *Trabalhadores e cidadãos. Nitro Química: A fábrica e as lutas operárias nos anos 50* (São Paulo: AnnaBlume and Sindicato dos Trabalhadores da Indústria Químicas e Plásticas de São Paulo, 1997).

8 Leon Fink, *The Maya of Morganton: Work and Community in the Nuevo New South* (Chapel Hill: University of North Carolina Press, 2003), is a stimulating recent example of the rich possibilities opened by this historiographic approach that links work, migration, and community.

9 An extensive bibliography deals with foreign immigration to Brazil. For an overview of major trends and debates in this area, see Boris Fausto, *Historiografia da imigração para o Brasil* (São Paulo: Editora Sumaré and Fundação de Amparo à Pesquisa do Estado de São Paulo, 1991).

10 Richard Whipp, *Patterns of Labour: Work and Social Change in the Pottery Industry* (London: Routledge, 1990), 163. For a more general assessment of the (often problematic) use of community studies by social historians, see the debate between Alan Macfarlane and C. J. Calhoun: Alan Macfarlane, "History, Anthropology and the Study of Communities," *Social History* 5, no. 5 (1977); C. J. Calhoun, "History, Anthropology and the Study of Communities: Some Problems in Macfarlane's Proposal," *Social History* 3, no. 3 (1978). In the field of sociology, obviously, there is a long tradition of studies that goes back to the founding of the discipline in the nineteenth century. For syntheses of the sociological debate about the concept and the problems encountered by social historians, see C. J. Calhoun, "Community: Toward a Variable Conceptualization for Comparative Research," *Social History* 5, no. 1 (1980); Greg Patmore, "Community and Australian Labour History," in *Challenges to Labour History*, ed. Terry Irving (Sydney: University of New South Wales Press, 1994); Talja Blokland and Michael Savage, "Networks, Class and Place," *International Journal of Urban and Regional Research* 25, no. 2 (2001); Eileen and Stephen Yeo. "On the Uses of 'Community': From Owenism to the Present," in *New Views of Co-operation*, ed. Stephen Yeo (London: Routledge, 1988).

11 See, e.g., David Crew, "Class and Community: Local Research on Working-Class History in Four Countries," *Historische Zeitschrift* 15 (1986): 290, and the books he cites in that article.

12 Rick Halpern, "Respatializing Marxism and Remapping Urban Space," *Journal of Urban History* 23, no. 2 (1997); Ira Katznelson, *Marxism and the City* (Oxford: Oxford University Press, 1992); Michael Savage, "Space, Networks and Class Formation," in *Social Class and Marxism: Defences and Challenges*, ed. Neville Kirk (Hants: Scholar Press, 1996).

13 Savage, "Space, Networks and Class Formation," 68.

14 See Andrew Herold, "Workers, Space, and Labor Geography," *International Labor and Working-Class History*, no. 64 (2003). See also Andrew Herold, *Labor Geographies: Workers and the Landscapes of Capitalism* (New York: Guilford, 2002); José Luis Oyon Bañales, "Historia urbana y historia obrera: Reflexiones sobre la vida obrera y su inscripción em el espacio urbano, 1900–1950," *Perspectivas Urbanas*, no. 2 (2002).

15 See, e.g., Adriano Luiz Duarte, "Cultura popular e cultura política no após-guerra: Redemocratização, populismo e desenvolvimentismo no bairro da Mooca, 1942–1973," Ph.D. diss., History Department, Instituto de Filosofia e Ciências Humanas, Universidade Estadual de Campinas, 2002; Adriano Luiz Duarte, "Os sentidos da comunidade: Notas para um estudo sobre bairros operários e identidade cultural," *Trajetos* 1, no. 2 (2002); Alexandre Fortes, *Nós do quarto distrito. A classe trabalhadora porto-alegrense e a era Vargas* (Rio de Janeiro: Garamond, 2004). An interesting parallel can be established with the historiography of work in Argentina. In relation to this, see Daniel James, *Doña Maria's Story: Life History, Memory, and Political Identity* (Durham, NC: Duke University Press, 2000); Mirta Lobato, *La vida en las fábricas: Trabajo, política y protesto en una comunidad obrera, Berisso (1904–1970)* (Buenos Aires: Prometeo Libros and Entrepassados, 2001).

16 Part of the argument developed in this section was previously presented in Adriano Duarte and Paulo Fontes, "O populismo visto da periferia: Adhemarismo e Janismo nos bairros da Mooca e São Miguel Paulista, 1947–1953," *Cadernos AEL* 11, vols. 20–21 (2004).

17 The studies by Juarez Rubens Brandão Lopes are of particular importance and had great influence in academic production about labor in Brazil in that period: See Juarez Rubens Brandão Lopes, *Sociedade industrial no Brasil* (São Paulo: Difel, 1964); Juarez Rubens Brandão Lopes, *Crise do Brasil arcaico* (São Paulo: Difel, 1967). See also Leôncio Martins Rodrigues, *Conflito industrial e sindicalismo no Brasil* (São Paulo: Difel, 1966); Fernando Henrique Cardoso, "Proletariado no Brasil: Situação e comportamento social," *Revista Brasiliense*, no. 41 (May–June 1962). The Argentine author Gino Germani was widely read by Brazilian sociologists and became a basic reference in Latin American modernization studies. See, among others, Gino Germani, *Sociologia da modernização. Estudos teóricos, metodológicos e aplicados à América Latina* (São Paulo: Mestre Jou, 1974).

18 Lopes, *Sociedade industrial no Brasil*, 23.

19 Vicente Unzer de Almeida and Octávio Teixeira Mendes Sobrinho, *Migração rural-urbana: Aspectos da convergência de população do interior e outras localidades para a capital do estado de São Paulo* (São Paulo: Secretaria da Agricultura do Estado de São Paulo, 1951), 16; emphasis added.

20 Eder Sader, *Quando novos personagens entraram em cena. Experiências e lutas dos trabalhadores da Grande São Paulo (1970–1980)* (Rio de Janeiro: Paz e Terra, 1988), 88–99. Sader counterpoises modernization theory's "optimism" against the images of exclusion and uprooting of the marginality theory developed in the late 1960s. Indeed, the two analyses' approaches depart from different assumptions about what the migration process represented for migrants. However, both ways of thinking tend to downplay the possibility of action and the ability of rural migrants to respond to the urban situation, something Sader well portrays.

21 See "Migrações, mobilidade de massas e consenso social na Argentina e no Brasil," in Germani, *Sociologia da modernização*, 138.

22 Such formulations, widely disseminated among academics at the time, are systematized in Rodrigues, *Conflito industrial e sindicalismo no Brasil*. Michael Hall and

Paulo Sérgio Pinheiro demonstrated subsequently the fragility of such explanations in pointing to the rural origin of the majority of the European immigrants, as well as their absence of factory experience and lack of political militancy in their countries of origin. See Michael Hall and Paulo Sérgio Pinheiro, "Imigração e movimento operário no Brasil: Uma interpretação," in *Trabalhadores no Brasil: Imigração e industrialização*, ed. José Luiz Del Roio (São Paulo: Ícone, 1990).

23 Rodrigues, *Conflito industrial e sindicalismo no Brasil*, 78.

24 Moisés Vinhas, *Operários e camponeses na revolução brasileira* (São Paulo: Fulgor, 1963).

25 A review of migration studies in universities and governmental organizations during the 1970s and 1980s is in Carlos A. Hasenbalg, "A pesquisa sobre sobre migrações, urbanização, relações raciais e pobreza no Brasil: 1970–1990," memograph, Série Estudos, Iuperj, Rio de Janeiro, 1991, 9. An important critique of dualism in modernization theory is in Francisco de Oliveira, "A economia brasileira: crítica à razão dualista," *Estudos Cebrap*, no. 2 (1972); Weffort, *O populismo na política brasileira*. For a specific analysis of sociological approaches to Brazilian labor in the 1950s and 1960s, see Maria Célia Paoli, Vera Silva Telles, and Eder Sader, "Pensando a classe operária: Os trabalhadores sujeitos ao imaginário acadêmico," *Revista Brasileira de História*, no. 6 (1984); José Sérgio Leite Lopes, "Sobre os trabalhadores da grande indústria na pequena cidade: Crítica e resgate da *Crise do Brasil Arcaico*," in *Cultura e identidade operária: Aspectos da cultura da classe trabalhadora*, ed. José Sérgio Leite Lopes (Rio de Janeiro: Marco Zero and Editora Universidade Federal do Rio de Janeiro, 1987).

26 Weffort, *O populismo na política brasileira*, 136.

27 Angela de Castro Gomes, "O populismo e as ciências sociais no Brasil: Notas sobre a trajetória de um conceito," in Ferreira, *O populismo e sua história*.

28 *Translator's note:* Due to the inability of the national bourgeoisie to become a hegemonic class, and in the absence of an autonomous and organized proletariat, the state occupied the power vacuum in the wake of a crisis of hegemony in the country that began in the early 1930s.

29 See, among others, Maria Célia Paoli, "Os trabalhadores urbanos na fala dos outros. Tempo, espaço e classe na história operária brasileira," in Leite Lopes, *Cultura e identidade operária*; Gomes, *A invenção do trabalhismo*; French, *The Brazilian Workers' ABC*. An overview of recent debates about populism and a review of critiques of the concept is in Ferreira, *O populismo e sua história*. Particularly the notion of "populist unionism" as a reference to the workers' movement of the 1930s through the 1960s has been intensely criticized. Besides the already cited texts, studies in this area can be found, among others, in José Sérgio Leite Lopes, *A tecelagem dos conflitos de classe na "cidade das chaminés"* (São Paulo: Marco Zero, 1988); José Ricardo Ramalho, *Estado-patrão e cultura operária: O caso FNM* (Rio de Janeiro: Paz e Terra, 1989); Marcelo Badaró Mattos, *Novos e velhos sindicalismos. Rio de Janeiro (1955–1988)* (Rio de Janeiro: Vício de Leitura, 1988). See also the essays collected in Fortes et al., *Na luta por direitos*; Marco Aurélio Santana, *Homens partidos. Comunistas e sindicatos no Brasil* (São Paulo: Boitempo, 2001).

30 French, *The Brazilian Workers' ABC*.

31 In this connection, see especially the essays by Angela de Castro Gomes, "O populismo e as ciências sociais no Brasil: notas sobre a trajetória de um conceito"; Jorge Ferreira, "O nome a coisa: o populismo na política brasileira," and Daniel Aarão Reis Filho, "O colapso do colapso do populismo: a propósito de uma herança maldita"in Ferreira, *O populismo e sua história*. In his most recent book, Ferreira deepens his analysis of *trabalhismo*: see Jorge Ferreira, *O imaginário trabalhista* (Rio de Janeiro: Civilização Brasileira, 2005).

32 See Jorge Ferreira. "Introdução," in Ferreira, *O populismo e sua história*, 13; Gomes, "O populismo e as ciências sociais no Brasil," 46–47.

33 Jorge Ferreira, "O nome e a coisa. O populismo na política brasileira," in Ferreira, *O populismo e sua história*.

34 Daniel Aarão Reis Filho, "O colapso do colapso do populismo ou a propósito de uma herança maldita," in *O populismo e sua história. Debate e crítica*, ed. Jorge Ferreira (Rio de Janeiro: Civilização Brasileira, 2001), 345–47.

35 Fortes, *Nós do quarto distrito*, esp. the epilogue titled "Trabalhadores e participação política na República Populista."

36 Over the length of its history, the DEOPS of São Paulo had several names. The latest, State Department of Political and Social Order (DEOPS), was implemented in 1975 and remained in force until the agency's termination in 1983. It is this name that is used to reference the document collection. In the text, however, I chose to use the name DOPS, which was in effect between 1945 and 1975 and was the best known to political militants and the general population during the entire period studied in this work.

37 For an analysis of the potential risks of research on the labor movement using police sources, particularly with the collection of the DEOPS, see Antonio Luigi Negro and Paulo Fontes, "Using Police Records in Labor History: A Case Study of Brazilian DOPS," *Labor: Studies in Working-Class History of the Americas* 5, no. 1 (2008).

38 Partido Comunista do Brasil (Communist Party of Brazil) was the official name of the party founded in 1922. In the early 1960s, the party changed its name to Partido Comunista Brasileiro (Brazilian Communist Party). A dissident group, claiming to be the original Communist party, founded another party in 1962, using the acronym PCdoB. Unless indicated otherwise, PCB refers to the Communist Party of Brazil founded in 1922.

39 This collection is presently in the IFCH Library at Unicamp.

40 For a list of the names of interviewees and dates of interviews, see the bibliography. Whenever possible, in quotations of statements throughout the text I tried to preserve as much as possible the orality of the interviews.

41 By analyzing the workers' memories I sought to view their testimony as a selective, socially determined retelling of the past, constructed retrospectively from the motivations and issues of the present. For a rapprochement with the intense current debate on oral history, see Rick Halpern, "Oral History and Labour History: A Historiographic Assessment after Twenty-five Years," *Journal of American History* 85, no. 2 (1998); Robert Perks and Alistair Thomson, *The Oral History Reader* (London:

Routledge, 1998); José Carlos Sebe bom Meihy, *(Re)introduzindo a história oral no Brasil* (São Paulo: Xamã, 1996); Marieta de Moraes Ferreira and Janaína Amado, eds., *Usos e abusos da história oral* (Rio de Janeiro: Fundação Getúlio Vargas, 1996); Michael Hall, "História oral: Os riscos da inocência," in *O direito à memória. Patrimônio histórico e cidadania,* ed. Departamento do Patrimônio Histórico de São Paulo (São Paulo: Secretaria Municipal de Cultura de São Paulo, 1982).

CHAPTER 1. A Cardboard Suitcase and a Backpack

1 Information taken from the testimony of Artur Pinto de Oliveira and Augusto Ferreira Lima. The testimony cited in this chapter was given to me by Artur Pinto de Oliveira, Augusto Ferreira Lima, Geraldo Rodrigues de Freitas, Jorge Gonçalves Lula, Maria José dos Santos Oliveira, and Afonso José da Silva.

2 *Translator's note:* Lit., "macaw's perch," named for the boards on which the migrants precariously sat.

3 *Translator's note:* São Paulo is simultaneously the name of the city, the *município* (county), and the state. In this text, the name will generally be used to mean the city, unless explicitly phrased in terms such as "the state of São Paulo" or clearly implied by context.

4 Data on migration flows from several Brazilian states to the county of São Paulo between 1900 and 1970 are in Manoel Tosta Berlinck and Daniel J. Hogan, *O desenvolvimento econômico do Brasil e as migrações internas para São Paulo: Uma análise histórica* (Campinas: Cadernos do Instituto de Filosofia e Ciências Humanas, Univerisdade Estadual de Campinas, 1974), 28.

5 See Alba Maria Morandi, *O trabalhador migrante nacional em São Paulo (1920–1923)* (São Paulo: Pontifícia Universidade Católica de São Paulo, 1978); Ely Souza Estrela, *Os sampauleiros: Cotidiano e representações* (São Paulo: Editora da Pontifícia Universidade Católica de São Paulo, 2003).

6 See Jeffrey Lesser, ed., *Searching for Home Abroad: Japanese Brazilians and Transnationalism* (Durham, NC: Duke University Press, 2003), 8.

7 Cf. Afonso Celso Miranda e Silva, "Departamento de Migrantes," in *Anais da Semana de Estudos Migratórios (6 a 11 de julho de 1970),* ed. Juarez Segalin and Jacyr Braido (São Paulo: Centro de Estudos Migratórios, 1970); Santa Helena Bosco and Antônio Jordão Netto, *Migrações: Estudo especial sobre as migrações internas para o Estado de São Paulo e seus efeitos* (São Paulo: Departamento de Imigração e Colonização da Secretaria da Agricultura do Estado de São Paulo, 1967); Odair da Cruz Paiva, *Caminhos cruzados. Migração e construção do Brasil moderno (1930–1950)* (Bauru: EDUSC, 2004). See also the newspaper *O Migrante,* May and June 1978, 11.

8 Humberto Dantas, "Movimentos de migrações internas em direção ao planalto paulista," *Boletim do Serviço de Imigração e Colonização,* no. 3 (March 1941): 81–83.

9 Cf. Dantas, "Movimentos . . . , 79; T. Pompeu Accioly Borges, *Migrações internas no Brasil* (Rio de Janeiro: Comissão Nacional de Política Agrária, 1955), quadro X.

10 Cf. *Revista do Arquivo Municipal* 75, no. 7 (April 1941): 147.

11 Cf. Cornélia Porto, Iraci da Costa, and Nélson Nozoe, "Movimentos migratórios no Brasil e seus condicionantes econômicos (1872–1980)," mimeograph, Convênio

Financiadora de Estudos e Projetos and Fundação Instituto de Pesquisas Econômicas, São Paulo, 1987.

12 See Douglas Graham and Sérgio Buarque de Holanda Filho, *Migration, Regional and Urban Growth and Development in Brazil: A Selective Analysis of the Historical Record, 1872–1970* (São Paulo: IPE/USP, 1971).

13 Cf. José Francisco de Camargo, *A cidade e o campo: O êxodo rural no Brasil* (Rio de Janeiro: Ao Livro Técnico, 1968), 38.

14 Cf. Carlos A. Hasenbalg, "A pesquisa sobre migrações, urbanização, relações raciais e pobreza no Brasil, 1979–1990," mimeograph, série estudos, Iuperj, Rio de Janeiro, 1991.

15 Cf. Francisco Weffort, "Nordestinos em São Paulo: Notas para um estudo sobre cultura nacional e cultura popular," in *A cultura do povo*, ed. José Valle Edênio (São Paulo: Cortez e Instituto de Estudos Especiais, 1988), 17; Eder Sader, *Quando novos personagens entraram em cena. Experiências e lutas dos trabalhadores da Grande São Paulo (1970–1980)* (Rio de Janeiro: Paz e Terra, 1988), 88.

16 Cf. Maria Judith de Brito Muszynski, *O impacto político das migrações internas: O caso de São Paulo (1945–1982)* (São Paulo: Índice de Desenvolvimento da Educação, 1986), 23.

17 Cf. Manoel Tosta Berlinck and Daniel J. Hogan, "Migração interna e adaptação na cidade de São Paulo: Uma análise preliminar," in *Anais do I Simpósio de Desenvolvimento Econômico e Social: Migrações internas e desenvolvimento regional* (Belo Horizonte: Centro de Desenvolvimento e Planejamento Regional, Universidade Federal de Minas Gerais, 1972), 12.

18 Cf. Renato Colistete, *Labour Relations and Industrial Performance in Brazil: Greater São Paulo, 1945–1960* (Houndmills: Palgrave, 2001), esp. chap. 1. See also Murilo Leal Pereira Neto, *A reinvenção da classe trabalhadora (1953–1964)* (Campinas: Editora da Unicamp, 2011), esp. chap. 1.

19 Cf. Borges, *Migrações internas no Brasil*, 25.

20 Luís Fernando Maria Teixeira, "O desajuste e a recuperação do trabalho rural," *Revista de Imigração e Colonização* 10 (January–December 1949), 265. According to Celso Furtado, in 1955 the "per capita income of the São Paulo region was . . . 4.7 times higher than that of the Northeast": Celso Furtado, *Formação econômica do Brasil*, 11th ed. (São Paulo: Companhia Editora Nacional, 1972), 239.

21 Cf. Celeste Souza Andrade, "Migrantes nacionais no estado de São Paulo," *Sociologia* 19, no. 2 (1952): 125–26.

22 Cf. Afrânio Garcia and Moacir Palmeira, "Rastros de casas-grandes e senzalas: Transformações sociais no mundo rural brasileiro durante o século XX," in *Brasil: Um século de transformações*, ed. Ignacy Sachs, Jorge Wilheim, and Paulo Sérgio Pinheiro (São Paulo: Companhia das Letras, 2001).

23 See Andrade, "Migrantes nacionais no estado de São Paulo," 125–26.

24 Cf. Maria José Villaça, *A força de trabalho no Brasil* (São Paulo: Pioneira e Edusp, 1967), 248.

25 Cf. Andrade, "Migrantes nacionais no estado de São Paulo," 123. For a specific analysis of the impact on workers of the crisis in the sugar economy, particularly in Pernambuco, see, among others, Thomas D. Rogers, "The Deepest Wounds: The

Laboring Landscapes of Sugar in Northeastern Brazil," Ph.D. diss., Duke University, Durham, NC, 2005; Anthony Pereira, *The End of Peasantry: The Rural Labor Movement in Northeast Brazil, 1961–1988* (Pittsburgh: University of Pittsburgh Press, 1997).

26 About the agrarian reform debate in the 1950s and 1960s, see, among others, Leonilde Sérvolo de Medeiros, *História dos movimentos sociais no campo* (Rio de Janeiro: Fase, 1989); Leonilde Sérvolo de Medeiros, *Reforma agrária no Brasil* (São Paulo: Editora da Fundação Perseu Abramo, 2003); Rudá Ricci, *Terra de ninguém* (Campinas: Editora da Unicamp, 1999); Cliff Welch, *The Seed Was Planted: The São Paulo Roots of Brazil's Rural Labor Movement (1924–1964)* (University Park: Pennsylvania State University Press, 1999); Delsy Gonçalves de Paula, Heloísa Starling, and Juarez Guimarães, eds., *Sentimento de reforma agrária, sentimento de república* (Belo Horizonte: Editora da UFMG, 2006); João Pedro Stédile, ed., *A questão agrária no Brasil* (São Paulo: Expressão Popular, 2004).

27 See Bertha Becker, "As migrações internas no Brasil: Reflexo de uma organização do espaço desequilibrada," *Revista Brasileira de Geografia* 30, no. 2 (April–June 1968).

28 Cf. Edison Nunes, "Algumas notas sobre o Nordeste brasileiro: A terra, o homem, secas," mimeograph, Cedec, São Paulo, August 1978, 9.

29 Cf. Andrade, "Migrantes nacionais no estado de São Paulo," 117.

30 Cf. Manoel Correia de Andrade, *A terra e o homem no Nordeste* (São Paulo: Brasiliense, 1964), 112; Marilda Aparecida de Menezes, *Redes e enredos nas trilhas dos migrantes: Um estudo de famílias de camponeses-migrantes* (Rio de Janeiro: Relume Dumará/João Pessoa, Editora UFPB, 2002); Estrela, *Os sampauleiros*, esp. chap. 1; Souza Barros, *Êxodo e fixação. Sugestões para uma política de colonização e aldeamento no Nordeste* (Rio de Janeiro: Ministério da Agricultura, 1953), 36. About the migrations to the Companhia de Tecidos Paulista, see José Sérgio Leite Lopes, *A tecelagem dos conflitos de classe na "cidade das chaminés"* (São Paulo: Marco Zero e Brasília, Editora da Universidade de Brasília, and Conselho Nacional de Desenvolvimento Científico e Tecnológico, 1988); Rosilene Alvim, *A sedução da cidade. Os operários-camponeses e a fábrica dos Ludgreen* (Rio de Janeiro: Graphia, 1997). About the migration of northeasterners to Amazônia, cf. Furtado, *Formação econômica do Brasil*, 127–35; Estanislau Fischlowitz, *Principais problemas da migração nordestina* (Rio de Janeiro: Ministério da Educação e Cultura, 1959), 43–44; Warren Dean, *Brazil and the Struggle for Rubber: A Study in Environmental History* (Cambridge: Cambridge University Press, 1987); Maria Verônica Secreto, *Soldados da borracha. Trabalhadores entre o sertão e a Amazônia no governo Vargas* (São Paulo: Editora da Fundação Perseu Abramo, 2007).

31 Souza Barros, "Nordestinos, pioneirismo e emigração," *O Observador Econômico e Financeiro* (December 1956).

32 "I suffered, but I arrived" is translated from the lyrics of the song "Pau-de-arara," composed by Guio de Morais and Luiz Gonzaga, 1951.

33 Cf. Borges, *Migrações internas no Brasil*, 16; Estrela, *Os sampauleiros*, chap. 2.

34 The scenes (without audio) of TV Tupi can be seen in the collection of the Cinemateca Brasileira (SP). Cf. Base Tupi, 4/7/1960, NE11802.11-VV15054N. The

material about the "Bahian train" was published in the newspaper *Última Hora* between July 7 and July 12, 1958.

35 Marcos Vinicios Vilaça, *Em torno da sociologia do caminhão* (Recife: Instituto Joaquim Nabuco de Pesquisas Sociais, 1961), 147–48.

36 *A Hora*, December 22, 1954. The São Paulo daily newspaper *A Hora* began publishing in the late 1940s. At first, it associated itself with the future President Jânio Quadros, who was then beginning his political career, but the newspaper's board broke with Quadros in the mid-1950s. It gave ample coverage to the city's peripheral neighborhoods and gained some popularity among their residents, but ceased publication in the early 1960s.

37 Cf. data from the Statistics Division of the Instituto Nacional de Imigração e Colonização, published in *Revista de Imigração e Colonização* 14–16, new series (1955).

38 AESP, DEOPS sector, dossier 118 844.

39 *Última Hora*, March 26, 1958; *Atas da Assembleia Legislativa de São Paulo*, 9th ordinary session, April 2, 1959.

40 *Atas da Assembleia Legislativa de São Paulo*, 9th ordinary session, April 2, 1959; *Revisa de Imigração e Colonização* 13, no. 1 (1952): 151; *A Hora*, March 6, 1956; *Última Hora*, July 9, 1958.

41 *Translator's note:* A *toada* is a style of rural ballad with recurring choruses.

42 Patativa do Assaré, "A triste partida."

43 Cf. Boris Fausto, "Imigração: Cortes e continuidades," in *História da vida privada: Contrastes de intimidade contemporânea*, ed. Lilia Moritz Schwarcz (São Paulo: Companhia das Letras, 1988), 14.

44 Vilaça, *Em torno da sociologia do caminhão*, 148.

45 Cf., among others, Vicente Unzer de Almeida and Octávio Teixeira Mendes Sobrinho, *Migração rural-urbana: Aspectos de convergência de população do interior e outras localidades para a capital do estado de São Paulo* (São Paulo: Secretaria de Agricultura do Estado de São Paulo, 1951); Fischlowitz, *Principais problemas da migração nordestina*; Juarez Brandão Lopes, *Sociedade industrial no Brasil* (São Paulo: Difel, 1964); Eunice Durham, "Os migrantes nacionais," in *São Paulo, espírito, povo, instituições* (São Paulo: Pioneira, 1968); Eunice Durham, *A caminho da cidade* (São Paulo: Perspectiva, 1976); Berlinck and Hogan, *O desenvolvimento econômico do Brasil e as migrações internas*; Gino Germani, *Sociologia da modernização. Estudos teóricos, metodológicos e aplicados à América Latina* (São Paulo: Mestre Jou, 1974); Gentil Dias Martins, *Depois do latifúndio. Continuidade e mudança na sociedade rural nordestina* (Brasília: Editora Universidade de Brasília, 1978); Andrade, *A terra e o homem no Nordeste*.

46 Alvim, *A sedução da cidade*, 3. Recently, various studies, especially about social relations in the Brazilian countryside, have attempted to emphasize the agency of workers in the process of migration: see, among others, A. R. Garcia Jr., *O sul: Caminho do roçado. Estratégias de reprodução camponesa e transformação social* (Brasília: Marco Zero, Editora de Universidade de Brasília, and Conselho Nacional de Desenvolvimento Científico e Tecnológico, 1989); Charles D'Almeida Santana, *Fartura e venturas camponesas. Trabalho, cotidiano e migrações. Bahia: 1950–1980* (São Paulo: Annablume, 1998); Estrela, *Os sampauleiros*; Menezes, *Redes e enredos nas trilhas dos*

migrantes; Robson Laverdi, *Tempos diversos, vidas entrelaçadas. Trajetórias itinerantes de trabalhadores no extremo oeste do Paraná* (Curitiba: Aos Quatro Ventos, 2005).

47 Cf. Alistair Thomson, "Moving Stories: Oral History and Migration Studies," *Oral History* 27, no. 1 (1999): 28.

48 Parallels can also be made with the historiography of the great African American migration from the South to the North of the United States between the 1910s and the 1950s: cf. Joe William Trotter Jr., ed., *The Great Migration in Historical Perspective: New Dimensions of Race, Class, and Gender* (Bloomington: Indiana University Press, 1991); Kimberley L. Phillips, *Alabama North: African-American Migrants, Community and Working-Class Activism in Cleveland, 1915–1945* (Chicago: University of Illinois Press, 1999); Ira Berlin, *The Making of African America: The Four Great Migrations* (New York: Viking, 2010).

49 Cf. Thomson, "Moving Stories," 28.

50 Luiz Cava Netto, "Contribuição do desenvolvimento e organização da comunidade e do planejamento socioeconômico ao problema dos deslocamentos populacionais (Migração Nordestina e êxodo rural)," in *Anais do encontro de técnicos promovido pela Secretaria de Saúde Pública e de Assistência Social do Estado de São Paulo—1962* (São Paulo: Cooperação e Intercâmbio de Serviços Sociais, 1965), 66.

51 *O Observador Econômico e Financeiro*, July 1957, 13.

52 Cf. Durham, *A caminho da cidade*, 63.

53 *Translator's note:* The ABC region is an industrial area in São Paulo state that includes the cities of Santo André, São Bernardo do Campo, and São Caetano do Sul.

54 Cf. Berlinck and Hogan, "Migração interna e adaptação na cidade de São Paulo," 33; Antônio de Almeida, "Um encontro de origens diversas: A presença de migrantes e imigrantes na composição da classe trabalhadora do ABC paulista," *Tempos Históricos* 1, no. 1 (March 1999); Almeida and Sobrinho, *Migração rural-urbana*, 27.

55 Cf. R. Parry Scott, "A lógica migratória camponesa e o capital: O Nordeste brasileiro," in *Emprego rural e migrações na América Latina*, ed. Renato Duarte (Recife: Fundação Joaquim Nabuco and Massangana, 1986), 88; Santana, *Fartura e venturas camponesas*.

56 Cf. Borges, *Migrações internas no Brasil*, 33; Fischlowitz, *Principais problemas da migração nordestina*, 97.

57 Cf. Welch, *The Seed Was Planted*, 164–6s5.

58 Cf. Netto, "Contribuição do desenvolvimento e organização da comunidade e do planejamento socioeconômico ao problema dos deslocamentos populacionais," 65.

59 Cf. Antônio Jordão Netto, "São Paulo e o problema das migrações internas," *Sociologia* 25, no. 3 (September 1963): 212.

60 Andrade, "Migrantes nacionais no estado de São Paulo," 125–26.

61 Cf. Cleópatra Poli, "Atitudes de operários de procedência rural (transição ou incorporação à vida urbana)," *Sociologia* 31 (1981): 53.

62 For a survey of European and North American literature on the role of social networks in migratory processes and their relation to labor history, see Michael P. Hanagan, "Labor History and the New Migration History: A Review Essay," *International Labor and Working-Class History*, no. 54 (Fall 1998).

63 See, e.g., the now classic Durham, *A caminho da cidade*. See also Alvim, *A sedução da cidade*; Célia Toledo Lucena, *Artes de lembrar e de inventar. (Re)lembranças de migrantes* (São Paulo: Arte e Ciência, 1999); Ronaldo Aurélio G. Garcia, *Migrantes mineiros em Franca: Memória e trabalho na cidade industrial (1960–1980)* (Franca: Faculdade de História, Direito e Serviço Social, Universidade Estadual Paulista "Júlio de Mesquita Filho," 1997); Dulce Maria Tourinho Baptista, "Nas terras do 'Deus-dará.' Nordestinos e suas redes sociais em São Paulo," Ph.D. diss., Pontifícia Universidade Católica de São Paulo, 1998.

64 Dantas, "Movimentos de migrações internas em direção ao planalto paulista," 85.

65 Cf. Alvim, *A sedução da cidade*; Garcia, *Migrantes mineiros em Franca*.

66 Cf. Durham, *A caminho da cidade*, 130–34.

67 Cf. Andrade, "Migrantes nacionais no estado de São Paulo," 118; Durham, *A caminho da cidade*, 138.

68 Roniwalter Jatobá, *O pavão misterioso e outras memórias* (São Paulo: Geração Editorial, 1999), 30–33.

69 Cf. Baptista, "Nas terras do 'Deus-dará,'" 108; Durham, *A caminho da cidade*, 132; Andrade, "Migrantes nacionais no estado de São Paulo," 126.

70 Cf. Bertram Hutchinson, "The Migrant Population of Urban Brazil,"*América Latina* 6, no. 2 (1963): 61. This phenomenon was not restricted to Brazil. Surveying internal migrations in Latin America and the Caribbean, Edward Ebanks also argues for the importance of networks of parents, friends, and countrymen in the migratory process: Cf. Edward Ebanks, *Determinantes socioeconómicos de la migración interna* (Santiago de Chile: Centro Latinoamericano de Demografía, 1993).

71 Cf. José Albertino Rodrigues, "Condições econômico-sociais da mão de obra em São Paulo," mimeograph, Dieese, São Paulo, April 1958, 8; and the communication of the U.S. Consulate in São Paulo titled "Brief Résumé of Labor Force in São Paulo," October 27, 1958, U.S. National Archives 832.06/10–2758, box 4308.

72 Cf. Andrade, "Migrantes nacionais no estado de São Paulo," 126; Estrela, *Os sampauleiros*; Menezes, *Redes e enredos nas trilhas dos migrantes*.

73 Cf. Hutchinson, "The Migrant Population of Urban Brazil," 68.

74 *Última Hora* was created in 1951 in Rio de Janeiro by the journalist Samuel Weimer, a political ally of President Getulio Vargas, and was circulating in São Paulo with great popularity by the following year. It was the main periodical politically close to the laborist and nationalistic forces in the 1950s and 1960s. *Última Hora* was known for its innovative graphic format, with big headlines and an abundance of pictures, as well as for its coverage of labor issues, sports, and everyday working-class life.

75 Cf. *Folha da Noite*, August 8, 1956; "Brief Résumé of Labor Force in São Paulo"; *Última Hora*, January 14, 1959.

76 Cf. Colistete, *Labour Relations and Industrial Performance in Brazil*, chap. 1; Rodrigues, "Condições econômico-sociais da mão de obra em São Paulo," 7–11.

77 Cf. Colistete, *Labour Relations and Industrial Performance in Brazil*.

78 See Barbara Weinstein, *For Social Peace in Brazil: Industrialists and the Remaking of the Working Class in São Paulo, 1920–1964* (Chapel Hill: University of North Carolina Press, 1996); Colistete, *Labour Relations and Industrial Performance in Brazil*.

79 Without a doubt, this was the case at Nitro Química: cf. Paulo Fontes, *Trabalha-dores e cidadãos. Nitro Química: a fábrica e as lutas operárias* (São Paulo: AnnaBlume and Sindicato dos Trabalhadores da Indústria Químicas e Plásticas de São Paulo, 1997), esp. chaps. 2–3.

80 Cf. Antônio Jordão Netto, "Algumas considerações a propósito da estrutura profis-sional de migrantes nacionais no estado de São Paulo," *Sociologia* 27, no. 4 (December 1965).

81 Cf. Bosco and Netto, *Migrações*, 73.

82 Cf. Armando Corrêa da Silva, "Estrutura e mobilidade social do proletariado urbano em São Paulo," *Revista Civilização Brasileira*, no. 13 (1967).

83 See, among others, Fischlowitz, *Principais problemas da migração nordestina*, esp. chap. 6; Rodrigues, "Condições econômico-sociais da mão de obra em São Paulo," 14; Leda Maria Fraenkel, "Questionamentos sobre o mercado de trabalho das regiões metropolitanas brasileiras e suas relações com as migrações internas," in *Encontro brasileiro de estudos populacionais: contribuições apresentadas*, ed. Instituto Brasileiro de Geografia e Estatística (Rio de Janeiro: Instituto Brasileiro de Geogra-fia e Estatística, 1976), 321.

84 Comissão Nacional de Planejamento do II Congresso dos Metalúrgicos, "Os met-alúrgicos e a industrialização," *Revista Brasiliense* (May–June 1960).

85 Cf. Fischlowitz, *Principais problemas da migração nordestina*, 91–92; Antonio Luigi Negro, "Servos do tempo," in *De JK a FHC. A reinvenção dos carros*, ed. Glauco Arbix and Mauro Zilbovicius (São Paulo: Scritta, 1997), 109. For the formation of the working class in the automobile industry of ABC, see Antonio Luigi Negro, *Linhas de Montagem. O industrialismo nacional-desenvolvimentista e a sindicalização dos trabalhadores* (São Paulo: Boitempo, 2004).

86 Cf. Colistete, *Labour Relations and Industrial Performance in Brazil*, 41.

87 Cf. Bosco and Netto, *Migrações*, 64–a; Celso Carlos da Silva Simões et al., "Algu-mas características da participação dos membros da família na força de trabalho: 1950–1970," in Instituto Brasileiro de Geografia e Estatística, *Encontro brasileiro de estudos populacionais*, 351.

88 Cf. Fischlowitz. *Principais problemas da migração nordestina*, 147–48; Fraenkel, "Questionamentos sobre o mercado de trabalho das regiões metropolitanas brasileiras e suas relações com as migrações internas," 328. Of the employed women in a sample taken by Armando Corrêa Silva, 57.4 percent declared themselves domestics: cf. Silva, "Estrutura e mobilidade social do proletariado urbano em São Paulo." See also Estrela, *Os sampauleiros*, 166–68.

89 *Última Hora*, August 31, 1955, 9.

90 *A Hora*, October 6, 1955.

91 *Atas da Assembleia Legislativa do Estado de São Paulo*, 144th ordinary session, Octo-ber 21, 1955. *Translator's note:* A Paulista is a person from São Paulo.

92 *Atas da Assembleia Legislativa do Estado de São Paulo*, 56th ordinary session, June 24, 1958; *Anais da Câmara Municipal de São Paulo*, 24th ordinary session, March 25, 1960.

93 Cf. Lopes, *Sociedade industrial no Brasil*, 68.

94 Carolina Martescelli, "Uma pesquisa sobre aceitação de grupos nacionais, grupos nacionais, grupos 'raciais' e grupos regionais em São Paulo," *Psicologia,* no. 3 (1950): 67.

95 Cf. Alexandre Fortes et al., *Na luta por direitos. Estudos recentes em história social do trabalho* (Campinas: Editora da Unicamp, 1999): 189. In 1950, the proportion of whites in the total population of the city reached 87 percent: cf. J. R. de Araújo Filho, "A população paulistana," in *A cidade de São Paulo. Estudos de geografia urbana,* ed. Aroldo de Azevedo (São Paulo: Companhia Editora Nacional, 1958). In his study of workers in Volta Redonda, Oliver Dinius also reported this correspondence between skin color and migrants' being identified as "Bahian." In spite of the predominant migration from Minas Gerais and Espírito Santo, the great number of black and mixed migrants were generically called Bahians in Volta Redonda: cf. Oliver Dinius, *Brazil's Steel City: Developmentalism, Strategic Power, and Industrial Relations in Volta Redonda, 1941–1964* (Stanford, CA: Stanford University Press, 2011).

96 Bosco and Netto, *Migrações,* 32, 66–68; Antonio Sérgio Alfredo Guimarães, *Classes, raças e democracia* (São Paulo: Editora 34, 2002).

97 Cf. Lopes, *Sociedade industrial no Brasil,* 91.

98 *Translator's note: A pexeira* (lit., fishwife) is a knife widely used by rural northeasterners.

99 Cf. Weffort, "Nordestinos em São Paulo." Other examples are in Estrela, *Os sampauleiros,* 180–89.

100 *Anais da Câmara Municipal de São Paulo,* 96th ordinary session, October 22, 1956; *O Dia,* October 21, 1956, 12.

101 Partido Socialista Brasileiro, "A imigração e o atual momento histórico," *Revista de Imigração e Colonização* 10 (January–December 1949): 21; Roberto Pinto de Souza, "Deslocamento da população rural," *Digesto Econômico,* no. 83 (October 1951); Luís Fernando Maria Teixeira, "O desajuste e a recuperação do trabalho rural," *Revista de Imigração e Colonização* 10 (January–December 1949): 263; Francisco Barbosa Leite, "O pau-de-arara," *Revista Brasileira de Geografia* 17, no. 2 (April–June 1955): 222.

102 *Translator's note:* The term *bandeirantes* (followers of the flag) refers to pioneers and colonizers of São Paulo and other areas of Brazil. They were known for their expeditions into the countryside to find gold and other precious metals and to enslave indigenous people. The term "bandeirante" became synonymous with "Paulista," a person born in São Paulo.

103 *A Hora,* March 16, 1956.

104 See Frederico de Castro Neves, *A multidão e a história: Saques e outras ações de massa no Ceará* (Rio de Janeiro: Relume Dumará, 2000); Marco Antônio Villa, *Vida e morte no sertão. História das secas no Nordeste nos séculos XIX e XX* (São Paulo: Ática, 2000); Monia Melo Ferrari, "A migração nordestina para São Paulo no segundo governo Vargas (1951–54)—Secas e desigualdades regionais," master's thesis, Univesidade Federal de Sãi Carlos, 2005.

105 *Diário Oficial do Estado de São Paulo,* September 1, 1955, 43, June 9, 1956, 57.

106 *Anais da Câmara Municipal de São Paulo,* 457th ordinary session, March 1, 1959; *A Hora,* March 16, 1956.

107 *O Observador Econômico e Financeiro,* no. 194 (March 1952): 4.

108 Netto, "Contribuição do desenvolvimento e organização da comunidade e do planejamento socioeconômico ao problema dos deslocamentos populacionais," 66–69.

109 *Translator's note:* The Canudos War, in the interior of the state of Bahia, resulted in the massacre in 1897 by federal troops of thousands of poor peasants. One of the bloodiest and most significant social conflicts in Brazilian history, it was immortalized in *Os Sertões* (1902), written by Euclides da Cunha, a journalist who witnessed the massacre: see Euclides da Cunha, *Rebellion in the Backlands* (Chicago: University of Chicago Press, 1957).

110 Durval Muniz de Albuquerque Jr., *A invenção do Nordeste e outras artes* (Recife: Fundação Joaquim Nabuco e São Paulo, Cortez, 1999), 57–8.

111 About the role of intellectuals and artists in the "creation" of the Northeast, see de Albuquerque Jr. *A invenção do Nordeste,* and Michel Zaidan Filho, *O fim do Nordeste e outros mitos* (São Paulo: Cortez, 2001). For an argument about the discursive construction of "racial inferiority" of the northeasterners, see Stanley Blake, "The Medicalization of Nordestinos: Public Health and Regional Identity in northeastern Brazil, 1889–1939," *The Americas* 60, no. 2 (2003).

112 Mônica Pimenta Velloso, "A brasilidade verde-amarela: Nacionalismo e regionalismo paulista," *Estudos Históricos* 6, no. 11 (1993). For an analysis of the role of romances in migration (in the construction of social memory and a regionalist discourse about the Northeast and northeasterners), see Mirandulina Maria Moreira Azevedo, "Migração e memória: A experiência dos Nordestinos," Ph.D. diss., Department of Geography, Faculdade de Filosofia, Letras e Ciências Humanas, Universidade de São Paulo, 2002, esp. chap. 4.

113 Cf. Barbara Weinstein, "Racializing Regional Difference: São Paulo versus Brazil, 1932," in *Race and Nation in Modern Latin America,* ed. Nancy Appelbaum, Anne Macpherson and Karin Rosemblatt (Chapel Hill: University of North Carolina Press, 2003).

114 Angela de Castro Gomes, "Ideologia e trabalho no Estado Novo," in *Repensando o Estado Novo,* ed. Dulce Pandolfi (Rio de Janeiro: Editora Fundação Getulio Vargas, 1999), 68.

115 João Manuel Cardoso de Mello and Fernando Novais, "Capitalismo tardio e sociabilidade moderna," in *História da vida privada. Contrastes da intimidade contemporânea,* ed. Lilia Schwarcs (São Paulo: Companhia das Letras, 1998).

116 Geraldo Sarno, dir., *Viramundo,* film, São Paulo, 1965. For a now classic interpretation of this film, see Jean-Claude Bernardet, "O modelo sociológico ou a voz do dono: *Viramundo,*" in *Cineastas e imagem do povo* (São Paulo: Companhia das Letras, 2003).

117 *Notícias de Hoje,* October 15, 1957.

118 *Notícias de Hoje,* October 26, 1957.

119 Marcelo Ridenti, *Em busca do povo brasileiro. Artistas da revolução, do CPC à era da TV* (Rio de Janeiro: Record, 2000), 21–23. *Translator's note:* The Popular Culture Center, an organization linked to the National Union of Students, was created in the early 1960s by leftist intellectuals who aimed to promote a "popular revolutionary art."

120 *A Hora*, June 21, 1954.

121 *O Observador Econômico e Financeiro*, no. 195 (April 1952): 3–4; emphasis added.

122 Maura Penna, *O que faz ser nordestino. Identidades sociais, interesses e o "escândalo" Erundina* (São Paulo: Cortez, 1992), 28–29; Nunes, "Algumas notas sobre o Nordeste brasileiro."

CHAPTER 2. Land of the Northeasterners

1 Mario da Natividade Valladão, *Dá conta de tua mordomia* (São Paulo: Igreja Batista de São Miguel Paulista, 1986).

2 Jorge Amado, "O jovem Ramiro," in *Homens e coisas do Partido Comunista* (Rio de Janeiro: Edições Horizonte, 1946).

3 For an analysis of the history of São Miguel, see Sylvio Bomtempi, *O bairro de São Miguel Paulista. A aldeia de São Miguel do Ururaí na história de São Paulo* (São Paulo: Departamento de Cultura da Prefeitura Municipal, 1970); Aristides Pimentel, "Cronologia comentada da história de São Miguel Paulista 1493–1990," mimeograph, São Paulo, undated; Juergen R. Langenbuch, *A estruturação da grande São Paulo. Estudo de geografia urbana* (Rio de Janeiro: Fundação IBGE), 1971.

4 Langenbuch, *A estuturação da grande São Paulo*, 170.

5 Jover Telles, *O movimento sindical no Brasil* (São Paulo: Ciências Humanas, 1981), 31.

6 *Translator's note:* The city of Volta Redonda is approximately halfway between São Paulo and Rio de Janeiro, which was then the federal capital.

7 On the history of Nitro Química, see Paulo Fontes, *Trabalhadores e cidadãos. Nitro Química: a A fábrica e as lutas operárias nos anos 50.* (São Paulo: AnnaBlume and Sindicato dos Trabalhadores da Indústria STI Químicas e Plásticas de São Paulo, 1997), esp. chaps. 1–2.

8 Teresa Caldeira, *A política dos outros. O cotidiano dos moradores da periferia e o que pensam do poder e dos poderosos* (São Paulo: Brasiliense, 1984), 15; Lúcio Kowarick, "A expansão metropolitana e suas contradições em São Paulo," *Caderno do Ceas*, no. 102 (1986): 14.

9 About the concept of "peripheral pattern of urban growth," see Lúcio Kowarick and Nabil Bonduki, "Espaço urbano e espaço político: Do populismo à redemocratização," in *Social Struggles and the City: The Case of São Paulo*, ed. Lúcio Kowarick (New York: Monthly Review Press, 1994); Teresa Caldeira, *City of Walls: Crime, Segregation, and Citizenship in São Paulo.* (Oakland: University of California Press, 2000), esp. chap. 6; Eder Sader, *Quando novos personagens entraram em cena. Experiências e lutas dos trabalhadores na Grande São Paulo (1970–1980).* (Rio de Janeiro: Paz e Terra, 1988), esp. chap. 2; Lúcia Maria Bógus, "Urbanização e metropolização: O caso de São Paulo," in *A luta pela cidade em São Paulo*, ed. Lúcia Maria Bógus and Luiz Eduardo Wanderley (São Paulo: Cortez, 1992).

10 About worker housing and the process of urbanization in São Paulo in the first half of the twentieth century, see Eva Alterman Blay, *Eu não tenho onde morar. Vilas operárias na cidade de São Paulo* (São Paulo: Nobel, 1985); Maria Auxiliadora Guzzo Decca, *A vida fora das fábricas. Cotidiano operário em São Paulo: 1920–1934*

(Rio de Janeiro: Paz e Terra, 1987); Raquel Rolnik, *A cidade e a lei: Legislação, política urbana e territórios na cidade de São Paulo* (São Paulo: Studio Nobel and Fapesp, 1997); Nabil Bonduki, *Origens da habitação social no Brasil. Arquitetura moderna, Lei do Inquilinato e difusão da casa própria* (São Paulo: Estação Liberdade, 1998); Lúcio Kowarick, *Escritos urbanos* (São Paulo: Editora 34, 2000); Bógus, "Urbanização e metropolização."

11 Nabil Bonduki, "Crise na habitação e a luta pela moradia no pós-guerra," in Kowarick, *Social Struggles and the City*.

12 Bonduki, *Origens da habitação social no Brasil*. Landlord-tenant conflicts in the mid-1940s, as seen through an analysis of court proceedings, are studied in Adriano Duarte, *Cidadania e exclusão. Brasil: 1937–1945* (Florianópolis: Editora da Universidade Federal de São Carlos, 1999).

13 Aroldo de Azevedo, *A cidade de São Paulo. Estudos de geografia urbana*, vol. 2 (São Paulo: Companhia Editora Nacional, 1958), 155.

14 Kowarick, *Social Struggles and the City*; Langenbuch, *A estruturação da grande São Paulo*; Caldeira, *City of Walls*; Nabil Bonduki and Raquel Rolnik, "Periferia da grande São Paulo. Reprodução do espaço como expediente de reprodução da força de trabalho," in *A produção capitalista da casa (e da cidade) no Brasil industrial*, ed. Ermínia Maricato (São Paulo: Alfa-Ômega, 1982); Arlete M. Rodrigues and Manoel Seabra, "Habitação e espaço social na cidade de São Paulo," *Boletim Paulista de Geografia*, no. 64 (1986); Fernando Henrique Cardoso, Cândido Procópio Ferreira, and Lúcio Kowarick, "Considerações sobre o desenvolvimento de São Paulo: Cultura e participação," in *Cultura e participação na cidade de São Paulo*, ed. Fernando Henrique Cardoso et al. (São Paulo: Centro Brasileiro de Analise e Planejamento, 1973).

15 Cf. Cardoso et al., "Considerações sobre o desenvolvimento de São Paulo," 8.

16 Armando Corrêa da Silva, "Estrutura e mobilidade social do proletariado urbano em São Paulo," *Revista Civilização Brasileira*, no. 13, (May 1967): 77.

17 Oracy Nogueira, "Distribuição residencial de operários de um estabelecimento industrial em São Paulo," *Sociologia* 11, no. 1 (1949): 38–39; Kowarick, *Escritos urbanos*, 27.

18 Kowarick, "A expansão metropolitana e suas contradições em São Paulo," 15.

19 Langenbuch, *A estruturação da grande São Paulo*, 189–90.

20 Bomtempi, *O bairro de São Miguel Paulista*, 159.

21 Caldeira, *A política dos outros*, 31; Langenbuch, *A estruturação da grande São Paulo*, 251; Sader, *Quando novos personagens entraram em cena*, 125.

22 Aroldo de Azevedo, "Subúrbios orientais de São Paulo," diss. for the chair in Brazilian geography, Faculdade de Filosofia, Ciências e Letras, Universidade de São Paulo, 1945, 129–32.

23 *O Estado de São Paulo*, August 16, 1957, cited in Caldeira, *A política dos outros*, 39–40.

24 *A Hora*, October 8, 1954; *O Dia*, November 29, 1956.

25 *Translator's note*: The term *grilagem* (lit., cricketing) comes from an old-time fraudsters' practice of putting a document in a drawer with crickets to make it look old.

26 *A Hora*, December 19, 1954.

27 Langenbuch, *A estruturação da grande São Paulo*, 266–67.

28 Langenbuch, *A estruturação da grande São Paulo*, 269. In first place among the places surveyed was the municipality of São Bernardo do Campo, where 46 percent of the resident population worked in local industries.

29 The population of the district of São Miguel Paulista in 1950 was 16,022 (excluding the neighborhood of Ermelino Matarazzo, which from an administrative point of view belonged to São Miguel) and the number of workers at Nitro Química the same year was about four thousand: cf. Livro de Empregados, 1950, Collection of Companhia Nitro Química Brasileira.

30 The interviews cited in this chapter were given to the author by Adelço de Almeida, Aurelino de Andrade, Nair Cecchini, Belarmino Pereira Duarte, José Caldini Filho, Helena de Oliveira da Fonseca, Geraldo Rodrigues de Freitas, Milton Furlan, Celina Garcia, Osvaldo Pires de Holanda, Moisés Igel, Salomé Lúcia Igel, José Cecílio Irmão, Gerolino Costa Jacobina, Roniwalter Jatobá, Augusto Ferreira Lima, Osvaldo Lino José Gonçalves Lula, Waldomiro Macedo, Benedito Miguel, Artur Pinto de Oliveira, Maria José dos Santos Oliveira, Oscar Alonso de Oliveira, Irene Ramalho, Fábio Ravaglia, Antônio Xavier dos Santos, Joaquim Anselmo dos Santos, Afonso José da Silva, and José Ferreira da Silva.

31 Prefeitura Municipal de São Paulo, *Atlas da administração regional de São Miguel Paulista e Ermelino Matarazzo* (São Paulo: Coordenadoria de Gestão de Pessoas / Confederation of Open Access Repositories / Companhia de Processamento de Dados do Município de São Paulo, 1975); Antônio Augusto Arantes Neto, "Produção cultural e revitalização em bairros populares: O caso de São Miguel Paulista," mimeograph, São Paulo, December 1978, 18; Marília Pontes Sposito, ed., "Memória do movimento popular de arte do bairro de São Miguel: Cultura, arte e educação," mimeograph, Núcleo de Estudos de Sociologia da Educação, Faculdade de Educação, USP, 1987, 16; Cleide Lugarini de Andrade, "As lutas sociais por moradia na cidade de São Paulo: a experiência de São Miguel Paulista e Ermelino Matarazzo," master's thesis, Department of Social Science, Pontifícia Universidade Católica de São Paulo, 1989, 69.

32 In this chapter, I used transcripts of interviews given to the Documentation Laboratory of the Universidade Cruzeiro do Sul: Maria Degersília Aragão, Bartolomeu de Araújo, Amauri da Cunha, Luís Gerônimo Ferreira, Maria Fernanda dos Santos Gomes, Maria Ferreira Jensen, Maria Pureza de Mendonça, José Souza Nery, Darcy Xavier Ribeiro, Josué Pereira da Silva, Benedita de Souza, José Damasceno de Souza, and José Venâncio.

33 *Correio da Zona Leste*, September–October 1975.

34 Carlos Neiva, "Como evitar as greves," *O Observador Econômico e Financeiro*, January 1944.

35 Speeches of São Paulo councilmen Benedito Rocha and Rio Branco Paranhos in homage to Tarcílio Bernardo, a councilman with a strong electoral base in São Miguel Paulista: *Anais da Câmara Municipal de São Paulo*, 117th extraordinary session, December 16, 1961. Speech of State Deputy Hélio Dejtiar: *Diário Oficial do Estado de São Paulo*, September 10, 1968, 56–57.

36 Gilberto Nascimento, "S. Miguel: O Nordeste em S. Paulo," *O Estado de São Paulo*, August 28, 1987.

37 Transcription of interview with Catarina de Jesus Crusato Cano, Collection of Companhia Nitro Química Brasileira.

38 Fontes, *Trabalhadores e cidadãos*, 79–84.

39 Fontes, *Trabalhadores e cidadãos*, esp. chap. 2.

40 Examples of similar strategies can be found in the Companhia Docas de Santos and in the Fábrica Nacional de Motores in the interior of the state of Rio de Janeiro: cf. Fernando Teixeira da Silva, *A carga e a culpa. Os operários das docas de Santos: Direitos e cultura de solidariedade* (São Paulo: Hucitec, 1995); José Ricardo Ramalho, *Estado-patrão e cultura operária: O caso FNM* (Rio de Janeiro: Paz e Terra, 1989).

41 Fábio Ravaglia, "Contribuição à história da Companhia Nitro Química Brasileira: 1935–1985," mimeograph, Companhia Nitro Química Brasileira, São Paulo, 1988, 9.

42 Ravaglia, "Contribuição à história da Companhia Nitro Química Brasileira."

43 Ravaglia, "Contribuição à história da Companhia Nitro Química Brasileira," 39.

44 AESP, DEOPS sector, dossier 50-A-27, fols. 125–28. In the late 1940s, Nitro's management periodically sent lists of recently hired employees to the DOPS so the police could run background checks on their political histories.

45 Ravaglia, "Contribuição à história da Companhia Nitro Química Brasileira."

46 Fontes. *Trabalhadores e cidadãos.*

47 Paul Willis, *Aprendendo a ser trabalhador: Escola, resistência e reprodução social* (Porto Alegre: Artes Médicas, 1991).

48 Renato Colistete, *Labour Relations and Industrial Performance in Brazil: Greater São Paulo, 1945–1960* (Houndmills: Palgrave, 2001), 64.

49 Ravaglia, "Contribuição à história da Companhia Nitro Química Brasileira," section SENAI.

50 *Nitro Jornal*, no. 43, September 1956.

51 Ravaglia, "Contribuição à história da Companhia Nitro Química Brasileira," 26.

52 *Nitro Notícias*, no. 14, September 1993.

53 On the idea of women's work as a "necessity," see Mirta Lobato, "Women Workers in the 'Cathedrals of Corned Beef': Structure and Subjectivity in the Argentine Meatpacking Industry," in *The Gendered Worlds of Latin American Women Workers: From Household and Factory to the Union Hall and Ballot Box*, ed. John French and Daniel James (Durham, NC: Duke University Press, 1997). See also the case of the women workers of Porto Alegre analyzed in Alexandre Fortes, *Nós do quarto distrito. A classe trabalhadora porto-alegrense e a era Vargas* (Rio de Janeiro: Garamond, 2004), esp. chap. 1. For an analysis of the role of the differences of gender in the definition of what was considered skilled work, see Elizabeth Souza Lobo, *A classe operária tem dois sexos: Trabalho, dominação e resistência* (São Paulo: Brasiliense and Secretaria Municipal de Cultura, 1991). Important parallels can be drawn with other Latin American countries. An Argentine example is in Mirta Lobato, *La vida en las fábricas. Trabajo, protesta y política em uma comunidad obrera, Berisso (1904–1970)* (Buenos Aires: Prometeo Libros and Entrepasados, 2001). An interesting Colombian case is analyzed in Ann Farnsworth-Alvear, *Dulcinea in the Factory: Myths, Morals, Men, and Women in Colombia's Industrial Experiment, 1905–1960* (Durham, NC: Duke University Press, 2000).

54 A gender division of factory sections based on different associations attributed to feminine and masculine work seems to have been common in other large Brazilian companies of the period, as well: cf. Rosilene Alvim, *A sedução da cidade. Os operários-camponeses e a fábrica dos Ludgreen* (Rio de Janeiro: Graphia, 1997).

55 *Jornal da Tarde*, April 25, 1966. The wave of dismissals in 1966 is analyzed later.

56 *Diário Oficial do Estado de São Paulo*, June 15, 1960.

57 AESP, DEOPS sector, dossier 50-A-27, fo1.132.

58 Minutes of monthly meeting of CIPA, July 18, 1958, Collection of Compahia Nitro Química Brasileira.

59 Cited in Antônia Sarah Aziz Rocha, "O bairro à sombra da chaminé. Um estudo sobre a formação da classe trabalhadora da Companhia Nitro Química Brasileira de São Miguel Paulista (1935–1960)," master's thesis, Pontifícia Universidade Católica de São Paulo, 1992, 59.

60 AESP, DEOPS sector, dossier 50-A-27, fol. 151.

61 Roniwalter Jatobá, *Crônicas da vida operária* (São Paulo: Global, 1988).

62 "Poesia de cordel: A grande explosão da Nitro Química Brasileira," poesia de cordel, August 15, 1947, Collection of Companhia Nitro Química Brasileira. *Translator's note:* A *cordel* is a literary genre popular in the Northeast, written frequently in rhymed form, originating in oral repertoire, and later printed in pamphlets.

63 *A Gazeta Esportiva*, June 18, 1947; emphasis added.

64 Arantes Neto, "Produção cultural e revitalização em bairros populares," 11.

65 *Anais da Câmara Municipal de São Paulo*, 447th ordinary session, April 22, 1959, and 59th ordinary session, June 17, 1960.

66 *Diário Oficial do Estado de São Paulo*, May 31, 1967, 40.

67 *Notícias de Hoje*, January 15, 1959; AESP, DEOPS sector, dossier 50-B-259, fol. 73.

68 Interviews with Waldomiro Macedo and Antônio Xavier dos Santos.

69 José Sérgio Leite Lopes, *A tecelagem dos conflitos de classe na "cidade das chaminés"* (São Paulo: Marco Zero e Brasília, Editora da Universidade de Brasília, and Conselho Nacional de Desenvolvimento Científico e Tecnológico, 1988), 82.

70 *Nitro Jornal*, no. 10, October 1953, and no. 4, April 1953.

71 Juarez Brandão Lopes, *Sociedade industrial no Brasil* (São Paulo: Difel, 1964), 57, 69.

72 Leôncio Martins Rodrigues, *Conflito industrial e sindicalismo no Brasil* (São Paulo: Difel, 1966), 75.

CHAPTER 3. Worker Community and Everyday Life

1 Richard Hoggart, *The Uses of Literacy: Aspects of Working Class Life* (London: Chatto and Windus, 1957). In Brazil, in addition to analyses of urban anthropology and sociology, there has been a renewed interest in the history of work as it relates to social relations in the neighborhood: see, among others, Odette Carvalho de Lima Seabra, "Urbanização: Bairro e vida de bairro," *Travessia* 13, no. 38 (September 2000); Alexandre Fortes, *Nós do quarto distrito. A classe trabalhadora porto-alegrense e a era Vargas* (Rio de Janeiro: Garamond, 2004); Adriano Duarte, "Cultura popular e cultura política no após-guerra: Redemocratização, populismo e desenvolvi-

mentismo no neighborhood da Mooca, 1942–1973," Ph.D. diss., Universidade Estadual de Campinas, 2002; Murilo Leal Pereira Neto, *A reinvenção da classe trabalhadora (1953–1964)* (Campinas: Editora da Unicamp, 2011), esp. chap. 2.

2 Manoel Berlinck and Daniel Hogan, "Migrações interna e adaptação na cidade de São Paulo: Uma análise preliminar," in *Anais do I Simpósio de Desenvolvimento Econômico e Social: Migrações internas e desenvolvimento regional* (Belo Horizonte: Centro de Desenvolvimento e Planejamento Regional, Universidade Federal de Minas Gerais, 1972).

3 Cf. Liliana Tamagno, "Nordestinos Experiencing São Paulo: Time, Space and Identity in Relation to Internal Migration," master's thesis, Uppsala University, 1984, 56.

4 *Correio Paulistano*, April 11, 1948.

5 Mário da Natividade Valladão, *Dá conta de tua mordomia* (São Paulo: Igreja Batista de São Miguel Paulista, 1986), 5.

6 The interviews cited in this chapter were given to me by Aurelino de Andrade, Nelson Bernardo, Palmira Bernardo, Manuel Caçador, Nair Cecchini, Antônio Mendes Correa, José Caldini Filho, Helena Oliveira da Fonseca, Geraldo Rodrigues Freitas, Milton Furlan, Celina Garcia, Lídia Castelani, Osvaldo Pires de Holanda, Regina Igel, Salomé Igel, Gerolino Costa Jacobina, Roniwalter Jatobá, Augusto Ferreira Lima, João Freitas Lírio, Jorge Gonçalves Lula, Waldomiro Macedo, Antônio Pereira da Mata, Benedito Miguel, Artur Pinto de Oliveira, Maria José dos Santos Oliveira, Ana Maria Silvério Rachid, Irene Ramalho, Fábio Ravaglia, Antônio Xavier dos Santos, Joaquim Anselmo dos Santos, Afonso José da Silva, José Ferreira da Silva, and Valdevino Raimundo da Silva.

7 AESP, DEOPS sector, record 110703.

8 In his studies of immigrants in France, Abdelmalek Sayad verifies this "educational" character of their housing: cf. Abdelmalek Sayad, *Imigração ou os paradoxos da alteridade* (São Paulo: Editora da Universidade de São Paulo, 1998), 74–75.

9 *Folha de São Miguel*, no. 29, October 24, 1954.

10 Book list of employees of Companhia Nitro Química Brasileira, April 26, 1956–April 25, 1957.

11 Fernando Henrique Cardoso, Cândido Procópio Ferreira, and Lúcio Kowarick, "Considerações sobre o desenvolvimento de São Paulo: Cultura e participação," in *Cultura e participação na cidade de São Paulo*, ed. Fernando Henrique Cardoso and Paul Israel Singer (São Paulo: Centro Brasileiro de Analise e Planejamento, 1973), 8; Nabil Bonduki, *Origens da habitação social no Brasil. Arquitetura moderna, Lei do Inquilinato e difusão da casa própria* (São Paulo: Estação Liberdade, 1998), 307–12.

12 Juarez Brandão Lopes, *Sociedade industrial no Brasil* (São Paulo: Difel, 1964), 69. *Translator's note: Mutirão is the singular; mutirões is the plural.*

13 Gentil Martins Dias, *Depois do latifúndio. Continuidade e mudança na sociedade rural nordestina* (Rio de Janeiro: Tempo Brasileiro and Editora da Editora de Universidade de Brasília, 1978), 125; Clóvis Caldeira, *Mutirão. Formas de ajuda mútua no meio rural* (São Paulo: Companhia Editora Nacional, 1956).

14 Myrna Therezinha Rego Viana, "São Miguel Paulista. O chão dos desterrados (Um estudo de migração e de urbanização)," Master's thesis, Geography Department,

Facultad de Filosofia, Letras e Ciências Humanas, Universidade de São Paulo, 1982, 88.

15 Testimony in Antônia Sarah Aziz Rocha, "O bairro à sombra da chaminé: Um estudo sobre a formação da classe trabalhadora da Companhia Nitro Química de São Miguel Paulista (1935–1960)," Master's thesis, Pontifícia Universidade Católica de São Paulo, 1992, 79; *O Dia*, September 28, 1956.

16 Rev. P. J. L. Lebret, "Sondagem preliminar a um estudo sobre a habitação em São Paulo," *Revista do Arquivo Municipal* (April–May 1951).

17 *Translator's note:* A *roda* is a "wheel" or circle of people.

18 Lúcio Kowarick, *A espoliaçã urbana* (São Paulo: Paz e Terra, 1983); Francisco de Oliveira, *Economia brasileira: Crítica à razão dualista* (São Paulo: Editora Brasiliense and Centro Brasileiro de Analise e Planejamento, 1971); Ermínia Maricato, *A produção capitalista da casa (e da cidade) no Brasil industrial* (São Paulo: Alfaômega, 1982); Bonduki, *Origens da habitação social no Brasil*, 308; James Holston, "Autoconstruction in Working-Class Brazil," *Cultural Anthropology* 6, no. 4 (November 1991); James Holston, *Insurgent Citizenship: Disjunctions of Democracy and Modernity in Brazil* (Princeton, NJ: Princeton University Press, 2008). An update of part of this debate occurred recently in the pages of the journal *Novos Estudos*, published by the Centro Brasileiro de Análise e Planejamento (CEBRAP): cf. Francisco de Oliveira, "O vício da virtude. Auto-construção e acumulação capitalista no Brasil," *Novos Estudos*, no. 74 (March 2006); Sérgio Ferro, "Notas sobre o 'vício da virtude,'" *Novos Estudos*, no. 76 (November 2006); João Marcos Lopes, "O Anão caolho," *Novos Estudos*, no. 76 (November 2006).

19 Antônio Augusto Arantes Neto, "Produção cultural e revitalização em bairros populares: O caso de São Miguel Paulista," mimeograph, São Paulo, December 1978, 35.

20 Paulo Fontes, *Trabalhadores e cidadãos. Nitro Química: A fábrica e as lutas operárias nos anos 50* (São Paulo: AnnaBlume and Sindicato dos Trabalhadores da Indústria Químicas e Plásticas de São Paulo, 1997), esp. chap. 2; Barbara Weinstein, *For Social Peace in Brazil: Industrialists and the Remaking of the Working Class in São Paulo, 1920–1964* (Chapel Hill: University of North Carolina Press, 1996).

21 *O Dia*, September 28, 1956.

22 José Jorge Farah Neto and Rodolfo Kussarev Jr., *Almanaque do futebol paulista* (São Paulo: Panini, 2001), 414.

23 *A Gazeta Esportiva* was the most important and popular newspaper specializing in sports in São Paulo from the 1940s to the 1980s.

24 M. Terleote, *Um puoco do boxe do Clube de Regatas Nitro Química*, Collection of the Companhia Nitro Química Brasileira.

25 Cf. the testimony in Arantes Neto, "Produção cultural e revitalização em bairros populares," 33.

26 *Nitro Jornal*, no. 47, January 1957.

27 Testimony collected in Arantes Neto, "Produção cultural e revitalização em bairros populares," 27–29; Teresa Caldeira, *A política dos outros. O cotidiano dos moradores da periferia e o que pensam do poder e dos poderosos* (São Paulo: Brasiliense, 1984), 36. On the religious festivals in the first decades of the twentieth century in an area next to São Miguel Paulista, see Edson Penha de Jesus, "Penha: De bairro rural a

bairro paulistano. Um estudo do processo de configuração do espaço penhense," Master's thesis, Geography Department, Facultad de Filosofia, Letras e Ciências Humanas, Universidade de São Paulo, 2006, 127–31.

28 Cf. the testimony in Arantes Neto, "Produção cultural e revitalização em bairros populares," 29.

29 *Folha de São Miguel*, no. 29, October 24, 1954.

30 Fátima M. Rodrigues Antunes, "Diversão ou trabalho? O futebol dentro da fábrica," *DO Leitura* 12, no. 141 (February 1994): 8–9.

31 Fontes, *Trabalhadores e cidadãos*, 47–78.

32 *Nitro Jornal*, no. 35, December 1955.

33 Weinstein, *For Social Peace in Brazil*, 258–59.

34 In relation to the number of teams in São Miguel, cf. Marília Pontes Sposito, ed., "Memória do movimento popular de arte do bairro de São Miguel: Cultura, arte e educação," mimeograph, Núcleo de Estudos de Sociologia da Educação, Faculdade de Educação, Universidade de São Paulo, 1987.

35 J. V. Freitas Marcondes, "Aspectos do trabalho e do lazer em São Paulo," in *São Paulo: Espírito, povo, instituições*, ed. J. V. Freitas Marcondes and Osmar Pimentel (São Paulo: Livraria Pioneira Editora, 1968), 358.

36 A detailed history of the popularization of soccer in Brazil in the early twentieth century and its relationship with the various popular communities of Rio de Janeiro is in Leonardo Affonso de Miranda Pereira, *Footballmania. Uma história social do futebol no Rio de Janeiro, 1902–1938* (Rio de Janeiro: Nova Fronteira, 2000). For a more contemporary anthropological analysis of the importance of amateur soccer in the social networks of the periphery of São Paulo, see José Guilherme Cantor Magnani, *Festa no pedaço. Cultura popular e lazer na cidade* (São Paulo: Editora Brasiliense, 1984); Daniel Veloso Hirata, "No meio de campo: O que está em jogo no futebol de várzea?" in *Nas tramas da cidade. Trajetórias urbanas e seus territórios*, ed. Vera da Silva Telles and Robert Cabanes (São Paulo: Humanitas, 2006).

37 Information obtained in an informal conversation with Joaquim Serafim da Silva.

38 The election of workers' queens and princesses was common in the worker organizations of the period: see, e.g., Murilo Leal Pereira Neto, "A operária têxtil em São Paulo nos anos 50: Rainha dos trabalhadores ou grande sindicalista lutadora?" *Revista UniABC* 1, no. 1 (2005). In the 1950s, SESI also adopted the practice: cf. Barbara Weinstein, "Unskilled Workers, Skilled Housewife: Constructing the Working-Class Woman in São Paulo, Brazil," in *The Gendered Worlds of Latin American Women Workers: From Household and Factory to the Union Hall and Ballot Box*, ed. John French and Daniel James (Durham, NC: Duke University Press, 1997), 92. A similar phenomenon occurred in Argentina: cf. Mirta Lobato, ed., *Cuando las mujeres reinaban. Belleza, virtud y poder en la Argentina del siglo XX* (Buenos Aires: Biblos, 2005).

39 Marcondes, "Aspectos do trabalho e do lazer em São Paulo," 358.

40 Cristina Meneguello, *Poeira de estrelas. O cinema hollywoodiano na mídia brasileira nas décadas de 40 e 50* (Campinas: Editora da Unicamp, 1996), 43–51.

41 Inimá Simões, *Salas de cinema em São Paulo* (São Paulo: PW, Secretaria Municipal de Cultura, and Secretaria Estadual de Cultura, 1990); Marcondes, "Aspectos do trabalho e do lazer em São Paulo," 359.

42 *Última Hora,* July 22–23, 1978, 11; *Jornal da Tarde,* April 19, 1973.

43 Geraldo Antônio, "As 10 personalidades de São Miguel Paulista" in *São Miguel Agora,* no. 6, August–September 1987, 40.

44 *Translator's note:* A *batucada* is a fast-paced, drum-driven samba style. A *pandeiro* is a type of tambourine with a tunable head.

45 "A inquietação de São Miguel Paulista: Entrevista de Edvaldo Santana," *Carta Maior,* January 24, 2007, http://www.agenciacartamaior.com.br.

46 Sidney Chalhoub, *Trabalho, lar e botequim. O cotidiano dos trabalhadores do Rio de Janeiro da Belle Époque* (São Paulo: Editora Brasiliense, 1986).

47 Maria Célia Paoli, "São Paulo operária e suas imagens (1900–1940)," in *Espaço e Debates,* 9, no. 33 (1991): 35; Luiz Antonio Machado da Silva, "O significado do botequim," in *Cidade: Usos e abusos,* ed. Daniel Joseph Hogan (São Paulo: Editora Brasiliense, 1978), 81; Adriano Duarte, *Cidadania e exclusão. Brasil: 1937–1945* (Florianópolis: Editora da Universidade Federal de São Carlos, 1999), 271; Adriano Duarte and Maria Celia Paoli, "São Paulo no plural: Espaço público e redes de sociabilidade," in *História da cidade de São Paulo. A cidade na primeira metade do século XX (1890–1954),* vol. 3, ed. Paula Porta (São Paulo: Paz e Terra, 2004).

48 *Translator's note:* A *cavaquinho* is a ukulele-like instrument with four pairs of strings, typically used to play sixteenth-note rhythms in samba.

49 *Translator's note:* A *chorinho* is an upbeat, cheerful Brazilian musical style.

50 *Hoje,* January 21, 1946; AESP, DEOPS sector, record 59.619.

51 Sposito, "Memória do movimento popular de arte do bairro de São Miguel"; Sérgio Lessa and Maristela Mafei, "Movimento Popular de Arte," *Movimento,* October 19–25, 1981; "A inquietação de São Miguel Paulista: Entrevista com Edvaldo Santana," *Carta Maior,* January 24, 2007, http://www.agenciacartamaior.com.br.

52 See, e.g., *Nitro Jornal,* May 1953, January 1954.

53 *Anais da Câmara Municipal de São Paulo,* 346th ordinary session, November 17, 1954, and 474th ordinary session, December 14, 1955.

54 Cf. *Anais da Câmara Municipal de São Paulo,* 380th ordinary session, March 16, 1955, 398th ordinary session, May 2, 1955, and 78th ordinary session, September 19, 1956.

55 *O Estado de São Paulo,* September 19, 1957; *Anais da Câmara Municipal de São Paulo,* 249th ordinary session, September 11, 1957.

56 *A Hora,* May 11, 1956.

57 Founded in 1875 as *A Província de São Paulo* (the name was changed in 1889 with the proclamation of the republic in Brazil), *O Estado de São Paulo* is the most traditional newspaper in the state. For many decades it was considered the most important paper connected with the local political and economic local elites.

58 *O Dia,* October 2, 1956; *O Estado de São Paulo,* September 24, 1957.

59 *Correio Paulistano,* April 11, 1948.

60 *Anais da Câmara Municipal de São Paulo,* 239th ordinary session, August 29, 1957, and 243rd ordinary session, September 3, 1957.

61 *Correio Paulistano,* April 11, 1948; *Folha de São Miguel,* November 28, 1953.

62 *Anais da Câmara Municipal de São Paulo,* 55th ordinary session, June 11, 1956.

63 *Correio Paulistano,* April 11, 1948; *Folha de São Miguel,* November 28, 1953; *O Estado de São Paulo,* April 17, 1955.

64 *Diário Oficial do Estado de São Paulo,* June 1, 1961, 13.

65 *Anais da Câmara Municipal de São Paulo,* 344th ordinary session, November 10, 1954.

66 *Anais da Câmara Municipal de São Paulo,* 278th ordinary session, April 30, 1954, and 477th ordinary session, December 21, 1955.

67 *Anais da Câmara Municipal de São Paulo,* 108th ordinary session, November 21, 1952.

68 Aurélio Gaudêncio Ferreira Gonçalves, Maria de Fátima Bandeira dos Santos, and Vera Lúcia Bandeira dos Santos, "São Miguel Paulista," winning essay in a contest held by the Rotary Club of São Miguel Paulista, Raimundo de Menezes Public Library of São Miguel Paulista 1968, 18–19; "O colégio de São Miguel," *São Miguel Agora,* no. 6, August–September 1987.

69 *O Dia,* February 19, 1960.

70 Cf. Juergen R. Langenbuch, *A estruturação da grande São Paulo. Estudo de geografia urbana* (Rio de Janeiro: Fundação Instituto Brasileiro de Geografia e Estatística, 1971), 277.

71 Public transportation was one of the principal failings of São Paulo's postwar urban infrastructure, generating great dissatisfaction and at least one general conflict in the city, a riot in 1947: see José Álvaro Moisés, "Protesto urbano e política: O quebra-quebra de 1947," in *Cidade, povo e poder* (Rio de Janeiro: Paz e Terra, 1985). For a critical view of Moisés's interpretation, see Adriano Duarte, "O 'dia de São Bartolomeu' e o 'carnaval sem fim': O quebra-quebra de ônibus e bondes na cidade de São Paulo em agosto de 1947," *Revista Brasileira de História,* no. 50 (2005).

72 *Anais da Câmara Municipal de São Paulo,* 230th ordinary session, August 14, 1957.

73 Langenbuch, *A estruturação da grande São Paulo,* 190.

74 Gonçalves et al., "São Miguel Paulista," 17. In relation to the line to Penha, see also Jesus, "Penha," 171–72.

75 *Anais da Câmara Municipal de São Paulo,* 30th ordinary session, April 30, 1956.

76 *Anais da Câmara Municipal de São Paulo,* 124th ordinary session, January 31, 1957.

77 *O Estado de São Paulo,* August 26, 1952, and September 22, 1948.

78 *Anais da Câmara Municipal de São Paulo,* 32nd ordinary session, April 19, 1960.

79 *Última Hora,* April 22, 1959.

80 *Anais da Câmara Municipal de São Paulo,* 210th ordinary session, October 9, 1953.

81 *Anais da Câmara Municipal de São Paulo,* 210th ordinary session, June 13, 1957, and 259th ordinary session, March 16, 1960.

82 *Correio Paulistano,* April 11, 1948.

83 Berlinck and Hogan, "Migrações interna e adaptação na cidade de São Paulo"; Eunice Durham, *A caminho da cidade* (São Paulo: Perspectiva, 1976).

84 *Hoje,* December 28, 1950. AESP, DEOPS sector, dossier 50Z-591, fol. 12.

85 *Boletim Eleitoral do Tribunal Regional do Estado de São Paulo,* no. 42, February 17, 1949.

86 David Crew, "Class and Community: Local Research on Working-Class History in Four Countries," *Historische Zeitschrift* 15 (1986): 279.

87 Aroldo de Azevedo, "Subúrbios orientais de São Paulo," diss. for the chair in Brazilian geography, Faculdade de Filosofia, Ciências e Letras, Universidade de São Paulo, 1945, 129–31.

88 *Translator's note:* This is a colloquial expression that means pompous or arrogant.

89 Rocha, "O bairro à à sombra da chaminé," 20.

90 Antônio, "As 10 maiores personalidades de São Miguel Paulista" in *São Miguel Agora*, no. 6, August–September 1987, 40.

91 Cf. the testimony cited in Arantes Neto, "Produção cultural e revitalização em bairros populares," 33–34.

92 Norbert Elias and John L. Scotson, *Os estabelecidos e os outsiders. Sociologia das relações de poder a partir de uma pequena comunidade* (Rio de Janeiro: Jorge Zahar, 2000).

93 *História do Esperanto Klubo "Zamenhof" em São Miguel Paulista*, São Paulo, 1999, 3. Personal Archives of Osvaldo Pires de Holanda.

94 AESP, DEOPS sector, dossier 43-Z-0, fol. 909.

95 Aristides Pimentel, "Cronologia comentada da história de São Miguel Paulista 1493–1990," mimeograph, undated, São Paulo, 44; Ana Maria Silvério Rachid, interview by the author.

96 AESP, DEOPS sector, dossier 50-A-27, fol. 198.

97 Cf. testimony of Julius Meksenas, quoted in Duarte, "Cultura popular e cultura política no após-guerra."

98 *Translator's note: Cangaceiros* were bandits in the Northeast in the nineteenth and early twentieth centuries.

99 Cf. *A Hora*, May 3, 1955, October 24, 1955. The scenes from TV Tupi can be seen at the Cinemateca Brasileira: Base Tupi, December 18, 1961, NE12347.13–VV15011N.

100 *Translator's note:* A *caboclo* is a person of mixed European and Indian descent.

101 Fábio Ravaglia, "Contribuição à história da Companhia Nitro Química Brasileira: 1935–1985," mimeograph, Companhia Nitro Química Brasileira, São Paulo, 1988, table "Motivo de saída da companhia (1935–1984)."

102 *A Hora*, March 2, 1955.

103 *O Jornal*, September 1978; *O Estado de São Paulo*, August 28, 1987.

104 E. P. Thompson, "Rough Music," in *Customs in Common: Studies in Traditional Popular Culture* (London: Merlin, 1991). On the dockworkers of Santos, see Fernando Teixeira da Silva, "Valentia e cultura do trabalho na estiva de Santos," in *Culturas de classe. Identidade e diversidade na formação do operariado*, ed. Cláudio Batalha, Fernando Teixeira da Silva and Alexandre Fortes (Campinas: Editora da Unicamp, 2004). On the Chilean miners, see Thomas Miller Klubock, *Contested Communities: Class, Gender and Politics in Chile's El Teneiente Copper Mine, 1904–1951* (Durham, NC: Duke University Press, 1998).

105 *Translator's note: Cabro-macho* (lit., billy goat) is a term common in the Northeast to designate a brave man.

106 Among others, Jeffrey Lesser and Barbara Weinstein, analyzing quite different cases, call attention to the importance of dress in the constructing of indemnificatory processes: see Jeffrey Lesser, *Negotiating National Identity: Immigrants, Minorities and the Struggle for Ethnicity in Brazil* (Durham, NC: Duke University Press, 1999); Barbara Weinstein, "The Model Worker of the Paulista Industrialists: The 'Operário Padrão' Campaign," *Radical History Review*, no. 61 (Winter 1995): 92–123.

107 On the relationship among Luiz Gonzaga, northeastern regionalism, and migrants, see Durval Muniz de Albuquerque Jr., *A invenção do Nordeste e outras artes* (Recife: Fundação Joaquim Nabuco, 1999), 151–64; Bryan McCann, *Hello, Hello Brazil: Popular Music in the Making of Modern Brazil* (Durham, NC: Duke University Press, 2004). For more information about the artistic career of the "king of *baião*," see Dominique Dreyfus, *Vida do viajante. A saga de Luiz Gonzaga* (São Paulo: Editora 34, 1996).

108 João Batista de Andrade, dir., *O Homem que Virou Suco*, 1989. On this film, see Frederico de Castro Neves, "Armadilhas nordestinas: O Homem que Virou Suco," in *A história vai ao cinema: 20 filmes brasileiros comentados por historiadores*, ed. Jorge Ferreira and Mariza Soares (Rio de Janeiro: Record, 2001).

109 Silva, "Valentia e cultura do trabalho na estiva de Santos." In Chapter 1 we also saw that certain employers cited the northeasterners' "reputation as tough guys" as a reason for not hiring them.

110 Interview with picket chief, Glassworkers Union, October 1958, Fundo Fábio Munhoz, Centro de Desenvolvimento Multidisciplinar, Universidade Estadual Paulista.

111 AESP, DEOPS sector, dossier 50-Z-591, fol. 37.

112 *Translator's note:* The Janistas were followers of Jânio Quadros, then the governor of the state of São Paulo.

113 *A Hora*, October 26, 1954.

114 On the practices of homogenization of groups from "outsider" into "established" that implies a resignification of identities, see Elias and Scotson, *Os estabelecidos e os outsiders*. For an interesting analysis of a particular process of identity construction of an ethnic community in Brazil, see Lesser, *Negotiating National Identity*.

115 Jesus, "Penha," 190–93; Duarte, "Cultura popular e cultura política no após-guerra," esp. chap. 5.

116 For an important analysis of ideas and representations about racial constructions involving the poor as "metanarratives" that shaped the actions and proposals of Brazilian educators during the first half of the twentieth century, see Jerry Dávila, *Diploma of Whiteness: Race and Social Policy in Brazil, 1917–1945* (Durham, NC: Duke University Press, 2003).

117 Lopes, *Sociedade industrial no Brasil*, 70.

118 João de Barros, *O que faz o nordestino em São Paulo*, quoted in Tamagno, "Nordestinos Experiencing São Paulo: Time, Space and Identity in Relation to Internal Migration," master's thesis, Uppsala University, 1984, 31. *Translator's note:* The final line, which translates literally as "an ugly face is shamelessness," refers to a popular saying about people who make ugly faces when the time comes to work.

119 Weinstein, *For Social Peace in Brazil*. Owners with a more positive rhetoric about the national worker also existed: see, e.g., the analysis of the automobile industry in Antonio Luigi Negro, *Linhas de montagem: O industrialismo nacional-desenvolvimentista e a sindicalização dos trabalhadores* (São Paulo: Boitempo, 2004), esp. chap. 3.

120 See, among others, Lopes, *Sociedade industrial no Brasil*; Durham, *A caminho da cidade*.

CHAPTER 4. The Right to Practice Politics

1 For a general view of the participation of Brazil in the Second World War and its impact on the internal politics of the country, see Leslie Bethell and Ian Roxborough, *Latin America between the Second World and the Cold War, 1944–1948* (Cambridge: Cambridge University Press, 1992).

2 The interviews quoted in this chapter were given to me by Adelço de Almeida, Aurelino de Andrade, Nelson Bernardo, Nair Cecchini, Antônio Mendes Corrêa, José Caldini Filho, Helena de Oliveira da Fonseca, Geraldo Rodrigues de Freitas, Lídia Castelani, Osvaldo Pires de Holanda, Augusto Ferreira Lima, João Freitas Lírio, José Gonçalves Lula, Waldomiro Macedo, Antônio Pereira da Mata, Artur Pinto de Oliveira, Maria José Santos Oliveira, Ana Maria Silvério Rachid, Antônio Xavier dos Santos, Joaquim Anselmo dos Santos, and Afonso José da Silva.

3 Sílvio Frank Alem, "Os trabalhadores e a redemocratização," master's thesis, Instituto de Filosofia e Ciências Humanas, Universidade Estadual de Campinas, 1981; Maria Célia Paoli, "Labour, Law and State in Brazil: 1930–1950," Ph.D. diss., University of London, 1988; Hélio da Costa, *Em busca da memória. Comissão de fábrica, partido e sindicato no pós-guerra* (São Paulo: Scritta, 1995).

4 That was also the case with the National Steel Company (CSN), whose Personnel Department was nicknamed the "Gestapo gang": cf. Oliver Dinius, *Brazil's Steel City: Developmentalism, Strategic Power, and Industrial Relations in Volta Redonda, 1941–1964* (Stanford, CA: Stanford University Press, 2011), chap. 3.

5 For an analysis of the letters sent to Vargas, see Jorge Ferreira, *Trabalhadores do Brasil: O imaginário popular* (Rio de Janeiro: Editora da Fundação Getúlio Vargas, 1997). For another interpretation of these letters, see José Roberto Franco Reis, "Cartas a Vargas: Entre o favor, o direito e a luta política pela sobrevivência (1937–45)," *Locus* 7, no. 2 (2001).

6 DOPS was abolished in 1983, as part of the re-democratization process. In the case of the state of São Paulo, the immense documentation gathered by the police over six decades was placed in the Public Archive of the State of São Paulo and was opened to the public in the 1990s. For an analysis of the structure and history of DOPS, see Maria Aparecida de Aquino, Marco Aurélio Vannucchi Leme de Mattos, and Walter Cruz Swensson Jr., eds., *No coração das trevas: O DEOPS/SP visto por dentro* (São Paulo: Arquivo do Estado, Imprensa Oficial, 2001). For a specific analysis of the action of the political police in unions and companies, see Antonio Luigi Negro and Paulo Fontes, "Using Police Records in Labor History: A Case Study of Brazilian DOPS," *Labor: Studies in Working-Class History of the Americas* 5, no. 1 (2008).

7 AESP, DEOPS sector, dossier 50-A-27, fol. 8. Beginning in 1908 and over the following decades, more than 250,000 Japanese immigrants arrived in Brazil (especially São Paulo). In 1960, Brazil had the largest Nikkei population (the term most Japanese Brazilians use to refer to themselves) in the world. During the dictatorship of the Estado Novo and especially during the Second World War, the Japanese community in Brazil suffered repression and persecution. The different reactions by the members of that community were fundamental in the construction of postwar ethnic identity by the Japanese-descended population. For an analysis of Japanese immigration to

Brazil and its process of identity construction, see Jeffrey Lesser, *Negotiating National Identity: Immigrants, Minorities and the Struggle for Ethnicity in Brazil* (Durham, NC: Duke University Press, 1999).

8 *Translator's note:* The Integralists were partisans of Brazilian Integralist Action (AIB), the political movement founded by the writer Plínio Salgado in 1932. This ultraconservative movement, symbolized by the color green, was inspired by aspects of the social doctrine of the Catholic Church and was also sympathetic to Italian fascism. Throughout the 1930s, the AIB gained enormous support and had much influence on various social sectors and on the government. After a failed uprising against Vargas in 1938, the AIB was shut down and banished from politics. With the end of the Second World War, the Integralists reorganized into the Popular Representation Party (PRP), which, with much less appeal and influence than it had had in the 1930s, participated in the political game and in elections from 1945 to 1964. On Integralism, see the classic studies Ricardo Benzaquen de Araújo, *Totalitarismo e revolução: O integralismo de Plínio Salgado* (Rio de Janeiro: Jorge Zahar, 1988); Marilena Chauí, "Apontamentos para uma crítica à Ação Integralista Brasileira," in *Ideologia e mobilização popular* (São Paulo: Paz e Terra, 1978).

9 AESP, DEOPS sector, dossier 50-A-27, fols. 12–13. Regarding the relationship between Integralism and fascism in São Paulo, see João Fábio Bertonha, *Fascismo, nazismo, integralismo* (São Paulo: Ática, 2000).

10 For an overview of the political scenario of 1945 and the creation of new political parties, see the classic study by Thomas Skidmore, *Politics in Brazil, 1930–1964* (New York: Oxford University Press, 1967).

11 Francisco Weffort, "Origens do sindicalismo populista no Brasil," *Estudos* CEBRAP 4 (April–June 1973); Ricardo Maranhão, *Sindicatos e democratização* (São Paulo: Editora Brasiliense, 1979); Alem, "Os trabalhadores e a redemocratização"; Paoli, "Labour, Law, and the State in Brazil"; Costa, *Em busca da memória*; John French, *The Brazilian Workers' ABC: Class Conflict and Alliances in Modern São Paulo* (Chapel Hill: University of North Carolina Press, 1992).

12 Maranhão, *Sindicatos e democratização*, 77; Jorge Amado, *Homens e coisas do Partido Comunista* (Rio de Janeiro: Edições Horizonte, 1946), 44; Paulo Teixeira Iumatti, *Diários políticos de Caio Prado Júnior: 1945* (São Paulo: Editora Brasiliense, 1998), 142. Even if this number might be exaggerated (in the entire ABC region, for example, the party had a thousand members in 1947: see French, *The Brazilian Workers' ABC*, 233), a large and surprising surge in PCB membership definitely occurred in São Miguel. It became the largest party in the area during those years.

13 Cf. Amado, *Homens e coisas do Partido Comunista*, 45.

14 AESP, DEOPS sector, record 59.619.

15 Teresa Caldeira also found people in São Miguel who remembered the visit of Prestes to the neighborhood: Teresa Caldeira, *A política dos outros. O cotidiano dos moradores da periferia e o que pensam do poder e dos poderosos* (São Paulo: Editora Brasiliense, 1984), 271.

16 AESP, DEOPS sector, dossier 20-Z-39, fol. 281.

17 AESP, DEOPS sector, record 59.544, vols. 1–3.

18 AESP, DEOPS sector, dossier 20-Z-39, fols. 251, 288; *Hoje*, November 18, 1945.

19 Cf. Antônio Carlos Felix Nunes, PC *linha leste. Fragmentos da vida partidária* (São Paulo: Editorial Livramento, 1980), 79–80.

20 Testimony of Cícero dos Santos, quoted in Antônia Sarah Azis Rocha, "O bairro à sombra da chaminé: Um estudo sobre a formaçõ da classe trabahadora da Compan-hia Nitro Química de São Miguel Paulista (1935–1960)," master's thesis, Pontifícia Universidade Católica de São Paulo, 1992, 36–37.

21 An analysis of *Hoje*, the newspaper of the Communist Party in São Paulo, including coverage of the urban demands of the popular neighborhoods at that moment, is in Pedro Estevam Rocha Pomar, "Comunicação, cultura de esquerda e contra-hegemonia: O jornal *Hoje* (1945–1952)," Ph.D. diss., Escola de Comuni-cação e Artes, Universidade de São Paulo, 2006.

22 *Hoje*, November 22, 1946.

23 Paulo Fontes, *Trabalhadores e cidadãos. Nitro Química: A fábrica e as lutas operárias nos anos 50* (São Paulo: AnnaBlume and Sindicato dos Trabalhadores da Indús-tria Químicas e Plásticas de São Paulo, 1997), 103–19; Annez Troyano, *Estado e sindicalismo* (São Paulo: Simbolo, 1978), 42–59.

24 For more detail about this specific strike, see Fontes, *Trabalhadores e cidadãos*, 109–12; Costa, *Em busca da memória*, 77–83; AESP, DEOPS sector, record 57.727.

25 Rocha, "O bairro à sombra da chaminé," 35.

26 Miguel Caires de Brito was elected first substitute deputy to the Constituent Assembly. He was seated after the Municipal Committee of the party obliged the railway worker Mário Scott, the deputy-elect, to resign in favor of Caires: cf. Móises Vinhas, *O Partidão: A luta por um partido de massas (1922–1974)* (São Paulo: Hucitec, 1982), 91; Dulce Pandolfi, *Camaradas e companheiros. História e memória do* PCB (Rio de Janeiro: Relume Dumará, 1995).

27 *Hoje*, January 21, 1946, December 20, 1946.

28 AESP, DEOPS sector, dossier 50-A-27, fol. 6.

29 *Boletim Eleitoral do Tribunal Regional Eleitoral de São Paulo*, no. 24, May 24, 1948, 268, 284, 300, 315.

30 *Boletim eleitoral do Tribunal Regional Eleitoral de São Paulo*, no. 10, October 15, 1947, 129.

31 *Boletim eleitoral do Tribunal Regional Eleitoral de São Paulo*, no. 7, October 10, 1947; Caldeira, *A política dos outros*, 43. On the support of the PCB for Barros, see French, *The Brazilian Workers' ABC*.

32 Aziz Simão, "O voto operário em São Paulo," *Revista Brasileira de Estudos Políticos* 1, no. 1 (December 1956).

33 On the PTB in São Paulo, see Maria Victoria Benevides, *O PTB e o trabalhismo. Partido e sindicato em São Paulo (1945–1964)* (São Paulo: Editora Brasiliense and Centro de Estudos de Cultura Contemporânea, 1989).

34 *Hoje*, January 21, 1946.

35 In this chapter, I used oral history interviews with Elza Alcântra de Araújo, Josué Pereira da Silvam Laboratory of Historical Documentation, Universidade Cruzeiro do Sul.

36 *Hoje*, January 21, 1946.

37 *Translator's note: Gostoso* (lit., tasty) can also mean "sexy."

38 Vinhas, *O Partidão*; French, *The Brazilian Workers' ABC*, 222–23; Pandolfi, *Camaradas e companheiros*, 168–70; Marco Aurélio Santana, *Homens partidos. Comunistas e sindicatos no Brasil* (São Paulo: Boitempo, 2001).

39 Auto de Fechamento, Comitê Distrital de Baquirivú do Partido Comunista do Brasil, Tribunal Regional Eleitoral de São Paulo (processos avulsos).

40 AESP, DEOPS sector, record 86.465.

41 Fontes, *Trabalhadores e cidadãos*, 117–19.

42 AESP, DEOPS sector, record 59.544.

43 Testimony of Severino Barbosa, quoted in Rocha, "O bairro à sombra da chaminé," 37. Teresa Delta in São Bernardo do Campo is another interesting case of co-optation of an emerging popular leader by Barros in that period: see French, *The Brazilian Workers' ABC*.

44 Armando Mazzo, *Memórias de um militante político e sindical no ABC* (São Bernardo do Campo: Prefeitura do Município de São Bernardo do Campo, 1991); Costa, *Em busca da memória*, 123–27; French, *The Brazilian Workers' ABC*.

45 AESP, DEOPS sector, record 4.272; Tribunal Regional Eleitoral de São Paulo, box 3247.

46 Costa, *Em busca da memória*, 225.

47 Edgard Carone, *O PCB: 1943–1964*, vol. 2 (São Paulo: Difel, 1982), 72; Pandolfi, *Camaradas e companheiros*, 170–71. For two different visions of the proposals of parallel unions, see Costa, *Em busca da memória*, esp. chap. 3; Augusto César Buonicore, "Sindicalismo vermelho: A política sindical do PCB entre 1948 e 1952," *Cadernos AEL* 7, nos. 12–13 (2000).

48 AESP, DEOPS sector, dossier 43-Z-0, fol. 395.

49 AESP, DEOPS sector, dossier 50-A-27, fols. 131–32.

50 AESP, DEOPS/São Paulo sector, dossier 50-A-27, fol. 128; Fontes, *Trabalhadores e cidadãos*, 120–24. The controversial union tax was established during the Estado Novo dictatorship in 1939, and with few modifications it persists to the present day. It consists of an involuntary annual contribution of a day's salary that the employer deducts from the pay of every worker. These resources are then split among the government (Labor Ministry), union federations, and the local unions.

51 AESP, DEOPS sector, dossier 50-Z-591, fols. 4–5, dossier 50-A-27, fol. 134.

52 *Conto de réis* was the expression used in Brazil and Portugal to indicate a million réis. As of 1942, the cruzeiro was adopted as the currency instead of the réis, but the expression "contos" continued in wide use, especially among the popular classes.

53 AESP, DEOPS/São Paulo sector, dossier 50-A-27, fol. 151.

54 Fontes, *Trabalhadores e cidadãos*, esp. chap. 2.

55 AESP, DEOPS sector, dossier 50-A-27, fols. 178b, 167.

56 AESP, DEOPS sector, dossier 50-A-27, fols. 77, 176, 184–85.

57 AESP, DEOPS sector, dossier 50-A-27, fol. 174; emphasis added.

58 AESP, DEOPS sector, dossier 50-A-27, fol. 174; Antonio Luigi Negro, *Linhas de montagem. O industrialismo nacional-desenvolvimentista e a sindicalização dos trabalhadores* (São Paulo: Boitempo, 2004); Barbara Weinstein, *(Re)formação da classe trabalhadora no Brasil, 1920–1964* (São Paulo, Editora Cortez, 2000), chap. 8; Paulo

Sérgio Pinheiro, "State and Labor in the Vargas Years (1930–1945)," paper presented at "State and Labor 1930s: A Comparative Perspective," Naples, 1993.

59 For an analysis of a case of a workers' community formed by immigrants where the association between communism and "foreigner" and "anti-national" was quite successful, see Mirta Lobato, *La vida en las fábricas. Trabajo, protesta y política em uma comunidad obrera, Berisso (1904–1970)* (Buenos Aires: Prometeo Libros and Entrepasados, 2001), 64–66.

60 Wilson João Zampieri and Avelar Cezar Imamura, *Padre Aleixo Monteiro Mafra. O pastor de almas de São Miguel Paulista* (São Paulo: Universidade Cruzeiro do Sul, 1998). Father Aleixo Mafra, a popular and prominent figure in the community of São Miguel for almost three decades, was responsible for the parish between 1941 and 1964.

61 Resoluções do Congresso Operário Católico Nacional, Rio de Janeiro, 1937, cited in Damião Duque de Farias, *Em defesa da ordem. Aspectos da práxis conservadora católica no meio operário em São Paulo (1930–1945)* (São Paulo: Hucitec, 1998), 191.

62 *Nitro Jornal*, no. 5, May 1953.

63 For an analysis of the origins and concepts of the Workers' Circles, see Farias, *Em defesa da ordem*; Jesse Jane Vieira de Souza, *Círculos operários: A Igreja Católica e o mundo do trabalho no Brasil* (Rio de Janeiro: Editora Universidade Federal do Rio de Janeiro, 2002). A specific analysis of the working of a Workers' Circle in a neighborhood of São Paulo is in Adriano Duarte, "Cultura popular e cultura política no após-guerra: Redemocratização, populismo e desenvolvimentismo no bairro da Mooca, 1942–1973," Ph.D. diss., Universidade Estadual de Campinas, 2002, chap. 3.

64 AESP, DEOPS sector, record 62.487.

65 AESP, DEOPS sector, record 62.487.

66 Fontes, *Trabalhadores e cidadãos*, esp. chaps. 4–5; Annez Troyano, *Estado e sindicalismo* (São Paulo: Símbolo, 1978).

67 *Nitro Jornal*, no. 49, April 1957.

68 Fontes, *Trabalhadores e cidadãos*, 139–41. In his study of the FNM, José Ricardo Ramalho also registered a similar mistrust by workers stemming from the closeness of the local Workers' Circle with the administration of the company: José Ricardo Ramalho, *Estado-patrão e cultura operária: O caso FNM* (Rio de Janeiro: Paz e Terra, 1989), 191.

69 For an analysis of the courses offered to working women by the SESI, see Barbara Weinstein, *For Social Peace in Brazil: Industrialists and the Remaking of the Working Class in São Paulo, 1920–1964* (Chapel Hill: University of North Carolina Press, 1996).

70 In relation to social movements in the eastern region of the state capital in the 1970s and their relation to the new position of the Catholic Church, see, among others, Eder Sader, *Quando novos personagens entraram em cena. Experiências e lutas dos trabalhadores na Grande São Paulo (1970–1980)* (Rio de Janeiro: Paz e Terra, 1988), esp. chaps. 3–4; Catherine Iffy, *Transformar a metrópole: Igreja Católica, territórios e mobilizações sociais em São Paulo 1970–2000* (São Paulo: Editora Unesp, 2011).

71 An earlier version of this section was published as Paulo Fontes and Adriano Duarte, "O populismo visto da periferia: Adhemarismo e janismo nos bairros da Mooca e São Miguel Paulista (1947–1953)," *Cadernos AEL* 11, nos. 20–21 (2004).

72 Benevides, *O PTB e o trabalhismo.*

73 French, *The Brazilian Workers' ABC*; Regina Sampaio, *Adhemar de Barros e o PSP* (São Paulo: Global, 1982); Duarte, "Cultura popular e cultura política no após-guerra."

74 Cf. interview with Mario Beni in Fernando Henrique Cardoso, "Partidos e deputados em São Paulo (o voto e a representação política)," in *Os partidos e as eleições no Brasil,* ed. Fernando Henrique Cardoso and Bolivar Lamounier (Rio de Janeiro: Paz e Terra, 1975), 51; Duarte, "Cultura popular e cultura política no após-guerra."

75 For an analysis of the importance of visits to voters' homes in a recent context, see Karina Kuschnir, "Cultura e participação política no Rio de Janeiro," in *Antropologia, voto e representação política,* ed. Moacir Palmeira and Marcio Goldman (Rio de Janeiro: Contracapa, 1996).

76 Sampaio, *Adhemar de Barros e o PSP.*

77 Francisco Weffort, *O populismo na política brasileira* (Rio de Janeiro: Paz e Terra, 1978), 125–26.

78 AESP, DEOPS sector, record 69.506.

79 AESP, DEOPS sector, dossiers 21-J-11, fol. 24, 30-J-53, fol. 147.

80 Cf. *Boletim Eleitoral do Tribunal Regional Eleitoral de São Paulo,* supp. no. 9, November 6, 1951.

81 Silvana Maria de Moura Walmsley, "Origens do janismo. São Paulo, 1948/1953," master's thesis, Instituto de Filosofia e Ciências Humanas, Universidade Estadual de Campinas, 1992.

82 *Translator's note: pinga,* also known as *cachaça* and *aguardente,* is a distilled liquor made from sugarcane.

83 Duarte, "Cultura popular e cultura política no após-guerra."

84 Walmsley, "Origens do janismo," 81.

85 Benevides, *O PTB e o trabalhismo,* 59; Walmsley, "Origens do janismo," 124; Vera Lúcia Michalany Chaia, *A liderança política de Jânio Quadros, 1947–1990* (São Paulo: Humanidades, 1992), 50.

86 Luiz Tenório de Lima, *Movimento sindical e luta de classes* (São Paulo: Oliveira Mendes, 1998), 24.

87 Chaia, *A liderança política de Jânio Quadros,* 59, 62.

88 Cardoso, "Partidos e deputados em São Paulo," 55; Chaia, *A liderança política de Jânio Quadros,* 72.

89 José Álvaro Moisés, "Classes populares e protesto urbano," Ph.D. diss., Facultad de Filosofia, Letras e Ciências Humanas, Universidade de São Paulo, 1978, 278; Bolívar Lamounier, "Comportamento eleitoral em São Paulo: Passado e presente," in *Os partidos e as eleições no Brasil,* ed. Fernando Henrique Cardoso and Bolivar Lamounier (Rio de Janeiro: Paz e Terra, 1975), 21. Barros and Quadros ran for election against each other for governor in 1954 (Quadros won), for president in 1960 (Quadros won), and for governor again in 1962 (Barros won). Even in the 1962 election, which took place after the impact had been felt of Quadros's resignation from the presidency in 1961, Quadros beat Barros in São Miguel: see Caldeira, *A política dos outros,* 46.

90 *Boletim eleitoral do Tribunal Regional Eleitoral de São Paulo,* January 31, 1955. Quadros was elected governor by a narrow margin over Barros. He obtained 34.2 percent

of the votes, versus 33.3 percent for his rival. The wide margin of victory that he obtained in the capital, once again thanks to the peripheral neighborhoods, was fundamental to his being elected: cf. Chaia, *A liderança política de Jânio Quadros*, 112–15.

91 Cf. Chaia, *A liderança política de Jânio Quadros*, 103.

92 Fontes, *Trabalhadores e cidadãos*, esp. chap. 5; Paulo Fontes, "'Centenas de estopins acesos ao mesmo tempo.' A greve dos 400 mil, piquetes e a organização dos trabalhadores em São Paulo (1957)," in *Na luta por direitos. Estudos recentes em história social do trabalho*, ed. Alexandre Fortes, Antonio Luigi Negro, Fernando Teixeira da Silva, Hélio da Costa, and Paulo Fontes (Campinas: Editora da Unicamp, 1999).

93 On Rio Branco Paranhos and other workers' and union lawyers in São Paulo in the 1950s and 1960s, see Larissa Rosa Corrêa, "Trabalhadores e os doutores da lei: Direitos e Justiça do Trabalho na cidade de São Paulo—1953 a 1964," *Histórica*, no. 27 (November 2007).

94 *Boletim eleitoral do Tribunal Regional Eleitoral de São Paulo*, no. 141, January 1960.

95 AESP, DEOPS sector, dossier 50-Z-591, fol. 57.

96 The defense of a foreign policy more independent of the U.S. sphere of influence would be one of the most serious points of conflict between Quadros and his base of support, especially with the UDN: see, among others, Chaia, *A liderança política de Jânio Quadros*, 214–18; Michael W. Weis, *Cold Warriors and Coups d'État: Brazilian-American Relations, 1945–1964* (Albuquerque: University of New Mexico Press, 1993).

97 *Boletim eleitoral do Tribunal Regional Eleitoral de São Paulo*, no. 150, October 1960.

98 *Boletim eleitoral do Tribunal Regional Eleitoral de São Paulo*, no. 120, February 1956.

99 AESP, DEOPS sector, dossiers 21-J-1, fol. 123, 284, 50-Z-591, fol. 37.

100 *Anais da Câmara Municipal de São Paulo*, 42nd ordinary session, May 11, 1956.

101 For an interesting analysis of politicians aiding their voters in a rural community, see Beatriz Heredia, "Política, família, comunidade," in *Antropologia, voto e representação política*, ed. Moacir Palmeira and Marcio Goldman (Rio de Janeiro: Contracapa, 1996).

102 *Última Hora*, August 20, 1958; emphasis added.

103 Cf. *Boletim Eleitoral Tribunal Regional Eleitoral de São Paulo*, no. 120, February 1956, no. 130, March 1957, no. 141, January 1960. In 1957, Andrade was classified as the fourth alternate state representative for the PSP, and Bernardo was classified as the third alternate for the PTN.

104 On the relationship between amateur soccer clubs and politics, see Odette Carvalho de Lima Seabra, "Urbanização e fragmentação: Cotidiano e vida de neighborhood na metamorfose da cidade em metrópole," diss., Department of Geography, Facultad de Filosofia, Letras e Ciências Humanas, Universidade de São Paulo, 2003; Adriano Duarte and Maria Célia Paoli, "São Paulo no plural: Espaço público e redes de sociabilidade," in *História da cidade de São Paulo. A cidade na primeira metade do século XX (1890–1954)*, vol. 3, ed. Paula Porta (São Paulo: Paz e Terra, 2004).

105 *Anais da Câmara Municipal de São Paulo*, 79th ordinary session, September 12, 1956, 416th ordinary session, July 19, 1963, 79th ordinary session, September 9, 1960.

106 *Anais da Câmara Municipal de São Paulo*, 254th ordinary session, September 18, 1957, 85th ordinary session, September 23, 1960.

CHAPTER 5. Workers and the Neighborhood

1 The reference to São Paulo as "a hotbed of social movements" is in José Álvaro Moisés, "Classes populares e protesto urbano," Ph.D. diss., Facultad de Filosofia, Letras e Ciências Humanas, Universidade de São Paulo, 1978. A history of the Neighborhood Friends Societies is in the same dissertation, esp. chaps. 5–6.

2 AESP, DEOPS sector, dossier 30-J-59, fols. 44, 51.

3 *Notícias de Hoje*, August 17, 1956, in AESP, DEOPS/São Paulo sector, dossier 30-J-59, fol. 55.

4 Moisés, "Classes populares e protesto urbano," 196–208.

5 "Fundada a Federação das Sociedades Amigos dos Neighborhoods," *A Hora*, August 24, 1954.

6 AESP, DEOPS sector, dossier 50-J-138, fol. 145.

7 AESP, DEOPS sector, dossier 50-J-138, fol. 160.

8 AESP, DEOPS sector, dossier 50-J-138, fols. 168, 176, 189; *Anais da Câmara Municipal de São Paulo*, 262nd session, September 30, 1957.

9 U.S. National Archives, Washington, DC, doc. no. 83201/2–2037, box 4308; AESP, DEOPS sector, dossier 50-J-138, fols. 126, 193.

10 *Última Hora*, June 16, 1958.

11 AESP, DEOPS sector, dossier 50-J-138, folder 1. See also Murilo Leal Pereira Neto, *A reinvenção da classe trabalhadora (1953–1964)* (Campinas: Editora da Unicamp, 2011), esp. chap. 4.

12 AESP, DEOPS sector, dossier 50-J-138, fol. d.

13 Public Record Office, London, FO 371/139125; AESP, DEOPS sector, dossier 50-J-138, fol. 323.

14 Fernando Henrique Cardoso and Paul Israel Singer, *Cultura e participação na cidade de São Paulo* (São Paulo: Centro Brasileiro de Analise e Planejamento, 1973), 12–13; Moisés, "Classes populares e protesto urbano," 182.

15 The testimony in this chapter was given to the author by Nelson Bernardo, Manuel Caçador, José Caldini Filho, Geraldo Rodrigues de Freitas, Osvaldo Pires de Holanda, Jorge Gonçalves Lula, Augusto Ferreira Lima, Waldomiro Macedo, Antônio Pereira da Mata, Artur Pinto de Oliveira, Joaquim Anselmo dos Santos, José Ferreira da Silva, and Valdevino Raimundo da Silva.

16 Quoted in Antônio Augusto Arantes Neto, "Produção cultural e revitalização em bairros populares: O caso de São Miguel Paulista," mimeograph, São Paulo, December 1978, 19–20.

17 *O Estado de São Paulo*, August 4, 1945.

18 Moisés, "Classes populares e protesto urbano," 228–36.

19 Paulo Fontes, *Trabalhadores e cidadãos. Nitro Química: A fábrica e as lutas operárias nos anos 50* (São Paulo: AnnaBlume and Sindicato dos Trabalhadores da Indústria Químicas e Plásticas de São Paulo, 1997), esp. chaps. 4–5.

20 Paulo Fontes, "Centenas de estopins acesos ao mesmo tempo." A greve dos 400 mil, piquetes e a organização dos trabalhadores em São Paulo (1957)," in *Na luta por direitos. Estudos recentes em história social do trabalho*, ed. Alexandre Fortes, Antonio Luigi Negro, Fernando Teixeira da Silva, Hélio da Costa, and Paulo Fontes (Campinas: Editora da Unicamp, 1999); Paulo Fontes and Francisco Barbosa de Macedo, "Strikes and Pickets in Brazil: Working-Class Mobilization in the 'Old' and 'New' Unionism, the Strikes of 1957 and 1980," *International Labor and Working Class History* 86 (2013); Antônio Luigi Negro, *Linhas de montagem. O industrialismo nacional-desenvolvimentista e a sindicalização dos trabalhadores* (São Paulo: Boitempo, 2004); Pereira Neto, *A reinvenção da classe trabalhadora*.

21 Prefeitura Municipal de São Paulo, *O poder em São Paulo: História da administração pública da cidade, 1554–1992* (São Paulo: Cortez, 1992), 89.

22 *Livro de atas do Movimento Popular Autonomista de São Miguel Paulista*, 1–3; *Estatutos do Movimento Popular Autonomista 16 de Junho*, 1. Raimundo de Menezes Public Library of São Miguel Paulista.

23 Moisés, "Classes populares e protesto urbano."

24 *Folha de São Miguel*, no. 32, November 28, 1953.

25 AESP, DEOPS sector, dossier 50-Z-591, fols. 24–25.

26 "Salva-te povo dos políticos separatistas!" pamphlet, personal collection of José Caldini Filho.

27 "Explicação necessária: Porque devemos voltar contra a autonomia," pamphlet, personal collection of José Caldini Filho.

28 AESP, DEOPS, dossier 50-Z-591, fols. 29–30

29 "Coação no plebiscito de São Miguel Paulista," newspaper clipping, personal collection of José Caldini Filho.

30 *Anais da Câmara Municipal de São Paulo*, 284th ordinary session, October 30, 1957.

31 *Folha de São Paulo*, December 23, 1958. The total number of voters in the elections of October 3, 1958, in São Miguel is in *Boletim Eleitoral do Tribunal Regional Eleitoral de São Paulo*, no. 136, October–December 1958.

32 AESP, DEOPS sector, dossier 50-Z-591, fol. 64.

33 *Livro de atas do Movimento Popular Autonomista de São Miguel Paulista*, 47.

34 AESP, DEOPS sector, dossier 50-Z-591, fol. 62.

35 *Livro de atas do Movimento Popular Autonomista de São Miguel Paulista*, 8, 24, 26, 42, 39.

36 *A Média*, no. 12, April 1963.

37 "Carta do Sindicato dos Químicos ao MPA," dated April 18, 1963, and signed by Gabriel Alves Viana, personal collection of Osvaldo Pires de Holanda.

38 *Novos Rumos*, March 22–28, 1963.

39 Moisés, "Classes populares e protesto urbano," 330–31, 369.

40 "Cartaz: Você é autonomista? Então peça aqui o seu distintivo. Oferta desta casa aos seus distintos clientes" and lyric of the "Hino da autonomia de São Miguel Paulista" (music by Antônio José da Silva, lyric by Osvaldo Pires de Holanda and Paulo de Luna), personal collection of Osvaldo Pires de Holanda.

41 Teresa Caldeira, *A política dos outros. O cotidiano dos moradores da periferia e o que pensam do poder e dos poderosos* (São Paulo: Editora Brasiliense, 1984), 271, 274–75.

42 *Boletim eleitoral do Tribunal Regional Eleitoral de São Paulo*, no. 150, October 1960.

43 Testimony of Gersino, quoted in Caldeira, *A política dos outros*, 271.

44 *Diário oficial do estado de São Paulo*, September 13, 1961, 50; *Anais da Câmara Municipal de São Paulo*, 299th ordinary session, June 25, 1962, 315th ordinary session, September 5, 1962, 26th ordinary session, April 6, 1964.

45 Fontes, *Trabalhadores e cidadãos*; Fábio Ravaglia, "Contribuição à história da Companhia Nitro Química Brasileira: 1935–1985," mimeograph, Companhia Nitro Química Brasileira, São Paulo, 1988, 15–23.

46 Ravaglia, "Contribuição à história da Companhia Nitro Química Brasileira," 18; AESP, DEOPS, dossier 50-B-259, fol. 26.

47 Larissa Rosa Corrêa, "Trabalhadores e os doutores da lei: Direitos e Justiça do Trabalho na cidade de São Paulo—1953 a 1964," *Histórica*, no. 27 (November 2007).

48 AESP, DEOPS sector, dossier 50-B-259, fol. 49.

49 For different analyses of the symbolic importance of the CLT in the political culture of Brazilian workers, see, among others, John French, *Afogados em leis. A CLT e a cultura política dos trabalhadores brasileiros* (São Paulo: Editora da Fundação Perseu Abramo, 2001); Angela de Castro Gomes, *A invenção do trabalhismo* (Rio de Janeiro: Editora Fundação Getulio Vargas, 2005); Maria Célia Paoli, "Labour, Law, and the State in Brazil, 1930–1950," Ph.D. diss., University of London, 1988.

50 Processo TRT/São Paulo, 67/63, A. Acordão no. 475/63, February 19, 1963, Biblioteca Adelço de Almeida.

51 This strike is remembered as the Strike of the 700,000. For more details, see Márcia de Paula Leite and Sidney Sólis, "O último vendaval: a greve dos 700 mil," *Cara a cara*, no. 2 (1978); Negro, *Linhas de montagem*; Pereira Neto, *A reinvenção da classe trabalhadora*, chap. 5.

52 *Notícias Populares*, October 29, 1963; *Novos Rumos*, November 1–7, 1963.

53 *Notícias Populares*, November 7, 1963.

54 AESP, DEOPS sector, dossier 50-B-259, fol. 173.

55 AESP, DEOPS sector, dossier 50-Z-591, fols. 67, 73.

56 For a critical analysis of the dominant political line of the PCB during the post-coup years and the rise of the ALN and other groups of armed struggle see, among others, Jacob Gorender, *Combate nas trevas. A esquerda brasileira: Das ilusões perdidas à luta armada* (São Paulo: Ática, 1987); Daniel Aarão Reis Filho, *A revolução faltou ao encontro* (São Paulo: Editora Brasiliense, 1991); Marcelo Ridenti, *O fantasma da revolução brasileira* (São Paulo: Editora Unesp and Fundação de Amparo à Pesquisa do Estado de São Paulo, 1993). For an excellent biography of Marighella, see Mario Magalhães, *Carlos Mariguella: O guerrilheiro que incendiou o mundo* (São Paulo: Companhia das Letras, 2012).

57 Edileuza Pimenta and Edson Teixeira, *Virgílio Gomes da Silva: De retirante a guerrilheiro* (São Paulo: Plena Editorial, 2009); Karim Roberta de Almeida, "Esquerda em armas: A trajetória da classe operária de São Miguel Paulista na luta armada (1968–1974)," typescript, Trabalho de Conclusão de Curso, Departamento de História, Universidade Cruzeiro do Sul, São Paulo, 2001.

58 *A Gazeta Esportiva*, April 6, 1966.

59 A Gazeta Esportiva, April 10, 1966; Jornal da Tarde, April 20, 1966, May 2, 1966; O Estado de São Paulo, August 10, 1969.
60 Jornal da Tarde, April 16, 1966.
61 Jornal da Tarde, April 25, 1966, April 15, 1966.
62 O Estado de São Paulo, April 21, 1966; A Gazeta Esportiva, April 24, 1966.
63 Jornal da Tarde, April 25, 1966; O Estado de São Paulo, August 10, 1969.

CONCLUSION

1 In addition to Weffort, José Álvaro Moisés, Fábio Munhoz, and Régis Andrade, among others, participated in the discussions and research. Part of the material collected by them is in Fundo Fábio Munhoz, Centro de Documentação e Memória, Universidade Estadual São Paulo.

2 Interview with a worker from Ceará (Companhia Siderúrgica Paulista), Fundo Fábio Munhoz, Centro de Documentação e Memória, Universidade Estadual São Paulo.

ARCHIVAL SOURCES

Adelço de Almeida Library, São Paulo Chemical Workers Union

Newspapers and pamphlets
Photographs
Union minutes

Archive of the Metropolitan Curia

Material about the parish of São Miguel Paulista

Center for Migratory Studies

Books and periodicals

Centro de Desenvolvimento Multidisciplinar (CEDEM), Universidade Estadual Paulista

Fundo Roberto Morena–PCB
Fundo ASMOB
Fundo Fábio Munhoz

Collections of Institutions in São Miguel Paulista

Baptist Church of São Miguel
Carlos Gomes Escola
Diogo de Faria School
D. Pedro School
Municipal Library of São Miguel Paulista
Registrar de São Miguel
Rotary Club de São Miguel

Companhia Nitro Química Brasileira Collection

Nitro Jornal
Photographs
Varied documentation

Documentation Laboratory, Universidade Cruzeiro do Sul
Photographs
Varied documentation

Edgard Leuenroth Archive, Universidade Estadual de Campinas
Newspaper collection

Instituto de Filosofia e Ciências Humanas Libraries, Universidade Estadual de Campinas
Books and periodicals

Judicial Archive
Criminal proceedings

Library and Documentation Center of the Legislative Assembly of São Paulo
Minutes of the sessions
Books and periodicals

Library of the Municipal Council of São Paulo
Minutes of sessions
Books and newspapers
Newspaper collection
Varied documentation

Library of the Regional Electoral Court
Electoral bulletins

Mário de Andrade Library
Books and periodicals
Newspaper collection

National Archives, Washington, DC
Diplomatic documentation

Public Archive of the State of São Paulo (Arquivo Público do Estado de São Paulo; AESP)
DEOPS Collection
Newspaper Collection

Public Record Office, London
Diplomatic documentation

National Library, Rio de Janeiro

Books and periodicals

Newspaper collection

Personal Collections

Nelson Bernardo

Nair Cecchini

José Caldini Filho

Osvaldo Pires de Holanda

Helena Oliveira Silveira

Roberto Simonsen Library, Federação das Indústrias do Estado de São Paulo (now incorporated into the library of the Instituto de Filosofia e Ciências Humanas, Universidade Estadual de Campinas)

Books and periodicals

Universidade de São Paulo Libraries (Facultad de Filosofia, Letras e Ciências Humanas, Faculdade de Arquitetura e Urbanismo, and Faculdade de Economia, Administração e Contabilidade)

Books and periodicals

University of Manchester Library, United Kingdom

Books and periodicals

Working Class Movement Library, Salford, United Kingdom

Books and periodicals

ORAL HISTORY INTERVIEWS

Library of Historical Documentation, Universidade Cruzeiro do Sul (UNICSUL)

Transcriptions of fifty-four interviews with neighborhood residents. The interviews were carried out by students of the history program of UNICSUL, coordinated by Professor Ana Bárbara Pederiva. The following are the names of those interviewed (with dates of interviews, when available):

Alcântra, Elvira Souza de (June 16, 2000)

Andrade, Fildecino Silva de (April 15, 2000)

Aoki, Kazume (May 8, 2000)

Aoki, Mikui (May 8, 2000)

Aragão, Alderi Campos (September 29, 2000)

Aragão, Maria Degersília (September 29, 2000)

Araújo, Bartolomeu de

Arcanjo, Sacha
Augusto, Miguel (April 20, 2000)
Cacian, Maria das Graças Lins
Caldini, Augusto
Carvalho, Juraci Pereira de (October 9, 2000)
Cunha, Amauri da (May 20, 2000)
Dias, Nelson (March 25, 2000)
Fernandes, Henriqueta Lopes (May 13, 2000)
Ferreira, Antônio Benedito Guedes (April 20, 2000)
Ferreira, Antônio Joaquim
Ferreira, Luiz Gerônimo
Geraldo, Laurentina C. (March 25, 2000)
Gomes, Maria Fernanda dos Santos (April 20, 2000)
Guimarães, Lucilene Sanches (March 25, 2000)
Jensen, Agenor Antônio
Jensen, Maria José
Jesus, Valter de (June 3, 2000)
Lima, Antônio Nilton de
Mateus, Regina Aparecida (May 1, 2000)
Matos, Vilma Garcia (September 21, 2000)
Mendonça, Maria Pureza de (September 29, 2000)
Mesquita, Sebastião A.
Nery, Júlio de Souza (April 1, 2000)
Paschoal, Iracema (October 16, 2000)
Pedro, José (June 15, 2000)
Pereira, Cícero Antônio (April 29, 2000)
Pimentel, Aristides (October 6, 2000)
Pires, Artur (March 30, 2000)
Ramos, Davi de
Ribeiro, Beatriz Maria
Ribeiro, Bernardete G.
Ribeiro, Darci Xavier
Ribeiro, Vilma Costa (October 13, 2000)
Santana, Josefa Batista Almeida (November 9, 2000)
Santos, Elza Jardelina dos
Santos, Maria Eunice dos (April 24, 2000)
Silva, Bartolomeu Tragino da
Silva, Gilberto Gonçalves da (April 29, 2000)
Silva, Josué Pereira da
Silva, Valdemir Lopes da (September 12, 2000)
Sobrinho, José Amaro (October 26, 2000)
Souza, Benedita de
Souza, Elza Alcântra de (April 29, 2000)
Souza, José Damasceno de (April 10, 2000)
Souza, Sebastião Azaria de (April 7, 2000)

Venâncio, José (April 8, 2000)

Vieira, Benedito Carlos dos Santos

Interviews by the Author

The cassettes and copies of the interview transcriptions are in the Raimundo de Menezes Public Library of São Miguel Paulista. Copies of the documentation and sources researched were also donated to the library.

Almeida, Adelço de (April 25, 1994)

Andrade, Aurelino Soares de (June 1, 1998, December 1, 2001)

Bernardo, Nelson (August 7, 2001)

Caçador, Manuel (March 14, 2000)

Caldini Filho, José (May 24, 2000)

Castelani, Lídia (February 23, 2000)

Cecchini, Nair (March 21, 2000)

Corrêa, Antônio Mendes (July 27, 2000)

Duarte, Belarmino Pereira (November 15, 1994)

Freitas, Geraldo Rodrigues de (November 15, 1994, August 3, 2000)

Furlan, Milton (October 15, 1997)

Garcia, Celina (September 19, 2000)

Holanda, Oswaldo Pires de (May 31, 2000)

Igel, Moisés (June 12, 2000)

Igel, Salomé Lúcia (June 12, 2000)

Irmão, José Cecílio (October 20, 1994)

Jacobina, Gerolino Costa (October 15, 1997)

Jatobá, Roniwalter (May 12, 2000)

Lima, Augusto Ferreira (May 18, 1998)

Lima, Luíz Tenório de (April 4, 1997, September 9, 1997)

Lino, Osvaldo (May 6, 1994)

Lírio, João Freitas (September 19, 2000)

Lula, Jorge Gonçalves (June 21, 2000)

Macedo, Waldomiro (May 23, 2000)

Mata, Antônio Pereira da (March 15, 2000)

Miguel, Benedito (May 19, 1998)

Oliveira, Artur Pinto de (April 16, 1998)

Oliveira, Maria José Santos (August 26, 1998)

Pimentel, Aristides (August 18, 1998)

Rachid, Ana Maria Silvério (June 17, 2000)

Raimundo, Valdevino da Silva (August 3, 2000)

Ramalho, Irene (May 21, 1998)

Ravaglia, Fábio (April 18, 1995)

Santos, Antônio Xavier dos (February 21, 2000)

Santos, Joaquim Anselmo dos (November 15, 1994, May 29, 2000, March 1, 2001)

Silva, Afonso José da (October 15, 1997)

Silva, José Ferreira da (December 8, 1994)

Silva, Júlio Paulino da (February 21, 2000)
Silveira, Helena Oliveira (June 16, 2000)
Souza, Oscar Alonso de (December 22, 1994)

SECONDARY SOURCES

Albuquerque, Durval Muniz de, Jr. *A invenção do Nordeste e outras artes*. Recife: Fundação Joaquim Nabuco, 1999.

Alem, Sílvio Frank. "Os trabalhadores e a redemocratização." Master's thesis, Instituto de Filosofia e Ciências Humanas, Universidade Estadual de Campinas, 1981.

Almeida, Antônio. "Um encontro de origens diversas: A presença de migrantes e imigrantes na composição da classe trabalhadora do ABC paulista." *Tempos Históricos* 1, no. 1 (March 1999).

Almeida, Karim Roberta de. "Esquerda em armas: A trajetória da classe operária de São Miguel Paulista na luta armada (1968–1974)." Typescript. Trabalho de Conclusão de Curso, Departamento de História, Universidade Cruzeiro do Sul, São Paulo, 2001.

Almeida, Vicente Unzer de, and Octávio Teixeira Mendes Sobrinho. *Migração rural-urbana: Aspectos de convergência de população do interior e outras localidades para a capital do estado de São Paulo*. São Paulo: Secretaria de Agricultura do Estado de São Paulo, 1951.

Alvim, Rosilene. *A sedução da cidade. Os operários-camponeses e a fábrica dos Ludgreen*. Rio de Janeiro: Graphia, 1997.

Amado, Jorge. *Homens e coisas do Partido Comunista*. Rio de Janeiro: Edições Horizonte, 1946.

———. "O jovem Ramiro." In *Homens e coisas do Partido Comunista*. Rio de Janeiro: Edições Horizonte, 1946.

Anderson, Benedict. *Imagined Communities*. London: Verso, 1983.

Andrade, Celeste Souza. "Migrantes nacionais no estado de São Paulo." *Sociologia* 19, no. 2 (1952).

Andrade, Cleide Lugarini de. "As lutas sociais por moradia na cidade de São Paulo: A experiência de São Miguel Paulista e Ermelino Matarazzo." Master's thesis, Department of Social Science, Pontifícia Universidade Católica de São Paulo, 1989.

Andrade, Manoel Correia. *A terra e o homem no Nordeste*. São Paulo: Editora Brasiliense, 1964.

Antônio, Geraldo. "As 10 personalidades de São Miguel Paulista" in *São Miguel Agora*, no. 6, August–September 1987.

Antunes, Fátima M. Rodrigues. "Diversão ou trabalho? O futebol dentro da fábrica." *DO Leitura* 12, no. 141 (February 1994).

Aquino, Maria Aparecida de, Marco Aurélio Vannucchi Leme de Mattos, and Walter Cruz Swensson Jr., eds. *No coração das trevas: O DEOPS/SP visto por dentro*. São Paulo: Arquivo do Estado, Imprensa Oficial, 2001.

Arantes Neto, Antônio Augusto. "Produção cultural e revitalização em bairros populares: O caso de São Miguel Paulista." Mimeograph. São Paulo, December 1978.

Araújo, Ricardo Benzaquen. *Totalitarismo e revolução: O integralismo de Plínio Salgado*. Rio de Janeiro: Jorge Zahar, 1988.

Azevedo, Aroldo de. *A cidade de São Paulo: Estudos de geografia urbana*, vol. 2. São Paulo: Companhia Editora Nacional, 1958.

————. "Subúrbios orientais de São Paulo." Diss. for the chair in Brazilian geography, Faculdade de Filosofia, Ciências e Letras, Universidade de São Paulo, 1945.

Azevedo, Mirandulina Maria Moreira. "Migração e memória: A experiência dos Nordestinos." Ph.D. diss., Geography Department, Facultad de Filosofia, Letras e Ciências Humanas, Universidade de São Paulo, 2002.

Bañales, José Luis Oyon. "História urbana y história obrera: Reflexiones sobre la vida obrera y su inscripción em el espacio urbani, 1900–1950." *Perspectivas Urbanas*, no. 2 (2002).

Baptista, Dulce Maria Tourinho. "Nas terras do 'Deus-dará'. Nordestinos e suas redes sociais em São Paulo." Ph.D. diss., Pontifícia Universidade Católica de São Paulo, 1998.

Barros, Souza. *Êxodo e fixação. Sugestões para uma política de colonização e aldeamento no Nordeste*. Rio de Janeiro: Ministério da Agricultura, 1953.

Batalha, Cláudio. "A historiografia da classe operária no Brasil: trajetória e tendências." In *Historiografia brasileira em perspectiva*, ed. Marcos Cezar de Freitas. São Paulo: Contexto and Universidade São Francisco, 1998.

Batalha, Cláudio, Fernando Teixeira da Silva, and Alexandre Fortes, eds. *Culturas de classe. Identidade e diversidade na formação do operariado*. Campinas: Editora da Unicamp, 2004.

Becker, Berta. "As migrações internas no Brasil: Reflexo de uma organização do espaço desiquilibrada." *Revista Brasileira de Geografia* 30, no. 2 (April–June 1968).

Berlin, Ira. *The Making of African America: The Four Great Migrations*. New York: Viking, 2010.

Berlinck, Manoel Tosta, and Daniel J. Hogan. "Migração interna e adaptação na cidade de São Paulo: Uma análise preliminar." In *Anais do I Simpósio de Desenvolvimento Econômico e Social: Migrações internas e desenvolvimento regional*. Belo Horizonte: Centro de Desenvolvimento e Planejamento Regional, Universidade Federal de Minas Gerais, 1972.

————. *O desenvolvimento econômico do Brasil e as migrações internas: Uma análise histórica*. Campinas: Cadernos do Instituto de Filosofia e Ciências Humanas, Universidade Estadual de Campinas, 1974.

Benevides, Maria Victoria. *O PTB e o trabalhismo. Partido e sindicato em São Paulo (1945–1964)*. São Paulo: Editora Brasiliense and Centro de Estudos de Cultura Contemporânea, 1989.

Bernardet, Jean-Claude. *Cineastas e imagem do povo*. São Paulo: Companhia das Letras, 2003.

Bertonha, João Fábio. *Fascismo, nazismo, integralismo*. São Paulo: Ática, 2000.

Bethell, Leslie, and Ian Roxborough. *Latin America between the Second World and the Cold War, 1944–1948*. Cambridge: Cambridge University Press, 1992.

Blanco, Alejandro. *Razón y modernidad. Gino Germani y la sociología em la Argentina*. Buenos Aires: Siglo XXI, 2006.

Blake, Stanley. "The Medicalization of Nordestinos: Public Health and Regional Identity in Northeastern Brazil, 1889–1939." *The Americas* 60, no. 2 (2003).

Blay, Eva Alterman. *Eu não tenho onde morar. Vilas operárias na cidade de São Paulo.* São Paulo: Nobel, 1985.

Blokland, Talja, and Michael Savage. "Networks, Class and Place." *International Journal of Urban and Regional Research* 25, no. 2 (2001).

Bógus, Lúcia Maria. "Urbanização e metropolização: O caso de São Paulo." In *A luta pela cidade em São Paulo,* ed. Lúcia Maria Bógus and Luiz Eduardo Wanderley. São Paulo: Cortez, 1992.

Bógus, Lúcia Maria, and Luiz Eduardo Wanderley, eds. *A luta pela cidade em São Paulo.* São Paulo: Cortez, 1992.

Bomtempi, Sylvio. *O bairro de São Miguel Paulista. A aldeia de São Miguel do Ururaí na história de São Paulo.* São Paulo: Departamento de Cultura da Prefeitura Municipal, 1970.

Bonduki, Nabil. *Origens da habitação social no Brasil. Arquitetura moderna, Lei do Inquilinato e difusão da casa própria.* São Paulo: Estação Liberdade, 1998.

Bonduki, Nabil, and Raquel Rolnik. "Periferia da grande São Paulo. Reprodução do espaço como expediente de reprodução da força de trabalho." In *A produção capitalista da casa (e da cidade) no Brasil industrial,* ed. Ermínia Maricato. São Paulo: Alfa-Ômega, 1982.

Borges, T. Pompeu Accioly. *Migrações internas no Brasil.* Rio de Janeiro: Comissão Nacional de Política Agrária, 1955.

Bosco, Santa Helena, and Antônio Jordão Netto. *Migrações: Estudo especial sobre as migrações internas para o estado de São Paulo e seus efeitos.* São Paulo: Departamento de Imigração e Colonização da Secretaria de Agricultura do Estado de São Paulo, 1967.

Braido, Jacyr, and Juarez Segalin, ed. *Anais da Semana de Estudos Migratórios (6 a 11 de julho de 1970).* São Paulo: Centro de Estudos Migratórios, 1970.

Buonicore, Augusto César. "Sindicalismo vermelho: A política sindical do PCB entre 1948 e 1952." *Cadernos AEL* 7, nos. 12–13 (2000).

Caldeira, Clóvis. *Mutirão. Formas de ajuda mútua no meio rural.* São Paulo: Companhia Editora Nacional, 1956.

Caldeira, Teresa. *A política dos outros. O cotidiano dos moradores da periferia e o que pensam do poder e dos poderosos.* São Paulo: Editora Brasiliense, 1984.

———. *City of Walls: Crime, Segregation, and Citizenship in São Paulo.* Oakland: University of California Press, 2000.

Calhoun, C. J. "Community: Toward a Variable Conceptualization for Comparative Research." *Social History* 5, no. 1 (1980).

———. "History, Anthropology and the study of Communities: Some Problems in Macfarlane's Proposal." *Social History* 3, no. 3 (1978).

Camargo, José Francisco. *A cidade e o campo: O êxodo rural no Brasil.* Rio de Janeiro: Ao Livro Técnico, 1968.

Cardoso, Fernando Henrique. "Partidos e deputados em São Paulo (o voto e a representação política)." In *Os partidos e as eleições no Brasil,* ed. Fernando Henrique Cardoso and Bolivar Lamounier. Rio de Janeiro: Paz e Terra, 1975.

———. "Proletariado no Brasil: Situação e comportamento social." *Revista Brasiliense*, no. 41 (May–June 1962).

Cardoso, Fernando Henrique, Cândido Procópio Ferreira, and Lúcio Kowarick. "Considerações sobre o desenvolvimento de São Paulo: Cultura e participação." In *Cultura e participação na cidade de São Paulo*, ed. Fernando Henrique Cardoso and Paul Isarel Singer. São Paulo: Centro Brasileiro de Analise e Planejamento, 1973.

Cardoso, Fernando Henrique, and Paul Israel Singer, eds. *Cultura e participação na cidade de São Paulo*. São Paulo: Centro Brasileiro de Analise e Planejamento, 1973.

Carone, Edgard. *O PCB: 1943–1964*, vol. 2. São Paulo: Difel, 1982.

Cavalcanti, Cláudio Antônio de Vasconcelos. "As lutas e os sonhos. Um estudo sobre os trabalhadores de São Paulo nos anos 30." Ph.D. diss., Department of Sociology, Facultad de Filosofia, Letras e Ciências Humanas, Universidade de São Paulo, 1996.

Chaia, Vera Lúcia Michalany. *A liderança política de Jânio Quadros, 1947–1990*. São Paulo: Humanidades, 1992.

Chalhoub, Sidney. *Trabalho, lar e botequim. O cotidiano dos trabalhadores no Rio de Janeiro da Belle Époque*. São Paulo: Editora Brasiliense, 1986.

Chalhoub, Sidney, and Fernando Teixeira Silva. "Sujeitos no imaginário acadêmico: Escravos e trabalhadores na historiografia brasileira desde os anos 1980." *Cadernos AEL* 14, no. 26 (2009).

Chauí, Marilena. "Apontamentos para uma crítica à Ação Integralista Brasileira." In *Ideologia e mobilização popular*. São Paulo: Paz e Terra, 1978.

Chaves, Marcelo Antônio. "Da periferia ao centro da(o) capital: Perfil dos trabalhadores do primeiro complexo cimenteiro do Brasil, São Paulo, 1925–1945." Master's thesis, History Department, Instituto de Filosofia e Ciências Humanas, Universidade Estadual de Campinas, Campinas, 2005.

Colistete, Renato. *Labour Relations and Industrial Performance in Brazil: Greater São Paulo, 1945–1960*. Houndmills: Palgrave, 2001.

Corrêa, Larissa Rosa. "Trabalhadores e os doutores da lei: Direitos e Justiça do Trabalho na cidade de São Paulo—1953 a 1964." *Histórica*, no. 27 (November 2007).

Costa, Emília Viotti. "Entrevista com Emília Viotti da Costa." In José Geraldo Vinci Moraes and José Marcio Rego, *Conversas com historiadores brasileiros*. São Paulo: Editora 34, 2002.

Costa, Hélio. *Em busca da memória. Comissão de fábrica, partido e sindicato no pós-guerra*. São Paulo: Scritta, 1995.

Crew, David. "Class and Community: Local Research on Working-Class History in Four Countries." *Historische Zeitschrift* 15 (1986).

Cunha, Euclides da. *Rebellion in the Backlands*. Chicago: University of Chicago Press, 1957.

Dávila, Jerry. *Diploma of Whiteness: Race and Social Policy in Brazil, 1917–1945*. Durham, NC: Duke University Press, 2003.

Dean, Warren. *Brazil and the Struggle for Rubber: A Study in Environmental History*. Cambridge: Cambridge University Press, 1987.

Decca, Maria Auxiliadora Guzzo. *A vida fora das fábricas. Cotidiano operário em São Paulo: 1920–1934*. Rio de Janeiro: Paz e Terra, 1987.

Dias, Gentil Martins. *Depois do latifúndio. Continuidade e mudança na sociedade rural nordestina.* Rio de Janeiro: Tempo Brasileiro and Editora Universidade de Brasília, 1978.

Dinius, Oliver. *Brazil's Steel City: Developmentalism, Strategic Power, and Industrial Relations in Volta Redonda, 1941–1964.* Stanford, CA: Stanford University Press, 2011.

Dreyfus, Dominique. *Vida do viajante. A saga de Luiz Gonzaga.* São Paulo: Editora 34, 1996.

Duarte, Adriano. *Cidadania e exclusão. Brasil: 1937–1945.* Florianópolis: Editora da Universidade Federal de São Carlos, 1999.

———. "Cultura popular e cultura política no após-guerra: Redemocratização, populismo e desenvolvimentismo no bairro da Mooca, 1942–1973." Ph.D. diss., Universidade Estadual de Campinas, 2002.

———. "O 'dia de São Bartolomeu' e o 'carnaval sem fim': O quebra-quebra de ônibus e bondes na cidade de São Paulo em agosto de 1947." *Revista Brasileira de História,* no. 50 (2005).

———. "Os sentidos da comunidade: notas para um estudo sobre bairros operários e identidade cultural." *Trajetos* 1, no. 2 (2002).

Duarte, Adriano, and Maria Célia Paoli. "São Paulo no plural: Espaço público e redes de sociabilidade." In *História da cidade de São Paulo. A cidade na primeira metade do século XX (1890–1954),* vol. 3, ed. Paula Porta. São Paulo: Paz e Terra, 2004.

Durham, Eunice. *A caminho da cidade.* São Paulo: Perspectiva, 1976.

———. "Os migrantes nacionais." In *São Paulo, espírito, povo, instituições.* São Paulo: Pioneira, 1968.

Ebanks, Edward. *Determinantes socioeconómicos de la migración interna.* Santiago de Chile: Centro Latinoamericano de Demografía, 1993.

Elias, Norbert, and John L. Scotson. *Os estabelecidos e os outsiders. Sociologia das relações de poder a partir de uma pequena comunidade.* Rio de Janeiro: Jorge Zahar, 2000.

Estrela, Ely Souza. *Os sampauleiros: Cotidiano e representações.* São Paulo: Editora da Pontifícia Universidade Católica de São Paulo, 2003.

Farah Neto, José Jorge, and Rodolfo Kussarev Jr. *Almanaque do futebol paulista.* São Paulo: Panini, 2001.

Farias, Damião Duque de. *Em defesa da ordem. Aspectos da práxis conservadora católica no meio operário em São Paulo (1930–1945).* São Paulo: Hucitec, 1998.

Farnsworth-Alvear, Ann. *Dulcinea in the Factory: Myths, Morals, Men, and Women in Colombia's Industrial Experiment, 1905–1960.* Durham, NC: Duke University Press, 2000.

Fausto, Boris. "Imigração: Cortes e continuidades." In *História da vida privada: Contrastes de intimidade contemporânea,* ed. Lilia Moritz Schwarcz. São Paulo: Companhia das Letras, 1988.

———. *Historiografia da imigração para São Paulo.* São Paulo: Editora Sumaré and Fundação de Amparo à Pesquisa do Estado de São Paulo, 1991.

Ferrari, Monia Melo. "A migração nordestina para São Paulo no segundo governo Vargas (1951–54)—Secas e desigualdades regionais." Master's thesis, Universidade Federal de São Carlos, 2005.

Ferreira, Jorge. "Introdução." In *O populismo e sua história. Debate e crítica,* ed. Jorge Ferreira. Rio de Janeiro: Civilização Brasileira, 2001.

———. *O imaginário trabalhista.* Rio de Janeiro: Civilização Brasileira, 2005.

———. "O nome e a coisa. O populismo na política brasileira." In *O populismo e sua história. Debate e crítica,* ed. Jorge Ferreira. Rio de Janeiro: Civilização Brasileira, 2001.

———, ed. *O populismo e sua história. Debate e crítica.* Rio de Janeiro: Civilização Brasileira, 2001.

———. *Trabalhadores do Brasil: O imaginário popular.* Rio de Janeiro: Editora da Fundação Getúlio Vargas, 1997.

Ferreira, Marieta de Moraes, and Janaína Amado, eds. *Usos e abusos da história oral.* Rio de Janeiro: Fundação Getúlio Vargas, 1996.

Ferro, Sérgio. "Notas sobre o 'vício da virtude.'" *Novos Estudos,* no. 76 (November 2006).

Fischlowitz, Estanislau. *Principais problemas da migração nordestina.* Rio de Janeiro: Ministério da Educação e Cultura, 1959.

Fink, Leon. *The Maya of Morganton: Work and Community in the Nuevo New South.* Chapel Hill: University of North Carolina Press, 2003.

Fontes, Paulo. "'Centenas de estopins acesos ao mesmo tempo.' A greve dos 400 mil, piquetes e a organização dos trabalhadores em São Paulo (1957)." In *Na luta por direitos. Estudos recentes em história social do trabalho,* ed. Alexandre Fortes, Antonio Luigi Negro, Fernando Teixeira da Silva, Hélio da Costa, and Paulo Fontes. Campinas: Editora da Unicamp, 1999.

———. *Trabalhadores e cidadãos. Nitro Química: A fábrica e as lutas operárias nos anos 50.* São Paulo: AnnaBlume and Sindicato dos Trabalhadores da Indústria Químicas e Plásticas de São Paulo, 1997.

———. "'With a Cardboard Suitcase in My Hand and a Pannier on My Back': Workers and Northeastern Migrations in the 1950s in São Paulo, Brazil." *Social History* 36, no. 1 (2011).

Fontes, Paulo, and Adriano Duarte. "O populismo visto da periferia: Adhemarismo e janismo nos bairros da Mooca e São Miguel Paulista (1947–1953)." *Cadernos AEL* 11, nos. 20–21 (2004).

Fontes, Paulo, and Francisco Barbosa de Macedo. "Strikes and Pickets in Brazil: Working-Class Mobilization in the 'Old' and 'New' Unionism, the Strikes of 1957 and 1980." *International Labor and Working Class History* 83 (2013).

Fortes, Alexandre. *Nós do quarto distrito. A classe trabalhadora porto-alegrense e a era Vargas.* Rio de Janeiro: Garamond, 2004.

Fortes, Alexandre, and Antonio Luigi Negro. "Historiografia, trabajo y ciudadanía en Brasil." *Entrepassados,* no. 15 (1998).

Fortes, Alexandre, Antonio Luigi Negro, Fernando Teixeira da Silva, Hélio da Costa, and Paulo Fontes. *Na luta por direitos. Estudos recentes em história social do trabalho.* Campinas: Editora da Unicamp, 1999.

Fraenkel, Leda Maria. "Questionamentos sobre o mercado de trabalho das regiões metropolitanas brasileiras e suas relações com as migrações internas." In Instituto Brasileiro de Geografia e Estatística, *Encontro brasileiro de estudos populacionais: Contribuições apresentadas.* Rio de Janeiro: Instituto Brasileiro de Geografia e Estatística, 1976.

French, John. *Afogados em leis. A CLT e a cultura política dos trabalhadores brasileiros.* São Paulo: Editora da Fundação Perseu Abramo, 2001.

————. *The Brazilian Workers' ABC: Class Conflict and Alliances in Modern São Paulo.* Chapel Hill: University of North Carolina Press, 1992.

————. "The Latin American Labor Studies Boom." *International Review of Social History* 2, no. 45 (2000).

Furtado, Celso. *Formação econômica do Brasil,* 11th ed. São Paulo: Companhia Editora Nacional, 1972.

Garcia, A. R., Jr. *O sul: O caminho do roçado. Estratégias de reprodução camponesa e transformação social.* Brasília: Marco Zero, Editora de Universidade de Brasília, and Conselho Nacional de Desenvolvimento Científico e Tecnológico, 1989.

Garcia, Ronaldo Aurélio G. *Migrantes mineiros em Franca: Memória e trabalho na cidade industrial (1960–1980).* Franca: Faculdade de História, Direito e Serviço Social, Universidade Estadual Paulista "Júlio de Mesquita Filho," 1997.

Germani, Gino. *Sociologia da modernização. Estudos teóricos, metodológicos e aplicados à América Latina.* São Paulo: Mestre Jou, 1974.

Gomes, Angela de Castro. *A invenção do trabalhismo.* São Paulo: Vértice, 1988.

————. "Ideologia e trabalho no Estado Novo." In *Repensando o New State,* ed. Dulce Pandolfi. Rio de Janeiro: Editora Fundação Getulio Vargas, 1999.

————. "O populismo e as ciências sociais no Brasil. Notas sobre a trajetória de um conceito." In *O populismo e sua história. Debate e crítica,* ed. Jorge Ferreira. Rio de Janeiro: Civilização Brasileira, 2001.

Gorender, Jacob. *Combate nas trevas. A esquerda brasileira: Das ilusões perdidas à luta armada.* São Paulo: Ática, 1987.

Graham, Douglas, and Sérgio Buarque de Holanda Filho. *Migration, Regional and Urban Growth and Development in Brazil: A Selective Analysis of the Historical Record, 1872–1970.* São Paulo: IPE, Universidade de São Paulo, 1971.

Guimarães, Antonio Sérgio Alfredo Guimarães. *Classes, raças e democracia.* São Paulo: Editora 34, 2002.

Gutman, Herbert. *Power and Culture: Essays on the American Working Class.* New York: New Press, 1987.

Gutierrez, Leandro H., and Luis Alberto Romero. "Barrio Societies, Libraries and Culture in the Popular Sectors of Buenos Aires in the Inter-War Period." In *Essays in Argentine Labour History (1870–1930),* ed. Jeremy Councilman. London: Macmillan, 1992.

Hall, Michael. "História oral: Os riscos da inocência." In *O direito à memória. Patrimônio histórico e cidadania,* ed. Departamento do Patrimônio Histórico de São Paulo. São Paulo: Secretaria Municipal de Cultura de São Paulo, 1982.

Hall, Michael, and Paulo Sérgio Pinheiro. "Imigração e movimento operário no Brasil: Uma interpretação." In José Luiz Del Roio, *Trabalhadores no Brasil: Imigração e industrialização.* São Paulo: Ícone, 1990.

Halpern, Rick. "Respatializing Marxism and Remapping Urban Space." *Journal of Urban History* 23, no. 2 (1997).

————. "Oral History and Labour History: A Historiographic Assessment after Twenty-five Years." *Journal of American History* 85, no. 2 (1998).

Hasenbalg, Carlos A. "A pesquisa sobre migrações, urbanização, relações raciais e pobreza no Brasil, 1979–1990." Mimeograph. Série estudos, Iuperj, Rio de Janeiro, 1991.

Haupt, Georges. "Por que a história do movimento operário?" *Revista Brasileira de História* 5, no. 10 (1985).

Heredia, Beatriz. "Política, família, comunidade," in *Antropologia, voto e representação política*, ed. Moacir Palmeira and Marcio Goldman. Rio de Janeiro: Contracapa, 1996.

Herold, Andrew. *Labor Geographies: Workers and the Landscapes of Capitalism.* New York: Guilford, 2002.

————. "Workers, Space, and Labor Geography." *International Labor and Working-Class History*, no. 64 (2003).

Hirata, Daniel Veloso. "No meio de campo: O que está em jogo no futebol de várzea?" In *Nas tramas da cidade. Trajetórias urbanas e seus territórios*, ed. Vera da Silva Telles and Robert Cabanes. São Paulo: Humanitas, 2006.

História do Esperanto Klubo "Zamenhof" em São Miguel Paulista. São Paulo, 1999. Personal Archives of Osvaldo Pires de Holanda.

Hobsbawm, Eric, and Terence Ranger. *The Age of Extremes: The Short Twentieth Century, 1914–1991.* New York: Vintage, 1994.

————. *A invenção das tradições.* Rio de Janeiro: Paz e Terra, 1984.

————. *The Invention of Tradition.* Cambridge: Cambridge University Press, 1983.

————. *Workers: Worlds of Labor.* New York City: Pantheon, 1984.

Hoggart, Richard. *The Uses of Literacy: Aspects of Working Class Life.* London: Chatto and Windus, 1957.

Holston, James. "Autoconstruction in Working-Class Brazil." *Cultural Anthropology* 6, no. 4 (1991).

————. *Insurgent Citizenship: Disjunctions of Democracy and Modernity in Brazil.* Princeton, NJ: Princeton University Press, 2008.

Hutchinson, Bertram. "The Migrant Population of Urban Brazil." *América Latina* 6, no. 2 (1963).

Iffy, Catherine. *Transformar a metrópole: Igreja católica, territórios e mobilizações sociais em São Paulo 1970–2000.* São Paulo: Editora Unesp, 2011.

Iumatti, Paulo Teixeira. *Diários políticos de Caio Prado Júnior: 1945.* São Paulo: Editora Brasiliense, 1998.

James, Daniel. *Doña Maria's Story: Life History, Memory, and Political Identity.* Durham, NC: Duke University Press, 2000.

————. "O que há de novo, o que há de velho? Os parâmetros emergentes da história do trabalho latino-americana." In *Trabalho, cultura e cidadania*, ed. Angela M. C. Araújo. São Paulo: Scritta, 1997.

Jatobá, Roniwalter. *Crônicas da vida operária.* São Paulo: Global, 1988

————. *O pavão misterioso e outras memórias.* São Paulo: Geração Editorial, 1999.

————. *Sabor de química.* Belo Horizonte: Oficina de Livros, 1976.

Jesus, Edson Penha de. "Penha: De bairro rural a bairro paulistano. Um estudo do processo de configuração do espaço penhense." Master's thesis, Geography Department, Facultad de Filosofia, Letras e Ciências Humanas, Universidade de São Paulo, 2006.

Katznelson, Ira. *Marxism and the City.* Oxford: Oxford University Press, 1992.

Klubock, Thomas Miller. *Contested Communities: Class, Gender and Politics in Chile's El Teneiente Copper Mine, 1904–1951.* Durham, NC: Duke University Press, 1998.

Kowarick, Lúcio. *A espoliação urbana.* São Paulo: Paz e Terra, 1983.

————. "A expansão metropolitana e suas contradições em São Paulo." *Caderno do Ceas*, no. 102 (1986).

————. *Escritos urbanos*. São Paulo: Editora 34, 2000.

————, ed. *As lutas sociais e a cidade—São Paulo: Passado e presente*. Rio de Janeiro: Paz e Terra, 1988.

————, ed. *Social Struggles and the City: The Case of São Paulo*. New York: Monthly Review, 1994.

Kowarick, Lúcio, and Nabil Bonduki. "Espaço urbano e espaço político: Do populismo à redemocratização." In *Social Struggles and the City: The Case of São Paulo*, ed. Lúcio Kowarick. New York: Monthly Review Press, 1994.

Kuschnir, Karina. "Cultura e participação política no Rio de Janeiro." In *Antropologia, voto e representação política*, ed. Moacir Palmeira and Marcio Goldman. Rio de Janeiro: Contracapa, 1996.

Lamounier, Bolívar. "Comportamento eleitoral em São Paulo: Passado e presente." In *Os partidos e as eleições no Brasil*, ed. Fernando Henrique Cardoso and Bolivar Lamounier. Rio de Janeiro: Paz e Terra, 1975.

Langenbuch, Juergen R. *A estruturação da grande São Paulo. Estudo de geografia urbana*. Rio de Janeiro: Fundação Instituto Brasileiro de Geografia e Estatística, 1971.

Lara, Silvia, and Joseli Mendonça, eds. *Direitos e justiças no Brasil. Ensaios de história social*. Campinas: Editora da Unicamp, 2006.

Laverdi, Robson. *Tempos diversos, vidas entrelaçadas. Trajetórias itinerantes de trabalhadores no extremo oeste do Paraná*. Curitiba: Aos Quatro Ventos, 2005.

Lebret, Rev. P. J. L. "Sondagem preliminar a um estudo sobre a habitação em São Paulo." *Revista do Arquivo Municipal* (April–May 1951).

Leite, Francisco Barbosa. "O pau-de-arara." *Revista Brasileira de Geografia* 17, no. 2 (1955).

Leite Lopes, José Sérgio. *A tecelagem dos conflitos de classe na "cidade das chaminés."* São Paulo: Marco Zero, 1988.

————, ed. *Cultura e identidade operária: Aspectos da cultura da classe trabalhadora*. Rio de Janeiro: Marco Zero and Editora Universidade Federal do Rio de Janeiro, 1987.

Lesser, Jeffrey. *Negotiating National Identity: Immigrants, Minorities and the Struggle for Ethnicity in Brazil*. Durham, NC: Duke University Press, 1999.

————, ed. *Searching for Home Abroad: Japanese Brazilians and Transnationalism*. Durham, NC: Duke University Press, 2003.

Lima, Luiz Tenório de. *Movimento sindical e luta de classes*. São Paulo: Oliveira Mendes, 1998.

Lobato, Mirta. *La vida en las fábricas. Trabajo, protesta y política em uma comunidad obrera, Berisso (1904–1970)*. Buenos Aires: Prometeo Libros and Entrepasados, 2001

————. "Women Workers in the 'Cathedrals of Corned Beef': Structure and Subjectivity in the Argentine Meatpacking Industry." In *The Gendered Worlds of Latin American Women Workers: From Household and Factory to the Union Hall and Ballot Box*, ed. John French and Daniel James. Durham, NC: Duke University Press, 1997.

————, ed. *Cuando las mujeres reinaban. Belleza, virtud y poder en la Argentina del siglo XX*. Buenos Aires: Biblos, 2005.

Lobo, Elizabeth Souza. *A classe operária tem dois sexos: Trabalho, dominação e resistência*. São Paulo: Brasiliense and Secretaria Municipal de Cultura, 1991.

Lopes, João Marcos. "O Anão caolho." *Novos Estudos*, no. 76 (November 2006).

Lopes, Juarez Brandão. *Crise do Brasil arcaico*. São Paulo: Difel, 1967.

———. *Sociedade industrial no Brasil*. São Paulo: Difel, 1964.

Lucena, Célia Toledo. *Artes de lembrar e de inventar. (Re)lembranças de migrantes*. São Paulo: Arte e Ciência, 1999.

Macfarlane, Alan. "History, Anthropology and the Study of Communities." *Social History* 2, no. 5 (1977).

Magalhães, Mario. *Carlos Mariguella: O guerrilheiro que incendiou o mundo*. São Paulo: Companhia das Letras, 2012.

Magnani, José Guilherme Cantor. *Festa no pedaço. Cultura popular e lazer na cidade*. São Paulo: Editora Brasiliense, 1984.

Maranhão, Ricardo. *Sindicatos e democratização*. São Paulo: Editora Brasiliense, 1979.

Marcondes, J. V. Freitas. "Aspectos do trabalho e do lazer em São Paulo." In *São Paulo: Espírito, povo, instituições*, ed. J. V. Freitas Marcondes and Osmar Pimentel. São Paulo: Livraria Pioneira Editora, 1968.

Maricato, Ermínia. *A produção capitalista da casa (e da cidade) no Brasil industrial*. São Paulo: Alfa-ômega, 1982.

Martescelli, Carolina. "Uma pesquisa sobre aceitação de grupos nacionais, grupos nacionais, grupos 'raciais' e grupos regionais em São Paulo." *Psicologia*, no. 3 (1950).

Mattos, Marcelo Badaró, ed. *Greves e repressão policial ao sindicalismo carioca (1945–1964)*. Rio de Janeiro: Faperj, Arquivo Público do Estado do Rio de Janeiro, 2003.

———. *Novos e velhos sindicalismos. Rio de Janeiro (1955–1988)*. Rio de Janeiro: Vício de Leitura, 1988.

Mazzo, Armando. *Memórias de um militante político e sindical no ABC*. São Bernardo do Campo: Prefeitura do Município de São Bernardo do Campo, 1991.

McCann, Bryan. *Hello, Hello Brazil: Popular Music in the Making of Modern Brazil*. Durham, NC: Duke University Press, 2004.

McClymer, John F. "The Study of Community and the 'New' Social History." *Journal of Urban History* 7, no. 1 (1980).

Medeiros, Leonilde Sérvolo. *História dos movimentos sociais no campo*. Rio de Janeiro: Fase, 1989.

———. *Reforma agrária no Brasil*. São Paulo: Editora da Fundação Perseu Abramo, 2003.

Meihy, José Carlos Sebe bom. *(Re)introduzindo a história oral no Brasil*. São Paulo: Xamã, 1996.

Mello, João Manuel Cardoso, and Fernando Novais. "Capitalismo tardio e sociabilidade moderna." In *História da vida privada: Contrastes da intimidade contemporânea*, ed. Lilia Schwarcz. São Paulo: Companhia das Letras, 1998.

Meneguello, Cristina. *Poeira de estrelas. O cinema hollywoodiano na mídia brasileira nas décadas de 40 e 50*. Campinas: Editora da Unicamp, 1996.

Menezes, Maria Aparecida. *Redes e enredos nas trilhas dos migrantes: Um estudo de famílias de camponeses-migrantes*. Rio de Janeiro: Relume Dumará/João Pessoa and Editora Universidade Federal da Paraíba, 2002.

Miranda Pereira, Leonardo Affonso de. *Footballmania. Uma história social do futebol no Rio de Janeiro, 1902–1938*. Rio de Janeiro: Nova Fronteira, 2000.

Moisés, José Álvaro. "Classes populares e protesto urbano." Ph.D. diss., Facultad de
Filosofia, Letras e Ciências Humanas, Universidade de São Paulo, 1978.

———. "Protesto urbano e política: O quebra-quebra de 1947." In *Cidade, povo e poder*.
Rio de Janeiro: Paz e Terra, 1985.

Morandi, Alba Maria. *O trabalhador migrante nacional em São Paulo (1920–1923)*. São
Paulo: Editora da Pontifícia Universidade Católica de São Paulo, 1978.

Muszynski, Maria Judith de Brito. *O impacto político das migrações internas: O caso
de São Paulo (1945–1982)*. São Paulo: Índice de Desenvolvimento da Educação do
Estado de São Paulo, 1986.

Negro, Antonio Luigi. *Linhas de montagem. O industrialismo nacional-desenvolvimentista
e a sindicalização dos trabalhadores*. São Paulo: Boitempo, 2004.

———. "Servos do tempo." In *De JK a FHC. A reinvenção dos carros*, ed. Glauco Arbix
and Mauro Zilbovicius. São Paulo: Scritta, 1997.

Negro, Antonio Luigi, and Paulo Fontes. "Using Police Records in Labor History: A
Case Study of Brazilian DOPS." *Labor: Studies in Working-Class History of the Americas* 5, no. 1 (2008).

Netto, Antonio Jordão. "Algumas considerações a propósito da estrutura profissional de
migrantes nacionais no estado de São Paulo." *Sociologia* 27, no. 4 (December 1965).

———. "São Paulo e o problema das migrações internas." *Sociologia* 25, no. 3 (September 1963).

Netto, Luiz Cava. "Contribuição do desenvolvimento e organização da comunidade e
do planejamento sócio-econômico ao problema dos deslocamentos populacionais
(migração nordestina e êxodo rural)." In *Anais do Encontro de Técnicos promovido pela
Secretaria de Saúde Pública e de Assistência Social do estado de São Paulo—1962*. São
Paulo: Cooperação e Intercâmbio de Serviços Sociais, 1965.

Neves, Frederico de Castro. *A multidão e a história: Saques e outras ações de massa no
Ceará*. Rio de Janeiro: Relume Dumará, 2000.

———. "Armadilhas nordestinas: O Homem que virou suco." In *A história vai ao
cinema: 20 filmes brasileiros comentados por historiadores*, ed. Jorge Ferreira and Mariza
Soares. Rio de Janeiro: Record, 2001.

Nogueira, Oracy. "Distribuição residencial de operários de um estabelecimento industrial em São Paulo." *Sociologia* 11, no. 1 (1949).

Nunes, Antônio Carlos Felix. *PC linha leste. Fragmentos da vida partidária*. São Paulo:
Editorial Livramento, 1980.

Nunes, Edison. "Algumas notas sobre o Nordeste brasileiro: A terra, o homem, secas."
Mimeograph. Centro de Estudos de Cultura Contemporânea, São Paulo, August
1978.

Oliveira, Francisco de. *Economia brasileira: Crítica à razão dualista*. São Paulo: Editora
Brasiliense and Centro Brasileiro de Analise e Planejamento, 1971.

———. "A economia brasileira: crítica à razão dualista." *Estudos CEBRAP*, no. 2 (1972).

———. "O vício da virtude. Auto-construção e acumulação capitalista no Brasil." *Novos
Estudos*, no. 74 (March 2006).

Paiva, Odair da Cruz. *Caminhos cruzados. Migração e construção do Brasil moderno
(1930–1950)*. Bauru: Editora da Universidade do Sagrado Coração, 2004.

Palmeira, Moacir, and Marcio Goldman, eds. *Antropologia, voto e representação política*. Rio de Janeiro: Contracapa, 1996.

Pandolfi, Dulce. *Camaradas e companheiros. História e memória do PCB*. Rio de Janeiro: Relume Dumará, 1995.

Paoli, Maria Célia. "Labour, Law, and the State in Brazil, 1930–1950." Ph.D. diss., University of London, 1988.

———. "São Paulo operária e suas imagens (1900–1940)." *Espaço e Debates* 9, no. 33 (1991).

Paoli, Maria Célia, Vera Silva Telles, and Eder Sader. "Pensando a classe operária: Os trabalhadores sujeitos ao imaginário acadêmico." *Revista Brasileira de História*, no. 6 (1984).

Pastore, José. "Migração, mobilidade social e desenvolvimento econômico." *Ciências Econômicas e Sociais* 6, no. 1 (1971).

Patmore, Greg. "Community and Australian Labour History." In *Challenges to Labour History*, ed. Terry Irving. Sydney: University of New South Wales Press, 1994.

Paula, Delsy Gonçalves de, Heloísa Starling, and Juarez Guimarães, eds. *Sentimento de reforma agrária, sentimento de república*. Belo Horizonte: Editora da Universidade Federal de Minas Gerais, 2006.

Paula Leite, Márcia de, and Sidney Sólis. "O último vendaval: A greve dos 700 mil." *Cara a cara*, no. 2 (1978).

Penna, Maura. *O que faz ser nordestino. Identidades sociais, interesses e o "escândalo" Erundina*. São Paulo: Cortez, 1992.

Pereira, Anthony. *The End of Peasantry: The Rural Labor Movement in Northeast Brazil, 1961–1988*. Pittsburgh: University of Pittsburgh Press, 1997.

Pereira Neto, Murilo Leal. "A operária têxtil em São Paulo nos anos 50: Rainha dos trabalhadores ou grande sindicalista lutadora?" *Revista UniABC* 1, no. 1 (2005).

———. *A reinvenção da classe trabalhadora (1953–1964)*. Campinas: Editora da Unicamp, 2011.

Perks, Robert, and Alistair Thomson. *The Oral History Reader*. London: Routledge, 1998.

Phillips, Kimberley L. *Alabama North: African-American Migrants, Community and Working-Class Activism in Cleveland, 1915–1945*. Chicago: University of Illinois Press, 1999.

Pimenta, Edileuza, and Edson Teixeira. *Virgílio Gomes da Silva: De retirante a guerrilheiro*. São Paulo: Plena Editorial, 2009.

Pimentel, Aristides. "Cronologia comentada da história de São Miguel Paulista 1493–1990." Mimeograph. Undated, São Paulo.

Pinheiro, Paulo Sérgio. "State and Labor in the Vargas Years (1930–1945)." Paper presented at "State and Labor 1930s: A Comparative Perspective," Naples, 1993.

Poli, Cleópatra. "Atitudes de operários de procedência rural (transição ou incorporação à vida urbana?)." *Sociologia* 31 (1981).

Pomar, Pedro Estevam Rocha. "Comunicação, cultura de esquerda e contra-hegemonia: O jornal *Hoje* (1945–1952)." Ph.D. diss., Escola de Comunicação e Artes, Universidade de São Paulo, 2006.

Porto, Cornélia, Iraci da Costa, and Nélson Nozoe. "Movimentos migratórios no Brasil e seus condicionantes econômicos (1872–1980)." Mimeograph. Convênio Financiadora de Estudos e Projetos and Fundação Instituto de Pesquisas Econômicas, São Paulo, 1987.

Prefeitura Municipal de São Paulo. *Atlas da administração regional de São Miguel Paulista e Ermelino Matarazzo*. São Paulo: Coordenadoria de Gestão de Pessoas/Confederation of Open Access Repositories / Companhia de Processamento de Dados do Município de São Paulo, 1975.

———. *O poder em São Paulo: História da administração pública da cidade, 1554–1992*. São Paulo: Cortez, 1992.

Ramalho, José Ricardo. *Estado-patrão e cultura operária: O caso FNM*. Rio de Janeiro: Paz e Terra, 1989.

Ravaglia, Fábio. "Contribuição à história da Companhia Nitro Química Brasileira: 1935–1985." Mimeograph. Companhia Nitro Química Brasileira, São Paulo, 1988.

Reis, José Roberto Franco. "Cartas a Vargas: Entre o favor, o direito e a luta política pela sobrevivência (1937–45)." *Locus* 7, no. 2 (2001).

Reis Filho, Daniel Aarão. *A revolução faltou ao encontro*. São Paulo, Editora Brasiliense, 1991.

———. "O colapso do colapso do populismo ou a propósito de uma herança maldita." In *O populismo e sua história. Debate e crítica*., ed. Jorge Ferreira. Rio de Janeiro: Civilização Brasileira, 2001.

Ricci, Rudá. *Terra de ninguém*. Campinas: Editora da Unicamp, 1999.

Ridenti, Marcelo. *Em busca do povo brasileiro. Artistas da revolução, do CPC à era da TV*. Rio de Janeiro: Record, 2000.

———. *O fantasma da revolução brasileira*. São Paulo: Editora Unesp and Fundação de Amparo à Pesquisa do Estado de São Paulo, 1993.

Rocha, Antônia Sarah Aziz. "O bairro à sombra da chaminé: Um estudo sobre a formação da classe trabalhadora da Companhia Nitro Química de São Miguel Paulista (1935–1960)." Master's thesis, Pontifícia Universidade Católica de São Paulo, 1992.

Rodrigues, Arlete M., and Manoel Seabra. "Habitação e espaço social na cidade de São Paulo." *Boletim Paulista de Geografia*, no. 64 (1986).

Rodrigues, José Albertino. "Condições econômico-sociais da mão de obra em São Paulo." Mimeograph. Dieese, São Paulo, April 1958.

Rodrigues, Leôncio Martins. *Conflito industrial e sindicalismo no Brasil*. São Paulo: Difel, 1966.

Rogers, Thomas D. "The Deepest Wounds: The Laboring Landscapes of Sugar in Northeastern Brazil." Ph.D. diss., Duke University, Durham, NC, 2005.

Rolnik, Raquel. *A cidade e a lei: Legislação, política urbana e territórios na cidade de São Paulo*. São Paulo: Studio Nobel and Fapesp, 1997.

Sader, Eder. *Quando novos personagens entraram em cena. Experiências e lutas dos trabalhadores na Grande São Paulo (1970–1980)*. Rio de Janeiro: Paz e Terra, 1988.

Sampaio, Regina. *Adhemar de Barros e o PSP*. São Paulo: Global, 1982.

Santana, Charles D'Almeida. *Fartura e venturas camponesas. Trabalho, cotidiano e migrações. Bahia: 1950–1980*. São Paulo: AnnaBlume e Universidade Federal de Feira de Santana, 1998.

Santana, Edvaldo. "Ruas de São Miguel." *Edvaldo Santana.* Eldorado, 2000. Compact disc.

Santana, Marco Aurélio. *Homens partidos. Comunistas e sindicatos no Brasil.* São Paulo, Boitempo, 2001.

Savage, Michael. "Class and Labour History." Paper presented at "The State of Labour and Working-Class History in Europe" conference, University of Manchester, February 1997.

———. "Space, Networks and Class Formation." In *Social Class and Marxism: Defences and Challenges,* ed. Neville Kirk. Hants: Scolar Press, 1996.

Sayad, Abdelmalek. *Imigração ou os paradoxos da alteridade.* São Paulo: Editora da Universidade de São Paulo, 1998.

Scott, R. Parry. "A lógica migratória camponesa e o capital: O Nordeste brasileiro." In *Emprego rural e migrações na América Latina,* ed. Renato Duarte. Recife: Fundação Joaquim Nabuco e Massangana, 1986.

Seabra, Odette Carvalho de Lima. "Urbanização: Bairro e vida de bairro," *Travessia* 13, no. 38 (September 2000).

———. "Urbanização e fragmentação: Cotidiano e vida de bairro na metamorfose da cidade em metrópole." Livre docência dissertation, Department of Geography, Facultad de Filosofia, Letras e Ciências Humanas, Universidade de São Paulo, 2003.

Secreto, Maria Verônica. *Soldados da borracha. Trabalhadores entre o sertão e a Amazônia no governo Vargas.* São Paulo: Editora da Fundação Perseu Abramo, 2007.

Sevcenko, Nicolau. *Orfeu extático na metrópole. São Paulo, sociedade e cultura nos frementes anos 20.* São Paulo: Companhia das Letras, 1998.

Silva, Afonso Celso Miranda. "Departamento de Migrantes." In *Anais da Semana de Estudos Migratórios (6 a 11 de julho de 1970),* ed. Juarez Segalin and Jacyr Braido. São Paulo: Centro de Estudos Migratórios, 1970.

Silva, Armando Corrêa da. "Estrutura e mobilidade social do proletariado urbano em São Paulo." *Revista Civilização Brasileira,* no. 13 (1967).

Silva, Fernando Teixeira da. *A carga e a culpa. Os operários das docas de Santos: Direitos e cultura de solidariedade.* São Paulo: Hucitec, 1995.

———. *Operários sem patrões. Os trabalhadores da cidade de Santos no entreguerras.* Campinas: Editora da Unicamp, 2003.

———. "Valentia e cultura do trabalho na estiva de Santos." In *Culturas de classe. Identidade e diversidade na formação do operariado,* ed. Cláudio Batalha, Fernando Teixeira da Silva, and Alexandre Fortes. Campinas: Editora da Unicamp, 2004.

Silva, Luiz Antonio Machado da. "O significado do botequim." In *Cidade: Usos e abusos,* ed. Daniel Joseph Hogan. São Paulo: Editora Brasiliense, 1978.

Silva, Maria Aparecida de Moraes, and Marilda Aparecida Menezes. *Migrações rurais no Brasil: velhas e novas questões.* Brasília: Nead, 2006.

Simão, Aziz. "O voto operário em São Paulo." *Revista Brasileira de Estudos Políticos* 1, no. 1 (December 1956).

Simões, Celso Cardoso da Silva, Luiz Antônio Pinto de Oliveira, and Jorge de Rezende. "Algumas características da participação dos membros da família na força de trabalho: 1950–1970." In *Encontro brasileiro de estudos populacionais: Contribuições apresentadas*, ed. Instituto Brasileiro de Geografia e Estatística. Rio de Janeiro: Instituto Brasileiro de Geografia e Estatística, 1976.

Simões, Inimá. *Salas de cinema em São Paulo*. São Paulo: PW, Secretaria Municipal de Cultura, and Secretaria Estadual de Cultura, 1990.

Skidmore, Thomas. *Politics in Brazil, 1930–1964*. New York: Oxford University Press, 1967.

Souza, Jesse Jane Vieira de. *Círculos operários: A Igreja Católica e o mundo do trabalho no Brasil*. Rio de Janeiro: Editora Universidade Federal do Rio de Janeiro, 2002.

Sposito, Marília Pontes, ed. "Memória do movimento popular de arte do bairro de São Miguel: Cultura, arte e educação." Mimeograph. Núcleo de Estudos de Sociologia da Educação, Faculdade de Educação, Universidade de São Paulo, 1987.

Stédile, João Pedro, ed. *A questão agrária no Brasil*. São Paulo: Expressão Popular, 2004.

Tamagno, Liliana. "Nordestinos Experiencing São Paulo: Time, Space and Identity in Relation to Internal Migration." Master's thesis, Uppsala University, 1984.

Telles, Jover. *O movimento sindical no Brasil*. São Paulo: Ciências Humanas, 1981.

Thiago, Cristiane Muniz. "Rio de Janeiro Operário: Memória dos trabalhadores do bairro do Jacaré." Master's thesis, Universidade Federal do Estado do Rio de Janeiro, 2007.

Thompson, E. P. *Customs in Common: Studies in Traditional Popular Culture*. London: Merlin, 1991.

———. *The Making of the English Working Class*. Harmondsworth: Penguin, 1968.

Thomson, Alistair. "Moving Stories: Oral History and Migration Studies." *Oral History* 27, no. 1 (1999).

Trotter, Joe William, Jr., ed. *The Great Migration in Historical Perspective: New Dimensions of Race, Class and Gender*. Bloomington: Indiana University Press, 1991.

Troyano, Annez. *Estado e sindicalismo*. São Paulo: Símbolo, 1978.

Valladão, Mario da Natividade. *Dá conta de tua mordomia*. São Paulo: Igreja Batista de São Miguel Paulista, 1986.

Velloso, Mônica Pimenta. "A brasilidade verde-amarela: Nacionalismo e regionalismo paulista," *Estudos Históricos* 6, no. 11 (1993).

Viana, Myrna Therezinha Rego. "São Miguel Paulista. O chão dos desterrados (Um estudo de migração e de urbanização)." Master's thesis, Geography Department, Facultad de Filosofia, Letras e Ciências Humanas, Universidade de São Paulo, 1982.

Vilaça, Marcos Vinicios. *Em torno da sociologia do caminhão*. Recife: Instituto Joaquim Nabuco de Pesquisas Sociais, 1961.

Villa, Marco Antônio. *Vida e morte no sertão. História das secas no Nordeste nos séculos XIX e XX*. São Paulo: Ática, 2000.

Vinhas, Moisés. *Operários e camponeses na revolução brasileira*. São Paulo: Fulgor, 1963.

———. *O Partidão: A luta por um partido de massas (1922–1974)*. São Paulo: Hucitec, 1982.

Walmsley, Silvana Maria de Moura. "Origens do janismo. São Paulo, 1948/1953." Master's thesis, Instituto de Filosofia e Ciências Humanas, Universidade Estadual de Campinas, 1992.

Weffort, Francisco. "Nordestinos em São Paulo: Notas para um estudo sobre cultura nacional e cultura popular." In *A cultura do povo*, ed. José Valle Edênio. São Paulo: Cortez e Instituto de Estudos Especiais, 1988.

———. *O populismo na política brasileira*. Rio de Janeiro: Paz e Terra, 1978.

———. "Origens do sindicalismo populista no Brasil." *Estudos CEBRAP* 4 (April–June 1973).

Weinstein, Barbara. *For Social Peace in Brazil: Industrialists and the Remaking of the Working Class in São Paulo, 1920–1964*. Chapel Hill: University of North Carolina Press, 1996.

———. "The Model Worker of the Paulista Industrialists: The 'Operário Padrão' Campaign." *Radical History Review*, no. 61 (Winter 1995).

———. "Racializing Regional Difference: São Paulo versus Brazil, 1932." In *Race and Nation in Modern Latin America*, ed. Nancy Appelbaum, Anne Macpherson, and Karin Rosemblatt. Chapel Hill: University of North Carolina Press, 2003.

———. *(Re)formação da classe trabalhadora no Brasil, 1920–1964*. São Paulo, Editora Cortez, 2000.

———. "Unskilled Workers, Skilled Housewife: Constructing the Working-Class Woman in São Paulo, Brazil." In *The Gendered Worlds of Latin American Women Workers: From Household and Factory to the Union Hall and Ballot Box*, ed. John French and Daniel James. Durham, NC: Duke University Press, 1997.

Weis, Michael W. *Cold Warriors and Coups d'État: Brazilian-American Relations, 1945–1964*. Albuquerque: University of New Mexico Press, 1993.

Welch, Cliff. *The Seed Was Planted: The São Paulo Roots of Brazil's Rural Labor Movement, 1924–1964*. University Park: Pennsylvania State University Press, 1999.

Wellman, Barry, and Barry Leighton. "Networks, Neighborhoods and Communities: Approaches to the Study of the Community Question." *Urban Affairs Quarterly* 14, no. 3 (1979).

Whipp, Richard. *Patterns of Labour: Work and Social Change in the Pottery Industry*. London: Routledge, 1990.

Willis, Paul. *Aprendendo a ser trabalhador: Escola, resistência e reprodução social*. Porto Alegre: Artes Médicas, 1991.

Yeo, Eileen, and Stephen Yeo. "On the Uses of 'Community': From Owenism to the Present." In *New Views of Co-operation*, ed. Stephen Yeo. London: Routledge, 1988.

Zaidan Filho, Michel. *O fim do Nordeste e outros mitos*. São Paulo: Cortez, 2001.

Zampieri, Wilson João, and Avelar Cezar Imamura. *Padre Aleixo Monteiro Mafra. O pastor de almas de São Miguel Paulista*. São Paulo: Universidade Cruzeiro do Sul, 1998.

Cinelândia (São Paulo), 93

Cine Lapenna, 93–94, 115. *See also* Lapenna family

Cine São José do Belém, 206

Cine São Miguel, 93, 155

Circulista movement, 154–57

class formation, 5–6

Clementino (worker), 206

Cleofas, João, 41

Club Cornmeal. *See* Clube Fubá

Clube Fubá, 95

CMTC (Companhia Municipal de Transporte Colectivo), 107–8

Communist Party of Brazil (Partido Comunista Brasileiro, PCB), x, 14, 45, 49, 132, 135–47, 179, 181; and autonomy, 193; criminalized, 151–54, 169; founded, 216n38; headquarters closed in São Miguel, 144; infighting, 203–4; Sunday meetings, 143

community: as concept, 5–6

Companhia Mirante, 103

Companhia Nitro Química Brasileira. *See* Nitro Química

Consolidated Labor Laws (CLT), 200; symbolic importance of, 247n49

Constitution of 1946, 187

construction sector, 34–35

Corrêa, Antônio Mendes, 124, 157, 188

Correio Paulistano, 80, 102–3, 110

Costa, João Romualdo da, 109

Costa, Oscar Pereira, 118

Coup of 1964, 8, 14, 153, 158, 185, 196, 202–3, 208, 212n4

Crispim, José Maria, 152

Cristiano, Luís, 162

Cruz, Maria da, 31

cruzeiro, as currency, 241n52

Cuban Revolution, 204

Cunha, Amauri da, 75, 82, 95–96, 101, 102, 103, 106–7

dancing, 94–96, 144, 184

Dantas, Humberto, 18, 30

Democratic National Union (União Democrática Nacional, UDN), 134, 141–42, 167, 168, 170

Department of Immigration and Colonization (Departamento de Imigração e Colonização, DIC), 18, 28

Department of Political and Social Order (Departamento de Ordem Político e Social, DOPS), x, 24, 80, 144–48, 181, 203; abolished, 238n6; at Nitro Química, 133–34, 137, 149–57, 172, 189, 198

Dia, O, 39, 84, 87, 100

Diniz, José, 190

Drought Polygon, 22

droughts, northeast: 16, 17, 22, 26, 29, 40–43, 46, 75

Duarte, Adriano, 126, 165

Duarte, Belarmino, 66

Dutra, Eurico, 140–41, 147, 166, 170

ecclesiastical base communities (*comunidades eclesiais de base*, CEBS), 158

education: as benefit of migration, 21

elections, 14

Ermelinio Matazzaro, 55, 108, 228n29

Esporte Club Bahia, 92

Esporte Club São Miguel, 90, 116, 162, 184

Estação do Norte (Estação Roosevelt), 16, 23, 24, 61, 121, 128

Estado de São Paulo, O, 100–101, 104, 108, 184, 198, 206

Estado Novo, 3, 52, 72, 131, 141, 154, 163; as dictatorship, 212n2; end of, 135, 138; union tax, 241n50

Estrada de Ferro Central, 18

Fábrica Nacional de Artefatos de Metal, 152

Factory Street (São Miguel). *See* Rua da Fábrica

Falcão, João Mendonça, 162

fascist sympathizers, 131–35, 163

Federation of Chemical Workers, 201

Federation of Neighborhood Friends Societies (Federação das Sociedades Amigos de Bairros e Vilas de São Paulo, FESAB), 180–82

Fernandes, Henriqueta Lopes, 82, 107, 108

Ferreira, Jorge, 9

Ferreira, Luís Gerônimo, 61, 62

Ferreira, Rogê, 190

Mesquita family, 206–7
Mesquita, Sebastião Adriano, 64
metallurgy sector, 35
Metalúrgica Cosmopoliti, 202
migrants: compared to slaves, 16, 25; disparaged, 40–41; illiteracy rate, 34; networks, 26–31
migration, domestic, 17–23; as carefully considered action, 27; circular, 29; compared with African American migration, 211n1, 221n48; as formative to working class, 13; indirect, 28; international, vii–viii, 7–8; and the job market, 32–37; northward, 19–20
migration, foreign: 213n9, 215n22; Japanese, 133, 238n7; Portuguese, 50. *See also* migration, domestic
Miguel, Benedito, 68, 101, 121
Minas Gerais: as source of migrants, viii–ix, 1, 17–19, 32, 44, 59, 60–61, 64, 87, 101, 208; as symbol of poverty, 170
minimum wage, 197
Ministry of Justice, 183
Ministry of Labor, 134, 145, 200–201
Miragaia family, 115–16, 162
modernization: as concept, 7, 214n20
Moisés, José Álvaro, 183, 187, 194
Mônaco, Agenor, 39, 181
Montanhani, Manoel de Almeida, 170
Monteiro, Pedro, 189
Montes Claros, 18, 24, 61
Mooca, 52, 57, 120, 126, 202
Moraes, José Ermirio de, 50, 60, 87, 198, 205–7
Morais, Joaquim, 140
Moussalhe Brothers, 152
movies, 93–94
music, 49, 60, 85, 137, 138, 144; *cordel* poets, 73, 129. *See also* dancing
mutirão (pl. *mutirões*), viii, 84–85, 112, 183
Mutti, José Augusto, 188

National Liberation Alliance (Aliança Libertadora Nacional, ALN), 204
National Renewal Alliance (Aliança Renovadora Nacional, ARENA), 198

National Service of Industrial Instruction (Serviço Nacional de Aprendizagem Industrial, SENAI), 33–34, 66–67, 157; negative view of worker, 129
National Steel Company (Companhia Siderúrgica Nacional, CSN), 51
Neighborhood Friends Societies (Sociedades de Amigos de Bairro, SABs), 167, 168, 178–86, 194, 201
Nery, Júlio de Souza, 61, 71
Neto, João Rodrigues, 121
Neto, Teixeira, 27
Netto, Antônio Jordão, 28
Netto, Luiz Cava, 27, 41–42
Neves, José Maria Costas, 104
New Directions. See Novos Rumos
Nitro Jornal, 76, 88, 155, 156
Nitro Química, viii, ix, 2–3, 15, 37, 102; attacked by Quadros, 166; and Catholic Church, 154–58; Communist cell at, 49, 135–47; dangerous working conditions, 71–75, 200–201; economic crisis at, 198–99; explosions at, 73; hiring policies of, 63–64; loss of influence, 192–93; mass dismissals at, 14, 204–7; "national interest" designation, 132; Nazi-fascist sympathies at, 132–33; nicknames at, 76–77; as polluter, 73–75, 176; pranks at, 76–77; provider of credit, 120; as rayon producer, 51, 204; recruitment of workers, 61; repression at, 153, 202; and São Miguel, 50–65, 114, 190; severance pay, 205–7; social networks at, 77; strikes and protest at, 44–45, 137–54, 184–85, 198–202; supervisors, 68–69; union at, 201; women, participation in workforce, 35, 69–71. *See also* Christmas bonus; Regatta Club of Nitro Química
Northeast: regionalist discourse surrounding, 42–43, 208; as source of migrants, viii, 1–2, 17, 32, 44, 60–65
northeasterners, viii–ix; associated with violence, 120–26; discriminated against, 36–37, 225n111; fleeing for home, 123; as symbol of migration, 17, 59–60
"northeastern question," 13, 210
Noticias de Hoje, 44, 75, 199